Living and Cursing in the Roman West

Also available from Bloomsbury

Ancient Magic and the Supernatural in the Modern Visual and Performing Arts,
edited by Filippo Carlà-Uhink and Irene Berti
Canidia, Rome's First Witch, Maxwell Teitel Paule
Magic in Ancient Greece and Rome, Lindsay C. Watson
Roman Britain, S. Ireland and Stephen R. Hill

Living and Cursing in the Roman West

Curse Tablets and Society

Stuart McKie

BLOOMSBURY ACADEMIC
LONDON • NEW YORK • OXFORD • NEW DELHI • SYDNEY

For Penny and Sophie

BLOOMSBURY ACADEMIC
Bloomsbury Publishing Plc
50 Bedford Square, London, WC1B 3DP, UK
1385 Broadway, New York, NY 10018, USA
29 Earlsfort Terrace, Dublin 2, Ireland

BLOOMSBURY, BLOOMSBURY ACADEMIC and the Diana logo are trademarks of Bloomsbury Publishing Plc

First published in Great Britain 2022
This paperback edition published 2024

Copyright © Stuart McKie, 2022

Stuart McKie has asserted his right under the Copyright, Designs and Patents Act, 1988, to be identified as Author of this work.

For legal purposes the Acknowledgements on p. vii constitute an extension of this copyright page.

Cover image: A curse tablet from Mainz, Germany, with nail in situ.
Courtesy GDKE, Landesarchäologie, Mainz.

All rights reserved. No part of this publication may be reproduced or transmitted in any form or by any means, electronic or mechanical, including photocopying, recording, or any information storage or retrieval system, without prior permission in writing from the publishers.

Bloomsbury Publishing Plc does not have any control over, or responsibility for, any third-party websites referred to or in this book. All internet addresses given in this book were correct at the time of going to press. The author and publisher regret any inconvenience caused if addresses have changed or sites have ceased to exist, but can accept no responsibility for any such changes.

A catalogue record for this book is available from the British Library.

Library of Congress Cataloging-in-Publication Data

Names: McKie, Stuart (Historian), author.
Title: Living and cursing in the Roman West: curse tablets and society /Stuart McKie.
Description: London; New York: Bloomsbury Academic, 2022. | Includes bibliographical references and index.
Identifiers: LCCN 2021052186 | ISBN 9781350102996 (hardback) | ISBN 9781350289352 (paperback) | ISBN 9781350103009 (ebook) | ISBN 9781350103016 (epub) | ISBN 9781350103023
Subjects: LCSH: Blessing and cursing–Rome. | Rites and ceremonies–Rome. | Tablets (Paleography) | Roman provinces–Religion. | Roman provinces–Religious life and customs. | Europe, Western–Antiquities, Roman.
Classification: LCC BL815.B54 M35 2022 | DDC 200.937–dc23/eng/20220517
LC record available at https://lccn.loc.gov/2021052186

ISBN: HB: 978-1-3501-0299-6
PB: 978-1-3502-8935-2
ePDF: 978-1-3501-0300-9
eBook: 978-1-3501-0301-6

Typeset by RefineCatch Ltd, Bungay, Suffolk

To find out more about our authors and books, visit www.bloomsbury.com and sign up for our newsletters.

Contents

List of Figures — vi
List of Tables — vi
Acknowledgements — vii
List of Abbreviations — viii

1 Introduction — 1
2 Cursing and Religion in the Roman West — 12
3 Rituals, Gestures and Movements — 23
4 Motives and Social Frameworks — 59
5 Agency, Power and Relationships — 104
6 Epilogue — 130

Appendix: Select Catalogue of Curses — 133
Notes — 245
Bibliography — 263
Index — 283

Figures

1.1	SD 492 from Mainz written by the wife of Florus. Image from Blänsdorf 2012, copyright GDKE Rheinland-Pfalz	2
2.1	Distribution map of curses across the western provinces. Copyright Matilde Grimaldi	14
3.1	Front and back of SD 306 from Bath. Author's photograph	36
3.2	Front and back of SD 484 from Mainz. Image from Blänsdorf 2012, copyright GDKE Rheinland-Pfalz	38
3.3	SD 345 from Clothall. Image from *RIB* Online, copyright CSAD	39
3.4	SD 213 from Bath. Image from Tomlin 1988, copyright Barry Cunliffe and Oxford University Committee for Archaeology	41
5.1	SD 215 and 220 from Bath (not to scale). Images from Tomlin 1988, copyright Barry Cunliffe and Oxford University Committee for Archaeology	114

Tables

2.1	Number of curses included from each region	17
3.1	Number of curses from different depositional contexts in each region	49
4.1	Totals of motive categories found on curse tablets from the western provinces of the Roman Empire	61
4.2	Totals of motives in each region	62

Acknowledgements

This book started life as a PhD thesis completed at the Open University between 2013–17, under the supervision of Emma-Jayne Graham, Phil Perkins and Ursula Rothe. I am still incredibly grateful for the support and guidance they gave me then, and for the advice and assistance offered since. The original project was funded by Baron Lorne Thyssen-Bornemisza, for whose support I remain thankful. Other members of the OU Classical Studies department, especially Eleanor Betts, Jess Hughes and Valerie Hope, deserve thanks for their insightful comments on parts or all of the manuscript. Adam Parker has been a constant supporter and close collaborator on the 'loony fringe' of Roman magic, and I am indebted to him for many enriching conversations, and for comments on the manuscript. I cannot thank Kate Cook enough for all the advice, encouragement, accountability and friendship she has given me.

My thanks are offered to many colleagues for their generous advice and help, especially Virginia Campbell, Pierre Chevet, Christopher Faraone, Richard Gordon, Louise Revell, Celia Sánchez Natalías, Lothar Schwinden and Roger Tomlin. Most of the work on the book was done while I was at Durham University, and I would like to thank Zara Chadha, Roy Gibson, Ted Kaizer, Polly Low and Amy Russell for all their help during that time. Staff at the Bill Bryson Library deserve high praise for their efforts in finding resources, even throughout the Covid pandemic. I would like to express my gratitude to everyone at Bloomsbury, especially Georgina Leighton, Lily Mac Mahon and Alice Wright. Barry Cunliffe, Matilde Grimaldi, Andrew Meadows and Marion Witteyer either produced images or gave permission for them to be used, for which I am grateful. Translations from Tomlin 1988 are copyright Oxford Committee for Archaeology and Roger Tomlin, and have been reproduced with permission. Translations from Gager 1992 are copyright Oxford Publishing Limited, and are reproduced with permission.

Lastly to my family: my parents Karen and Nick, my brother Mike and of course my wife Juli, who has been my rock throughout. This book could not have been written without you all.

Abbreviations

Abbreviations of journal names follow those of L'Année Philologique, and abbreviations of ancient authors and their works follow the Oxford Classical Dictionary. All curse tablets are cited either by their number in SD or, if not included by Sánchez Natalías, by their number in another major corpus. Those in bold are included in the Appendix at the end of this book.

AE	*l'Année Epigraphique*
CIL	*Corpus Inscriptionum Latinarum*
dfx	Kropp (2008)
DT	Audollent (1904)
DTM	Blänsdorf (2012a)
Gager	Gager (1992)
LCT	Urbanova (2018)
NGCT	Jordan (2000)
PGM	Betz (1992)
RIB	*Roman Inscriptions of Britain.*
RIG	Lambert (2002)
SD	Sánchez Natalías (forthcoming)
SEG	*Supplementum Epigraphicum Graecum*
SGD	Jordan (1985)
Suppl. Mag.	Daniel and Maltomini (1990–2)
TabSulis	Tomlin (1988)
Tremel	Tremel (2004)
Uley	Tomlin (1993)

1

Introduction

In one form or another, the ritual of cursing an enemy by inscribing a piece of lead existed for over 1,000 years in the regions around the Mediterranean, and for 500 years in the regions of northern Europe that became part of the Roman Empire. Despite numerous attempts by religious and legal authorities to outlaw the practices, they succeeded in addressing difficult moments in the everyday lives of people in the Graeco-Roman world. One such person was an unnamed woman who lived in Mainz. At some point in the late first or early second century AD, she lost all the money left to her by her (presumably) late husband. According to her version of events – the only version we have – the fortune had been stolen by a certain Ulattius Severus, clearly someone she trusted: perhaps a relative or her guardian. Having no legal right to pursue her case through the courts, this woman turned to the gods in her time of need. She went to the temple of Magna Mater, where she had heard from friends or acquaintances that it was possible to perform a cursing ritual against thieves and embezzlers. She procured a thick sheet of lead, perhaps from the priests at the temple and possibly for a small fee, and inscribed her curse against the man who had betrayed her (**SD 492,** Figure 1.1).

> I ask you, Lady Mater Magna, that you avenge me in the matter of the fortune of my husband Florus. The one who has deceived me, Ulattius Severus: just as I write this wrongly, so shall everything that he does, everything he undertakes, everything should go wrongly for him. Like salt and water shall it go for him. Everything he has taken away from me from the fortune of my husband Florus, I ask you Lady Mater Magna, that for this you avenge me.

The priests directed her to a pit behind the temple, which was lined with the burnt remains of animal and plant matter that others had given to the goddess. After taking in her enclosed, smoky surroundings, she spoke the words that would invoke the vengeful power of the goddess, and finally threw her tablet into the piles of ash at the bottom of the pit. We will never know the outcome of

DTM 3 (Inv.-Nr. 1,29), Rückseite

Figure 1.1 SD 492 from Mainz written by the wife of Florus. Image from Blänsdorf 2012, copyright GDKE Rheinland-Pfalz.

this event, but it is likely that the wife of Florus walked out of the temple feeling that she had done something to rectify the wrongs done to her. She may have reported back to the friends who had told her about the rituals performed at the temple, setting the rumour mill in motion. If word reached Ulattius Severus, it may have sowed a seed of doubt in his mind, meaning the next time a business arrangement turned sour, or the next time he suffered an illness or injury, he may have begun to worry about the divine implications of his dealings with Florus' wife.

Some of what I have presented here is, of course, creative speculation, but it nevertheless demonstrates the significance of curse tablets for the social lives of the people who produced them. Although what often survives is only a few scratched lines, barely legible on corroded lead sheets, these objects, and the rituals of which they were part, were explicitly directed towards the faults and failings in the relationships that connected people to others around them. Community life in the ancient world – as in any human society throughout history – was never lived in total harmony, and rituals such as cursing offered means through which ancient people could define, negotiate and at times destroy the relationships they made with others. In doing so, they drew upon influences from local, regional and global beliefs and practices, connecting their actions to those of countless others across the Roman Empire. At the same time, ancient cursing rituals were totally adaptable, allowing individual people to make them relevant to their own circumstances, like Florus' wife attacking the business dealings of her embezzling guardian. What survives are hundreds of individual appeals to the gods, with huge variations in language, style, content and form.

The focus of this book is on these individual situations and how, by closely examining the curse tablets and the contexts in which they were produced, modern historians can develop a greater understanding of the lives of their makers. In the past, much scholarship on curse tablets has been concerned with attempting to fit them into schemes of categorization, based on either motive or language use, or has used them as evidence for changes in Latin or Greek language.[1] Where their ritual importance has been recognized, it has, until very recently, been done within a pan-Imperial tradition of magical practice and belief.[2] Such macro-scale analysis is unsustainable, and fundamentally misses the point of curse tablets, which were individualized reactions to personal crises. In this book I will take a significantly different approach to the curses from the Roman west by examining them within the physical and social contexts of the communities in which they were produced. My central aim is to show that curse tablets were an important means of addressing moments of crisis, and that cursing rituals were creatively performed, taking inspiration from the world around them in those moments of crisis. To do so, I will build on several recent developments in the study of ancient religion, especially the Lived Ancient Religion approach, as well as the sensory and material turns in archaeology. Curse tablet scholarship is beginning to feel the presence of these new approaches, but this book represents a paradigm shift in the analysis of these fascinating ancient objects.

Lived ancient religion

Scholars of contemporary religion have long recognized the immense importance of framing religion as lived experience. Drawing on Heidegger and Merleau-Ponty, and closely related to ideas of 'vernacular' and 'everyday' religion, the 'lived religion' approach contends that religion is fundamentally based in daily practice and patterns of social life, not abstract belief.[3] As Primiano argued, 'official religion' has no objective existence that can be separated from the combined actions of individuals, up to and including religious or civic leaders.[4] Privileging belief and measuring it against some dogmatic standard is a 'highly western, protestant conceptualisation of religion'[5] that makes little sense in other historical and cultural environments, including the Roman Empire. Religion is not handed down by authorities and then mindlessly replicated, but is produced by the actions of humans, enacted within social contexts that provide shared experiences and learned practices.[6] It is therefore complex, multifaceted and often messy, full of contradictions and inconsistencies as individuals adopt and adapt religious practices to make them meaningful in their everyday lives. Attending to individual experience means also being more aware of the impact of sensory perception and memory on the generation of religion, as well as the intersections between religion and other factors in human life, such as age, gender, race and class.[7]

Lived religion approaches have great potential for advancing our understanding of Roman religion, as has been amply shown by recent projects led by Rüpke.[8] When applying these approaches to the ancient world, the Lived Ancient Religion (LAR) Projects retained the questioning of institutionalized models of religion and the refocusing of enquiry onto individual experience, but, perhaps naturally for historians and archaeologists, added an interest in religious change over time. Rüpke offers the following description of how to use the Lived Ancient Religion model:

> ... scattered evidence should be contextualised and interpreted by relating it to individual agents, their use of space and time, their formation of social coalitions, their negotiation with religious specialists or providers, and their attempts to make sense of religion in a situational manner and thus render religion effective.[9]

Applying this model has revitalized Roman religion, overhauling older images of lifeless, automatic repetition of rituals in favour of a vibrant, creative and changeable religious world in which the actions of individuals had a cumulative effect on the direction of wider religious movements.[10] Curse tablets have been part of these discussions, but have not yet attracted sustained attention. The time is therefore right for a full analysis of curses from a 'lived religion' perspective. Rüpke's description of the model chimes very well with the aims of this book, which will focus especially on spatial and temporal contexts, the social relationships formed around cursing rituals, and the ways in which people used curses to not only make sense of their world, but to change it.

Agency and power

At the centre of the idea of religion as the product of lived experience is the concept of agency, which can be most usefully described as the ability to 'make a difference in the world.'¹¹ Since the work of Bourdieu and Giddens, agency has been understood in relationship with 'structure', which is anything that guides, encourages or limits agency.¹² These two concepts exist in a recursive relationship, each challenging and developing the other. In other words, the actions that people take are influenced by explicit instructions received from authority figures, codes of conduct, expected behavioural standards and so on. At the same time, the actions of individuals feed back into those structures, developing them, and producing change over time.¹³ People learn how to act in the world not just through their own experiences, but also through witnessing the actions of others and having conversations with the people around them. The wife of Florus, who cursed her embezzling guardian in first-century Mainz, may have made her curse after seeking advice from friends or the priests of the temple, and onlookers may have taken inspiration from her actions to produce their own future curses. Relationships are therefore firmly at the heart of agency, either among people or between people and objects, because agency emerges from how people interact with the humans, animals and objects around them.¹⁴ Theorists such as Gell, Hodder and Latour have proposed models where material objects and human beings are intimately connected, and are equally responsible for the production of agency.¹⁵ The physical properties of objects have the capacity to guide or limit human agency. For example, the soft, malleable quality of lead makes it a good material for writing, but as a physical experience it is very different from writing with ink on paper, and those differences informed the ways that people performed cursing rituals. In theoretical terms, we might say that curses emerged from the relationships between the human curser and the physical materials. Thinking about religion through the lens of agency adds another dimension, as humans engage in relationships with gods, spirits, ancestors and other superhuman figures, who might not be physically, materially present, but all of whom are believed to have the ability to affect the real world.¹⁶

Graham's recent book has made a powerful case for placing 'more-than-human things' – objects, the natural environment, animals, the intangible divine and so on – on an equal footing with humans in the production of religious agency, inspired by post-humanist theories loosely grouped under the label of 'new materialism'.¹⁷ From this kind of perspective, it becomes more apparent how religious experiences emerge from the physical and relational interactions between things. To give a specific example, a human might *intend* to perform a sacrifice, but cannot actually do one without the mutual, active engagement of knives, bowls, altars and sheep, not to mention the physical matter of their own body. All these things perform the sacrifice together, bundled into an assemblage that creates religious agency as it acts. Graham takes this another step further, arguing that the lived experiences of doing religion generated what she calls 'proximal religious knowledge'. In other words, 'people knew how, why, and when to act *based on their experience* ... rather than merely with reference to shared doctrine'.[18] Distal knowledge – shared and generally accepted frameworks of practice, which, in religious contexts, we might also call dogma or tradition – was then created by the accumulation of lived experiences, either direct performance or witnessing others performing ritualized actions.

The interpretation of ancient religion from a new materialist perspective is no doubt refreshing, and I am convinced by many of Graham's conclusions. However, as others have already pointed out, these kinds of theoretical approaches can have the tendency to obscure some important facts of life, namely the existence of unequal structures of power.[19] It is essential to recognize that agents cannot uniformly deploy their agency, but must act within the structures, cultural ideas and ways of behaving in which they are embedded. Power can therefore be defined as the capacity to constrain or encourage the agency of others, through determining or changing the incentives, costs or benefits of certain actions.[20] Power can also be described as someone's ability to challenge the limitations placed on them by others.[21] Exercising power is discretional – people can decide whether to wield power or not – and can also be describe as potential, in that people who *appear* powerful *are* powerful, because it affects how other treat them, even if they have not actually done anything.[22] Much like agency, we see that power emerges from relationships, rather than being an essential characteristic of an agent, or being a resource that they can spend or use.[23] Woolf has recently invoked the image of overlapping 'webs of power': networks through which people exercised their influence, but in which they were all entangled.[24] The closer to the centre of such webs a person was, the greater their ability to exert power over others. As Gardner has reminded us on several occasions, it is essential that Roman archaeologists and historians keep in mind that people in the Roman Empire lived in situations of unequal power and coercive force.[25] As individuals totally under the power of others, enslaved people are the most obvious victims of these conditions, but they also apply to free people, especially those considered marginal in some way, such as women or non-citizens.[26] The unequal distribution of power had a direct impact on the agency of individuals as they sought to get things done, not only in terms of enabling or hampering the ability for someone to do something for themselves, but also their ability to affect what someone else does.

Anthropology

To bring power back into the picture of Roman religion for this book, I have drawn on anthropological and ethnographic work done in colonial and post-colonial contexts in the modern world, which shows very clearly the place of lived religious experience in the navigation and expression of power structures. Moreover, the strong tradition of social anthropology concerned with witchcraft, sorcery, rumour and gossip is very relevant for a book focused on curse tablets. From the pioneering work of Malinowski and Evans-Pritchard, through Douglas in the 1970s and on into the late twentieth and early twenty-first centuries, scholars in this field have studied the social, economic and political contexts in which cursing and other related practices were performed.[27] Although these contexts necessarily differ depending on the society under study, the clustering of such practices at 'times of sickness and death, periods of achievement and success and of failure and abjection' is very strong.[28] In a number of societies, the practice of witchcraft or sorcery is amoral, or at least morally ambiguous, depending on the subjective perceptions and justifications of the individuals involved.[29] Rumour and gossip play an important role in the contexts that surround people's engagement in magical rituals, not just in spurring accusations of witchcraft and the beginnings of witch hunts, but also the perceived need to take supernatural precautions against the actions of others.[30] Anthropologists have shown that sorcery practices like Roman cursing are regular features of the breakdown in personal relationships and in providing alternative sources of agency and power for individuals who might otherwise be marginalized in a society.[31] Indeed, such practices make abundantly clear the belief in the potential for human agency to reshape the world, often in combination with supernatural agents. These ideas will become especially relevant in Chapters 4 and 5, where I will explore the notions of agency and power in Roman cursing in greater detail.

Magic

By invoking anthropological work on witchcraft and sorcery, I have raised a term that is as contested as any other covered in this introduction: magic. In the words of Edmonds, the harmful, secret, strange and selfish nature of curse tablets means that they 'fall within everyone's intuitive definition of magic'[32] and the titles of most recent scholarly works that discuss curses – '*Magical Practice in the Latin West*', '*Materia Magica*' '*Contesti Magici*', '*Choosing Magic*' to name just a few monographs and edited volumes – leave little doubt that he is right.[33] However, the use of the term 'magic' to describe these or any object or ritualized activity, from Roman or any other human society, has attracted considerable academic disagreement over the years.[34] Much of the debate has been centred on whether magic should be considered a part of or separate from 'proper' religion. In the early twentieth century, Frazer argued that magic was a primitive form of belief that gave way to organized religion as civilization evolved and gave more meaning to the world around it.[35] More recent scholars have rejected the idea that magic and religion are separate entities, some – including Otto – calling for the abandonment of the term 'magic' entirely.[36] In contrast, Versnel and others have argued that, at least in regards to the study of the ancient Mediterranean, the two are inextricably intertwined, and therefore we cannot wholly do away with magic without surrendering our ability to discuss the topic.[37] We cannot fall back on purely using ancient terminology, as Otto would have us do: Stratton, Edmonds and others have shown that the Greek and Latin words μαγεια/*magia* are no less prejudiced than 'magic' in modern English.[38] The discourse of magic in Greek and Latin literature performed specific cultural and social functions, primarily for the urban elite, and we should question how useful it is in illuminating the practices of people outside those groups. However, at the same time, I do not think that rigid academic definitions of terms like 'magic' are particularly helpful, or indeed actually possible to achieve. Definitions proposed by scholars such as Versnel, Luck and Chadwick are either too narrowly prescriptive, or so wide that they become vague.[39]

A moderate position has begun to appear between the extremes of functionalists and deconstructionists, one which sees magic as a 'fuzzy concept', related to religion but distinct from it in sometimes self-conscious ways.[40] From this position, lived experience is essential, because it was the individual's perception or rationalization of actions performed by themselves or others that decided whether they were understood as 'religious' or 'magical.' Significantly, this allows for the same action to be understood in different ways depending on perspective. In other words, one woman's legitimate appeal to the goddess can be another woman's malign sorcery.

All forms of ritualized activity, however they were labelled, were part of the lived experience of those who practised them, and all informed one another. As we will see throughout this book, curse tablets demonstrate this exceptionally well, in that every aspect of the creation of the curses was affected by the context in which it was performed, and in turn affected wider structures of belief and practice. From the perspective of lived religion, the question is no longer about defining 'religion' and 'magic', but about how these activities operate in the lives of real people. The men and women who made curse tablets in the Roman west did so by creatively drawing on the beliefs and practices common in their religious and social contexts, blurring the boundaries between what could have been considered 'proper' religious actions and 'magical' practice. It is unlikely that many of these individuals were interested in, or even aware of, the debates over acceptable religious practice among the elite at Rome. Throughout this book I will argue that their concern was to create the most successful curse possible to address their own circumstances. To achieve this, they took inspiration from the world around them at the time of ritual performance and were influenced by the social relationships and structures in which they were embedded.

Outline of the book

This book concerns curse tablets produced by people who lived in the western provinces of the Roman Empire. I have included all tablets from Italia, Africa, Hispania, Gallia, Britannia, Germania, Raetia, Noricum and Pannonia that are at least roughly datable to the first five centuries AD. By including all curse tablets within these chronological and geographical boundaries, regardless of the language they were written in (Latin, Greek or Celtic), this book captures the wide variety of cursing practices across the Roman imperial period. The corpus covered in this book is far from homogenous, exhibiting only weak evidence for widespread 'traditions', despite what some past scholarship might have concluded. In total, the study rests on 607 tablets from 126 different locations across the region (see Figure 2.1). The majority of these come either from large cities in the central Mediterranean – namely Rome, Carthage and Sousse – or the three temple sites at Bath, Uley and Mainz in the north-western provinces. Away from these significant collections, almost all curse tablets were found alone or in pairs, spread widely across the study area. In Chapter 2 I will outline the chronological and geographic spread in more detail, before giving a summary of the religious and cultural backdrops against which cursing rituals were performed.

In Chapter 3, I analyse the ritual process of cursing in detail, taking it step by step from the procurement of the blank lead tablet through to deposition. The lived, physical experience of performing a cursing ritual is the central focus of the chapter, taking inspiration from the Lived Ancient Religion approach outlined above, as well as wider studies in sensory experience and emerging 'new materialist' archaeologies. My aim is to challenge the conceptualization of curses as inert written texts to be mined for linguistic or philological data, and instead to emphasize their nature as the product of a series of creative and ritually significant moments, in which the actions of individual cursers were affected by the physical contexts in which they were embedded. The final form of the curse was not just a simple copy of what the curser had in their head, but emerged out of embodied interactions between humans and objects, the aim of which was to transform blank sheets of lead into powerful curses with the capacity to affect the real world. In the chapter I will also counter the image of lone practitioners acting in total secrecy. From the moment at which they purchased their materials to the time when they finally deposited their curse, the people who performed these rituals were constantly interacting with others, and sometimes even acted in groups.

Having established *how* a person made a curse tablet, in Chapter 4 I turn to the question of *why*. Since Audollent's foundational collection, curses have been sorted into categories depending on the motives expressed in the texts, and the five groupings of competition, erotic, juridical, business, and prayers for justice have found wide acceptance. In this chapter I critique this scheme. First, I explore in detail the social contexts that could have made particular kinds of cursing attractive at particular times, revealing how much more important these are than pan-Mediterranean trends. Second, I use anthropological studies of modern cultures to ask new questions of the ancient evidence, showing that there are deeper underlying social frameworks beneath the motives stated on the tablets. Curse tablets will be established as part of local responses to situations of crisis and conflict, embedded in ongoing relationships and networks of gossip and rumour. Curses gave individuals the ability to attack enemies from a position of relative safety, with the aim of harming the target's public standing while simultaneously protecting their own.

The final substantial chapter, Chapter 5, further develops the idea that curses played an important role in ongoing relationships between people. Using agency and power as starting points, the chapter explores how cursing rituals presented opportunities for individuals to act in their lives, and especially to address problems that they were otherwise powerless to solve. Cursing operated alongside the law, courtship, rumour and gossip, and either supplemented these other avenues of action or replaced them when they failed. Through the listing of targets, curse tablets afforded people an opportunity to identify people they believed to be their enemies: affirming or reaffirming lines of rivalry in social situations that could often be complex. The nature of cursing rituals allowed them to take a step further by using the supernatural power they believed it granted them to reorganize relationships in ways that suited them better. This is most evident on the erotic attraction and separation curses, but in Chapter 5 I argue that it is visible on other kinds of curse too. Finally in this chapter, I explore naming strategies on Roman curses, in terms of the ways in which cursers used the names of their targets to not only make them physically present in the ritual, but also to subvert existing hierarchies and power structures. This chapter is followed by a short epilogue in which I bring together all the strands of the argument, and suggest potential avenues for future work.

2

Cursing and Religion in the Roman West

If we are to explore the importance of cursing rituals for the lives of the people who used them, we must first understand where the practice of cursing came from and how it got to the various places discussed in this book. It is also important to sketch, as briefly as possible, the developments in the religious world of the western Roman provinces. Of course, this is a complex picture so can only be treated with broad brush strokes here. Nevertheless, it is essential to have a sense of the backdrop if we are to think about the wider significance of a single ritual practice. My focus throughout will be on religion as a lived experience. In other words, how did the experience of 'doing' religion change for people across the western provinces of the Roman Empire, and how did cursing fit into that experience? The chapter will begin to make the case for the importance of wider social and cultural developments in the analysis of curse tablets. For example, I will demonstrate how the seeming growth in popularity of curing closely mirrors the changes in the epigraphic habit, as well as changing understandings of religious knowledge and experience.

The origin and spread of curse tablets in the west

Before starting the outline of how cursing spread across the Roman west, it is important to raise two important issues. The first is determining what counts as a 'curse tablet'. The following definition, put forward by Jordan, has become canon in curse tablet studies. He said that curse tablets were 'inscribed pieces of lead, usually in the form of small, thin sheets, intended to influence, by supernatural means, the actions or welfare of persons or animals against their will'.[1] The only alteration to be made is the materials on which curses could be written. As Jordan himself later pointed out, there is no reason to exclude curses inscribed on materials other than lead if they fulfil the other criteria of the definition.[2] Indeed, the identification of curses as objects that seek to influence people against their will excludes other ritual texts on lead or lead alloy, such the plague amulet from London.[3] I have therefore considered any text that fulfils Jordan's definition, regardless of writing medium or language (curses in Latin, Greek and Celtic have been included), as long as it was found in the west of the Roman Empire. For clarity in my discussions, I have used the provincial divisions of the Principate, but modern toponyms. As there are so few curses from the Danubian provinces (Pannonia, Raetia and Noricum), for the purposes of regional analysis I have treated them as a single unit.

The second thing to note is that dating curse tablets is notoriously difficult. Many were excavated in the nineteenth or early twentieth century, and so suffer from a lack of good archaeological reporting.[4] Particularly in Britain, many twentieth- and twenty-first-century discoveries of curse tablets were made by metal detectorists, creating the same problem of inaccurate or missing contextual data. Even with some professional archaeological excavations, accurate dating is impossible because of the contexts into which the tablets were deposited. To take a particularly important example, the bottom of the sacred spring at Bath is a continually churning bed of quicksand, so neither relative nor absolute dating of the curse tablets can be done on the basis of stratigraphy.[5] In the case of Bath, and indeed tablets from elsewhere, tentative dating can be done based on palaeography and linguistics, though, giving at least a rough idea of the century in which a curse may have been written.[6] Yet even taking these possibilities into account there still remain almost fifty curses from the west that cannot be dated at all. For the sake of completeness, I have included these texts in this book.

The earliest surviving Greek tablets come from late sixth or early fifth century BC Sicily and were found in the cemetery at Selinunte.[7] There were certainly antecedents to this, and similarities have been identified between Greek practices and various earlier cultures of the Mediterranean and West Asia.[8] However, the use of inscribed lead tablets seems to have been an innovation of the Greek world,[9] and the practice quickly appeared in Attica from the late fifth century onwards, where it became popular in attacks on legal and political opponents.[10] Cursing was also turned to other ends, primarily love and commerce, by Athenians and other Greeks over the course of the Classical and Hellenistic periods.

From around the fourth century BC, the practice of writing curses on lead was adopted by Etruscans and Samnites in Italia.[11] It is difficult to determine the motives behind these curses as they tend to consist of lists of names only, occasionally accompanied by simple curse formulas, but there are suggestions that they could relate to legal or commercial dealings. At roughly the same time,

1. Alcácer do Sal
2. Altino
3. Amelie-les-Bains
4. Ampurias
5. Arezzo
6. Arlon
7. Autun
8. Avenches
9. Aylesford
10. Bad Kreuznach
11. Bath
12. Bodegraven
13. Bologna
14. Bolonia
15. Bordighera
16. Brandon
17. Brean Down
18. Bregenz
19. Broomhill
20. Budapest
21. Caerleon
22. Caistor St. Edmund
23. Calvi Risorta
24. Camarina
25. Capua
26. Carthage
27. Casabermeja
28. Centuripe
29. Chagnon
30. Chamalières
31. Châteaubleau
32. Chesterton
33. Classe
34. Clothall
35. Cologne
36. Concordia
37. Constantine
38. Córdoba
39. Cremona
40. Cuma
41. Dax
42. Dodford
43. Donnerskirchen
44. East Farleigh
45. Écija
46. Eining
47. El Jem
48. Évreux
49. Farley Heath
50. Fontanaccia
51. Frankfurt
52. Groß-Gerau
53. Haidra
54. Hamble Estuary
55. Hockwold-cum-Wilton
56. Italica
57. Kelvedon
58. Kempraten
59. Kempten
60. Khoms
61. Krefeld-Gellep
62. Le Mans
63. Le Mas-Marcou, Le Monastère

Figure 2.1 Distribution map of curses across the western provinces. Copyright Matilde Grimaldi.

64. Leicester
65. Leintwardine
66. Les Martres-de-Veyre
67. Lezoux
68. L'Hospitalet-du-Larzac
69. Lidgate
70. Ljubljana
71. London
72. Lydney Park
73. Lyon
74. Maar (Trier-Nord)
75. Mainz
76. Malton
77. Mariana
78. Marlborough
79. Marsala
80. Mautern
81. Mérida
82. Messina
83. Minturno
84. Montfo
85. Murol
86. Neustadt-an-der-Donau
87. Old Harlow
88. Orosei
89. Ostia
90. Pagan's Hill
91. Peiting
92. Perugia
93. Petronell
94. Pompeii
95. Pontaix
96. Pozzuoli
97. Ptuj
98. Puckeridge-Braughing
99. Pula
100. Pupput, Suq-el-Abiod
101. Quartier Saint-Marcel, Paris
102. Ratcliffe-on-Soar
103. Reggio Calabria
104. Rom
105. Rome
106. Roßdorf
107. Rothwell
108. Rottweil
109. Sagunt
110. Salerno
111. San Benedetto dei Marsi
112. San Severino Marche
113. Silchester
114. Sisak
115. Sousse
116. Szombathely
117. Thetford
118. Tongres
119. Torano Castello
120. Towcester
121. Trier
122. Uley
123. Verona
124. Wanborough
125. Wilhering
126. Wilten bei Innsbruck

the practice of cursing may have also been adopted by Iberian-speaking people in Hispania, although such a suggestion is hypothetical because we can no longer read their language.[12] The earliest Latin curse comes from Samnite territory, namely a second century BC grave at Pompeii, and the discovery of twenty further Latin texts from republican Italia (including Rome itself), Samos and Hispania (a different part of the region to the Iberian examples) attests to the adaptation of this practice throughout the expanding Roman world.[13]

As we move into the Imperial period, where this book is primarily focused, the evidence shows a much wider use of cursing across almost the entire Roman west. In the first century AD, many curses still come from Hispania and southern Italia, although there are a few examples from the north of the peninsula and North Africa. Most are of uncertain or unspecified motive, but there are four erotic curses (**SD 1, 70, 140, DT 304**), two against thieves (**SD 121, 141**) and the three tablets from Ampurias that attack Roman officials, seemingly over a land dispute (**SD 134-6**). In this period, the first curses are found north of the Alps. The spread across the northern provinces was thin at the beginning, with mostly isolated finds from Gallia, Britannia and the Danubian region. The exception seems to be Germania, where large numbers of curses were found at Bad Kreuznach and Mainz, most of which date to the late first or early second century AD. The Bad Kreuznach curses mostly concern legal trials, but those from Mainz are predominantly 'prayers for justice' including some texts that curse thieves. A curse found recently near some Roman houses in Tongeren, and securely dated to the late first century, provides the earliest western examples of the *charaktêres* and *voces magicae* that would become so prevalent in Italia and Africa in later centuries.[14]

From the second and third centuries, the practice of cursing seems to become increasingly concentrated in specific locations. In Britannia, the temples of Sulis Minerva at Bath and Mercury at Uley saw surges of activity in this period, as did the cemeteries at Sousse and Carthage in Africa. The rise at the latter two sites can be attributed to the growth of competitive chariot racing, combined with freelance religious experts making use of new ritual traditions seemingly being developed in Egypt. As will be discussed in Chapters 3 and 4, the combination of these two factors is unique in the west under the Principate and does not seem to emerge again until Late Antiquity, predominantly in the east. Although there is weak evidence for the spread of Graeco-Egyptian traditions of cursing elsewhere in the second and third century west, most curses in this period were what I will call 'self-authored' texts, made by the curser themselves, using whatever knowledge and understanding they had to hand.[15] Self-authored curses

Table 2.1 Number of curses included from each region

Region	Number of curses
Britannia	204
Africa	117
Italia	134
Germania	58
Gallia	53
Danubian provinces	26
Hispania	16

are widely distributed across most provinces in this period – Gallia, Germania, Hispania, Britannia, Italia and the Danubian region – in single finds or very small groups of four at most.

Only in Britannia does this wider distribution carry on into Late Antiquity. Both the temple sites of Bath and Uley continued attracting curses to the end of the fourth century, and there are at least fifteen curses from elsewhere in the province that could be dated to the same century. On the continent, the practice of cursing disappears entirely from Hispania and Germania after the end of the third century, and there are only two later texts from Africa. In Italia and Gallia, curse tablets from the fourth and fifth centuries have only been found in two large cities: Rome and Trier. At Rome, two major collections dominate the picture: the so-called 'Sethian tablets' from a columbarium near Porta San Sebastiano, which are almost exclusively directed towards chariot racers, and the relatively recent finds from the spring of Anna Perenna.[16] The two collections were not connected to each other, despite being roughly contemporary. Those found at Porta San Sebastiano were the product of either a single professional practitioner or a closely connected group, whereas the Anna Perenna curses appear to have been self-authored.[17] The curses found in the amphitheatre at Trier contain suggestions of professional input, in the presence of *voces magicae* and *charaktêres*.[18] These are perhaps the last curses to be deposited in the Roman west, potentially dating to as late as the mid-fifth century. From this point onwards, cursing with lead tablets was no longer a feature of life in the regions of the former Western Roman Empire. The reason for the disappearance of the ritual is beyond the scope of this book, but no doubt it lies in the political, social and cultural changes brought about in the fourth and fifth centuries, including the increasing dominance of Christianity over the religious landscape of Western Europe.

There are several conclusions to be drawn from this brief sketch. The first is that curse tablet writing broadly conforms to the general trend of the Roman 'Epigraphic Habit', with a gradual increase from the beginning of the Principate up to a peak in the second and third centuries, followed by a significant drop-off.[19] To some extent, therefore, we can see the increased popularity of cursing as part of a wider movement towards written forms of religious expression over the early Imperial period, including inscribed votives and funerary monuments. The spread of literacy among non-elites will also have contributed to these trends. Latin was the dominant language of cursing everywhere in the west, although there are significant numbers of Greek curses from Italia and Africa, as well as a small but important body of texts in Celtic from Britannia and Gallia. The practice spread with the expansion of Roman power, and, outside Britannia, appears to be predominantly focused on large cities such as Mainz, Trier, Rome and Carthage. On this final point, the nature of both professional and amateur archaeological investigation must be considered. Metal detecting is tolerated more in Britain than other parts of Europe, which must contribute to the apparent wider distribution of curses across that province when compared with the areas of, for example, modern France, Spain, Austria and Germany, where the practice is much more heavily restricted.[20] However, even curses found during archaeological excavations, undertaken by either early antiquarians or modern professionals, produce curses as much through chance as anything else, especially at cemetery sites where curses are often found alone or in pairs. To use Bath as an example again, the Sacred Spring was drained and excavated because the water was contaminated, rather than for purely scholarly investigation, and only half of the deposit was explored. As such, we should not put too much stress on the patterns of distribution across space and time such as those charted here. The central argument of this book contends that such pan-Imperial narratives are inadequate on several levels, and that there is far more to be gained from a fine-grained approach that sees cursing within the contexts of the lives of the individuals who made them: in other words, cursing as a lived experience.

Religious contexts

It remains to describe the religious contexts of the Roman Empire in which the practice of cursing was embedded. Of course, this is a huge subject, on which there has been increasingly fruitful scholarly discussion in recent years, inspired in no small part by the same theoretical and methodological drives that inspired this book.[21] Roman religion is no longer seen as a dry, lifeless thing that was unthinkingly and unchangingly repeated across the centuries, but instead as a multifaceted, ever-changing, and often contradictory amalgam of beliefs and practices that varied considerably across time and space.[22] This is especially true in the provinces, where Roman religion was continuously being brought into relationships with local beliefs and practices, some of which may have pre-dated the Roman conquests.[23] The resulting picture is diverse and colourful, and it would be foolish to try to contain the whole thing in this short chapter. Nevertheless, there are some important points to draw out, so that the following analysis of the curse tablets from the Roman west can be seen in its proper context. The people who made these curses were steeped in this religious world, and their cursing practices were informed by their broader experiences and understandings. It is exactly the point of the lived religion approach to think about religion as part of an individual's whole life, and as embedded in wider contexts.

One of the most important factors to consider is the imperial context of Roman religion. Although many religious beliefs and practices will have remained on smaller scales, from the first century onwards (or earlier in some places) there was also an Empire-wide layer, superimposed on local and regional religion, which made connections between local or regional traditions and the overarching structures of Rome. The imperial cult is its most explicit manifestation, seen in the widespread dedications for the safety of the sitting emperor and worship of his deified predecessors, and often concentrated on supra-regional centres such as the Sanctuary of the Three Gauls at Lyon.[24] Alongside this, the worship of other imperial deities, such as Jupiter Optimus Maximus, Victoria, and Mars, was adopted and adapted to suit local needs, beliefs and practices.[25] The rituals that people performed across the provinces appear strikingly similar: vows, prayers and sacrifices were all performed along what some scholars have seen as increasingly 'Roman' lines. Moreover, the presence of objects such as curse tablets, amulets and inscribed gemstones in the western provinces demonstrate that a wide range of forms of religious belief and practice spread with Roman power. The conditions of Empire – relative internal peace, developed trade links, increased monetization and so on – facilitated greater movements of goods, ideas and people (forced or voluntary) around the Roman world. In the increasingly cosmopolitan cities of the Mediterranean, interest in new religious experiences grew, especially among the elite. At the same time, conquest, subjugation and ongoing imperial rule caused ruptures in local religious traditions across the Empire, facilitating the movement of what Wendt calls 'freelance religious specialists'.[26]

Previous generations of scholars conceptualized this through the lens of 'Romanization': the top-down imposition of Roman religious practices on the people of the provinces. Since the 1990s, the application of post-colonial methodologies by archaeologists has successfully overhauled this model.[27] The agency of local people in their own changing culture and society is now well established. Although the Romans were indeed an invading, colonizing power, cultural change only happened with the active participation of the people themselves, who adopted and adapted incoming Roman cultural forms to suit their own needs and preferences. By taking this approach we can more readily account for local and regional variation in eating habits, dress, architecture, language and, of course, religion, within the wider global context of the Roman Empire.[28] We can also more easily see instances of resistance to, or total rejection of, the cultural forms brought in with the Romans.[29] The 'lived religion' approach that I am taking in this book sits comfortably within these wider theoretical considerations, because they all put the agency and lived experience of the individual at centre stage, with all the wider contexts as an essential backdrop that informed their actions. Curse tablets are an excellent example of these processes, as people in different parts of the Empire adopted the practice, but only with adaptations to address not just personal crises, but also local or regional circumstances that were themselves nested within the overarching socio-cultural structures of the Roman Empire.

Alongside the imperial context of religion, and directly related to it, are developments in the formalization of religious knowledge. As Rüpke has recently shown, over the course of the imperial period, religious expression increasingly required the involvement, in one way or another, of specialists.[30] At even the most basic level, individual religious expression came to rely on an array of professionals including potters, masons, sculptors, fresco painters and garden designers, as the material components involved in religious ritual became increasingly complex.[31] Civic priests, in connection with local aristocracies, were also important figures in this development, because of their involvement in the regulation of time through the sacred calendar, the provision of buildings and space for worship, and the funding of large-scale sacrifices.[32] Such men and women were therefore essential for the religious life of their communities through their organization and maintenance of festivals and temples.[33]

However, as people who acted as a source of religious expertise, they did not hold a monopoly. The range of individuals who claimed knowledge of or access to the supernatural grew exponentially in the Roman imperial period, especially in cities.[34] Such people appear frequently in Roman literature as figures of ridicule or fear, but beneath the derision and stereotyping it is possible to glean some information about their real-world counterparts. They provided an array of different services, including healing, divination, initiation and philosophical advice, as well as selling religious objects such as amulets, votives and curse tablets. Some, like the witches of Lucian's *Dialogues of the Hetairai*, stayed in one place, building up a solid base of regular clients in a particular city.[35] Others, like the soothsayers that Columella and Cato warn about in their agricultural handbooks, were itinerant, travelling through the countryside or from town to town.[36] Most of the time they were at least tolerated by the civic and religious authorities across the Empire, but there were occasional purges, particularly in the city of Rome. Augustus famously burned more than 2,000 'prophetic texts' when he became *pontifex maximus*, and several of his successors expelled magicians, astrologers and other 'freelance religious specialists' from the city.[37] As Wendt points out, the main targets of these actions were probably the well-positioned individuals posing direct and blatant threats to political or military stability, rather than small-scale dream interpreters or potion sellers.[38] Nevertheless, it does suggest a more general feeling that freelance experts were somehow undesirable, which is compounded by the almost exclusively negative portrayal of witches and *magi* in Roman literature.[39] Exactly what sources of knowledge these experts drew on is a complicated, and ultimately unanswerable question because of the huge variety of options. Some will have appealed to exotic traditions from the east, especially Egypt and Persia, while others might have claimed connections to powerful lineages of practitioners.[40] If there were any shared principle, it was that their claims to knowledge and authority were based on themselves as individuals: *they* had the hidden knowledge or the personal connection to the divine that could solve a client's particular problem.

As we will see in Chapter 3, it is not always easy to say with confidence when a curse tablet was produced with the involvement of a specialist, although there are obvious examples from Rome, Carthage and Sousse in particular. Elsewhere in the Empire, most curses were 'self-authored' in the sense that they cursers themselves wrote the actual tablet, drawing on whatever knowledge was available to them through family, friends and others in their local communities, as well as their own lived experiences. As Graham has argued, religious knowledge is not simply a matter of institutionally defined doctrine, but is generated by individuals through their embodied experience in the world.[41] The lived religion approach I have taken in this book is explicitly aimed at uncovering these individual ways of experiencing and understanding religion.

To summarize: the spread and development of cursing practices in the Roman imperial period is closely related to wider changes in the culture, society and politics of the Roman Empire. Although this might seem like a trite and obvious statement, it is one that I think is worth making. There is a strong temptation to separate magical practices, such as cursing, away from 'normal' Roman society and therefore to see them as something disconnected from the wider world. The lived religion approach taken in this book demonstrates that this view is untenable. The people who made curse tablets were embedded in local, regional and global contexts, and generated knowledge and understanding of the world through their lived experience. They brought all that experience to the ritual of cursing, which they adapted to suit whatever personal situation they were in. The purpose of the rest of this book is to explore the ways in which cursing fit into the lives of those who performed these rituals.

3

Rituals, Gestures and Movements

Introduction

Curse tablets are the physical remains of a series of actions, gestures and movements that could have included writing, speaking, folding, nailing and depositing. It was these actions that constituted the curse ritual, not just the final written text, as they played a crucial role in creating a powerful curse that affected people in the real world. Yet although these actions were of critical importance to the efficacy of the curse, they have been relatively neglected in scholarship to date.[1] In this chapter I will challenge the focus of previous scholars on the written formulas at the expense of the lived experience of performing a cursing ritual. My argument rests on a reconceptualization of curse tablets as the end products of a series of ritually significant actions, gestures and movements, rather than as just inscribed texts. Thinking of the tablets in this way embraces their materiality and will bring into the foreground the ways in which lead tablets and human bodies interacted to create a curse.[2] A 'lived religion' approach is central to this argument because it requires that the cursers be seen as thinking and feeling individuals, who are intimately bound up with the material realities of the people, places and things around them. The impact of this kind of perspective on scholarly understanding of object production has been convincingly argued by (among many others) Ingold. In what has become an influential article, Ingold argued that the activity of basket weaving can be seen as the epitome of human technical activity, in that it demonstrates the skilled interaction between the practitioner and her materials, as well as the rhythmic, narrative quality of skilled action, in which every action grows out of the one before.[3] When making a basket, Ingold argues that the final form of the object is never exactly what the weaver had in mind originally, but only comes into being gradually, through a pattern of skilled movement in response to the material realities of the fibres being used. Weaving requires care, judgement and dexterity, and must be grounded in an attentive involvement with the materials. Building from this observation, recent movements in archaeological theory that are loosely grouped under 'new materialism' have argued that objects themselves are actively involved in processes such as weaving.[4] The fibres that a weaver uses to make a basket are not passive, but because of their physical properties (or 'affordances') have a direct effect on the form of the finished product. In this chapter I will argue that thinking about curse tablets in a similar way to Ingold's basket can reveal new insights into their production and use. I will argue that each curse tablet was 'woven' by the curser in a ritual that was informed by the materiality of the lead and their own understanding of the process.

Although 'ritual' as a term has a long history in the discipline of archaeology, recent work has overhauled many of the older debates. Following the work of Bell, archaeologists now tend to think less about 'rituals' and more about the 'ritualization' of objects and activities, in the sense that people distinguish ways of doing things in ritual contexts from other, more quotidian activities.[5] Ritualized actions are deliberately framed as different to 'routine reality' and therefore generate a 'quality of specialness'.[6] Archaeologists now also recognize the active role played by material things in creating and sustaining ritualized actions.[7] For example, a person intending to sacrifice an animal cannot actually do so without the animal, as well as a knife, an altar, fire, fuel and so on. The qualities (termed 'affordances' in the theoretical literature) of each object affect the performance of the ritual. In Roman studies, Graham's recent book is at the cutting edge in applying theories from the 'new materialism' to make a very strong case for the essential contribution of 'more-than-human' things to the ritualization of activities and the creation of religious agency.[8] She argues that religion is created by context-specific interactions within assemblages of things, including human bodies, objects, natural environments, animals and divinities. Human intentions are important, but cannot be realized without engagement with the physical world, and as such the material affordances of that world make just as significant a contribution to ritualized activities as do human intentions.[9] For our purposes here, it is important to recognize that although a curser might have had the idea of their curse in their heads before beginning the ritual, the curse itself emerged only from their direct, embodied engagement with material things: not just lead tablets, styli and nails, but also the waters of a sacred spring or the earth of a grave. As I will argue in this chapter, all these things had the potential to affect the lived experience of performing a cursing ritual, making each one unique.

The idea of transformation has become central to the study of ritual activity in several academic fields.[10] Through ritualized performances, power and meaning are given to spaces, objects and people. One example of this comes from West Africa, where the performance of rituals by masked individuals gives the masks power and agency, and also temporarily transforms the individual into a being with supernatural power.[11] Space is also transformed by ritual performance: processions, for example, generate traditional routes that take on religious significance and must be adhered to in future performances, regardless of subsequent changes in geography.[12] Cursing rituals were inherently transformative on many levels. In a similar way to the African mask rituals, ancient cursing sought to transform raw materials into powerful objects with the ability to directly influence people or animals in the real world against their will. As part of this aim, the ritual attempted various other transformations and transmissions; in theft curses, for example, the stolen object or the thieves themselves could be transformed into divine property through formulas that gave them to a goddess. These and other curses could attempt to transform parts of the victim's body through sympathetic formulas, for example 'just as salt becomes liquid in water, so shall his limbs and marrow waste away' (**SD 493**).

Many recent discussions of ritual in archaeology have worked from the assumption that they are regularly and repeatedly performed by the same people.[13] However, cursing rituals in the Roman west do not readily conform to this pattern. Curses were emergency rituals, performed only in response to rare moments of personal crisis. Outside small groups of freelance religious experts (whom I will discuss shortly), there is little evidence to suggest that any curser produced more than one tablet, and therefore it is probable that very few of them had any experience of conducting the rituals, although it is possible that they may have witnessed them being performed by others. This adds a level of tension and unfamiliarity to cursing that is non-existent in more general archaeological treatments of ritual. The cursers would have been entering uncharted territory, rather than going over well-worn ground. Although they may have sought advice from family, friends or religious authorities, the anxiety over getting something wrong would have been much higher than for someone repeating a ritual they had conducted many times before. Each tablet was produced for a specific reason, in response to a moment of uncertainty and possibly intense anger, frustration and fear in the life of the curser.[14] Again, this adds further emotional dimensions to the ritual acts, which would have been different for everyone depending on their situation. Thinking from a 'lived religion' perspective is important here, as we need to treat the cursers as embedded in their worlds, and intimately bound up with the physical, cultural and personal surroundings that I will continue to discuss throughout this book.

At this point it is important to draw this discussion together and to state the definition of ritual that I will use here. Cursing rituals in the west were highly individualistic performances based on each curser's motives for cursing, as well as their understanding of local traditions, embedded in the contexts of their location at the time of performance. These included elements of physical, temporal and social context – architecture, weather conditions, cultural sensitivities, individual circumstance, memory and so on – but also the materiality of the tablets and other objects used during the performance. I deem an action to have been part of the cursing ritual if it related in any way to the transformation of the blank sheet of lead into a powerful curse through which a person believed they could influence the real world. Aside from the writing of words onto the tablet this could include, but was not limited to, spoken words, bodily movement and gesture, manipulation or mutilation of the tablet or associated objects (such as dolls) and deposition. Specialist knowledge or training was not necessarily required on the part of the individual cursers, although some cursers did choose to go through a professional, and others may have sought advice from various sources within each local context.

Freelance religious experts in the Roman west

An exploration of the potential involvement of religious specialists in the creation of curse tablets in the Roman west is necessary here. Where curse tablets appear in literary sources, they are often produced by a specialist of one kind or another. Old women usually make curses in Latin literature, such as, for example, in Ovid's *Fasti* and Apuleius' *Metamorphoses*.[15] Tacitus records instances where various members of the imperial family were accused of consulting religious experts of different kinds, including male astrologers and *magi*, in order to attack each other, sometimes with curse tablets.[16] On top of these literary accounts, the evidence of the *PGM* attests to the existence of specialists making curses within the Graeco-Egyptian tradition.[17] That there were religious specialists who could make curse tablets is therefore not in doubt, and it might be thought that the existence of such specialists calls into question the arguments of this book, which is reframing curse tablets onto the individual experience of making them and their place in the social lives of those who did. It is therefore important to have a close look at the curses from the Roman west to establish how many may have been produced by specialists, or under their influence, and how many were 'self-authored', in the sense of being made directly by the people concerned with the matters addressed on the tablet.[18]

Of the 607 curses collected for this study, 167 bear evidence for the involvement of specialists. These are the tablets that contain *voces magicae*, *charaktêres* or complex drawings, or which appeal to exotic deities or spirits, the knowledge of which probably required some training, and perhaps access to instructional texts such as those preserved in the *PGM*. Of these, 139 come from the large cities of Carthage, Sousse and Rome, with a much smaller group of nine tablets from Trier and isolated finds from elsewhere in all regions except Britannia (see below). From the African cities, the curses that were made by specialists address erotic motives or attack chariot racers and their horses. The circus curses appear to cluster in groups, with several targeting the same victims and using the same or similar magical formulae, suggesting the work of individual specialists or closely related groups.[19] The same can be said for the city of Rome, where the best evidence for specialist production of curses is the group found in the columbarium near Porta San Sebastiano on the Via Appia.[20] Again, these curses relate to chariot racing, and suggest the work of either individuals or a small group who shared the same knowledge.

What kinds of specialists were involved? Scholarship on 'freelance religious experts' in the Roman Empire recognizes a range of possibilities, sometimes arranged in a hierarchy from village wise women to highly mobile and literate individuals.[21] Both ends of the hierarchy attracted attention from ancient authors. At the lower end, local religious specialists were conceptualized as being concerned with matters of the heart, but also with providing herbal remedies and protective amulets.[22] From the Augustan period onwards, this level of specialist was routinely morphed into the sensationalized figure of the witch: a troubling, feminine source of power that challenged the male dominance of society.[23] At the other end of the hierarchy was an array of different figures, including astrologers and adherents of philosophical schools that dabbled with divination, necromancy and theurgy. From the way they are characterized in the literature, their focus was on predicting the future and on establishing closer connections to the divine through secret knowledge of ritual activities.[24] These were the specialists who became connected to the imperial family and other prominent individuals and were also the ones regularly targeted by official attempts to stamp out ritual practices deemed unacceptable.[25] Somewhere between these two extremes must lie the individuals responsible for the curse tablets found in Carthage, Sousse and Rome. Although their knowledge and abilities surpassed non-literate specialists, there is little sense from the curses that they were connected to members of the elite, or that they were interested in the kinds of ritual practices that characterize the upper reaches of the hierarchy just described. The texts of the curses demonstrate connections to other parts of the Roman world, especially Egypt, through the evocation of deities such as Osiris and Seth, and the use of *voces magicae* and *charaktêres* found in the PGM. Whether the specialists themselves travelled directly from Egypt themselves, as Gordon imagines for the authors of the North African circus curses, is impossible to tell, but it is relatively safe to assume, at the very least, that they were in possession of texts that ultimately originated in Egypt.[26]

It is also very difficult to say how long these specialists were established in the places where curse tablets have been found. Dating curses is notoriously difficult, and often we can be no more precise that ascribing individual tablets to a particular century. Nevertheless, the repeated use of the same formulas or the targeting of the same victims across multiple curses – particularly prevalent in the circus curses from Carthage, Sousse and Rome – is evidence for flurries of activity by individual specialists concentrated in short spaces of time. In Chapter 4, I will argue that this may have resulted from periods of more intense rivalry between the racing factions. From the perspective of freelance religious specialists, such occasions would be perfect opportunities to diversify their offerings, or to travel to new locations in search of business. In the competitive atmosphere of large cities, religious specialists were willing to add new skills to their repertoire, and moved with the interests or needs of their potential clients. The individuals that Dio Chrysostom, Juvenal and Tertullian grumble about, preaching cod-philosophies, interpreting dreams or performing conjuring tricks for crowds in marketplaces or outside temples, are presumably also those who could turn their hands to making curse tablets if the demand existed.[27] Wendt makes the valuable point that these are not market conditions in the strict sense, because freelance religious experts often created the demand themselves by convincing people that their services were valuable. The few curses against *venatores* found in Carthage, discussed in Chapter 4, may represent a failed attempt at diversification into a market that could not sustain the demand. As I will argue, beast hunting did not attract the same levels of spectator rivalry as chariot racing, and so very few people felt the need to resort to cursing to ensure a favourable result.[28]

Away from the four big cities, the evidence for the involvement of freelance religious experts in the production of curse tablets is thinly and widely dispersed. There are only nineteen tablets that might fit into the category: four from other sites in Africa, seven from Italia outside Rome, two from Gallia outside Trier, two from Germania, one from Hispania and three from the Danubian provinces.[29]

Such a distribution makes it impossible to offer any interpretation without unreasonable speculation. We cannot know, for example, whether these sole tablets were produced by travelling experts who brought knowledge of *voces magicae* and the rest with them, or whether this is evidence of established local specialists integrating new elements into their existing practice. If it shows anything, it is that the knowledge of Graeco-Egyptian magical traditions penetrated only very weakly into the Roman west, at least in terms of the production of curse tablets.[30] The vast majority of curse tablets from the Roman west, at least away from the big cities, shows no signs of having been made by freelance religious experts with knowledge of Graeco-Egyptian traditions, but instead appear to have been 'self-authored' by an individual or group of individuals. Other people might still have been involved in the process. Family or friends might give advice on local traditions of cursing, as might local religious specialists of different kinds. It is not impossible to imagine some level of involvement by temple authorities at Bath, Uley and Mainz, for example, where the ritual seems to have been well established. Some of these traditions must have moved beyond the temple centres, as shown by the wide-spread use of mutually exclusive alternatives in British curses. In social contexts where literacy was rare, acquaintances who could write might be enlisted to aid in the creation of the curse, although there is only one clear example of a curse being written by someone other than the named cursers (**SD 350** from Ratcliffe-on-Soar).[31] Throughout this book I will counter the image of the lone practitioner acting in total secrecy, which is common in the literary testimonies and which has been followed by some earlier scholars. As I will demonstrate, these rituals were important moments in the social lives of those who practised them, and they involved more than just those immediately affected.

Creating a curse tablet

The process of creating a 'self-authored' curse tablet can be broken down into six steps. After the initial trigger – for example, the theft of personal items or the announcement of a legal trial – the curser made the decision to compose a curse tablet (1). They then needed to obtain the required physical materials – usually a sheet of lead and a stylus, in some cases also one or more nails for piercing – and perhaps also some advice on how to go about the process (2). This probably came in the form of either knowledge circulating within the community and passed on by friends or family, or, in certain contexts, directly from professional magicians or religious specialists based in temples. In general, people seem to have taken writing as the first step in physically altering the tablet (3). This makes sense in terms of the transformation of the lead sheet into the curse, as writing physically ingrained the intention into the material, and transformed it into an object with power.[32] This power could then be enhanced by further manipulation or mutilation (4) – commonly this involved folding, rolling or nailing – and would probably have been accompanied by an oral prayer (5). The final step was to deposit the tablet in a significant place (6), usually a temple, watery place, entertainment venue or cemetery. Step one, motivations for cursing, will be discussed in Chapter 4. Therefore, in this chapter I will explore in detail the other five ritual steps: obtaining the tablet, writing, manipulating or mutilating the tablet, speaking words and the final act of deposition. Other than writing, few of the other actions that went into the production of the tablets were explicitly recorded in the texts. This makes reconstructing the ritual a challenge, but the physical state of the tablet itself is as a record of the actions of the curser up to the point of deposition. By working backwards from that point, through the process of the ritual creation of the curse tablet, I argue that the series of actions that led to the finished product can be reconstructed.

To gain further insights into the creation of a curse tablet, I have conducted some experiments myself. These were limited by the resources available to me (modern materials produced using industrialized techniques), but my intention was to replicate the experience in as close a manner as possible. I obtained 1 millimetre-thick sheet lead, which is the approximate thickness of many of the tablets found in the western provinces of the Roman Empire and experimented with writing on and manipulating the material. I tested a variety of writing styles, including plain texts as well as reversed lettering. I also experimented with folding, rolling and piercing the tablets to assess the ease or difficulty of these actions. Although far from a rigorous scientific endeavour, the results of these experiments have given me a different sense of working with these materials and have therefore given greater insights into the experience of conducting a cursing ritual in the Roman world. In what follows I will discuss the results of my own experimentation in the relevant sections.

Obtaining the tablet

There is no clear evidence, from any site in the west, for exactly where the cursers obtained the raw materials needed to make a curse.[33] At the very least, each required a relatively flat tablet and a stylus to write with, and in some cases a nail for piercing. Scholars usually assume that curses were written on tablets made from pure lead – to the point where this material has entered Jordan's standard definition of a curse tablet – and that is presumably what many are indeed made from. However, the tablets themselves have never been subjected to chemical analysis, with only two exceptions. Seventy-five of the 130 curses from Bath were examined, revealing that only fourteen tablets contained at least two-thirds lead, with only four of these being pure lead.[34] In most of the other tablets, the lead was alloyed with tin, in a composition that resembles modern pewter. Significantly, none of the Bath tablets are identical in chemical composition and thickness, suggesting that they were not mass-produced. As there was a concentration of pewter production in the region around Bath from at least the third century, this would suggest that the tablets were off-cuts or side-line products of local industrial production.[35]

The second group of curses to undergo chemical analysis were ninety-six of those from Carthage. These were also found to include other metals, most notably copper and tin. The curses appear to have been mostly produced using local lead, but with some using material imported from across the Empire.[36] As with the Bath tablets, it seems reasonable to conclude that individuals were making use of whatever lead or lead-alloy was available in their local areas. Away from Bath and Carthage, such conclusions are harder to draw because of the lack of chemical analysis. However, lead was a common material in the Roman provinces and so it is unlikely that it would have been difficult to obtain in the quantities needed to produce a curse.[37]

Lead and lead-alloy are by far the most common materials used for curse tablets in the Roman west, and for the ancient world overall. Apart from its ready availability, scholars have long recognized the symbolic meanings given to lead in Greek and Roman thought.[38] It was associated with death because of its dull colour, its weightiness, and the fact that it was cold to the touch. These associations were transferred to the victims in recipes in the *PGM* and on some curse tablets, although not frequently outside the Greek east.[39] On Latin curses, the heaviness of lead is most commonly mentioned, usually in formulas alluding to the quick falling of lead when deposited, as on **SD 157** (Montfo), **470** (Bad Kreuznach) and **530** (Petronell). Some of the Mainz tablets draw connections between the melting of lead and the fate of the victims, which related to their deposition in fire pits, as I will discuss later in this chapter. Cousins has recently suggested that the significance of pewter as a material may have been overlooked, citing Pliny the Elder and Suetonius who both hint that it was considered a cheap substitute for silver.⁴⁰ If this is the case, Cousins argues, then we might view the Bath curses as 'positive and orthodox' religious offerings, rather than emphasizing the dark, chthonic associations that normally go with lead. I do not think we can push any of these associations too far. For some individuals there certainly were deeper meanings to the material they chose for their curse, but for others the tablet, whether pure or alloyed lead, must have simply been a convenient writing surface. Moreover, although modern scholars privilege lead as the prime material for cursing, we have no way of knowing how many were written on perishable materials. Papyrus curses have survived only in Egypt, and although Ovid mentions curses on wax, none have been found by modern archaeologists for obvious reasons.⁴¹

In very few cases – only nine out of the 607 in this study – curses have been found written on imperishable materials other than metal sheets. Unfortunately, we can only guess at the reasons for choosing materials other than lead on these occasions because the curses themselves give few definitive answers. Indeed, most raise tantalising but unsolvable questions. To take one example, the erotic curse from Maar was apparently inscribed on a cinerary urn (**SD 173**). Was this done before or after the burial? If before, what involvement did the family of the deceased have in the ritual? If after, how and why was this particular urn chosen? Another curse, presumably from Rome but without specific provenance, was written in ink on the *inside* of a cinerary urn (**SD 16**). Muzzioli reasoned that this must have been written before the ashes were placed inside, and therefore must have been written by whoever oversaw the funeral rites, or at least with their consent.⁴² The formulas in this curse make explicit use of both the urn's material form and intended purpose, requesting that the victim, a man called Collecticius, be restrained inside with the soul of the dead person and carried off to the underworld. The curse from Rome written on a lamp also refers to the object itself, this time making it an offering brought to the spirits of the dead by the victim (**SD 3**). As noted by Sánchez Natalías, by also making the victim's name part of the offering – through the formula 'Helenus gives his name to the infernals' – this curse creates direct connections between the lamp (and its light), the victim's name and their life.⁴³ The final two exceptional cases to discuss here are the curses inscribed on stone: one from Merida (Hispania) and the other from Pompeii. The Pompeiian example was nailed to a tomb in a prominent position below the epitaph, and reveals a series of developments between two men: Publius Vesonius Phileros, for whom the tomb was built, and Marcus Orfellius, a friend who was also going to be buried here (**SD 72**).⁴⁴ However, after Orfellius betrayed their friendship by bringing legal charges against him,

Phileros not only cut him from these burial arrangements, but by means of the curse, from any peaceful rest in the underworld. The very public nature of this curse is a reaction to the public disloyalty that Orfellius had shown his former friend. The breakdown of this relationship may have been widely known, so Phileros was publicly demonstrating the serious consequences of betraying his *amicitia*. The inscription blends traditions of cursing with language typical of funerary epigraphy: it addresses passers-by with the phrase '*hospes paullisper morare*' (stranger, stay a short while), and goes on to exhort them to learn a moral lesson from the story being told.[45] In this way, the curse itself is almost hidden in plain sight, or at the very least comes across as justified in the circumstances.[46] The other stone curse targets a thief but gives no indication as to why it was not written on lead (**SD 120**). The language addresses the goddess in very flattering terms and justifies the punishment of the victim, but no more so than many British equivalents that were not displayed.[47] We might suggest that the intention was to associate the curse with other votive inscriptions, perhaps displayed in a temple. Unfortunately, the lack of original depositional context makes it hard to go beyond conjecture.

To return to lead, the source of the materials is an important question, but one that does not have secure answers. If indeed they were off-cuts or side-line products of local industries, the cursers could well have obtained them directly from the producers. The presumption among most modern scholars is that they would have been relatively cheap to purchase, following Tomlin in pointing towards the low value of some objects reported stolen on the Bath curses.[48] At temple sites such as Bath and Mainz, where cursing was common, the temple may have kept a store of blank tablets that the cursers could buy, and specialist practitioners in Carthage, Sousse and Rome are likely to have kept their own store of materials too. However the tablet was procured, the process would have required some form of social interaction with another person, and therefore could have been the first time that the curser had expressed their intention to someone else. Even if they did not state explicitly that they were buying the object to make a curse tablet, in a society where this kind of ritual action was relatively common, working out the intention would not have been difficult. This would be enhanced in the small communities of the western provinces, where the misfortunes of individuals would have been more widely known to others.[49] For the curser this could have elicited a whole range of emotions, on which the temptation is to speculate endlessly. It could have been a moment of anxiety, fearing having their intentions revealed to others, or perhaps it could have been a moment of resolve, with a definite sense that the ritual was going to be performed and that justice was going to be served. Each curser would have reacted to the experience differently, depending on their own individual circumstances.

Written words

The central position of the written word in Roman religion is now well established. Despite a lack of any single sacred book, Roman religion did place importance and power on certain writings, such as collections of oracles, recipe books and priestly texts.[50] Pliny the Elder mentions that priests read the words of their prayers from books,[51] meaning that collections of words must have existed, although none have survived. As well as instructions used by priests, ordinary worshippers in urban settings could consult publicly displayed calendars to ensure their own correct observance of festivals and other rituals. Through these written texts, the authorities maintained their control of religion through their power to organize time and to restrict access to communications with the gods.[52] Alongside these, Roman temples were covered with other writings, not just durable stone inscriptions but also messages to the gods written by private individuals on perishable materials such as wood, papyrus and wax.[53] These could have been formal records of fulfilled or promised vows, or casual inscriptions and graffiti of visitors.[54] Scholars have argued that writing something down and leaving it in the temple helped to define the place of the individual within the religious system; if the individuals were explicitly named, it confirmed and memorialized their presence at the temple at a specific time.[55]

Until recently, philological readings of texts such as these have taken precedent, focussing on their content, for example their scripts, language and semantic meanings. In the last decade or so, scholars have moved away from these analyses towards examining the contexts and materiality of texts, looking at the mechanics of writing and problematizing the definitions of 'reader' and 'writer'.[56] Piquette and Whitehouse have argued that writing is inextricably embedded in material worlds, and is therefore directly informed by the properties of the materials used and cultural knowledge of things like script forms.[57] Writing is possible only through direct bodily engagement with the materials, and demands certain postures and gestures involving the entire body – not just the hands, but also the arms, face, eyes and head.[58] The form of the materials used in writing are shaped accordingly, for example the size to which many (although not all) curse tablets were cut made them easy to inscribe while being held in one hand. This meant that they could be inscribed without a specific writing surface, perhaps using the upper leg for support.[59] The comportment of the writer's body during the act of writing would have made it obvious to onlookers what they were doing, especially at temple sites such as Bath, Uley and Mainz where cursing was relatively common.

Unlike writing with ink on paper, writing on lead is not a process of adding to the surface of the material, but of physically carving the words *into* it,[60] meaning that the writing surface itself plays an active role in the process. The action of inscribing into lead or lead alloy removes the top layer of dull, oxidized metal, such that the text of the inscription catches the light and shines against the rest of the tablet. This could have enhanced the otherworldly experience of the act of writing, especially for anyone who had no experience of writing on such materials. The varying nature of the materials used would have created a range of possible lived experiences here, depending on exactly what the curser was writing on. According to Tomlin, pewter and other lead or tin alloys would have provided a smoother writing surface than pure lead and could have been cast into thinner tablets.[61] This may have made the task easier, and possibly would have made it closer to the experience of writing on thin sheets of papyrus or wood, which may have been a more common experience for practised writers.

On this point we must also consider again the nine tablets written or inscribed on ceramic or stone. These may have been harder to achieve, requiring concentration and perhaps repeated scratching with the stylus or the involvement of a professional mason in the case of the two stone curses. However, as ostraca are ubiquitous across the Roman Empire, so there is no reason to think that inscribing pottery was any more unusual for these individuals than writing on lead was for the other cursers. In one of these cases, the Châteaubleau curse, it is one of many Celtic texts inscribed on roof tiles found in that town, so it seems to be part of a local writing tradition peculiar to that area.[62]

Alongside the material there were other practical concerns. The tablets were often irregular in shape, there were casting flaws to avoid, as well as interference caused by whatever method was used to ensure a flat surface, usually hammering or scraping (Figure 3.1). Many cursers adapted their writing style to compensate for bumps, dips and holes in the tablet, and often changed the direction of the words to fit better onto the tablet. This would have been easier to achieve for those who had experience of writing in their everyday lives, and could therefore transfer the skill into the unfamiliar context of cursing.[63] The widely varying quality of the handwriting on display shows that experience and practice were not compulsory criteria for composing curses, and the small collection of

Figure 3.1 Front and back of a curse from Bath. Author's photograph.

pseudo-inscriptions from Bath point to a culture in which even illiterate people could petition the deities in this manner.⁶⁴ Away from the activities of professionals in Rome, Carthage and Sousse there is no repetition of curser names anywhere from the west, and with the possible exception of **SD 215** and **361**,⁶⁵ there are no two self-authored tablets written in the same hand, so even for practised writers the experience of composing a curse tablet would have been unfamiliar. No doubt they would have been aware of the significance of the new purpose to which they were turning their skill, and the added power involved in writing for this purpose.

Most of the curses from the western provinces were written entirely by individual hands, but a small number of tablets show more than one. Apart from one from Larzac,⁶⁶ all of these are from either Bath or Mainz. Of the seven examples from Bath, two have the curser's name written in a different hand to the main body of the text (**SD 271** and **210**) and three have the victims' names written in a different hand (SD 218, 283, **206**). The other two consist of a jumble of texts in several hands written over and around each other (SD 219, 309). The precise circumstances behind these tablets are impossible to reconstruct, but it seems clear that on these few occasions the curses were not written by a single person. Perhaps the main cursers were not confident in their ability to write more than their own names or the names of their victims and entrusted the more complex formulas to a more literate person, perhaps a friend, family member or temple attendant. The cases of SD 219 and 309 might suggest that several individuals were present at the ritual and took turns in writing their intentions on the tablet as it was passed between them. In this respect they have some similarities to the two Mainz curses with multiple authors (**SD 490** and

491), which both have a different script on the two sides of the tablet. Again, the most likely possibility is that the tablet was passed between two individuals for them to write their respective sections of the curse. The texts on the two sides of **SD 491** were sufficiently different for the editor to suggest that they might even be two separate curses. Whether this conclusion is accurate or not, more than one individual was involved in the ritual on this occasion.

At this point, a brief excursus on ancient literacy is relevant. Harris, whose monograph *Ancient Literacy* is still the most comprehensive work on the subject, concluded that literacy levels in the imperial period never rose above 10 per cent of the population.[67] This view of literacy as the preserve of the elite is a common one, but has been challenged both by evidence that Harris chose to ignore and by new evidence that has come to light since the publication of his book, particularly the Vindolanda tablets and many of the curse tablets studied in this book.[68] Harris took a very restrictive view of literacy, confining himself to material relevant to the elite and ignoring the participation of semi-literate and non-literate people with written culture.[69] In reality, there would have been a huge range of competencies in reading and writing in the ancient world, and it is probable that more could read than could write.[70] Semi- and non-literate people could be involved in the production of written texts, for example as bronze workers or stonemasons,[71] and also in the reception of texts, through oral performance by others or simply knowing that certain texts were important in some way, without being able to decode them fully.[72] The evidence of the curse tablets, particularly the British examples, has forced a reassessment of levels of written proficiency, especially in rural communities like Uley and Ratcliffe-on-Soar (Notts.).[73] The existence of an unpublished tablet from Uley that is in Latin but written in Greek letters is particularly surprising (SD 436), given that the same feature is more commonly found among professionally produced tablets from North Africa (e.g. **DT 231, 252, 267, 270, 304**). We evidently need to think more carefully about provincial and rural literacy away from the imperial centre. The curses written in Celtic using the Latin alphabet found in Britannia and Gallia should also force a reassessment of literacy in the west. As a result, there is no reason to think that all the cursers who wrote curse tablets in the western provinces more broadly were part of Harris' literate 10 per cent. The skills needed to write a curse were not only available to the educated elite, and the individuals named on the curses themselves demonstrate that the ritual was available to those of all social classes.

To return to writing curse tablets, one example from Mainz illustrates the creative and performative nature of the ritual perfectly (**SD 484**, Figure 3.2). The

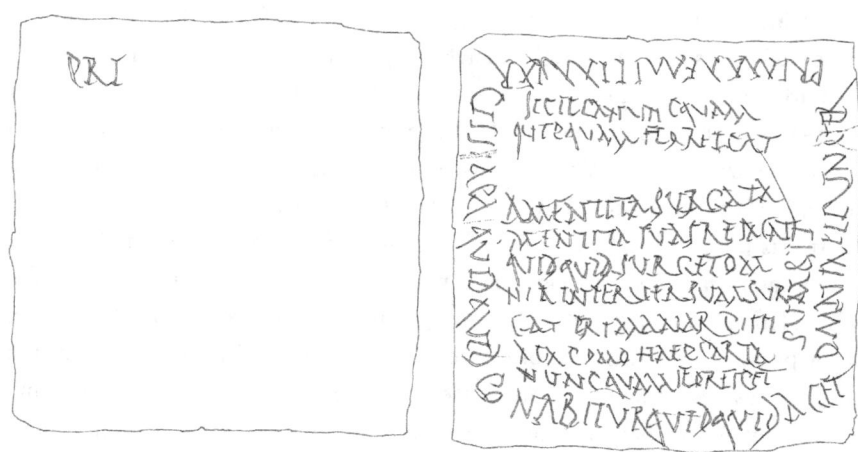

Figure 3.2 Front and back of a curse from Mainz. Image from Blänsdorf 2012, copyright GDKE Rheinland-Pfalz.

curser began writing normally on one side then changed their mind, turning over the tablet and starting again in what they may have considered a more magical style: spiralling the text around the outside. When all four sides were full, the curser started writing in the centre of the space left in the middle, and when the space ran out again, they wrote the last two lines at the top of the tablet. The curser did not have a plan before they started, but made it up as they went along, fitting their text both to their own interpretation of magical writing and to the material affordances of the tablet. The movements of flipping and rotating the tablet and the physical action of carving the words into the metal with a stylus are woven into the text – to use the terminology of Ingold's basket – and all would have had significance to the curser as they were performing the ritual.

Many other writers of curse tablets chose to manipulate the form of their writing, not just by using edge text but other strategies as well. Standard Latin texts were written from left to right, with the letters all formed facing the same direction, and with subsequent lines written under each other. Many curse tablets followed these writing conventions, but some chose to actively reject them in various ways.[74] The most common manipulation, which featured on forty-one tablets from the study area, was to write in retrograde, from right to left. Some writers mirrored their letters, reversing them from their normal direction. Mirrored letters are found on a total of fourteen tablets, where cursers chose to do things such as mirror each instance of the same letter, for example all the 'E's on SD 208 from Bath. One particular curser took this idea to the

Figure 3.3 Curse from Clothall. Image from *RIB* Online, copyright CSAD.

extreme, mirroring most of the 'C's, 'D's and 'S's, also inscribing some of the 'A's upside down and some of the 'E's and 'I's sideways (**SD 345**, Figure 3.3).

Other writing styles found on some tablets include writing some words or whole lines upside down, writing in boustrophedon – alternating right to left and left to right – and writing from the bottom up rather than top down. In places where professional magicians worked, certain methods of textual manipulation became part of standard practice. For example, eight competition curses from Carthage have text that tapers, with each line progressively shorter than the one above it (e.g. **DT 234**). Many curses at Carthage and Sousse used the strategy of edge text, usually bordering the tablet with *voces magicae* or *charaktêres* in a manner that was much more pre-planned than the ad hoc bordering of the Mainz curse discussed above (e.g. **DT 252**). Sequences of repeated vowels and drawings are also found repeatedly on curses presumably produced by professionals that had an awareness of Graeco-Egyptian magical traditions.[75]

In the 'self-authored' curses there are no strong patterns of textual manipulation, and I would argue that none should be sought. Each of these tablets is the product of a series of creative moments, influenced by the world in which the cursers were embedded. Some had plans before they started, but others clearly made it up as they went along, manipulating their inscription in whatever way they saw fit, often haphazardly and with mistakes.[76] The aim of doing so was probably to make the words harder to read, and therefore more mysterious. The twisting of the words could also directly enhance the twisting and binding that the curse was intending to unleash onto the victim. Clear evidence for this belief comes from a tablet found in a cemetery in Cologne (**SD 464**); the words are written in retrograde and includes the line 'you act perversely, even as this writing is perverse'. Three other curses, all from Germania or Noricum, make similar explicit mentions of the manipulation of the text: one from Krefeld-Gellep (**SD 462**) says 'just as this has been written perversely, so will the gods despise them', followed by a list of names written in retrograde. A curse from Rottweil (**SD 479**) includes the line 'as the gods make that man or that woman wrong like this (word) is wrong', in which some letters in the second *aversum* are written upside down. Finally, from Mautern (**SD 526**) comes a curse on which the victim's name has been written upside down, followed by the line: 'Thus Silvia, you see your husband turned upside down, just as his name is written.' The cursers have directly connected the 'perverse' writing to the actions or fates of their victims, making it the explicit source of the tablet's transformative potential.

Manipulation and mutilation

It was not just the text that could be manipulated, but also the tablet itself, and actions of manipulation and mutilation were very common features of cursing rituals across the Roman west.[77] Around 48 per cent of the 607 tablets (291 in total) from the study area were either folded or rolled, and 10 per cent were pierced (sixty-two in total). Within these groups, there is no set pattern. The number and direction of folds, the tightness of the roll or the location of the nail holes were all chosen by the individual cursers as they engaged with the physical qualities of tablet itself. Most cursers seem to have folded the tablet so that the words were covered, and where the tablet was inscribed on both sides it was usually the first side that was hidden. However, it was equally acceptable to leave the tablet unfolded, as more than half of cursers did. When nails were used, they usually hit part of the text, meaning that the nails were driven through the tablets after they were inscribed (e.g. **SD 132**). However, sometimes they missed the text, which means that in these cases the curser either left an area clear for nailing when writing, or pierced the tablet before it was inscribed (e.g. **SD 221**). There is an interesting case from Bath, where the writing has been carefully coordinated on both sides so that both instances of the name of one of the victims, Anniola, would be hit by the nail (**SD 213**, Figure 3.4).

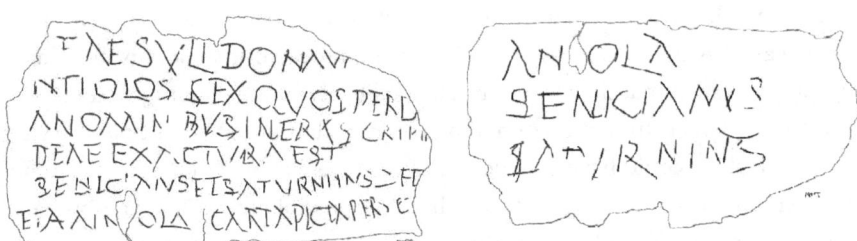

Figure 3.4 Curse from Bath. Image from Tomlin 1988, copyright Barry Cunliffe and Oxford University Committee for Archaeology.

These actions were intended to make the curse more likely to succeed. Folding and rolling may have acted to conceal the words, sealing them in until read by the deities or the spirits of the dead, and could also have had connotations of fixing and binding, as they enveloped the words, keeping them in place. They would have been relatively easy to achieve by hand for most able-bodied cursers, as lead is a soft and malleable material. From my own experimentation I have found that multiple folds become progressively more difficult to perform, which is perhaps the reason why most tablets are folded only once or twice.

Folding and fixing the tablet in these ways connected the curse tablets to bodily gestures of binding, which were well known across the Graeco-Roman world but appear rarely in literary sources. As I have discussed elsewhere, evidence of a range of sources, from Aulus Gellius to Pliny the Elder and the *PGM* demonstrates that Graeco-Roman culture attached meaning to gestures of tying and binding, interpreting them as suspicious and potentially dangerous for the smooth running of normal society.[78] Something as simple as crossing the legs or interlacing the fingers, which would seem innocuous to a modern observer, could be interpreted as an attempt to inhibit public business if performed in the right (or wrong) place and time.[79] The actions of folding and rolling a curse tablet should be seen within these traditions, as a folded curse tablet is conceptually similar to folded arms or bound clothing. People seeking to directly influence events in cursing rituals could use this to their advantage, but their intentions would be recognizable to any onlooker. Alongside the culturally determined meanings of folding, rolling and nailing, the actions also helped transfer pain and suffering onto the victim, who was intimately connected to the tablet by the inclusion of their name in the written curse.[80] Naming in this context did not just make the tablet symbolically stand for the victim, but made it physically part of their body, which could be burned in a fire, drowned in water or made to suffer pain through inflicted wounds. The above-mentioned curse against Anniola is a case in point, as the repeated instances of her name were aligned such that they would be stabbed by the same piercing action.

On some tablets the action of nailing was repeated, and the multiple stabbing of the lead sheet could have produced a cathartic effect in the curser.[81] From my own experiments I have determined that it is possible to push a nail by hand through a sheet of lead of the thickness of many of the tablets (around 1 millimetre), but not without some physical exertion. Piercing thicker tablets, or doing so after folding, would have required either considerable strength or a tool such as a hammer. In either case, the physical and destructive nature of the action could have helped relieve some of the emotions and tensions felt by the curser in the moment of ritual performance: anger at the victim for whatever they had done, hopelessness in the face of perceived injustice, or uncertainty about what would happen in the future. One of the Uley tablets was repeatedly stabbed with some force after inscribing (SD 433), an action which is perhaps a result of the curser taking out their emotions on the tablet. Another extreme example of mutilation is the sole tablet from the Roman cemetery at Clothall, discussed above for its strange writing style. After inscribing their curse with backwards, upside down and sideways letters, the curser then drove five nails through the tablet, four of which survive. They also made smaller holes in the centre of the tablet, through which they passed thin lead wire that acted as a binding.

Although rare, some cursers added the killing of animals to the cursing ritual. The tablet from Chagnon was accompanied by the killing of a puppy (**SD 160**), the creation of one of the Frankfurt curses seems to have involved the ritual 'silencing' of a songbird (**SD 477**), and one from Carthage includes the follow, grisly formula (**DT 222**): 'even as I twisted out and bound the tongue from this live chicken, thus shall the tongues of my enemies, having opposed me, become silent.' These three juridical curses are joined by a competition curse, also from Carthage (**Gager 12**), that asks 'just as this rooster has been bound by its feet, hands, and head, so bind the legs and hands and head and heart of Victoricus the charioteer of the Blue team.' All four texts use the suffering or death of the animals as sympathetic formulas intended to directly influence the victims, and none refer to the animals as offerings to the gods in the manner of more standard blood sacrifice. In that sense they can be taken as extensions of the manipulation and mutilation of the other materials involved in the ritual, as actions intended to enhance the binding power of the curse, making it harder for the victim to resist.

All of these were gestures and actions that required certain postures and movements, and these would have been immediately recognizable to any onlookers. Hammering a nail into a folded tablet creates noise too, which may have attracted attention if done in public. This may not have been such an issue at the temple sites of Bath and Mainz, where cursers were guided to secluded locations by the architectural arrangement of the buildings and therefore were unlikely to have been watched or overheard. At other, more open sites like Uley, those around the curser could easily have come to conclusions as to what they were doing by the sights and sounds of their actions. From this, rumour and gossip may have spread through the community, perhaps making their way to the victims themselves.

Spoken words

It would be naïve to assume that there was no spoken component of cursing rituals in the western Roman provinces: orally delivered prayers were the most important part of many aspects of Roman religion. In the words of Pliny the Elder, 'a sacrifice without a prayer is thought to have no effect, or not to count as a proper consultation of the gods'.[82] Although formal prayers for official sacrifices may have been written down, as discussed above, it was the oral recitation of them by the priests that gave them religious force and meaning. This follows on from some ancient philosophical discussions, in particular Plato and Aristotle, who argued that spoken words were more honest and powerful than written words. These authors claimed that the written word had little importance in and of itself, and only stood for speech.[83] This might be hard for people in the modern world to grasp, and Ingold has argued that the development of print literacy since the Renaissance has profoundly impacted on the perception of language in modern Europe.[84] Speech is now seen as the emulation of written language, which has been institutionalized and standardized, removing much of what gives spoken utterances their 'illocutionary force': in other words their power to produce effects in the people and things around the speaker. In many non-literate societies around the world, spoken words are a kind of energy that is especially potent in the context of magic.[85] For the Songhay people of Niger in West Africa, the actual sounds of magical incantations are what are thought to have the effect on the victim. They are described as 'magic arrows' that fly from the sorcerer and physically strike the victim, causing lethargy, nausea or diarrhoea.[86] Similar beliefs were held in the Roman world too, where words were seen as gestures in themselves: physical actions thrown into the world by the movement of the lips and face.[87]

Quite apart from all of this, the presence of an oral component to cursing rituals is apparent from even a cursory glance at the written inscriptions on many of the tablets. A minority include long texts that set out the victim's name(s), why they are being cursed and the punishments expected. Many curses contain only lists of names or even less descriptive formulas such as *nomen furis* ('the name of the thief', e.g. **SD 307**). The assumption with these tablets is that the address to the deities, the motive for the curse and the expected punishments were all spoken aloud by the curser while they were either writing, manipulating or depositing the tablet or, perhaps even in discussion with a professional practitioner. For some people, these words would have been spoken in the presence of the supernatural figures that were expected to carry out the curse, either in temples of the gods or in places where the restless dead lingered, and so speaking aloud could be more effective as a method of communication than leaving a written request. This also feeds back into the earlier discussion of literacy levels among cursers in the west. Those with less-developed writing skills may have only felt comfortable writing names on the tablet itself, especially at a moment of heightened emotion and stress when concentrating on writing could be too difficult. For those with more experience of writing it would have been easier, especially if they had planned their curse beforehand, as some tablets suggest by their complex rhetorical structure (e.g. **SD 494**). Even these elaborate curses are likely to have had some oral component, perhaps a reading of the text or a brief committal prayer when deposited.

The exact form of oral prayer spoken over each curse tablet is lost to us because spoken words are ephemeral and temporary, vanishing as soon as the sound waves dissipate. However, linguistic studies of the curse texts have attempted to reconstruct the oral components, assuming that they did not differ significantly from the written words on the tablets.[88] These are important analyses, because ultimately it was the words spoken or written by the curser that affected the transformations inherent in the cursing rituals. Kropp notes two different classes of formulas in the Latin curse tablets: performative and transformative.[89] Performative terms encompass statements of manipulation (i.e. piercing, binding, submerging, melting), committal (i.e. handing over or giving), request (i.e. 'kill him') and cursing.[90] These formulas do not simply refer to the actions performed, but play an essential role in the performance of the ritual: without them the rituals would have no effect.[91] As well as these performative functions, the words of curse formulas can also be transformative. The best examples are the sympathetic formulas, for example (**SD 157**) 'just as this lead disappears and falls, thus falls their youth, limbs, life, ox, grain and goods.' Through these words the cursers hoped to affect direct, immediate physical transformations in the real world. Formulas such as this, which Kropp calls 'godless', had no explicit addressee, but worked through the brute force of the utterances alone, much like the magic arrows of the Songhay.[92]

Alongside the conclusions drawn from linguistics, taking a lived religion approach reminds us of the importance of contextual factors. The location of the ritual performance will have impacted what was said, as well as how those words were said. Depending on who was nearby, within sight or hearing range, the curser may have felt more or less confident and comfortable voicing their curse aloud. As I will demonstrate later in this chapter, people may have been familiar with making an appeal to chthonic gods or the spirits of the dead in cemeteries, but these actions could also be perceived as potentially frightening or even illegal, depending on exactly what the individual was doing.[93] At the temple sites, the cursers may have felt more confident or comfortable in expressing a prayer out loud, especially if they phrased their curse in respectful or flattering terms, like 'most holy goddess Sulis' (on **SD 215**). Although they may have never composed a curse tablet before, each individual curser may have had previous experience of conducting (or at least witnessing) other rituals in the temple and these familiar memories will have influenced their feelings, perhaps making them bolder, and surer of success if they believed past prayers had been granted. Especially at Bath and Mainz, where cursers were guided to enclosed or private spaces, the anxiety of being overheard or overlooked would have been lower, creating a more intimate moment of communication between them and the deities.

Ancient Roman prayer was not a solely oral performance. Various ancient authors make it clear that certain gestures or movements of the body were enacted while the worshipper was speaking the words of the prayer. Hands could be raised towards the sky, a statue or altar,[94] or could touch the earth if terrestrial or chthonic gods were being invoked.[95] There is abundant evidence for Roman worshippers spinning clockwise on the spot, although ancient writers were uncertain of the precise meaning of the action.[96] As Corbeill rightly points out, modern scholars too easily forget that Roman prayer required physical as well as verbal activity.[97] Although impossible to know for certain, it seems reasonable to suggest that gestures or movements such as these might have been performed during a cursing ritual, perhaps just before deposition.

Deposition

The final step in the process of creating a curse tablet was deposition. Here we must return to a question raised earlier in this chapter, albeit briefly: where were the cursers when they performed the ritual actions required to make a curse? This strikes at the heart of attempting to explore the lived experience of cursing, because locations have a significant impact on the way people act. Physical surroundings affect sensory perception and bodily movement, guiding people to behave in particular ways. The nature and understanding of a place inform the kinds of activities a person undertakes there, and conversely, the meaning of a place is ascribed by the kinds of activities performed there. This is not the place for a deep exploration of the 'spatial turn' in Roman studies, but suffice to say that these ideas are now well established, and that they have an important impact on any study of lived experience in the ancient world.[98] In terms of analysing the curse tablets, it must be admitted that we cannot know for certain exactly where the previous steps of the process were performed, and indeed there was unlikely to have been a uniform experience for all cursers. Some individuals may have chosen to inscribe their lead tablet in their own homes, while others might have wanted to perform the whole ritual in the place the tablet would eventually be deposited. One instinct might be to think that, on the one hand, curses addressing non-chthonic deities in public temples, such as Sulis Minerva at Bath, were performed wholly in those sanctuaries, because they may have been considered conceptually like prayers or other rituals performed in such places. Indeed, these tend to be the locations in which so-called 'prayers for justice' were deposited. On the other hand, one might suppose that curses ultimately deposited in graves or entertainment venues might have been prepared somewhere else, so that the curser or religious specialist could spend as little time as possible in places where unquiet spirits roamed, performing actions that might have carried the death penalty if caught in the act. However, these assumptions stem from the dichotomy between legitimate, open prayers for justice and secretive, dark binding spells that was not necessarily part of the understanding of all cursers. Indeed, as I will discuss in Chapter 4, any action of cursing could be justified by the curser as a legitimate response to insurmountable odds or the misdeeds of others.

Considerations of space also raise the issue of time: if we are asking *where* curses were deposited, then we should also be asking *when*. Unfortunately, the evidence is too deficient to give a detailed answer to the question, although the same presumptions about the legitimacy of the act have tended to crop up again. For example, the familiar image of people depositing curse tablets in graves places them at night, seeking the cover of darkness to hide their actions. However, there is no reason to suggest this was the situation for every individual. Not all will have felt the need to hide their actions. Nevertheless, cursers will have needed to negotiate timing in many locations, especially temples. The suggestion from ancient literary evidence is that such buildings were not always accessible but were opened in the morning and closed again at night. The sacred calendar might have had an impact too; some cursers might have wanted to avoid busy festivals, or conversely to have appealed to the deities on days considered significant or auspicious.[99] Access to entertainment venues and cemeteries might have also been restricted at various times of day or night, or again there may have been preferable moments that were felt to be more effective times to place a curse. Some instructions for curse tablets in the *PGM*, specify a time for parts of the ritual to be performed, but as already discussed here, knowledge of these kinds of texts did not spread particularly widely in the Roman west.[100]

We can at least say that cursers needed to be in the appointed place to deposit their tablet, even if the preceding steps were performed elsewhere. How they chose a specific location will have depended on several factors, perhaps the most important of which was the deity or supernatural figure they intended to invoke in the curse. An interesting puzzle, akin to the chicken-egg question, is which was chosen first: deity or location? To put it another way, and to use a specific example (**SD 451**), did Muconius appeal to Neptune because he knew he would deposit his tablet in the River Hamble, or did he deposit his tablet in the Hamble because he had already decided to invoke Neptune? Of course, there is no way to provide a concrete answer here, but it is nevertheless important for challenging our assumptions. One might be tempted to think that a curser travelled to a particular place because they already knew they wanted to invoke a particular deity, but it is equally possible that proximity to an individual's home or workplace might determine the location of deposition, and therefore also the beings addressed in their curse. It is interesting that even in locations that developed long-standing and well-known traditions of cursing, such as the temple of Magna Mater in Mainz or the Spring of Anna Perenna in Rome, there is little sense that people travelled long distances to make use of them.

Nevertheless, most, if not all, cursers did move to a specific place to deposit their curse, usually somewhere with sacred significance, where communications with the gods was considered easier or more effective because they were believed to reside in them. To a modern mind, the most common image of an ancient sacred place is a traditional temple, in the sense of a building housing a statue and sited on consecrated ground, but this was not always how these places appeared. People in the Roman world believed that supernatural forces were present in a wide variety of locations, including houses, cemeteries, 'secular' public buildings and landscape features such as rivers, trees and mountains. Hunt's landmark book on sacred trees has forced a rethink of the nature of sacrality in the Roman world, away from narrow legalistic definitions of *sacer* and *consecratio*.[101] Her analysis, and the recent work of other scholars, shows that the exact nature of the relationship between a place and the divine was rarely unambiguous, but was multi-layered, diverse, changed over time, and depended on a range of different conditions including the circumstances of the individual worshipper.[102] Above all, understanding and lived experience of the sacrality of a particular place were informed by the awareness of past actions performed there, either through personal involvement as a performer or witness, through conversations with friends, relatives or religious specialists, or through the viewing of material traces left behind by others. Through all of this, individuals would be more confident in the efficacy of their own actions, as they followed established ritualized traditions in these places.

Curses were left in most of the major places where supernatural beings could be present: above all graves, watery places (springs, rivers, beaches, baths and lakes) and temples, but also entertainment venues (amphitheatres and circuses) and domestic settings. Some depositional contexts were more popular in some regions of the west than in others: watery places, for example, seem to have attracted more curses in Britannia and Gallia than elsewhere, whereas there are many more curses from cemeteries in Africa and Italia than the northern provinces (Table 3.1).[103]

These trends can be explained by considering differing traditions of cursing. In Italia and Africa religious specialists were more active in the production of curse tablets, and these individuals were possibly influenced by Graeco-Egyptian practices that tended to invoke underworld powers in cursing rituals, making graves the most effective places for people to communicate with them.[104] Even away from these eastern traditions, dominant in the big cities but not necessarily everywhere else, many Roman authors attest to the long-standing association in Italia between malicious cursing and necromancy, and there is good reason to think that such associations might have influenced real practice. To put it another way, a person might choose to deposit their curse in a grave because they had heard or read stories about the activities of witches and other magical figures, and therefore tried to mimic that practice in some way.[105] Away from the Mediterranean, and especially in Britannia, watery places become more prominent. In her recent discussion of the curse tablets from the spring at

Table 3.1 Number of curses from different depositional contexts (where known) in each region

	Africa	Britannia	Danube	Gallia	Germania	Italia	Hispania
Amphitheatre	12	4	1	22			
Bath		2					
Beach		2					
Circus	3						
Fort		2					
Grave	91	2	8	10	17	94	5
House		2	3	2	1	3	2
Lake						1	
Odeon	1						
Pit/Well		3		3		2	
River		4	2		1	3	
Road				1			
Spring	4	117		10		22	
Temple		50	6	2	35	1	2

Bath, Cousins drew comparisons between depositional practice in the Roman period and the late Iron Age.[106] Like Cousins, I do not think we should be looking for simple and direct continuities across the centuries, but there may still have been understandings of ritual deposition in watery contexts that did survive, albeit adapted and reimagined in the new cultural contexts of Roman imperial rule.[107] There was certainly a continued belief in the efficacy of rivers, springs, wells and coastal sites as locations for creating connections between humans and divine or chthonic entities. However, at least on the curse tablets, the powers addressed in these places were understood in new ways during the Roman period. All four of the British riverine curses name Neptune as the divine addressee (SD 340, **441**, 449, and **451**), and the Bath tablets were deposited in a location influenced heavily by Roman imperialist iconography and dedicated to a new hybrid goddess created by the fusion of local and 'Roman' divinities.[108]

At various times, scholars have suggested that some curse tablets, particularly those deposited in temples, may have been displayed somewhere before deposition to publicize the fact that the curse had been placed.[109] Without this step, it was argued, it would be impossible for the victim to know that they had been cursed, and therefore the words would have no effect. Kiernan in particular has argued that publicly displayed curse tablets could be similar to the *nuncupatio* part of votive rituals, in the sense that they record a contract between humans and gods.[110] As I have discussed elsewhere, I find these arguments unconvincing, as there is plenty of evidence both from the ancient world as well as anthropological studies of more recent cultures that suggest that there is no need for a victim to be explicitly aware of a curse for its intended outcomes to appear.[111] Rumour, gossip, guilt or shame can all influence psychosomatic symptoms that resemble malign magic. It is only after symptoms are manifest that a search for evidence of cursing is suggested, usually by a freelance religious specialist enlisted after medical professionals are unable to produce a cure.[112] Victim testimonies from the ancient world are rare, but the story of the chameleon in the classroom of Libanius is illuminating. The orator had been suffering from inexplicable bouts of gout, as well as the inability to speak to his students, causing fear and alarm in both himself and his friends. Doctors could offer no cure and the symptoms continued to worsen, until eventually a search of his classroom was conducted, and the offending chameleon produced. Someone had removed one of its front legs and stitched the other into its mouth, silencing it.[113] These mutilations of the chameleon were enough to explain the gout and the speechlessness, symptoms which had struck Libanius before specific knowledge of the curse had come to light.[114] A similar situation is visible in the circumstances surrounding the sickness and eventual death of Germanicus as reported by Tacitus.[115] It is only after Germanicus had begun to demonstrate serious ill health that a thorough search of his house was conducted, and evidence of malign magic brought to light. Although it may seem strange to modern eyes, in Roman society the belief in magic, or at least the fear of its results, was endemic. This is summed up in the words of Pliny the Elder, who stated that 'there is no-one who does not fear to be bound by dreadful curses'.[116] In this kind of cultural climate, every individual would have known whether something they had done could have made them a target for a curse, especially if they were part of a common target group like lawyers, orators or thieves.[117] Quite apart from this widespread culture of fear, the cursers themselves would trust the power of the gods to enact the curse, and no further strategies would be necessary in their mind. In fact, keeping the curse between themselves and the gods or spirits involved could enhance its possibility of success, because without knowledge that the curse had been placed there was no chance of the victim attempting to protect themselves with amulets, warding gestures or counter-curses.[118] All this considered, I would argue that most cursers deposited their curse as soon as they could, rather than displaying it somewhere first.

For reasons of space, I am not discussing the lived experience of this part of the ritual in much detail here. Each of the 126 places where curses were deposited in the Roman west had unique architectural and natural affordances and would have evoked unique memories and meanings for the cursers. We can never know how each individual act of depositing a tablet was affected by factors such as weather, time of day and the presence or absence of other people, not to mention the curser's age, gender, ethnicity or physical and emotional state. Trying to produce any kind of general overview would risk collapsing a kaleidoscope of possible lived experiences into an amorphous mass, with banal generalizations the only likely outcome. Close attention to the archaeological contexts of deposition locations can overcome some of these difficulties but would require far more space than possible here. The recent work of Veale, Cousins, Salvo and Graham shows the valuable outputs of this kind of approach when the excavation records are of sufficient quality.[119] Unfortunately many of the curses found in the late nineteenth and early twentieth century, including most of those from Italia and Africa, lack the kinds of detailed records needed for this kind of analysis.

However, we can be a little more confident in interpreting the meanings that may have been attached to the action of deposition, rather than trying to reconstruct the phenomenology of the action itself. As I have already begun to outline in this section, the act of depositing a curse tablet was, in some respects, one of communication: passing a message from the human curser to the divine or chthonic entities expected to receive and enact the curse. The presence of the relevant beings in the place meant that depositing a curse there was experienced as directly, physically handing it to them. Confidence in the perception of efficacy would be bolstered by the physical remains, or personal memories, of past communications in the same or similar locations. Especially for those deposited in temples, curse tablets were considered a normal part of the range of possible communication strategies between the human and the supernatural.[120] At the sacred springs of Sulis Minerva and Anna Perenna, the curses were found alongside other objects, including coins, vessels of clay or metal, jewellery and more, and it seems likely that cursers would have understood the actions of depositing curses as part of the same strategy of communicating with the relevant goddess. The fire pit behind the *cella* of Magna Mater at Mainz held not just the curse tablets, but also burnt remains of animal and plant matter, as well as coins and lamps that may have been thrown in as the fires died down. At Uley it is unclear where the curses were deposited as they were found scattered in demolition layers, but as those contexts also contained other votive objects it would be reasonable to suggest that here too, curses were conceptually linked to other things given to the god.[121] On all these sites, the objects deposited were being given to the gods or goddesses in order to open lines of communication, whether to instigate or complete a formal vow, celebrate the completion of a life stage or pilgrimage, or request the punishment of a wrongdoer.[122] There is nothing in the treatment of tablets to suggest that they were viewed as separate, and indeed their connections to other forms of human-divine communication would have enhanced their perceived efficacy.

From the perspective of communication, depositing a curse in a funerary context followed the same logic as leaving one in a temple.[123] These were places where supernatural forces were thought to live, and so therefore places where communication with them was easier. Funerary epigraphy and architecture attest to the common understanding of burial places as the houses of the dead or their place of eternal rest.[124] Tombs could be richly decorated, both inside and out, and provided with gardens and vineyards for the enjoyment of not just the deceased but also for the living family members who regularly attended them.[125] On the dead person's birthday, the anniversary of their death and during the nine-day festival of *Parentalia*, grave sites would have been hives of activity, as family and friends gathered to share in feasts and make offerings to those who had passed.[126] To facilitate these activities, some tombs in Latium and Campania were furnished with seating areas, ovens and wells, and dining tables have been found in cemeteries across the western Roman provinces.[127] The addition of libation tubes to graves in Italia and Africa made offering wine and other liquids to the dead even more direct.[128] Across the Empire, burials were accompanied by a huge range of objects, deposited either at the moment of burial or at later dates. The Roman cemeteries at Carthage, where dozens of curse tablets were deposited, also yielded bronze mirrors, ivory needles, dice and knives, coins, lamps and terracotta figurines when excavated.[129] In his discussion of the *Parentalia*, Ovid describes the food and other things left at tombs as offerings to the *Manes*, the deified spirits of the dead, aimed at appeasing them and ensuring their favour towards those who remain.[130] Both Plutarch and Cicero are equally clear that prayers and offerings to the dead were considered a matter of pious duty, akin to worshipping any other god.[131]

When thinking about depositing curses in graves, it has been all too easy for scholars to imagine practitioners sneaking around in dark, silent cemeteries, engaging in activities that would be unusual or shocking, even to an ancient audience.[132] However, Roman cemeteries were rarely quiet or empty places, and depositing things in tombs was not necessarily an unfamiliar lived experience for individuals, especially when the intent was to communicate with the spirits of the dead. To be sure, depictions of witches in cemeteries stress the horror and revulsion they elicit, but these are literary constructions aiming at provoking exactly those emotions. Canidia, Erichtho and the others engage in cannibalism, corpse desecration and even necrophilia, all of which would have been far from the minds of real cursers.[133] Many people will have been familiar with the experience of going to cemeteries and asking favours of the spirits of the dead.[134] It is probable that some cursers felt fear or trepidation at addressing or manipulating the spirits of the dead, but we should not assume this was a universal reaction, nor that it was necessarily different from the feelings experienced when approaching any divine figure. Direct addresses to the *dii manes*, *dii inferi* or named figures such as Persephone or Pluto are common in cemetery curses, and these powers were often ritually given the bodies and names of the victims, just like in curses left in temples. A curse from the Italian city of Minturno, acts as a good example here (**SD 56**):

> Infernal gods, to you I commend, if you have any power, and I hand over Tyche of Charisius, (and) whatever she does, so that everything should attack against her. Infernal gods, to you I commend her limbs, colour, shape, head, hair, shadow, brain, forehead, eyebrows, mouth, nose, chin, cheeks, lips, words, face, neck, liver, shoulders, heart, lungs, intestines, belly, arms, fingers, hands, navel, bladder, thighs, knees, shins, ankles, soles, toes. Infernal gods, if I will see her waste away, I will gladly [offer] you that sacrifice every year to the *di parentes* (?) ... property should waste away.

In excruciating detail, the whole body of the victim has been handed over to the gods of the underworld for destruction, but that should not distract us from the fact that the curse itself is framed in a much less sensationalized manner. The last line is particularly telling; despite a break in the text causing some uncertainty in the translation, the mention of annual sacrifices and the *di parentes* explicitly connects this curse to normal religious practice undertaken in cemetery contexts. Several other cemetery curses also used votive or prayerful language when handing over the victims to the underworld gods, such as *voveo* (e.g. **SD 469**) or *precor* (e.g. DT 273), or promise offerings if their curses are successful (e.g. **Gager 93**). All of this, combined with the giving of the physical tablet to the gods or the dead, suggests that the deposition of curses in cemeteries could be understood within the bounds of normal practice in these places. This is nowhere clearer than in the cemeteries of Sousse and Carthage, where curse tablets were frequently rolled and inserted into the ceramic tubes intended for liquid offerings to the *manes*.¹³⁵ At the same time, the lived, physical experience of pushing a rolled lead tablet into a tube is obviously different to pouring liquid. Wine or other drinks poured as libations would have disappeared into the tube much more quickly and easily, perhaps leaving only a few drops splashed at the opening, or dripped on the hands. By contrast, a rolled curse tablet might have required some effort to fit into the hole, especially if the tube was particularly narrow. Indeed, some curses became stuck inside the tubes, where they were found by excavators centuries later.¹³⁶ These different sensory experiences will have marked out the deposition of curse tablets as different to other forms of offering made in cemeteries, even if they were understood within the same set of broad understandings.¹³⁷

Amphitheatres and circuses present an interesting blend between temple sites and cemeteries, in that they were conceived as places where both divine and chthonic forces could be encountered.¹³⁸ Entertainment venues across the Empire often had permanent religious structures, perhaps taking inspiration from the Circus Maximus, which housed shrines to Sol and Luna, Cybele and others.¹³⁹ Even in arenas that did not have built shrines, it is likely that temporary *pulvinaria* were set up to receive divine images when games were given during festivals.¹⁴⁰ Curses at both the Trier and London amphitheatres appeal to Diana and Mars; as the traditional overseers of combat and hunting, these two would have had special relevance in this context (London: **SD 343**; Trier: **SD 183, 189**). At the same time, circuses and amphitheatres were places where humans and animals often died, so, like cemeteries, were locations in which the powers of the underworld could be contacted. Curses deposited in the amphitheatre and circus of Carthage mention Hermes (DT 246), Chaos (**DT 251**) and Persephone (NGCT 91), as well as less identifiable chthonic powers (e.g. DT 250), and at Petronell (Pannonia) the curse is addressed to Dispater, Aeracura and Cerberus (**SD 530**). Even in Britannia, the single curse from the amphitheatre at Caerleon invokes Nemesis (**SD 337**). As places with multiple uses and meanings, cursers depositing their curses in entertainment venues could follow their own interpretations of such spaces.

Part of the action of deposition as a form of communication is the idea of boundary crossing. The curses passed, both literally and figuratively, from the ordinary mortal world into the possession of the divine or chthonic powers expected to carry out the curse. This boundary crossing was the final stage in the ritual transformation of the sheet of lead purchased at the beginning of the process, after which it would be understood as a powerful curse, able to affect humans and animals in whatever way the curser had wished. The locations most commonly chosen for deposition – temples, graves, amphitheatres and water – were all thought of as liminal places, where transition between worlds was made possible by the presence of supernatural entities, as well as the actions of humans. Most cursers would have performed some actions of boundary crossing even before they reached the specific location of deposition. Temples were often surrounded by walls or stones that marked the edge of the space given to the gods, which people had to cross into to worship.[141] This was certainly the case at Bath and Mainz, where imposing walls separated the sacred space of the temple precinct from its surroundings. At Bath, there was another boundary to cross inside the precinct because the sacred spring was enclosed within its own circuit of walls. Access was possible either through a narrow doorway from the temple side, or through three windows in the opposite wall, and opinion is somewhat divided on which was most often used. Both Revell and Cousins argue that the heavy wear on the doorway indicates that it was the primary mode of access,[142] but Cunliffe pointed out that the locations of votive offerings in the spring, including the curses, mean they were more likely to have been thrown through the windows, from a deposition gallery created from what had previously been a corridor in the adjoining bath complex.[143] Either way, the curses and/or the cursers themselves were moving into a part of the complex occupied by the goddess. Any objects deposited in the spring would have vanished immediately on contact with the opaque water, further heightening the sense of giving the object to the deity.[144] At Mainz, deposition occurred into brick-lined fire pits behind the *cella* of Magna Mater, following the dominant form of private offerings on the site, which consisted of burning animal and vegetable sacrifices in pits.[145] The finds of charred and melted lumps of lead alongside the more complete tablets are evidence not only of just how many more than the thirty-four complete curses were actually dedicated, but also of how prevalent this method of deposition was on the site.[146] At least three of the cursers had planned this final action before writing their tablet, as they included sympathetic formulas transferring the burning and melting of the lead onto the bodies of the victims (**SD 488, 498,** 499).

Those who went to cemeteries will have crossed the boundaries of the city to access the extramural burial grounds required by both custom and law, transitioning from the world of peaceful civilian life into the domain of warfare and death.[147] All of the amphitheatres and circuses in which curse tablets were deposited were also located on the edges of their respective settlements, intentionally placing them in liminal spaces.[148] Wiedemann has argued that amphitheatres were combative, liminal spaces where civilization confronted nature, where justice confronted criminals, and where the Roman state confronted its enemies.[149] As places where people often died, amphitheatres and circuses were open doors between the living world and the underworld, as demonstrated by the 'fatal charades' in which people dressed as Pluto and Mercury would drag the dead bodies from the sand.[150] Cursers depositing tablets in cemeteries, amphitheatres and circuses harnessed these movements and used them to induce travel across the threshold in both directions: the curse itself was moving from the living to the dead, and then the power of the dead was expected to move back into the world of the living to harm the victim. At arenas and cemeteries (e.g. **SD 470** from Bad Kreuznach), cursers used formulas of falling or descending. Sometimes the formulas specified that the victim be dragged down, or taken against their will, perhaps evoking the myth of Persephone (e.g. **SD 48**). In all these cases, the cursers were also aware of the physical act of dropping their tablet into the ground or into a libation tube, envisioning their curse not just falling to the bottom of a hole, but all the way down into the underworld, taking their victims with them.

Alongside the reasons of communication and boundary crossing, the act of deposition may have had a cathartic effect on the curser. Cousins has argued that depositing curses against thieves at Bath may have been a method for dealing with the loss of a stolen item through a sense of regained control; the curser was symbolically regaining control over the stolen property by giving it to the goddess.[151] Like nailing or folding, the action of deposition aided in the purging of negative emotions from the cursers, helping them feel as if they had performed a concrete action to address a situation in which they might otherwise feel powerless. As I will discuss in Chapter 4, this was the case across the different motive categories, so Cousins' argument has wider applicability. Again, my argument here is that the action of depositing the tablet contributed as much to this cathartic effect as any other part of the ritual, including the written words.

There may have been a communal aspect to some performances of the deposition part of the cursing ritual, especially in those cases where multiple authors are evident. It is even possible that several cursers came together at the same time to deposit their individual tablets, whether related to the same event or not. Unfortunately, the find contexts of most of the curses in this study make it very difficult to determine if there were any depositional relationships between them. For example (as noted in Chapter 2), the constantly shifting sediment at the bottom of Sulis Minerva's spring obliterates any stratigraphy, and at Uley the curses were found mixed in demolition layers created when the temple was levelled. Curses excavated from cemeteries sometimes offer a slightly better picture, where multiple tablets were deposited in the same graves, as at Bad Kreuznach. For example, two curses were found together, both naming Fructus Gracilis as a victim, so it is relatively safe to assume that they were related (SD 466 and **467**). The three curses from a grave in Ampurias (**SD 134, 135, 136**), which target the same individuals, are also clearly related, although there is nothing to suggest that they were written by more than one person. Poor excavation records for the large caches of curses from cemeteries at Rome, Carthage and Sousse make it very difficult to say anything for certain about them, despite repeated victims and formulas giving compelling evidence that they are related. The so-called Sethian tablets were all found in the same columbarium near the Porta San Sebastiano on the Via Appia, but the excavators did not record which came from which urn.[152] At Sousse, there are records of eleven curses being found in the same two graves, but beyond these we are mostly in the dark about the exact find contexts of individual tablets, a situation that is repeated for the curses from Carthage.[153]

Cursing together might have strengthened group solidarity in the face of a shared problem, and the large-scale legal trial in evidence at Bad Kreuznach would certainly fit that description. However, in some of the cases from there, the association between tablets creates more confusion, rather than less. Two tablets found together in the same grave both name Sinto Valentis as a victim, which might suggest a connection in terms of intention (**SD 468, 470**). However, the curser of one of these, a man called Quartio, is named as a victim on the other, which makes the association much more complicated. Quartio was almost certainly not cursing himself, and it is hard to imagine a situation in which he could be being secretly cursed by the person he was standing next to at the graveside. The indication here is certainly not one of a simplistic division between prosecution and defence, but of tangled and overlapping webs of relationships between individuals within a community. This will be discussed further in the next two chapters.

Conclusions

Curses were created through the embodied engagement of human bodies with material things. Most obviously this meant the lead tablet or other object on which the curse was written and the stylus with which the words were inscribed, but it also could have included nails for piercing as well as the things at the deposition location, such as water, built structures, soil or sand. The agency of the curse – its capacity to bring about changes in the world – emerged from all these engagements, and through the active participation of all the things involved. The curser had their own intentions, and perhaps ideas about what their curse should look like or contain, but they could not act without engaging with material things. The final curse was not necessarily exactly what was in their head at the beginning of the process, but was determined in the moment by the physical realities of the world around them, just like the weaver making Ingold's Basket. The material, size, shape and condition of the writing medium impacted the physical experience of writing the curse and of manipulating or mutilating it. The location chosen for deposition created a range of possible lived experiences of the final act in the process: pushing a rolled lead tablet into a libation tube would have been totally different to digging a hole in the sand of an amphitheatre, or dropping something into a sacred spring. Moreover, even two cursers performing the same action will have experienced it differently, depending on the physical condition of their own bodies: factors such as their age, gender and health affected what was and was not possible.

Curses may have also been the product of multiple human bodies; freelance religious specialists, family, or friends could have offered advice or taken part in one or more steps of the ritualized process. Where formulas are repeated on multiple tablets, or curses cluster in particular locations, knowledge about how to perform an effective cursing ritual must have existed and circulated. Individual cursers drew on whatever knowledge and resources were available to them to produce the most effective curse possible. As such, curses were part of wider debates around how to best approach and communicate with supernatural powers, and were connected to culturally defined strategies that attempted to ensure success in religious endeavours. Far from 'growing like a fungus on the substratum of religion',[154] curses informed and were informed by votive practice, funerary cult, prayer and divine justice: elements that might be termed as more 'normal' Roman religious behaviour. In the lived experience of the people who made curse tablets, all these things were closely connected, and all affected the way they acted in their lives.

4

Motives and Social Frameworks

In the previous chapter I argued for the central role played by physical and religious contexts in the form and function of cursing rituals. As I have made clear, it is impossible for modern scholars to understand ancient curses without taking into consideration the settings in which the rituals were performed. However, arrival at the location of deposition was not the beginning of the process. Every cursing ritual performed in the Roman west was carried out with an intention on the part of the curser, and each intention was particular to that individual: they were all responding to a specific crisis in their lives. Fortunately for us, many of the tablets include details of these specific events, so reconstruction of the motives behind some of the curses is possible. This chapter sets out to explore the reasons why people in the western provinces of the Roman Empire sought the intervention of supernatural powers in the form of curse tablets. In doing so, I will not simply be asking about the issues that the curses were directly trying to address, but also the underlying social structures that made cursing a possible reaction to the situations that presented themselves to the cursers. Again, this is an argument of context, of lived experience. Instead of studying curse tablets as inert texts, this chapter seeks to examine them as embedded within the communities and societies in which they were an important feature of life. Taking this approach is vital because it allows us to assess properly how cursing rituals fitted into broader strategies for getting on with life.

To make a clearer distinction between the analysis of some previous scholarship and my own embedded perspective, this chapter will be divided between 'motives' and 'social frameworks'. I am defining 'motive' as the issues referenced on the tablets themselves, whether implicitly or explicitly. These describe the events that triggered the curser to write the curse in the first place, and they have been the focus of scholarly observation and categorization over the past century. It is the 'motive' visible on the tablet (either implicitly or explicitly) that causes it to be categorized as an erotic, juridical, competition or commercial curse, or a prayer for justice. Usually this can be determined from a specific statement in the curse text, the identification of a victim by their occupation (chariot racer, gladiator, lawyer and so on) or some other clue in the curse language. These categories were developed by Faraone and Versnel, based on the pioneering work of Audollent.[1] This model, which is to be found in almost every major work on curse tablets from Audollent onwards,[2] focusses on the short period of time centred on the performance of the cursing ritual, from the event that prompted the curse through to the successful deposition of the finished tablet.

However, to focus solely on the issues addressed by the individual tablets is to ignore or deny the social contexts in which they were made. People in the Roman west lived within complex webs of relationships with the other people around them and had at their disposal a variety of strategies for negotiating their way through them. Magic, including curse tablets, was just one option available when an individual wanted to harm a rival or promote their own interests. It was perfectly possible not to employ such methods and instead to do something else, or nothing at all. In cases of theft, for example, the individual could have confronted the accused directly or pursued them through the legal system. Countless millions of Romans dealt with their problems without resorting to cursing the people who caused them; however, the very existence of curse tablets indicates that in certain circumstances, and to certain people, cursing those whom they believed had done them wrong was a reasonable or logical option, and offered more chance of success than the other options that their social context presented.

To answer the question "why did people curse?", I intend to look past the motives stated on each tablet, and on which most scholars since Audollent have focussed, into the deeper, longer-term 'social frameworks' that both created the circumstances in which curse tablets could be used and shaped the forms and features of the individual tablets themselves. The origins of these frameworks can be found on various scales of interaction within Roman society, from widely held beliefs about the nature and outcomes of human and divine justice, to an individual's desire to see personal rivals humiliated in public. My analysis builds on the work that previous scholars have done in outlining the motive categories, but takes it further to examine the possible reasons why people in the Roman west chose to alleviate personal crises with curse tablets.

Motives

Over a century of curse-tablet scholarship, from Audollent onwards, five categories of motive have been established and reinforced: competition;

commercial matters; juridical matters, love (the four categories of archetypal 'binding' curses); and prayers for justice. These categories have been built on surveys of the entire corpus of surviving Graeco-Roman curse tablets, and are certainly a useful tool when conducting discussions of ancient magical practice in general, or, because of the wider variety of motives and the larger body of surviving evidence, when focusing on the Greek curses in particular. Both Gager and Eidinow divided their studies of cursing along the lines of these categories, allowing trends and similarities to be identified.[3] However, as has been occasionally pointed out by scholars, curses fitting into these categories are not evenly spread across time and space, with some more popular than others in various specific historical and social contexts.[4] As Eidinow noted, the validity of the existing taxonomy must remain an object of enquiry, and its use must be conditioned by close observations of the details of individual tablets.[5]

Of the 607 tablets collected in this study, the text on 161 is too corrupted to give any sign of the motive. Of the remaining 446, just under a third (141 tablets) are fully legible but do not specify a motive. This includes a variety of curses, from simple lists of names to texts that are solely made up of magical words, characters or drawings. Of those with definable motives, another third (145 tablets) were prompted by instances of theft or some other wrongdoing, putting them into Versnel's 'prayers for justice' category (see Table 4.1). Almost three quarters (101, or 71 per cent) of these prayers for justice are from Britannia, predominantly from the large collections found at Bath and Uley, and in fact prayers for justice are the only recognizable motive category present in Britannia at all. Outside this province, there are significant concentrations of different motives in particular places around the Empire that will be discussed throughout this chapter. Here it will suffice to say that a context-specific analysis of motive

Table 4.1 Totals of motive categories found on curse tablets from the western provinces of the Roman Empire

Motive	Number of tablets
Prayers for justice	145
Unspecified	141
Competition	84
Juridical	43
Love	30
Other	3

categories reveals much more than might be visible when the data is taken at a pan-Imperial level.

In the first half of this chapter, I will take a fresh, context-specific look at the Audollent/Faraone categories and assess their relevance for the curses from the Roman west. I will argue that, although they do have some usefulness for analysing this body of evidence, they leave unanswered many questions about the position of curses in wider Roman society. Therefore, in the second half of the chapter I will move beyond them and attempt to delve deeper into the social contexts in which the tablets were made.

Theft curses

Theft curses, part of the 'prayers for justice' category, come almost exclusively from Britannia (Table 4.2). Most of the items stolen were portable objects or small amounts of cash, probably taken by opportunistic thieves, but there are a few cases of stolen livestock (**SD 350**), burglary from homes (**SD 304**), or the embezzlement of loans or deposits (**SD 492**), all of which would have required a certain amount of premeditation or planning on the part of the thief. Tomlin has suggested that many of the items recorded on the Bath curses were stolen from the baths themselves.[6] Bathhouse thieves were enough of a menace in the Roman world to warrant an entire section of law codes in the writings of jurists,[7] so this conclusion has merit. However, some of the objects reported missing on the Bath tablets, such as Civilis' ploughshare (**SD 236**) and the items robbed from Deomiorix's house (**SD 304**), could not have been stolen in the bathhouse. These and the many curses against thieves from other contexts show that they were not always composed directly after discovering the theft, especially where they were

Table 4.2 Totals of motives in each region

	Britannia	Gallia	Germania	Hispania	Danube	Italia	Africa
Theft	98	6	9	6	5	3	0
Competition	0	0	0	1	0	22	61
Love	0	1	2	1	4	5	17
Juridical	0	6	11	3	6	4	13
Other prayers for justice	3	1	4	1	1	6	1
Unspecified	26	14	23	2	4	60	12

deposited at sites that were a considerable distance from population centres, as with the temple of Mercury at Uley, which was at least three kilometres from the nearest settlements.[8]

Scholars have usually classed curses against thieves as 'prayers for justice', the category coined by Versnel in 1991 and subsequently defended throughout his later work.[9] The distinction between prayers for justice and binding curses rests on several potential criteria, namely:

- The curser is named, rather than anonymous.
- His/her actions are justified or defended.
- The curser requests that they be spared any possible adverse effects.
- Language of flattery or supplication is used, rather than coercive or binding formulas.
- Tablets appeal to, and are deposited in the sanctuaries of, non-chthonic deities.[10]

No tablet is expected to adhere to all of these at once, and indeed some of the characteristics are apparent on curses traditionally placed in the other categories. Nevertheless, the general points stand up very well to the evidence, including the tablets from the Roman west. There is, however, a problem with some of the terminology and language often used by scholars when describing or explaining these tablets. Versnel himself has been at pains to emphasize the legitimate, sanctioned nature of the language in prayers for justice, to the point where he doubts that they can even be called 'magic' – hence the use of the word 'prayer'.[11] The image that Versnel and others have created around these tablets is one of people legitimately seeking due recompense from a higher authority after the wrongdoing of another person. This image has masked the often violent nature of the punishments meted out by these tablets, which can brutally attack the victim's mind, body and social relationships, effectively isolating them from the community. Unlike the juridical, competition and love spells, very few of the prayers for justice aim to gain influence over the victim in the short term, but seek to inflict punishments that are without end, or that result in their death.[12] As an example, consider this curse from Groß-Gerau, in Germania Superior (**SD 483**):

> The person who stole the cloak of Verio or his possessions, he who made his possessions smaller, may his thoughts and memories be destroyed, whether a woman or those who have reduced the property of Verio; worms, tumours and vermin shall invade his hands, head and feet, they shall invade his limbs and marrow.

Despite the slightly confused text, the general sense can be decoded: Verio has condemned the victim to horrific infestations across their whole body, inside and out, for the relatively minor crime of stealing a cloak.[13] Similarly, a curse from Petronell in Pannonia (**SD 530**) requires that Eudemus, the suspected thief of a cooking pot, be 'kill[ed] with the worst death, led to the infernals with bound hands, in service to the infernal gods'. This is not justice in the strictest sense of the term, which would imply punishments being decided with impartiality and rationality to fit the nature and severity of the offence. It certainly bears no relation to Roman law, which saw theft as mostly a private matter, and only required convicted thieves to pay a fine equal to the value of the stolen item, plus a little extra in compensation.[14] Instead, the emotional sense of these texts and many others should be considered more as a demand for vengeance, seeking the disproportionate punishment of perceived wrongdoers far beyond the normal limits of justice as defined by the legal system.[15] This could lead to a potential motivation for cursing against thieves that scholars have rarely considered, namely the failing of Roman law to punish such people to an extent that would appease victims of crime.[16] The fact that theft cursing was so prevalent in Britannia could also point to the existence of a more robust response to theft in the indigenous culture, something that went unsatisfied by the Roman system.[17] It is certainly worth exploring the legal and juridical contexts in which theft curses and other prayers for justice were created.

The legal system may have been hard to access for people towards the bottom of the social scale, especially enslaved people, for whom it would have been impossible to prosecute thieves. Roman property laws were clear that the possessions of dependants – not only enslaved people but also women and children – remained the property of the *paterfamilias*, and therefore it was up to him to bring legal action in the event of theft.[18] As a result, enslaved people such as Servandus, the author of a curse from Leicester against the thief of a cloak (**SD 456**), had little choice but to appeal to the gods for help. Access to the courts was in theory open to all free citizens, but in reality depended on the 'vagaries of travel and the inclinations of Roman officials.'[19] The law was administered by the emperor's representatives in the province, most importantly the governor, but also the staff of legates and military officers to whom the governor could delegate policing and legal responsibilities depending on the many other duties and concerns that pressed on his time.[20] Although the magistrates made regular circuits of their jurisdictions, they could not reach every corner of a province, nor would they have had the time or disposition to hear every case.[21] It would therefore have been easier to access a judge in large, important towns and more difficult for the residents of smaller or more rural settlements. The system of petitions may have made up for this patchy coverage in some places, giving a voice to those who might otherwise have been unable to access Roman justice. However, as Connolly notes, even these required a level of education and resources that was out of the reach of many.[22] In these circumstances, and in these social contexts where the belief in magic was endemic, it would not have been illogical to turn to extra-legal channels at times of personal stress such as becoming the victim of theft.[23]

Although the punishment of thieves in Roman law began with fairly mild impositions of fines, Ulpian states that by the mid-second century it had become increasingly common to prosecute them according to criminal law, opening up the potential for corporal and capital punishments for lower-class thieves.[24] According to Harries, this may have been driven by developments in social perceptions of crime and punishment, which no longer focused on compensating victims but instead valued exacting revenge from convicts and deterring others.[25] It is possible that the increasingly gory punishments outlined in the theft curses from Britannia mirrored this development. Cursers on theft curses rarely ask for their possessions back, preferring to symbolically give them to the gods, thereby making the theft a more serious crime, and making the gods more likely to pursue and punish the thief. The tablet from Caistor St. Edmund is particularly descriptive (**SD 441**):

> Vroc ... sius carries off from Nase ... a wreath, bracelets, a cap, a mirror (?), a head-dress, a pair of leggings, ten pewter vessels, whether he be man or woman, boy or girl. If you want the pair of leggings, they shall become yours at the price of his blood, so that he, Neptune, shall seek him out, and a cloak and head-dress and bracelets, fifteen denarii, the cap. Then the thief holds onto the wreath at the cost of his blood in accordance with the transaction on the above written sheet.

In this case, Neptune is expected to go after the thief, recover the goods and exact payment in blood – a common formula, and usually interpreted as a metaphor for capital punishment[26] – in much the same way that a Roman magistrate would do. The curser received no monetary remuneration but was instead compensated by witnessing the pain or death of the thief. As argued by Versnel and Chaniotis, the acting out of punishments in public was a key feature of Graeco-Roman concepts of divine justice.[27] This will be explored further below, but for now it will suffice to say that the evidence suggests that the presence of an audience was important both as a manifestation of divine power and as a form of social control. The gods needed to be seen to punish wrongdoers for belief in their judicial power to continue, and so public displays of confession and atonement were occasionally demanded.[28] In the motivations behind their actions, the cursers were influenced by these widely circulated ideas of divine justice, as well as what they understood about human justice.

It was not just the thieves themselves who were targeted in curses, but also anyone even tangentially connected to the crime. Some cursers included formulas intended to widen the curse to include witnesses or accomplices, or even the family of the thief. This text from Bath is illustrative of the trend (**SD 302**):

> Basilia presents to the temple of Mars (her) silver ring. If slave or free man has been involved, or knows anything about it, he may be accursed in (his) blood and eyes and all his limbs, or even with all his intestines eaten away: he who has stolen the ring or was a witness is done for.

The intention must be to inflict suffering on those connected to the crime, possibly in the hope that they will force the thief to return to the temple and confess. Punishing people who assisted thieves is consistent with Roman law, which stated that accomplices to theft had in effect committed the crime themselves and should therefore be prosecuted as thieves.[29] Other curses went further, extending the punishment to the family of the suspected thief. This is stipulated in at least three theft texts (**SD 246, 352, 443**). The best example is the fragmentary text of a curse from Bath (**SD 246**):

> ...has stolen, that...the price [of them and] exact this through [his] blood and [health] and (those) of his family, and not allow them [to drink or] eat or defecate or [urinate] before he has...[releas]ed this.

The intention of this curse is clear: the family of the thief is to suffer as much for the crime as the thief himself. Another fragmentary Bath curse is even more explicit (**SD 214**):

> A petition. (I ask) you Victory (The Avenger?)...Cunomolius (son?) of Minicus, Minervina (his?) wife, Cunitius (their?) slave, Senovara (his?) wife, Lavidendus (their?) slave, Mattonius (their?) slave, Catinius (son?) of Exsactor...Methianus ...I give...// enemy (?)

The curser on this text has gone to extreme lengths to ensure that whole households are punished by the curse, naming husbands, wives, fathers and enslaved people. This idea of distributing the punishment beyond the criminals and accomplices onto potentially innocent family members stems from a desire for vengeance rather than justice, and certainly does not feature in the Roman law codes. Perhaps this expansive application of punishment was another reason to curse thieves rather than pursue them through the courts: the gods could cause suffering far greater than any sentence a Roman magistrate could deliver.

Although I agree that theft curses should remain in the prayers for justice category, the evidence presented here shows that at times Versnel overstates his case. When these curses are put into the context of Roman law, the full force of their vengeful nature is revealed. It is much harder to argue that the cursers were seeking fair justice for the crimes committed against them when the punishments they demand for their victims are compared to those that would have been laid down by a Roman magistrate had the case come to court. Although they may have seen the system as letting them down when prosecuting thieves, the cursers certainly tapped into wider thoughts about the public nature of justice, and I will discuss this in more detail later in this chapter.

Competition curses

If the British theft texts were set aside, the image of cursing in the western half of the Empire would be dominated by those against charioteers and their horses, at least in numerical terms. However, and barring two exceptions (**SD 132** from Écija, Hispania and SGD 149 from Khoms, Africa) these come exclusively from three cities – Rome, Carthage and Sousse – and, when find-spot and content are considered, should be narrowed down even further to very specific circumstances. Put another way, the existence of many circus curses from the study region should not tempt us to think that this practice was widespread in the population, when in fact it seems to have been restricted to use by particular individuals, perhaps in moments of particular crisis or uncertainty.

Scholarship has tended to argue for three possible groups of people who would be interested in cursing charioteers and their horses: fans, rival charioteers and the organizers of the factions for whom they raced.[30] Gordon argues that the curses listing large numbers of drivers and horses are likely to have been commissioned by faction or stable owners, who would have been the only people with access to such detailed information about rival teams, and would also have been the people who risked the most when particular teams lost in the circus.[31] Unfortunately, there is little surviving evidence about faction management and the organization of chariot racing in the Imperial period. Even for the city of Rome, scholarship is mostly in the dark, but the situation in the provinces is even murkier. The most that can be said is that both factions and stables seem to have been run by private businessmen of equestrian rank, although with increasing imperial involvement at Rome across the first three to four centuries AD.[32] In North Africa, private interests seem to have survived longer, and the circus-themed mosaics of wealthy houses in both Carthage and Sousse suggest that some individuals became wealthy from providing horses and drivers for the races.[33] These fortunes would have been staked on the continued success of their teams in competition for fame and prize money, meaning that consistent failure to run winning horses and drivers could have serious financial implications for the backers. Gordon goes on to argue that only the curses that target individual or smaller numbers of drivers and their teams can be attributed to punters or rival charioteers, because their risks would be connected to the performance of the specific individuals on whom they were betting, or against whom they were competing.

This interpretation is attractive, especially for those texts from Sousse that include more than forty horses. Gordon is right to point out that we know virtually nothing about the advertising of games, so cannot know if the horses and drivers appearing in each event were publicly communicated beforehand.[34] However, his argument that these curses are only likely to have been written by those with financial interests in the outcomes of races is not totally convincing. Even before the organized and highly politicized factions found in the eastern cities of Late Antiquity, chariot-racing fans were passionate about their teams. As Cameron has amply shown, rivalry between the Green and Blue factions existed from at least the Julio-Claudian period, dividing Roman society from the imperial family downwards.[35] Although these rivalries did not escalate to riots or organized pitched battles before the fifth century, they were nevertheless lively and occasionally violent.[36] Chariot racing fans were certainly passionate enough to have an interest in the outcome of races, whether they had placed a wager or not. Although on an entirely different scale, the example of modern sports fans may be illustrative here. Fans who identify strongly with a particular team make their role as a follower a central component of their social identity, meaning that their team's performance becomes an important component in their own self-worth.[37] When the team loses, these fans experience a loss in self-esteem and can become aggressive or violent, even more so when that loss was unexpected.[38] Recent studies of American sports fans (mostly baseball or college basketball) have shown that a sizeable minority of fans would consider acting illegally or violently against players and coaches of opposing teams, if they thought it would result in a positive outcome for their own side.[39] To take one example, 34 per cent of college basketball fans surveyed would be at least minimally willing to break a rival player's leg to assist their own team.[40] Other studies show the prevalence of desperate or 'superstitious' behaviour that some fans would engage in to help their team to victory.[41] The psychological impact of victory or defeat for a favoured team is enough to elicit such actions, without the addition of financial risk. Returning to the Roman evidence, it seems reasonable to suggest that at least some chariot racing fans in the imperial period might have felt similarly about their chosen faction, and might therefore have engaged in cursing rituals to influence the outcome of races. Cameron's identification of small bands of hard-core supporters of athletes, gladiators, charioteers and dancers, predominantly composed of young men, would chime well with the identification of small minorities of highly identifying sports fans in the modern world.[42]

The question of why the same charioteers were targeted multiple times is a challenging one to answer, but is important for considering the contexts in which these texts were written. Although the same names occur repeatedly, they are often in different orders and associated with different horses, so presumably the curses target races held on different days. Unfortunately, the curses themselves rarely give details of the specific events, meaning we cannot know how closely related they were in time.[43] However, it seems likely to me that curses against the same or similar charioteers and horses must be concentrated around particular times, perhaps of especially intense rivalry between the factions. Studies of modern fan behaviour emphasize that rivalries can change over time, and often become stronger in response to events such as a particular run of success for one side. Fans of teams that repeatedly fail to win competitions are more likely to consider desperate or violent acts than those who follow more successful teams.[44] Similar situations may be behind some of the chariot racing curses from Rome, Carthage and Sousse: individuals driven to taking extreme measures to attempt to resolve a particular situation of anxiety and psychological stress caused by the inability of their team to win against the others, perhaps across a period of weeks or months. This could apply equally to any of the three types of people to whom these curses are usually attributed: faction owners, fans and the charioteers themselves.

Chariot racing is the dominant competition mentioned on the curse tablets, but a small minority refer to other events. Eleven curses found in the amphitheatre of Carthage target *venatores* – beast hunters – who would have performed there (DT 246, **247**, 248, 249, **250, 251, 252**, 253, 254; dfx 11.1.1/33, 11.1.1/37), fighting wild animals in single combat or hunting groups of herbivores for the entertainment of spectators.[45] Although beast hunts were performed for entertainment in arenas in Rome and across the Empire, these events seem to have been particularly popular in North Africa, as the evidence of mosaics with hunting and arena themes attests.[46] Furthermore, these North African mosaics are among the small but clear body of evidence for sodalities of *venatores*: formal organizations that provided trained hunters as well as beasts for events in the arena.[47] A dozen or so have been identified, with names such as Telegenii, Pentasii and Taurisci.[48] They also acted as burial associations for the *venatores* themselves, erecting monuments for each other when they died.[49] Some African Red Slip Ware vessels may also have been decorated with the emblems and logos of these organizations, accompanied by legends such as TELEGENI NIKA (Telegeni be victorious!), which could suggest fan identification with the different sodalities, and therefore some level of competition between them.[50] However, this does not come out in the curses. Most target individual *venatores*, as in this example (**DT 247**):

> Strike down, banish, wound Gallicus, whom Prima bore, in this hour in the amphitheatre at the games and ... bind his hand ... may he not bind the bear, the bears ... bind his feet, limbs, senses, marrow. Bind Gallicus, whom Prima bore, so that he cannot kill either the bear or the bull with a single blow, nor kill them with two blows, nor kill the bull or the bear with three blows. May you achieve this by the names of the living and almighty gods now, now, quickly, quickly. May the bear crush him and wound him.

As can be seen, the victim is identified only by his maternal lineage, with no associated faction. Of the two beast-hunter curses that targets multiple victims, only one links them together: DT 248 refers to the three targets – Ziolus, son of Restuta, Zelica the *apparitor*, and Adescila, son of Victoria – as 'sons of Aemilianus' (*filios Aemiliani*). Whether this means they were literally brothers, albeit with different mothers, or members of a troupe run by Aemilianus is uncertain.[51] In any case, naming the organization to which a *venator* belonged does not seem to have been necessary or relevant in the way that naming a charioteer's faction was, perhaps because the competition between them was less intense, or because fan identification was lower than for the circus factions. Fagan has argued that because bouts were relatively short and performers were rotated frequently, amphitheatre events were less suited to spectator rivalry and aggression, which resulted in far fewer violent disturbances than in the theatre or circus.[52] This being the case, it seems less likely that the beast-hunter curses were produced either by highly identified fans or by the organizers of the factions, but were rather provoked by individual conflicts between the performers themselves. This might also explain the very small number of such curses:

without the more intense fan rivalries of the circus, cursing beast hunters only made sense in quite specific, personal circumstances, and did not attract a wider significance or popular appeal. At Carthage, we might be seeing the inventiveness of freelance religious specialists, attempting to drum up demand for a new service. As it turned out, the nature of beast-hunting was not as promising as chariot racing, at least for cursing.

Juridical curses

Curses relating to legal trials make up 14 per cent of the tablets for which a motive could be identified (forty-three of 302). Of these, eleven were from Carthage and nine were from Bad Kreuznach, with the rest being found in ones, twos or threes at sites across Italia, Hispania, Gallia, Germania, Pannonia and Raetia.

It is interesting that, particularly in the northern provinces, many juridical curses were found in small towns or villages with no obvious administrative functions. Places such as Bad Kreuznach are unlikely to have been on the court circuit of the governor, and so probably were not the towns in which the trials would have taken place. Most of these tablets were found in graves, so the deposition locations may have been chosen for any of several reasons including, as discussed in the previous chapter, even for the convenience of the cemetery to the curser's home.

Juridical curses are often directed towards the speech, responses and answers of the victims, therefore hampering their ability to effectively fight the case. In fact, attacks on the victim's powers of speech have been so closely associated with juridical cursing that some texts are put into this category with no further evidence of connection to a trial (e.g. **SD 522** and **DT 300**). Most juridical curses name multiple victims: only five target (or appear to target) lone individuals (SD 161, **478, 522, DT 300**, 303). The text below shows it was not just the litigants that were targeted, but also anyone else who was connected to the trial – in this case an *adiutorium*, a technical term for a legal assistant (**SD 467**):

> I bring Fructus Gracilis and Aureus the *adiutorium* to those below. Thus may he not be able to respond to questioning.

Other juridical curses explicitly name legates (**SD 136**), lawyers (**SD 160**), the court clerk (**SD 473**), informers (SD 471) and witnesses (**SD 176**). By expanding the curse out to hit witnesses and informers, the juridical curses were driven by the same impulses as the theft curses that also targeted witnesses and family members of the named victims. Considering that it was the speech, responses and answers of these people that were targeted, it is likely that the curses were written and deposited immediately before the commencement of the trial or while it was in progress. These are pre-emptive strikes made before the victims appeared in court, and therefore they are attempts to influence future events to secure a positive outcome for the curser. The time in the run-up to a trial is also likely to be the most stressful for those involved, as anxiety and uncertainty take hold. These juridical curses could have cathartic benefits, in that they give the cursers an active outlet for these anxieties instead of passively waiting for the trial to commence. From occasional references in ancient literary sources, it seems that anyone who made public speeches in the Roman world could be a potential target for curses, and the belief in magical attacks of this kind could have disastrous effects on their performance, and therefore on the outcome of the trial.[53] In most cases it is unclear whether these curses were written by the prosecution or defence, as the victims are mostly referred to as *inimici*: enemies. The only exception is the Chagnon text (**SD 160**), which asks that the lawyers of the victims be unable to defend them, implying that the curse was made by the prosecution.

The curses from Bad Kreuznach deserve closer analysis. The curses from this cemetery form at least two groups, which can be constructed based on the names of the victims. The largest group consists of five individual curses: **SD 468, 469, 470**, 471 and **473**. Between them these five curses name almost forty victims, five of whom (Atticinus son of Ammo, Optatus son of Silo, Terentius Att(iss)o, Sinto son of Valens and Ma(n)suetus) appear on more than one of the tablets. The exact nature of the trials to which these curses relate is unfortunately unknown, but it must have been a dramatic, large-scale event considering the sheer number of people involved in such a small community. The names repeated across several tablets may have been the instigators of a conspiracy or the leaders of a local faction of some kind. Unfortunately, we have no clear idea of exactly who made the curses as most of them were composed anonymously. We have already encountered the strange case of Quartio Severus, who appears as a victim on another tablet found in the same grave, and therefore possibly deposited in the same action, as his own tablet. The most satisfying explanation for this confusing situation is that as the trial progressed, and as the list of witnesses, litigants, lawyers and other associated people grew and changed, it was apparent to one side or the other that new curses were required. They cast their net as widely as possible, including the wives and enslaved people of prominent individuals, so that the curse hit everyone involved in the case, no matter how tangentially.[54] It is important to remember that the relationships between two sides in a trial do not begin with its commencement, nor do they end at its conclusion. Members of a community, especially in small settlements like Bad Kreuznach, were part of complex and ever-changing social networks involving positive and negative ties of conflict and alliance.[55] Whether or not all these people would appear in front of the magistrates hearing this case was to a certain degree irrelevant to the cursers; their perception as enemies motivated their inclusion on the curses. This is corroborated by the repeated naming of the victims as *inimici*, and the inclusion of formulas like 'any other enemies' (**SD 470**).

The three curses from Ampurias should be discussed here too (**SD 134, 135, 136**), as they also all relate to a single incident. All three tablets were deposited in the same cemetery, although in different cinerary urns, and have been securely dated to the late 70s or early 80s AD.[56] Two consist solely of a list of the names of the victims in the nominative, with only the third including any more detail (**SD 135**):

> May the Olossitani, Sempronius Campanus Fidentinus, my adversaries, not oppose me unfairly // Fulvus the Augustan legate, Rufus the Augustan legate, Maturus the Augustan procurator, council of the legate, advocates of the Indicetani.

Almost uniquely among Latin curse tablets, these texts target officials of the Roman government of the province: T. Aurelius Fulvus, Q. Pomponius Rufus and Marius Maturus, respectively the governor of Hispania Tarraconensis (*legatus Augusti pro praetore*), his *legatus iuridicus* and *procurator Augusti*.[57] The three can be identified as politicians of some note in early Flavian Rome: Maturus also governed the province of Alpes Maritimae, and both Fulvus and Rufus attained the consulship.[58] Fulvus was also the paternal grandfather of the future emperor Antoninus Pius, making him the only named individual on all of the curse tablets from the Roman west with a direct connection to the imperial family. Alongside these named individuals, the curser has also targeted another unknown man, Sempronius Campanus Fidentinus, as well as two local communities, the Indicatani and the Olossitani, and their legal representatives. The exact historical context in which these texts were produced is a matter of debate, and probably unresolvable. Solin and Gager, among others, interpret this as a border dispute between the two communities, with the Olossitani cursing both the Romans and the Indicetani.[59] However, Marco Simón (following Fabre, Mayer and Rodà) has convincingly argued that all parties mentioned on the tablets are victims, and that the curser is an unnamed third party, perhaps someone who stood to lose out in a redistribution of land around Ampurias after the grant of *ius Latii* to Hispania by Vespasian in AD 70.[60] Whatever the specific legal circumstances, from a lived religion perspective it is somewhat puzzling that the curser felt it necessary to deposit three separate but almost identical curses, presumably on three different occasions. Unlike on the Bad Kreuznach tablets, the list of targets does not change substantially, so the second and third curses were not motivated by new people becoming involved in the dispute. Perhaps the tablets were deposited on successive days, as deliberation over the issue dragged on. The curser may have felt that repeating the ritual was necessary to ensure continued coverage or to amplify the curse.

The collection of juridical curses from the Roman west clearly demonstrates that people were actively engaged in the formal legal system across the provinces, despite the irregular and inconsistent access that was discussed above. Although the picture is far from complete, the curses suggest a limited but well-structured process, with litigants represented by lawyers who argued their case before a judge. Witnesses were evidently called to give evidence, and it seems that, much like in the city of Rome itself, crowds of family, friends, clients and others could be present while the trial was being heard.[61] The cursers on the juridical curses knew this and used it to their advantage by including as many people who could have an impact on the trial as possible.

This analysis of the juridical curses has revealed the many similarities among them, such as attacking the speech of victims, deposition of the tablets in graves and the invocations of underworld powers. In Africa and Italia, both deposition in graves and the invocation of underworld powers are found in a variety of other types of curse, particularly competition curses, but outside these regions, curses displaying these characteristics are almost exclusively juridical. This suggests that, especially in Gallia, Germania and Hispania, the knowledge of what constituted an appropriate and successful curse in this context may have circulated as a complete whole and may have gone along with the knowledge and expertise needed to pursue a case through the provincial legal system. In other words, this specific method of producing a curse tablet may have become closely associated with juridical cursing, and at times may even have become an accepted part of the process of bringing a case to trial in the provinces. The features of this category of curse were specifically intended to work as direct attacks on the performance of litigants, lawyers and witnesses, in an effort to ensure the success of the curser's side of the trial. This, then, is another example of people performing cursing rituals that suit their needs in specific contexts and circumstances.

Erotic curses

The fact that there are only thirty erotic curses from the Roman west could easily be cause for surprise, especially if the testimony of Latin literature is taken as any kind of guide for the intentions behind the use of magic in Rome. The witches familiar from the work of Apuleius, Horace, Ovid and others are almost exclusively focused on the pursuit of lovers by magical means, either for their clients or for themselves, and the use of inscribed lead tablets feature within the store of magical objects used in their work.[62] In contrast, the city of Rome has produced only three erotic curses, with the bulk of those in the western Empire coming from Carthage and Sousse. The discrepancy between the material and literary evidence has been dealt with by other scholars,[63] and it is not within the scope of this book to delve too deeply into the literary depictions of cursing. However, it is important to point it out here, because the temptation to draw upon the literature is strongest when discussing erotic magic. If there is one thing that can be seen in the literature, it is that there were a dazzling array of possible rituals that could be used to charm a lover, and that therefore the use of inscribed lead tablets was just one weapon in the potential arsenal. The thirty tablets examined here are presumably only the tip of the iceberg of magical responses to matters of the heart.

The erotic curses from the study area can be further subdivided into attraction and separation spells, of which there are nineteen and eleven respectively. Unlike in Faraone's analysis of the earlier Greek material, among the tablets analysed here there is no strong division between those seeking *eros* – uncontrollable desire – and those intended to promote *philia* – affection between partners in existing relationships.[64] All of the attraction spells seek *eros* in their target, as will be discussed below. The attraction spells are almost exclusively from Africa and exhibit good evidence for a coherent tradition. The influence from Graeco-Egyptian traditions is particularly strong, with the inclusion of magical words, *charaktêres*, and the invocation of Egyptian daemons suggesting the involvement of professional practitioners with access to instruction manuals and recipe books like those preserved in the *PGM*. This most telling example is a curse from Carthage (**DT 230**), which has blank spaces left within the text for the insertion of the name of the victim, perhaps suggesting that it was produced for purchase 'off the shelf'.

Almost all the attraction spells were produced by (or on behalf of) men and targeted a woman, always named and presumably therefore known to the man who desired her. This is an important point to dwell on in terms of the lived experience of producing these curses: they were created with a concrete goal in mind – the attraction of a specific woman to a specific man – rather than a general desire to find love with an otherwise unknown partner. The cursers were also not interested in brief flings or one-night stands, but generally sought to establish long-term relationships. In one curse, Martialis asks that his target be 'held back for all time in love and desire' for him (**DT 231**), in another, Bonosa is to be inflicted with a 'holy, unbroken love … until the day of her death' (**DT 267**) and in yet another, Optatus and Vera are to be 'bound together through all eternal time' (**dfx 11.2.1/36**).

The two curses explicitly written by (or for) women (**DT 270** and **Gager 36**, both from Sousse) follow the same patterns as the male-authored texts, targeting specific named individuals and attempting to create long-lasting relationships. In the latter, Domitiana invokes the God of Abraham and Jacob to torture a certain Urbanus with sleeplessness and mental anguish until he 'takes her into his house as his wife.' This curse ends with a series of wishes that make Domitiana's goal abundantly clear:

> unite them in marriage and as spouses in love for all the time of their lives. Make him as her obedient slave, so that he will desire no other woman or maiden apart from Domitiana alone, to whom Candida gave birth, and will keep her as his spouse for all the time of their lives.

None of the tablets, except the curse from Peiting, Raetia (**SD 524**) in which a man appears to be targeting women he enslaves, give any details of any existing relationships between the men and women named on the curses. This text, as with all the attraction spells, raises tantalising questions about why exactly the cursers felt it necessary to go to the extreme lengths of placing a curse upon the target. Are these cases of unrequited love, or of bitter ex-partners? Had they already made advances through other means but been spurned? Interpreting attraction spells hinges on how we imagine they were composed. How much input did the cursers have once they had enlisted the help of a specialist? If some of the curses were mass produced, as the gaps in the text from Carthage suggest, it necessarily dampens some of the more emotional interpretations that would otherwise be possible. Indeed, Graf has argued that there is no place in the careful composition of these texts for spontaneous, passionate outbursts of feeling on the part of the authors.[65] I think this is something of an extreme view, and that we should not totally discount the emotional stake held in the production of such texts. Even if they were mediated through the work of a specialist, it is difficult to read these texts as the totally passionless product of a retail transaction. Winkler's classic anthropological reading of the erotic curses places them within the context of ancient Mediterranean ideas of *eros* as a disease affecting body, mind and soul.[66] From this perspective, writing or commissioning an erotic curse becomes an attempt to cure an illness through a regaining of control over the situation and the transference of emotional torment from curser to victim.[67] For this reason, many of the curses ask for the victims to burn with passion and desire, to be stricken with insomnia, restlessness and loss of appetite. As Winkler argues, these are possibly the very symptoms being felt by the curser as their affections for the victim went unreciprocated.[68] The involvement of a specialist does not make the emotional situation of the curser any less real or less keenly felt, just as the involvement of a doctor does not make the symptoms of a physical illness or injury any less painful for the patient. This is an attractive interpretation, but perhaps risks creating too sympathetic a picture of the cursers who, it must not be forgotten, were attempting to harness supernatural powers to force an unwilling victim, almost always a woman, into a life-long sexual relationship. Not only was the victim seemingly unwilling to engage in this relationship, but evidently their wider families often were too. Six of the nineteen attraction curses from the western provinces include some variation of the command that the victim forget their fathers, mothers, relatives and friends (e.g. **DT 266**). Both Winkler and Faraone interpreted these formulas through the lens of restricted, segregated treatment of young women in the ancient world, concluding that these curses must have targeted virgin daughters kept away from the public eye by controlling parents.[69] However, both Dickie and Pachoumi have raised the important point that the curses often talk about their victims as if they are already sexually active, asking that they forget all other men or women and give their attention to the curser only.[70] Dickie goes too far in assuming that this must mean the targets are prostitutes; we cannot possibly be expected to imagine that the only sexually active, unmarried women in Roman society were those paid for their services. Although moralists, and perhaps some parents, might have baulked at the idea, there can be no serious doubt that some couples had sex before they were married, or that some women had experience of sexual partners other than their eventual spouses. Williams correctly points out that the late republican and Augustan love poets present personas that are clearly experienced lovers and who resist the pressure to marry.[71] Their female lovers are clearly not their wives, but are equally not all enslaved women or prostitutes, despite those being the only groups among whom free men were expected to find casual sexual partners. Indeed, both Ovid and Martial say that sex with free women is preferable to enslaved or freedwomen.[72] Although moral, social, and even legal restrictions on extra-marital sex for women should be considered, the existence of such constraints on behaviour are often more suggestive of its presence in a society rather than its absence, especially when repeated bans are required. In other words, if the Roman authorities felt the need to continually proclaim how wrong it was for women to take lovers outside marriage, then these restrictions were probably being circumvented. At the same time, the very existence of attraction curses speaks to circumstances where women could make themselves unavailable to some men, to the extent that these men resorted to extreme, otherworldly measures to pursue them. As I will discuss in the next chapter, the alternative future that these curses imagine is one that can only come into existence after a violent breaking of the woman's existing social relationships.

Turning from the attraction to the separation curses, the differences between the two collections are stark. Where the attraction spells are, for the most part, concentrated in North Africa, the separation spells are more widely and thinly dispersed, and crucially do not come from Carthage or Sousse. All are isolated finds: two from different locations in Rome (**SD 1** and NGCT 85), another two from separate locations in Italia (**SD 70** and **DT 198**), and one each from Hispania (**SD 140**), Pannonia (**SD 527**), Raetia (**SD 521**) and Noricum (**SD 526**). There are few traces of connections to the Graeco-Egyptian magical tradition, entirely unlike the attraction spells already discussed. Instead, these texts seem to have been produced on an ad hoc basis, with the cursers making the curses that seemed most appropriate to achieve their aim, which was either the splitting of an existing couple or the preventing of the victim finding a partner. The former is more common, accounting for six of the eight curses. The curse, from Calvi Risorta (Italia) provides a good example of these, and is also the only one to explicitly name the curser, which in this case is a woman named Quartia Satia (**SD 70**):

> Pluto and the underworld gods, (I hand over) Gaius Babullius and his fucker Tertia Salvia. Pluto, receive into the underworld the promise of Quarta Satia.

Only two curses attempt to prevent people from finding a partner, and both come from the Danubian provinces: one somewhat vague tablet from Bregenz in Raetia and this more specific text from Ptuj in Pannonia: 'Paulina should be turned away from all men and bound, so that she cannot do any harm. Close off Firmina from all men.'

For most of these texts we are again left guessing over the exact circumstances that would drive a person to seek supernatural aid in breaking up a couple or keeping a person single. Scholars have generally assumed that these texts represent love triangles of some sort, with the curser desiring one of the members of the couple.[73] The curse is therefore intended to drive the two apart so that the curser can make their move on whichever partner they desired. The text from Sagunt in Hispania is illustrative (**SD 140**): 'Quintula should never again be with Fortunalis.' However, the separation curses are not always so clear-cut. One of the two from Rome demonstrates the difficulties in teasing out the appropriate social contexts (**SD 1**):

> Danae, new slave of Capito: may you receive and accept this offering, and may you consume Danae. You may not have Eutychia, wife of Soterichos.

This curse could have been written by Soterichos himself, jealous of the attention given to his wife by a newcomer. The fact that Danae is enslaved might suggest the same status for Eutychia and Soterichos, meaning that their marriage was not a formal arrangement and therefore could be dissolved easily.[74] If Danae is a woman, as the name would suggest, this text would include the only mention of a same-sex relationship on the western erotic curses.[75] Other separation curses clearly did come from outside a married couple: the curse from Cuma (**DT 198**) attempts to split Valeria Quadratilla from her husband Vitruvius Felix, apparently because she 'broke faith' with him. The one from Mautern in Noricum (**SD 526**) may also intend to split a married couple, twisting the husband away from his wife and handing him over to the underworld gods. There is little clear evidence among these texts for the situations outlined by Ripat, in which a wife is cursing an enslaved woman currently engaged in a sexual relationship with her husband.[76] In Ripat's interpretation, the separation curses are a wife's last resort to preserve her position of favour and respect within the household. As mentioned above, the only text with a confirmed female curser is Quarta Satia's curse. While it is possible that Gaius Babullius could be her husband, if Ripat's argument is right, and Quarta is seeking to preserve her position in the household by attacking a potential rival for his affections, then it seems strange that she would curse both partners in the extra-marital affair, rather than just Tertia Salvia. Ultimately the exact circumstances are irretrievable, for this and the many of the other attraction and separation curses, and although speculation on individual cases is tempting it is probably unhelpful. However, I think we might more confidently speak about the wider social situations in which these curses were used, and the image they present of erotic relationships in the Roman world. They certainly suggest a strong current of rumour and gossip, and I will discuss this aspect of erotic magic later in this chapter.

By and large, the tradition of using curses to attract lovers did not reach north of the Alps.[77] Of the thirty curses with erotic motives collected for this study, only seven come from the Northern provinces. Aside from the four already discussed (the attraction spell from Peiting and the three separation spells from Pannonia, Raetia and Noricum), the others are of very uncertain motive. The identification of them as erotic curses rests on the hopeful interpretations of some very unclear Latin, and there are no texts that come anywhere near the elaborate tablets produced in the Graeco-Egyptian traditions. The only Gallic tablet seemingly motivated by love is from a cemetery in a northern district of Trier (**SD 173**):

> Artus (is a) fucker ... I bind Artus the fucker, (son?) of Dercomognus.

As discussed in Chapter 3, this curse was not inscribed on a sheet of lead, but scratched onto a pot. The brief curse formula tells us very little: the curser intended to bind someone who they described as a *fututor* – an obscene word which is often found in epigrams and graffiti.[78] The term specifically relates to the action of vaginal penetration and is almost always a label for men, so this could be another curse written by a woman.[79] Interpretations of the inscription have differed over time, with restoration of *Art(um)* a particular point of contention.[80] Here I have followed Urbanová in translating Artus as a proper name, making him the victim. Whether this is an attraction or separation curse is unclear, assuming that there even is an erotic motive. The text could be turning his abilities as a *fututor* towards the curser, or away from his current lover, or perhaps even both. Alternatively, *fututor* could be a simple slur, with no direct connection to the motive of the curse other than to add insult to injury.

Another tablet, this time from Bad Kreuznach, may have an erotic motive, but again the text is too unclear to make a definitive judgement (**SD 472**):

> The names have been given, delivered, entrusted to the infernals, so that they seize them by force. Silonia, Surus, Caenus, Secundus. That which has been vowed urges you. I love him.

The presence of *amo* would suggest love being involved, but the relevance of *illum amo* to the rest of the curse is unclear. There are multiple victims on the curse – three men and a woman – and nothing that clarifies which of them, if any, is the object of *amo*. *Sponsus* could be a passive perfect participle, as I have translated here, but it can also mean a betrothed man. In that case, perhaps the curse was written by someone who was jilted by their fiancée. It could have been written by the bridegroom himself, but the masculine pronoun in the *illum amo* formula suggests that the author could equally have been the female half of the couple. If there is anything certain to say about this curse, it is not about the motive but about the method of the curse: it adheres strongly to the local cursing traditions present in first-century Bad Kreuznach. Like the others found in that context, the curser gave the names of the victims to the gods of the underworld, and deposited their tablet in a grave to ensure the message was more likely to reach its intended audience. If it is an erotic curse, this tablet shows more similarities to the other curses made in the social context of Bad Kreuznach than to the Graeco-Egyptian traditions that developed elsewhere.

We are perhaps on firmer ground with one of the tablets from Groß-Gerau (**SD 482**), in which the curser asks to be avenged because a certain Priscilla 'married mistakenly' (*nubere erravit*). However, the text is phrased as a prayer for justice rather than either an attraction or separation spell, in that there is no sense that Priscilla should be split from her new husband, or that she should fall (back?) in love with the curser. Instead, Attis and Magna Mater are asked to punish Priscilla for betraying sacred secrets, presumably of the cult of those deities.[81] Versnel suggests that this may be a false accusation, meant to make the gods angry with the victim and therefore more concerned with carrying out the punishment.[82]

To summarize erotic magic in the western provinces, there are two separate traditions at work. On the one hand, there are the attraction spells, predominantly from North Africa and heavily influenced by Graeco-Egyptian manuals and perhaps produced by specialists. These form a cohesive corpus, using similar formulas and *charaktêres*, and making similar requests for the fates of their victims. However, there is enough variation to suggest some element of input on the part of the curser. In other words, they were not all mass produced by specialists to be purchased 'off the shelf'. On the other hand, there are the separation curses, spread thinly and widely across the Empire outside North Africa and with little inspiration from eastern practices. As with the other genres of curse in these regions, cursers relied on their own knowledge of local traditions of production, address and deposition to inform the rituals they performed, resulting in a body of texts that seems incoherent and idiosyncratic to modern readers. It is reasonable to conclude that, even if an awareness of the possibility of using magic to resolve matters of the heart existed more widely in the west, the kinds of erotic magic rituals preserved in the papyri, and the specialists who could use them, did not circulate much beyond Carthage and Sousse.

Attempts to make sense of erotic curses are difficult because the specific circumstances that provoked them are ultimately lost to us. The generalizations scholars have made on the positions and personalities of both the cursers and victims are unsatisfactory because they fail to do justice to the kaleidoscope of potential erotic experiences that were possible for men and women, even in the sexually restricted world of Imperial Rome. If the erotic curses tell us anything, it is that the repression of female sexuality that appears in some of the literary evidence is an ideal that was not followed by all, regardless of the censure and ridicule that such activity might attract. Both men and women could pursue their passions and desires, in extreme cases resorting to the supernatural to aid in achieving their aims.

Motives in the Roman west

An analysis of the motives behind curse tablets from the Roman west reveals an array of possible reasons to engage with the ritual, from the righteous fury of crime victims to the desperate actions of racing fans and the frustrated passions of spurned lovers. Making sense of these motives on a general level is difficult, and no simple narrative emerges that describes why some people cursed others. To attempt to construct one would do violence to the creative individuality of these texts. Curses were always the product of individual people embedded in their own social and cultural lives, conducting these rituals to address situations particular to them in that moment. Nevertheless, each curse was part of traditions of practice that transcended the individual, and that informed the curser of what constituted an effective curse for their particular purpose. The different motive categories are not evenly distributed but are concentrated in time and space. Cursing against chariot racers occurred in Carthage and Sousse for brief moments through the second and third centuries, and then again in late fourth/early fifth century Rome, perhaps connected to intense rivalry between factions. There were flurries of curses against legal opponents in places like Bad Kreuznach and Ampurias when particular issues were causing intense divisions within local communities. Perhaps the only exceptions to this rule are the British theft curses, which seem to have had a much more enduring popularity, no doubt helped by the establishment of Bath and Uley as centres for cursing thieves.

My argument here is contextual, as it has been throughout this study. In this section I have thought about how the curse tablets fitted into the lives of the people who used them. These lives were embedded into local and regional social, political and religious contexts, and as a result every action taken was influenced by them. The cursers were also influenced by their own personal motive for cursing, tailoring words and actions to fit these intentions. The close similarities across the category of juridical curses show that certain features were associated with certain motives. However, as the remainder of this chapter will demonstrate, these short-term goals were not the only social factors that influenced both the decision to curse and the form that each curse took.

Social frameworks

So far, this chapter has discussed the curse tablets from the western provinces in terms of the Audollent/Faraone motive categories that are omnipresent in existing scholarship. However, these categories suggest a simplistic model of curse-tablet production, which starts with the circumstance that triggers the writing of the curse – such as the theft of a personal item or the announcement of a legal trial – and which ends with the successful deposition of the tablet.

In the previous 'motives' model, there are two categories of person – the cursers and the victims – and the relationship between the two is considered simplistic and mono-directional, in other words that the curser is attempting to harm or control the victim because of whatever specific event triggered the curse tablet. The model takes at face value the motives of the curse tablets, and assumes that the curser was 'justified' in writing the tablet because of a real situation that had developed in their life.[83] What is missing, therefore, is a critical analysis of the motives of curse tablets: in the words of Gordon, "why should we believe what the writers [of curse tablets] claim about the wrong done to them? What did the other side have to say?"[84] To focus only on the motives stated in the tablets ignores the complexity of human interactions in life, as well as the wider social contexts in which the curses were created.

The rest of this chapter will suggest ways in which we can think about these questions by exploring the deeper social frameworks that may have underlain the motives stated on the tablets. These are not mutually exclusive, and I am not suggesting that curse tablets should be, or even *can* be, sorted into categories based on them. Instead, the headings of this section should be taken as thematic guides for the discussion, rather than the construction of a new taxonomy to supplant that of Audollent and Faraone. Under the first two headings, *agonistic contexts* and *coping mechanisms*, I will be applying models suggested by previous scholars to the evidence from the west. As will become apparent, I think that the attempts to rationalize ancient cursing, according to modern ideas of 'rationality', that these models suggest is unwise. My own interpretation, influenced by the lived ancient religion approach, is to contextualize curses in the lives of the people who used them. This will be done by firmly locating curse tablets in the context of the social relationships between individuals and within communities. My argument throughout is based on the understanding that the relationships between cursers and victims do not begin and end with the writing and deposition of a curse tablet, but are considerably more complicated, spanning far greater lengths of time both before and after the specific circumstance that triggered the curse and the performance of the cursing ritual.

A crucial point raised by the first half of this chapter is that curses belonging to the standard motive categories are strongly concentrated in particular areas. The question leading on from this conclusion is why curse tablets were used for only some of these reasons in some places but not others. Although not on the same scale as the great cities of the Mediterranean, gladiatorial combat and chariot racing were nevertheless popular in some cities of Britannia, Gallia and Germania, and it would be impossible to claim that people in the north-west never had problems with matters of the heart, so why did they not attract curse tablets as they did elsewhere in the Roman Empire? From the other direction, it would be equally impossible to argue that theft was uncommon outside Roman Britain, so why did relatively few people in other places turn to cursing after having personal items stolen? The answers to these questions contain caveats for any scholar attempting to study ancient magic using archaeological evidence. Others have pointed out that these distributions could be meaningless, purely a result of the vagaries of the archaeological record.[85] That is no doubt a factor, but to me the trends seem too strong to be totally random. It is difficult to argue from silence, but it is possible that either the traditions of cursing for different motives did not spread beyond specific places, or that they did not catch on because people had other strategies to deal with these situations. Ultimately, the focus of enquiry must be on the surviving lead tablets, but we do not know, and we will probably never know, if there were other practices with only oral, ephemeral or perishable components that applied to erotic, commercial or competitive motives in the north-west, or to theft outside Britain.[86]

Agonistic contexts and risk

Some work has already been done in appreciating the social contexts of cursing, and various models and theories have been suggested. However, most scholars who have approached these questions have done so with a focus on Greek curses and have tended to rationalize the use of curse tablets in ancient society.

Faraone argued that the essential feature of all four types of 'binding' curses was their reference to relationships between rivals, be they traders, lovers, litigants or athletes.[87] In his view, the cursers were the perennial underdogs, protecting themselves against certain defeat in whatever activities they were engaged in. To them, magical attacks on their rivals seemed the only way to tip the scales in their favour, and the fear of defeat would outweigh the legal or moral taboos attached to such rituals.[88] This 'agonistic context', as Faraone termed it, is certainly apparent in the Archaic and Classical Greek texts he cites as evidence, and extended into the Roman period with the increased popularity of chariot racing and other forms of competitive entertainment.[89]

Eidinow has built on this agonistic model and introduced the concept of risk into the study of ancient cursing.[90] In her analysis, curse tablets were used in times of crisis or perceived danger to mitigate that danger and to protect the curser. In these moments, other people were identified as potential risks because of their aggressive actions – in love, legal trials, business or the arena – and needed to be bound and controlled to avoid damaging the curser.[91] Considering cursing in this way, as motivated by the fear or suspicion of future events, Eidinow's conclusions align with the idea of religion as lived experience, informing and informed by the cares and concerns of individual people at particular moments in their lives. In the words of Thomas, humans are 'historical beings', who 'act on the basis of understandings which are culturally installed and historically specific' to their present moment.[92] The information people have can be negative as well as positive, and does not always come to the individual as unfiltered truth. Eidinow identified envy and jealousy as motivating factors in the act of writing curse tablets,[93] and this is an area that I argue has further potential, and which I will explore further below.

The analysis of curse tablets as fitting into the agonistic context of ancient society is clearly relevant for some of the texts from the Roman west. I have already discussed the competition curses that seek to influence circus races or beast-hunts – agonistic contexts in the literal sense of the word – as well as juridical and erotic tablets that reveal other situations of competition between groups or individuals. Whether we should always imagine these texts as written by underdogs, as Faraone suggests, is unclear. As mentioned above, modern sports fans might contemplate ever more desperate or violent actions to help their favourite team if they are repeatedly unsuccessful, so it is possible that circus curses were written after a particularly severe string of losses by one faction or another. Gordon's analysis of risk, especially financial risk, as a factor in circus cursing has also already been examined here, but it is worth repeating that money is not the only thing at stake for highly engaged sports fans. The emotional and psychological impacts of defeat for a favoured team might have been felt more keenly than any hit on their coin purses. For the erotic curses, Winkler imagines desperate young men as the typical curser, unable to win their intended lover by other means.[94] Other scholars have rightly drawn attention to the potential risks – emotional, financial and social – involved in the making or breaking of romantic relationships, especially for women.[95] The juridical curses from the Roman west can certainly be analysed through the concept of risk, as Eidinow does for the similar texts dating to Classical Athens.[96] Personal reputation and financial security hung on the verdict of legal trials, to say nothing of the lives of those who, depending on the nature of the crime, could be executed if the judge returned a guilty verdict.[97] However, the lack of specific details in all of the juridical curses often leaves us in the dark when trying to probe deeper into the kinds of trials that might be involved. Even at Bad Kreuznach, where multiple curses relate to the same event, we know nothing about the individuals involved, and so cannot confirm whether Faraone's conclusion about 'perennial underdogs' holds true.

Faraone's analysis of the agonistic context of cursing cannot be applied to the large number of theft curses from Britain and elsewhere. Even Eidinow's introduction of the concept of risk can only go so far with these texts: they are undoubtedly attempting to deal with a situation of personal crisis, but are not motivated by future uncertainties in the way that other kinds of curses are. Even more concerning are the huge numbers of tablets for which no clear motive can be discerned. When all we have is a list of names or a vague mention of wrongdoing, it is impossible to tell if the curser was experiencing a situation of competition or risk. If we are not going to reject half of the available texts, other models need to be proposed.

Coping mechanisms

According to other scholars, magic acted as a coping mechanism for the difficulties of living life in the ancient world.[98] Magical practices allowed people to feel some sort of control over their future: not only were they often explicitly concerned with revealing or controlling future events, but built into rituals such as curse-tablet production was the cathartic benefit of action over inaction.[99] In this way of thinking, curses helped people deal with the injustices of their lives, especially people who had no access to the Roman legal system: people towards whom the system was actively opposed or who found it inadequate. Curses directly helped people redress these imbalances by invoking a higher power to help resolve their personal crises.

Magic as a coping strategy is applicable to victims as well as cursers. Knowing that magical attacks were possible meant that victims could explain away their own failures and point to 'others' who were deemed responsible. The accounts of Cicero and Libanius have already been mentioned, but there are other examples. Pliny reports a case in which some landowners explained the low yields of their farms by accusing a foreign freedman, one Gaius Furius Cresimus, of magically transferring crops into his fields from theirs.[100] This is a particularly illuminating instance, as the accused man defends himself with a display of his dedication to the Roman virtues of rustic simplicity and hard work, thereby challenging his status as an outsider. His Roman credentials thus secured, the charges are duly dropped and Cresimus is embraced by his community.

Graf places magical medicine into the same category of coping strategies, in that it often explains unexplainable diseases, such as epilepsy, as having supernatural causes.[101] Not only is this evident in the writing of ancient doctors and other healers, but also in the confession *stelae* from Asia Minor. These texts, dating from the early imperial period, record occasions on which people approached temple authorities and confessed their wrongdoing in an attempt to alleviate an illness they believed was divine punishment.[102] Rituals such as these are not direct evidence for the situation in the western provinces, but I would argue that they can be seen as contextual manifestations of wider belief. The reasons that confession *stelae* are only found in certain regions of Asia Minor must lie in the particular social and religious contexts of those areas.[103] Nevertheless they certainly reveal something of the beliefs about divine justice that existed in the Roman Empire. They show that certain rituals could provide some sense of control for the participant. The world might be at the whim of supernatural powers, but humans could appeal to or directly control these powers to directly influence their own lives. This model has many merits when applied to the curses from the Roman west, especially the theft curses, which can be understood as part of a mechanism for coping with the loss of personal objects. However, in my opinion this is too much of a rationalization to adequately explain the enduring popularity of cursing throughout the Roman period. Without demonstrable results beyond simply making the curser feel a little better, the ritual would not have been continually practised by successive generations of people at sites such as Bath or Uley, which appear to have seen cursing activity for at least 200 years. There must have been deeper social factors at work, and it is these that I intend to explore in the following discussion.

The models and analyses proposed by previous scholars and discussed here have broken the ground on considering the social contexts of curse-tablet use, but I argue that considerably more work is needed. This is another area in which the study of ancient religion and magic has lagged behind comparable work in other areas of Roman studies, and which could be immeasurably enriched by interdisciplinary thought. Although what follows will be grounded in the evidence of the curse tablets found throughout the western Roman provinces, I will also bring in work carried out by ethnographers and anthropologists with contemporary traditional cultures that have practices comparable to ancient cursing. Studies of these communities can help us to think differently and explore new possibilities by showing us fresh ways to interrogate our existing evidence. Of course, this is not a new opinion in the broader study of the Roman provinces, and many archaeologists and ancient historians have benefitted greatly from the reflective and considered incorporation of anthropological comparisons into their work.[104] However, the study of Roman curse tablets has largely remained immune to these movements, for reasons that are not particularly clear. Perhaps it is because work in this field remained a largely philological exercise for much of the twentieth century, which insulated it from wider methodological movements in archaeology and ancient history. Also significant is the fact that ancient magic has been mostly neglected by mainstream classical scholars because it seems to reveal a side of ancient society far removed from their constructed image of 'pure philosophy and true religion.'[105] The vision of the Roman Empire as exceptional has been systematically deconstructed by postcolonial and postmodern archaeology, and the study of curse tablets is beginning to catch up.

Magic in anthropology

The social contexts of magical beliefs and practices have been the focus of anthropologists' research since the early twentieth century, from the pioneering work of Malinowski and Evans-Pritchard through to Douglas in the 1970s.[106]

Kapferer's fieldwork with Sinhalese Buddhists in Sri Lanka is of particular interest to this study.[107] As a society it bears close resemblance to the social situation in the Roman Empire, in that it is a literate society with clear hierarchies and strong internal divisions. Sri Lankan cursing rituals are remarkably like those found in some parts of the Roman west, as they are conducted in temples using material components such as wax images and inscribed metal tablets. Perishable objects such as coconuts or eggs are also important, often having the victim's name written on the before being ritually deposited or destroyed.[108] The people who use them attempt to attack sexual partners, the speech of participants in criminal cases, or suspected thieves.[109] Although Kapferer notes these short-term motives, the bulk of his study is devoted to exploring the underlying social motivations for engaging in rituals such as cursing. This is the major difference between the studies of magic conducted by ancient historians, who have mostly been concerned with classifying their evidence based on textual features, and anthropologists, who have, since Evans-Prichard, always considered the social contexts of the rituals and beliefs that they study. I will be applying the anthropologists' approach to the ancient evidence in the remainder of this chapter.

As I have already stated, I intend to use the work of anthropologists and ethnographers to think in different ways about the motivations behind Roman curses by interrogating the evidence in new ways. However, there are several caveats that need to be discussed before this can be done. As Brown noted half a century ago, ancient historians and anthropologists approach this debate from different directions.[110] Anthropologists come at magic from the point of view of the accuser – always assuming that the accusation of magic is false – rather than from the witch or sorcerer themselves. Researchers in the field rarely, if ever, witness these rituals being practised, either because they are done quickly and in secret or because in reality they are never actually performed at all, only existing in the fears of the general population.[111] People in these societies rarely admit to practicing sorcery or witchcraft because of the serious consequences that can follow such confessions, so the anthropologist's main source of information for details of specific rituals comes from the accusations levelled at suspected sorcerers or witches by those who have been attacked, or from third parties who claim to have been witnesses. This has led anthropologists to focus their studies on how suspected witches and sorcerers relate to their social contexts, the social impacts of beliefs about how witches and sorcerers act, the context and significance of witch-hunts, and so on. In contrast, scholars of Roman magic start with the significant quantity of surviving evidence for magical practice itself, including the *PGM*, amulets, dolls and curse tablets. With this body of evidence, it has been easy for previous scholars to lose sight of the human agent behind the beliefs and practices outlined in the texts, and therefore also the social contexts into which they fitted.[112] These differences in evidence and approach make linking our two disciplines difficult, but in the rest of this chapter I will argue that it is not only possible but necessary if we are to fully understand the practice of ancient magic in its social context.

Rumour and gossip

The ethnographers and anthropologists who have studied traditional societies recognize magic as an extension of rumour and gossip. When relationships between people degenerate to a significantly low point, especially where jealousy or envy are involved, magical attacks are often the next step after malicious gossiping or spreading rumours,[113] as they turn what are already aggressive words into powerful speech acts.[114] Magical attacks also maintain the secrecy and plausible deniability of gossip and rumour, something important in face-to-face societies that place a significant emphasis on public reputation, such as, for example, the Trobriand Islanders in the Pacific.[115] In this context, direct confrontation, or 'hard words' as they are known to the islanders, could be considered dangerous as they expose the attacker to the potential for embarrassment or counter-attack, both of which can damage social standing. The case in Sri Lanka is similar: on the island, magical attacks are seen as safer because they avoid the legal dangers of direct physical assault, as well as the social risk of publicly exposing the curser's malevolence.[116]

These observations can certainly be applied to the ancient world: in classical Athens and late republican Rome, the two historical contexts for which we have the most evidence, rumour and gossip were endemic and clearly more common tools for the destruction of rivals than outright public confrontation.[117] They became valuable weapons in the ongoing struggle for personal advancement that was central to life in these social contexts. There is no reason to think this was not also true outside large cities, despite the smaller scale of the communities. In fact, the smaller the community, the more likely it is that members would have known intimate details of each other's lives, and the less likely they would have been to directly confront rivals out of fear of retribution.[118] This is arguably the situation visible on some of the theft curses, for example this text from Bath (**SD 259**):

> ... I Arminia, complain to you, Sulis, [that] you consume Verecundinus (son of) Terentius, who has stolen ... two silver coins from me. You are not to permit him to sit or lie or ... or to walk or (to have) sleep or health, since you are to consume (him) as soon as possible; and again ... not to reach ...

Even though Arminia, and some other cursers like her, seem to have known the names of the thieves who stole their belongings, they chose to seek retribution through depositing a curse tablet, rather than directly confronting them. The juridical curses from Carthage, Ampurias, Bad Kreuznach and other sites have a different sense, in that the cursers had already confronted their opponents, or were at least planning on doing so soon, in the form of bringing their case to court. In this scenario, magical attacks with curse tablets act to strengthen and extend 'hard words' rather than to replace them.

There is a similar sense of replacing or strengthening 'hard words' in the erotic curses, both those relating to attraction and separation. If the separation curses do stem from love triangle situations, then they could have been deemed a safer method for the third party to break up the existing or potential couple than direct confrontation. As discussed above, I am not totally convinced by Ripat's interpretation of these texts as being written by wives whose husbands have begun favouring other women, but nevertheless her wider point about gossip swirling around love triangles is surely correct.[119] Knowledge about matters of the heart circulates freely within gossip networks, often maliciously directed towards people thought to be behaving inappropriately or who might be on the losing end of a shift in attention.[120] The damaged party can be the target of gossip, but importantly they can also be the source, spreading spiteful rumours about the people who have spurned them. The reputational damage of such gossip can be significant, as it undermines the public standing of individuals who might otherwise have appeared morally upright. It is only a small step from spreading such gossip to engaging in aggressive magical attacks, especially for those who might have had no other options available to them. The same can also be said for attraction spells, which Winkler has already characterized as the 'sneak attacks' of erotic warfare.[121] Publicly exposing their erotic desires leaves a person vulnerable, open to the potential for ridicule, rejection or censure depending on the target. This is exacerbated if the object of a person's desire is off-limits because of social constraints or has already rejected advances made through more conventional channels.[122]

From the other side, being the subject of rumours and gossip can elicit magical responses. Several curses that are usually categorized as 'juridical', because they attack the vocal faculties of the victims, could in fact be attempting to silence malicious informal speech, rather than public opposition in court.[123] A good example is a curse from Bregenz (**SD 520**), which curses 'Domitius Niger, Lollius, Iulius Severus and Severus, the slave of Niger, the opponents (*adversarii*) of Brutta and anyone else who speaks against her (*quisquis adversus eum loquat*)'. Five curses from Carthage (DT 217, 219, 224, 303, dfx 11.1.1/2) plus one each from Budapest (**SD 532**), London (**SD 339**) and Marsala (**SD 109**), also ask that the victims be unable to speak against the curser, or seek to bind 'hostile tongues' (*lingua inimica*). As is so often the case with curse tablets, it is impossible to reconstruct the specific circumstances that provoked the individual texts. However, the targeting of speech, especially malicious or hostile speech, certainly evokes the possibility of gossip being spread about the curser, and does not require the context of formal legal proceedings. As I will discuss in the rest of this chapter, rumours and gossip can have serious negative effects on the lives of people, and so any measure that can be used to suppress it would be very attractive.

Was cursing public or private?

There is a trade-off inherent in choosing magical attack over 'hard words' in that, although it is safer and arguably more powerful to use a ritual such as cursing to harm someone, it is less predictable because it relies on both the successful execution of the cursing ritual and the mediation of an unpredictable supernatural being, rather than the unavoidable consequences of direct public confrontation.[124] There is a tension here between the public and private aspects of cursing rituals, and this is an important strand of anthropological arguments on the topic. Privacy, even secrecy, is evidently valued in sorcery rituals in various cultures, to the point where few anthropologists record ever witnessing them being practised.[125] In the Sri Lankan coastal village of Seenigama, the cursing shrine is located behind a wall on a small island, making it very difficult to see what is happening from the mainland.[126] Feddema, who has studied the shrine, was only able to record the rituals after obtaining special permission to enter the shrine and witness the cursing procedure himself.[127] The secrecy created here and in other cultures protects the cursers from any negative consequences that may be attached to the practice of sorcery, and also prevents the victims from learning the exact nature of the attack, and therefore being able to protect themselves with the correct counter-measures. However, in the Sri Lankan example, for instance, other members of the community can still see cursers visiting the shrine by boat, and rumours about their intentions often spread quickly among neighbours, family and friends.[128]

Secrecy was clearly important in the western Roman provinces too, to the extent that some temples, such as Bath and Mainz, constructed dedicated areas specifically for conducting these rites, much like the cursing shrine in Sri Lanka. Existing scholarly opinion emphasizes secrecy in Roman curse-tablet rituals because of the perception that they were either somehow taboo or explicitly illegal. Following the ancient literary depictions of witches, deposition is usually imagined as happening under cover of darkness, especially for those curses that were left in cemeteries or entertainment venues.[129] However, all these venues were still public places, which could be occupied by other people regardless of the time of day or night, as discussed in Chapter 3. Even the most inconspicuous setting still offered the potential for being watched by onlookers or heard by eavesdroppers, whether intentional or accidental. In the face-to-face communities of the ancient world, any suspicious activity would likely be noticed and reported through the grapevines of rumour and gossip, especially in times of conflict or stress.[130] Scholars have often wondered if curse tablets worked because they were displayed publicly before being deposited, otherwise there would be no way for the victim to know they had been cursed, and therefore no way for the desired effects to manifest themselves.[131] If we factor in the power of rumours and gossip to spread information around a community, as anthropologists have done and as I argue we should do for Roman society, then this public display of the physical tablet becomes unnecessary. All that is required is an onlooker or eavesdropper, followed by a casual word to a friend or relative, to set the rumour mill churning.[132] From then on, the feedback loop of gossip would do all the work. The evidence from Soweto in South Africa, as well as Sri Lanka, shows that community members soon become aware when others are gossiping about them, and, because of the close links between the two, often suspect magical attacks as a result.[133]

Another aspect of the public/private tension within ancient cursing is the public nature of some of the punishments set out on the tablets. From the theft curses come seventeen examples that require the victim to make some form of atonement in a temple, as well as the nine that ask that the victim be compelled to return the stolen property to the cursers themselves. One example from Uley reads (SD 370):

> To you I commend ... the man who has cheated me of the denarii he owed me. I give, I offer, I destine, I depute one hundred thousand denarii to the god

Mercury, that he may bring them to the temple and treasury of the mightiest god ... lack of sleep, with unknown diseases and adverse ailments ... half-naked, toothless, tremulous, gouty, beyond human pity.

In this case we can see what the curser intends for the victim: they are to suffer so greatly for their crime that they have no choice but to go to the temple of Mercury – in doing so displaying their horrific illnesses to the community – and surrender the stolen money to the god. This creates a picture that aligns with the concepts of divine justice visible in other parts of the Empire, in particular the confession *stelae* from Asia Minor, which demanded some form of confession or public atonement in the presence of the gods.[134] Of course the gods were not the only audience at public temples, and other members of the community could witness whatever act of atonement was prescribed, resulting in a humiliating loss of reputation for the victim as they were, in effect, publicly displaying their criminal activities. The punishments for the victim in the above text are designed to make them the object of humiliation and ridicule, as Mercury is to make them 'half-naked, toothless, tremulous, gouty, and beyond human pity'. Versnel identifies an element of *Schadenfreude* here, and describes it as a feature of juridical curses as well as prayers for justice.[135]

Juridical curses that target the speech faculties of litigants, lawyers and witnesses were primarily attempting to stop them successfully putting across their case in court, but would have had the secondary effect of causing public embarrassment for the suddenly dumb-struck speaker, making them the object of ridicule and scorn. For lawyers this was an attack on their professional reputation, something that had the potential to become a subject of gossip and that could be used as ammunition by subsequent opponents.[136] The best example of this from the west is on one of the tablets from Frankfurt (**SD 478**):

I ask the spirits of the dead and the infernal gods that Marius Fronto, enemy of Sextus, be untrustworthy and not be able to speak against Sextus, thus Fronto is made mute, when he will approach the consular legate ...

In this case, the attack on Fronto's reputation is obvious: not only is his ability to speak limited, but if he does manage to speak the curse ensures that no one will trust him. There is a hint of public humiliation too. The curse specifies that he is to be struck dumb when he approaches the judge to argue his case, and therefore at the moment when he is the focus of the attention of the entire courtroom.

The competition curses are also interested in the public humiliation of their targets. The overwhelming majority of curses against charioteers and their horses are explicit in targeting their victims during races, when they would be performing in front of tens or even hundreds of thousands of spectators.[137] The ways in which this targeting was manifested in the text of the curses differ in the various locations, with some of the Carthaginian curses being particularly detailed. Seven of the curses from the cemeteries outside the town include variations on the following formulas (**DT 234**):

> Bind their race, feet, victory, strength, life, quickness, cut out their limbs, drive them mad, so that tomorrow in the circus they will neither run around (the turning point), nor win, nor even come out of the starting blocks, nor go around the turning point, but may they fall with their charioteers Dionysius of the Blues and Lamurus and Restutianus, and these allied charioteers of the Greens: Protus and Felix and Narcissus. Bind their hands, take away their victory, their success and their sight, so that they are not able to see their opponents when steering the car, but tear them from their cars and throw them to the ground, so that they fall and are dragged through the entire racetrack, but especially at the turning point, along with their horses.

As Gordon has argued, these quasi-narratives build on stereotypical depictions of chariot races common in Mediterranean literary and visual arts from Homer onwards.[138] They focus on the essential moments of the race, but these are also the moments of greatest danger, where it was most likely for teams to crash. This would have made them the most significant for the outcome of the race, and so therefore presumably the points at which the crowd were paying most attention. Wishing rivals to fall at the starting blocks or the turning points maximized the public nature of their failure, and so the *Schadenfreude* for those whose teams would then go on to win unopposed. For charioteers who, like the lawyers previously discussed, had reputations that were naturally built on their ability to win, anything that compromised their chances had the potential to be seriously damaging. The epigraphic record readily attests to the notoriety gained by consistently successful drivers.[139] Losers risked not only the ignominy of defeat, assuming they survived the race, but also more serious outcomes made possible by the precarity of their positions as enslaved men.

At the temple of Mater Magna and Isis in Mainz, several of the recurring curse formulas spell out the destruction of social standing in explicit terms. Three of the tablets found on the site (**SD 491, 493,** 507) include some variation of the phrase '*ut exitum spectent*' – 'thus they shall watch [the victim's] death'.[140] It is generally accepted that this violent language should probably be taken as symbolic rather than literal, partly because the tablets usually also condemn the victims to other fates that would be impossible or superfluous if they were going to be killed.[141] For example, one asks that (**SD 493**):

> ...just as he watches [the blood or the ritual] of the *galli*, the *magali* and the priests of Bellona... [he who committed] the fraud of this money... [so should] they watch his death. And just as salt [will become liquid] in [water], so shall his limbs and marrow waste away. Tomorrow [he should come], and say that he has committed the crime. I give to you the instruction in religious form, that you fulfil my wish and that I will happily and willingly reciprocate, when you have made over them a horrible death.

A dead thief cannot return stolen goods or money, nor can they come to the temple to confess their crime, as requested in the above text. Death could potentially mean a more symbolic death in the eyes of the community: a death of reputation or social standing brought on by confessing to criminal activity in the presence of gods and men. Another tablet from Mainz directly attacks the victim's reputation within their community, calling for them to be cut off from other people (**SD 494**):

> ...just as the *galli* or the priests of Bellona have cut or castrated themselves, so shall loyalty, reputation and ability be cut off, and just as they are not numbered among men, so should he not be...

It is unclear from the rest of this tablet what exactly the victim, a certain Quintus, has done to warrant such punishment. He is described as someone 'who has turned away from himself and his life principles and has acted badly' (*auersum se suisque rationibus uitaeque male consummantem*), so perhaps the curser considered him to have transgressed the boundaries of socially acceptable behaviour in some way. In any case, this curse demonstrates that attacking social relationships was considered a punishment on par with causing bodily pain. Lists of curse targets such as this usually contain body parts, such as, for example, the excessively complete list on the tablet from Minturno in Italia (**SD 56**), which curses the victim's 'limbs, colour, shape, head, hair, shadow, brain, forehead, eyebrows, mouth, nose, chin, cheeks, lips, words, face, neck, liver, shoulders, heart, lungs, intestines, belly, arms, fingers, hands, navel, bladder, thighs, knees, shins, ankles, soles, toes'. The appearance of 'loyalty, reputation and ability' in such a list on the above curse of Quintus is unusual, but nevertheless suggests that they were seen as intimate parts of the victim's person that could be damaged by magical means.[142]

Kapferer has shown how Sinhalese sorcery practices fit into wider Buddhist themes of justice and punishment. The rituals practised in modern Sri Lanka make sense to the people who use them because they fit into their understanding of their historical, social and political contexts.[143] The theft curses from the Roman west tapped into widely held beliefs about the nature of divine punishment, condemning their victims to illnesses regularly thought to have supernatural causes. Chief among these were blindness and insanity, both of which had no known cause or treatment in contemporary medicine.[144] Because of this, the gods – either acting for their own reasons or at the bidding or coercion of humans – were usually thought to be the cause of such ailments. Chaniotis noted that over half of the confession *stelae* from Asia Minor describe the illnesses suffered by those involved as relating to either the eyes or the mind, showing that these were clearly the prime targets for divine anger.[145] There appears to be a similar situation among the curse tablets from the Roman west directed towards thieves, in that the eyes and mind are among the most frequent body parts targeted by cursers (e.g. **SD 210**, which curses both). The purpose of directing a curse towards parts of the body most regularly attacked by divine punishment was to give the suspected thief no choice but to confess their crime to the gods and perform a propitiatory rite. Again, this would be acted out in places where an audience was possible, meaning that the victim's reputation and social standing could be damaged. The public nature of these punishments ties the curse tablets into wider Roman concepts of legal punishment and justice, as well as divine. There seems to have been a broad consensus among lawmakers and philosophers throughout the Roman period that the prime purpose of punishment was deterrence, and as a result extreme examples were required to scare off those who might be tempted to break the law.[146] Accordingly, aggravated death sentences became the norm under the Empire, with crucifixion and *damnatio ad bestias* the most frequent for those considered *humiliores*.[147] Prominent public executions such as these alienated the convict from normal society, making them an object of ridicule, and trivializing their death into a form of mass entertainment.[148] It seems likely that that some authors of curse tablets from the west took these concepts of state-administered justice and applied them to their own personal needs.

Social tension

In times of personal crisis or stress, people often have some idea about who is to blame. Communities never function in total harmony, and there will always be resentments, fear and suspicion between people who live side by side.[149] Anthropologists have recognized that, in these contexts, rumour, gossip and magic thrive because they have the effect of nurturing pre-existing tensions and amplifying the fears and suspicions that people hold about the abilities and intentions of their enemies. In social contexts in which the belief in magic is endemic, life is lived with the presumption of malice. Anyone with sufficient motive can access the knowledge, skills and materials required to perform malicious magic, and they will seek to harm others simply because they can.[150] In the ethnographic literature this is shown to elicit various responses, predominantly protective charms and rituals designed to break or reverse the effects of malicious magic.[151] In certain societies, particularly in Africa, witch-hunts can break out at times of heightened social tension, and the people who are targeted tend to be known individuals who have been blamed for specific misfortunes.[152]

Similar responses are visible in the Graeco-Roman world. On the one hand there are the charms, amulets and rituals designed to defend against magical attacks for which there is ample ancient evidence, and which were so common in the ancient world that Ogden has referred to the conflict between curse tablets and protective amulets as a magical 'arms race'.[153] On the other hand, the presumption of malice could provoke pre-emptive strikes in an attempt to get ahead of seemingly inevitable attacks that were bound to come from known or unknown enemies. These phenomena are easier for anthropologists to observe through participant interviews, but are harder to detect in the ancient evidence because we cannot access the exact thought processes that preceded the performance of the cursing ritual. However, a few formulas suggest that perhaps such motivations were at work.

At Mainz, cursers sometimes included formulas that barred the victim from overturning the curse using magical or religious rituals, as shown by this example (**SD 491**):

> ...these should not be able to be redeemed with woollen offerings. Neither through lead nor through gold nor through silver can they redeem themselves from your divine power, unless dogs, worms and other monsters devour them...

Here the curser is explicitly stating that the victim cannot break the curse with animal sacrifices, offerings of money or counter-curses. This shows that, from the perspective of the curser, it was at least conceivable that their victims might engage in similar rituals, either to protect from curses or to directly attack back.

In another tablet deposited at the same temple, the curser is equally specific in heading off protective rituals (**SD 486**):

> ...and that he cannot redeem himself with money or anything else, neither from you nor from some other god, except with a bad death ...

Again, the curser is aware that their victim could escape the curse by appealing to the gods or by making certain offerings and has taken definitive steps to make such attempts impossible. Away from Mainz, a curse from Budapest targets victims who make 'antepistula' (**Barta 2015**), which the editor translated as 'counter-curses', and commands that they be made 'mute and silent.' Another from Carthage (**DT 250**) commands the various daemons invoked by the curse to 'Pass through every remedy and every amulet and every defence and every anointing of oil' to attack Maurussus the Beast Hunter. Across all these examples there is a clear sense that appeals to the gods, whether through cursing or offering sacrifices, could be used for opposing purposes and therefore had the potential to compete against each other. It is interesting that they all include the names of their victims. Presumably the cursers knew their victims, and were at least vaguely aware of the methods they might use to try to protect themselves.

In the words of Ashforth, 'acts of witchcraft are not usually perpetrated by strangers'.[154] The pre-existing social tensions and resentments within small communities, nurtured and sustained by the ever-present forces of gossip and rumour, can supply names of known enemies who individuals would naturally assume to be the cause of any new misfortune. In cultures across the world, the use of magic is inextricably tied to complex webs of relationships between family and acquaintances. Among both the Cewa in southern Africa and Sinhalese Buddhists in Sri Lanka, magical attacks are perpetrated only within established kinship systems and can provoke feelings of intense fear and suspicion among relatives and acquaintances.[155]

For competition and erotic attraction curses, the names of the targets would have been supplied by obvious means; in both, the love interest or the rival competitors would have been clear in the minds of the curser, and known from their own desires or their awareness of upcoming events. For other kinds of curse, and indeed for those with no discernible motive, more complex process must be at work. This supplying of names from existing social relationships is seemingly evident on the Bad Kreuznach and Carthage juridical curses, where the cursers seem to have a good idea of those who could potentially be involved in the suit before the trial had begun. The theft curses with long lists of victims may have been provoked by similar suspicions about potential enemies within a community. Tomlin implied just such a motivation for a curse that was written after the theft of a cloak from the slave quarters of a house in Roman Leicester (**SD 456**). The curser, Servandus, could not have known exactly which of the other people enslaved in the household stole his cloak (if any), and if he could not narrow his suspicions down, then the only option left would be to curse them all and let the god apply the punishment to the correct culprit. Servandus is exceptional in that he had a ready-made list of suspects in the roll call of other enslaved people in the household. Other cursers were not so fortunate, and probably relied on their own witnessing of suspicious behaviour to identify potential suspects or, if that was lacking, gossip and rumours spread around their community. People who lost money or other goods may naturally have suspected not only those in their community who had a reputation for crime or untrustworthy behaviour, but also those considered enemies because of past conflicts or pre-existing resentments.[156]

On the curse tablets from the west, instances of cursers naming their victims far outweigh those with non-specific formulas (273 to fifty-seven), mostly of individuals or pairs, but in some exceptional cases running to twenty or even thirty names. The longest lists of victims tend to be on either competition or juridical curses, both of which went to great lengths to ensure that the curse hit everyone involved in the trial or race. The majority of those that use non-specific formulas to target their victims are curses against thieves (forty-nine of fifty-seven). This is to be expected: it would have been rare that a victim of burglary, pickpocketing or bath-house theft would have known the identity of the culprit, especially if no witnesses came forward or if the incident was too minor to go to court. It was in these circumstances that cursers made fullest use of the mutually exclusive alternative formulas so popular in Roman Britain – 'whether male or female, whether slave of free' – so that the thief would suffer no matter who they were.[157] The exception to this seems to be curses against those who stole money, half of which have named victims (twelve of twenty-four). Some of these complain of the theft of large sums, stretching to thousands or even tens of thousands of *denarii*, so they are probably embezzled deposits or loans. However, some of the longest lists of victims appear on curses against thieves of relatively minor sums, or objects such as cloaks or jewellery. It is clearly foolish to imagine a conspiracy of almost twenty people involved in the theft of six silver coins (**SD 303**) or a simple cloak (**SD 456**), so there must be something else at work in these instances. I have argued here that it is possible that the victims named on curse tablets from the Roman west were people in the community that the curser already thought of as rivals or enemies, and therefore the people who would naturally be suspected of causing any new misfortune.

Conclusions

This chapter has sought to answer a seemingly simple question: why did people curse? From the texts of the tablets themselves, the most basic answer to this question, following Jordan's now iconic definition, is that an individual made a curse tablet in an attempt to use supernatural beings to gain control over people or animals in order to influence the outcome of events.[158] The factors of lived experience to which these rituals were turned across the Graeco-Roman world have been broken down into a number of general categories by modern scholars since Audollent, and all but the 'commercial' curses are present in the Roman west. However, I have argued throughout this chapter that this classification of motives is not a satisfactory answer to the question, and that there are more complex social frameworks involved. These may not be detailed explicitly in the curse texts themselves, but nevertheless they need to be examined and discussed if the study of ancient cursing is to progress. To get to the heart of the problem, the question we are asking needs to be reworded: instead of asking 'why did people curse?', we should instead be asking 'why did people curse and not do something else? Or do nothing?'. These new questions demand that curse tablets be seen not as isolated phenomena, but as potential strategies for dealing with crises that beset individuals during their lives.

In these cultural settings, curse tablets were part of local responses to situations of conflict. Becoming the victim of theft, preparing to face trial in court, finding oneself unlucky in love, or facing an uncertain result in a chariot race sometimes provoked the performance of cursing rituals in the Roman west because individuals saw them as the most effective solution to the situation in which they found themselves. One interpretation of cursing is as a method of regaining control over a situation that might otherwise seem outside the ability of the individual to resolve. In the cases of curses against thieves, conducting the rituals may have been more accessible, and may have seemed more effective or more satisfying, than pursuing official legal prosecution in the courts. For the low-level crimes reported in some of the curse tablets, like the theft of a cloak or a pair of gloves, legal resolution was likely out of reach for many people. Erotic, juridical and competition curses gave cursers hope that an uncertain future event might be resolved in their favour, a concern potentially made more pressing by the experience of past failures. Sports fans turn to increasingly desperate measures as their chosen team continues to lose, and erstwhile lovers were perhaps more likely to consider cursing the target of their desire if more standard approaches had been spurned. Cursers of juridical curses may be responding to the anxiety felt by the approach of a significant trial, in which fortunes, reputations or even lives might be at risk.

By using work carried out by ethnographers and anthropologists I have shown that, just like similar practices found across traditional societies, the underlying frameworks behind Roman cursing rituals have their roots in the social structures in which the cursers were embedded. Cursing gave people the ability to act safely, avoiding direct public confrontation by virtue of the secrecy inherent in many of the settings in which the rituals took place. In this way, cursing was intimately linked to gossip and rumour, both of which have an element of plausible deniability, but which could operate as devastating attacks on enemies. When viewed from this perspective, the action of enacting a cursing ritual becomes a strategy for preserving one's own reputation whilst simultaneously attempting to damage that of rivals or enemies. To achieve this, many cursers directly assaulted their victim's reputation by causing them to become the object of ridicule or mockery in temples, law courts or arenas, where audiences could gloat over their divinely sanctioned misery. Cursers could have justified using magical attacks in certain circumstances because of the perceived wrongdoing of the victims, especially suspected thieves. In this way, Roman cursing is like the morally ambiguous sorcery practices observed by anthropologists who have worked in Africa and Sri Lanka.

It is the public face of the punishments that was perhaps the most compelling reason to use curse tablets in the ways visible in the western evidence. The writers of curses of all types expected the success of their curse to be outwardly displayed, through the public confession of the accused thief, the dramatic crashes imagined for rival chariot teams, or the shame felt by a suddenly dumbstruck orator. Visible success certainly contributed to the perpetuation of curse tablets as a legitimate and effective response to crisis situations, as communal gossip and rumours would have spread suspicions of magical activity perpetrated against the affected individuals.

This chapter has begun to make the case for the significance of cursing in ongoing social relationships in the western Roman provinces, but there are several lines of thought still to be pursued. There is more to be said on the connections between cursing rituals and expressions of power in the provinces, especially in terms of the sources of power that cursing rituals used, and the ways in which they negotiated existing power structures. Perhaps the most significant questions that have been raised but not answered in this chapter are those around the relationships between cursers and their victims. I have already mentioned the importance of naming and the use of mutually exclusive alternative formulas, and the discussion of these will be developed further in the next chapter.

5

Agency, Power and Relationships

Introduction

At their most basic level, curse tablets are an attempt by a person to affect their world. The complex formulas, the appeals to arcane tradition and the multi-step ritual processes can distract us from the fact that the people who engaged in these actions wanted concrete, observable things to happen because of what they did. As discussed in the previous chapter, the text of curse tablets sometimes gives an indication of what the intended result was, or why a curse was being placed in the first place. However, with 300 or so curses either too fragmentary or too vague to determine a motive, I have made it clear that approaches other than simply ascribing a motive are needed. In this chapter, I will continue exploring interpersonal relationships, thinking about the agency that these rituals gave people to begin, alter or end their connections with others. Agency is at the heart of the 'lived religion' approach, which emphasizes the expanded potential that religion gives to individuals' ability to act in their social contexts by involving non- or super-human agents.[1] We might also talk about religious action as potentially adding to the power of individuals, which would naturally be an attractive prospect to those who might otherwise be considered power*less*.

Curse tablets, like many other ritual actions, are fundamentally concerned with the expression and manipulation of power in various forms. As we saw in Chapter 3, every movement and gesture involved in the production of a curse was intended to make it more effective, and the language of the curses was designed to ensure that the power of the gods or the spirits of the dead would be fully brought to bear on the victims. In this way, cursing had a direct effect on the relationships between the parties involved, with potentially significant consequences for both them and their wider community. This chapter will explore the agency and power afforded by curses, in the sense of their ability to act in social situations and the importance of those actions. I will discuss the ways in which cursing gave individuals the ability to define and alter their place in the world, not just within their immediate social circles but also the wider economic, political and religious contexts of the Roman Empire. To do this, I will explore how both cursers and victims were identified on curse tablets, in terms of the naming strategies used.

Agency and power

Theoretical background

All curse tablets are an attempt to make something happen: a crash during a chariot race, the punishment of a thief, the striking-dumb of a witness, the suffering of a rival or enemy. In this sense, curses can be thought of as part of the curser's agency, or in other words their ability to act within their social, political, economic and cultural contexts. The debates over how to apply the concept of agency in archaeology and related disciplines have been fierce and are ongoing, but nevertheless have had a profound and lasting effect.[2] Although a detailed synopsis of all the scholarship around this debate is outside the scope of this study, it seems pertinent to offer a brief overview. Most archaeological applications of agency theory are ultimately based on the work of Giddens and Bourdieu in the 1970s and 1980s.[3] The basic premise of their models is that human action and social structures are inseparably connected, as they simultaneously constrain, enable and construct each other.[4] Humans are not considered to be mindless automata, but make decisions and act based on their understanding, knowledge, skills and experience of life in their own particular contexts. Therefore agency is not an essential characteristic, nor something that a person or object 'has', but is a product of relationships between people, and between people and things.[5] Post-humanist archaeology, as described by Graham, is especially keen to see agency through a flat ontological lens, where all things – humans, objects, the environment and so on – are equally involved in the production of agency.[6] Applying the concept to the study of religion means considering another complicating factor, namely the gods, spirits, ancestors and other forces who are ascribed agency by believers, but who (in the words of Rüpke) were 'not indubitably present'.[7]

In the introduction to this book, I began developing a criticism of flat-ontological archaeology by discussing the concept of power. Power, in terms of the capacity to constrain or enable the agency of others, is an ever-present aspect of life in human societies, including the Roman Empire. Individuals in the

Roman west could not act with total freedom, but were constrained by the social, political, cultural and economic structures in which they were embedded. Power, like agency, was produced by relationships between people and between people and things, and can therefore also be discussed as a 'lived experience'. By this I mean that each individual would have different experiences of exercising power, or being the target of the power of others, depending on their particular circumstances. Everyone could potentially constrain or enable the agency of others, but those in privileged positions, because of their social status, gender, age, ethnicity or wealth, will have found it easier, or have had more opportunities to do so.

Deficient agency and structures of Roman power

When applied to curse tablets from the Roman west, thinking in terms of agency and power helps us to contextualize the individual cursers, setting them firmly within their immediate social relationships as well as wider Roman economic, political and cultural structures. As discussed in Chapter 4, cursing was sometimes a way for a person to act with relative safety to attack a rival or enemy, while preserving their own position or reputation. Curses worked alongside other social structures, such as, for example, the legal system, rumour and gossip, and courtship, as ways for individuals to pursue their goals. Moreover, curses could supplement or replace efforts made through these (perhaps) more legitimate channels of action when they were either lacking or found to be ineffectual for one reason or another.[8] Faraone and Gordon have recently restated the interpretation of cursing as applying supernatural agency to augment the deficient agency of the person placing the curse: in other words, bringing the power of the gods to bear on a situation in which a human would otherwise find themselves unable to effectively act.[9]

If this interpretation is correct, we should expect to see cursing taken up more readily by those who were marginalized by the power structures of the Roman Empire, such as women, non-citizens and enslaved people. Both the political and religious structures of the Roman Empire were dominated by free, wealthy, adult males, and overlapped to the extent that many urban priesthoods were integrated into their career progression and were used as outlets for displays of generosity. This was as true in the provinces as in the city of Rome itself, as members of local elites became priests of the imperial cult or paid for monumental temples.[10] As a result, Roman society, in both the centre and at the periphery, made the experiences of these men normative, and denigrated the lived experiences women, children, enslaved people and the poor.[11] Power – in terms of the ways in which in enabled individual agency – was unequal, being more readily available to elite men than to others.

In the cities of the Roman provinces, the official, public approaches to the gods were (with a few exceptions) controlled by elite men and women in their capacity as priestly mediators between the gods and humanity.[12] They funded the construction of temples in towns across the Empire, as attested by the many dedicatory inscriptions erected to commemorate the occasions, and they conducted the central rituals of animal sacrifice in these places.[13] The erection of private votive dedications, which has been the focus of much scholarly attention over the years,[14] was often an arena for displays of prestige and wealth as much as a form of religious worship, with affluent men and women erecting larger monuments or using exotic materials so that their offering would stand out from smaller, less expensive examples.[15] Cursing rituals in the Roman west were perhaps a reaction against this situation, as they offered the cursers a direct line of communication to the gods that circumvented the religious structures dominated by the elite. Little money was needed for a person to access the cursing rituals,[16] and from the surviving evidence there seems to be no difference between a 'rich' curse tablet and a 'poor' one. Moreover, if I am right that curses were not made public before deposition, then there was even less room for displaying wealth or prestige in the ritual. This is particularly pertinent in the temple sites of Bath, Uley and Mainz, where the relative expense of other ritualized actions would be more apparent, but may be equally applicable to other contexts as well. Cursing rituals gave marginalized groups of people access to the supernatural, which they could then direct wherever they saw fit. The low cost of the ritual would be attractive to these disempowered groups, meaning that they could access it regardless of personal wealth. The ability to use supernatural power to augment their own agency in this way also helped them to overcome other inequalities in their lives, particularly regarding the legal system, which was heavily biased towards elite male interests.[17]

Given the potential for cursing to open alternative sources of power, it is surprising that there were relatively few that directly attacked the structures that excluded certain groups of people. In other times and places, aggressive magical practices like Roman cursing are used by subalterns to attack those who dominate or subjugate them.[18] By contrast, politicians, magistrates and other authority figures appear only very rarely on Roman curses. The three tablets from Ampurias that curse the governor, legate and procurator of Hispania Tarraconensis fall into this category although, as discussed in Chapter 4, it is difficult to determine the specific background. A recently published curse, with no known provenance but perhaps from Moesia (admittedly slightly outside the primary study area of this book), might be along similar lines, and might even curse the same Q. Pomponius Rufus mentioned on the Ampurias tablets.[19] In this new text, Rufus is again accompanied by other Roman officials, although this time exclusively military: two or three tribunes, three centurions, a *primuspilus* and a standard-bearer (*signifer*). The curse includes nothing more than the list of victims' names, so is equally impossible to fully interpret. However, the targeting of numerous officials, with their titles, suggests a complaint against the Roman state or military as a structure, rather than these men individually. A tablet from Bologna that curses 'Fistus the senator' does the opposite (**SD 118**); although Fistus is identified by his public position, he is alone, and the text gives no indication that it relates to anything more than a personal matter.

Aside from politicians or army officers, the other figures who appear on curse tablets as perpetuators of structures of subjugation are enslavers. The recent work of Alvar Nuño has investigated the cursing practices of enslaved people and the ways in which this practice helped them navigate the realities of their lived experience.[20] Again, it is surprising how very few enslaved people attempted to use curse tablets to directly harm the men and women who enslaved them; Alvar Nuño identifies only two examples, both written in Greek and from the city of Rome.[21] In one case, an anonymous enslaved man, who was being forced to work as a doctor's assistant, curses his enslaver for refusing to let him return home after his brother's death (**Gager 79**). The curse targets not just the enslaver, but also the whole land of Italia and the gates of Rome, all of which are conceived as being part of the man's enslavement. In the other, the curse attempts to stop a woman called Clodia Valeria Sophrone purchasing another woman, Politoria, and forcing her to work in something like a textile mill or brothel (**Gager 78**).[22] Both curses contain *voces magicae*, which suggests they were produced by specialists, rather than the enslaved people themselves. If that is the case, then Politoria and the unnamed doctor's assistant had enough relative freedom to find a specialist, express their wishes and presumably negotiate payment. Where they can be identified as such, enslaved people are as likely to be found cursing other enslaved people as those who subjugated them.[23] There are two texts involving thefts from slave quarters: Servandus' curse, mentioned in Chapter 4, as well as one from Sagunt, Hispania, on which Felicio accuses Heracla of embezzling some money (**SD 142**). In Budapest there is a curse made by a group of three enslaved people, Amoena, Felicio and Oceanus, who were trying to stop the tongues of at least eight other people, most of whom were also enslaved (**SD

532). Alvar Nuño's interpretation of this curse being related to gossip and accusation within a household is convincing.[24] There were complex systems of hierarchy among people enslaved in the same household, related to a range of factors such as closeness to the enslavers or levels of training and education. For the enslaved people, the quality of their existence was directly related to their position in this hierarchy, and it could even be a matter of life and death.[25] Therefore, any rumour or accusation that could jeopardize their situation would be a potential source of fear and uncertainty, justifying the use of curse tablets, at least from their perspective.

Sources of power and agency

If we are going to interpret cursing rituals as way of extending or augmenting the agency of the cursers, it is important to investigate the precise ways in which this was believed to happen. In this sense, we are talking about 'power' as I defined it above: a capacity to constrain or encourage the agency of others, or to challenge the limits placed by others. There are three kinds of power involved in cursing rituals: (1) the supernatural power of gods, spirits, daemons and so on; (2) the power that emerged from practising the ritual itself; and (3) the power gained from knowledge of how to perform the ritual (including skills such as literacy).

Supernatural power

The systems and structures of divine power were just as regulated as those of human power, and it was important in all religious rituals for worshippers to correctly situate themselves within them. The tablets are not consistent in this matter, with individual cursers appealing to and making use of a diverse range of supernatural agents, depending on a range of factors. Perhaps the most significant factor in a curser's choice on this matter is the location in which they would ultimately deposit their tablet, as highlighted in Chapter 3. We cannot be totally sure how much these decisions were down to deep considerations of ritual efficacy or religious appropriateness, and how much they were opportunistic uses of whatever was immediately available. Nevertheless, it is certainly the case that cursers often made direct, explicit use of the supernatural beings located in the places where their tablet would be deposited. At temples and watery places, the power of the curses mostly came from the deities to whom the cursers appealed.[26] On many such tablets, the resident gods or goddesses received the victims or stolen objects into their power or were asked to influence the victim in some way. There was a certain amount of respect in some of these addresses, as cursers used flattering titles for the deities (e.g. 'most holy goddess Sulis' on **SD 215**). This respect shows that the cursers recognized their inferior position relative to the gods, and that it was only with the gods' consent that their intentions would be fulfilled.[27] Theft curses were most concerned with maintaining good relations with the gods in these ways, and these were the curses that were mostly deposited in temples dedicated to non-chthonic deities such as Sulis Minerva, Mercury and Mater Magna. It is possible that the sense of these places as locations for respectful communications with the gods influenced the tone of the cursers' address, although we should not forget the vengeful, often violent nature of some of the punishments meted out onto suspected thieves.

People who deposited their curses in cemeteries and entertainment venues followed some of the same thought processes here, in terms of choosing places where supernatural beings were believed to be present and then attempting to bring their power to bear on a specific situation. In Chapter 3 I outlined the ways in which depositing curses in these locations was related to other practices carried out there, especially votive practice. However, unlike temples curses, those deposited in funerary contexts invoked a much wider range of supernatural beings, most, but not all of which had clear chthonic associations. Perhaps not unexpectedly, the spirits of the dead (named variously as *manes, inferii* or *nekudaimones*) and well-known underworld deities (Pluto, Persephone, Hecate and so on) feature very heavily, but there are also a dazzling array of other daemons, gods and spirits, some of whom were connected to Graeco-Egyptian traditions of magical practice. There are some unusual outliers, such as the curse from Évreux, in Gallia, which invokes 'Greatest Jupiter' (SD 168). As discussed in Chapter 3, the choice of addressee was informed by a combination of existing local traditions, availability or convenience and individual creativity. In terms of agency, the gods and daemons speak for themselves; these were entities with potential abilities far above that available to mere mortals. Some of the curses produced in the Graeco-Egyptian tradition make this point explicitly, naming beings who 'hold the power of fire, of water, of the earth and of the air' (**Gager 10**) or '[shake] the entire world, who break the back of the mountains and casts them up out of the water' (**Gager 36**). The spirits of the dead themselves were also imagined as beings with the ability to influence the living world: a belief not only confined to cursing practice, but a foundational principle of all Roman funerary cult.[28] Some curse tablets, especially those that were made by freelance religious experts, include complicated relationships between the different beings invoked. Many used *voces magicae* to summon or control forces such as the spirits of the dead, as in this example from Carthage (Gager 9): 'I invoke you, spirit of one untimely dead, whoever you are, by the mighty names SALBATHBAL AUTHGEROTABAL BASUTHATEO ALEO SAMABETHOR.' In others, the first entities invoked are expected to deliver the victim to other, more violent beings, for example in the following self-authored curse from Budapest (**Barta 2015**): 'Dis Pater, Aeracura, Mercury of Cyllene, I dictate the following names to you, hand them over to the dreadful dogs [i.e. Cerberus].'

Despite variety in the supernatural addressees of funerary curses, all were expected to operate in similar ways. The most common strategy was to send the victim down to the underworld. 'Giving' the victim is as common here as it is in temple texts, both in self-authored tablets and those produced by specialists.[29] As discussed in Chapter 3, the symbolic crossing of the boundaries between the worlds of the living and dead is given great significance, and there are some allusions to victims being hauled unwillingly to the underworld as in the Persephone myth. However, the influence of the supernatural beings was not confined to cemeteries and the underworld itself, but could be brought out into the physical world, at least temporarily, to target the victims there. Most of the African chariot racing curses require the invoked beings to attack the drivers and their horses during the race itself, and several attraction spells ask that the intended lover be physically driven, in the throes of erotic torment, to the curser.

The ritual itself

Although many cursing rituals were performed in places understood as sacred, and took inspiration from other rituals practised there, they were not exactly the same as them. Curses often used direct, coercive language to affect the victims without the intervention of any supernatural being, even though they might have been deposited somewhere in which such entities were believed to dwell. The power of the curse emerges from the performance of the ritual itself, including spoken words, movements and gestures. An example is this curse from Mainz (**SD 498**):

> ...just like this will melt away, thus may the neck, the limbs, the marrow, the property melt away...

The objects involved in the rituals were crucial, as it was through the possession, preparation and manipulation of the lead tablets (in this case melting one in fire) that this power over others emerged and was asserted, in conjunction with the written and spoken words of the curse. Certain formulas and phrases attest to this, such as, for example, on the curse from Montfo (**SD 157**):

> Just as this lead disappears and falls, thus falls their youth, limbs, life, ox, grain and goods those who did me wrong, namely Asuetemeos, Secundina who stole it, and Verres Tearus and Amarantis and all that is yours, oh gods, I forbid (them) by all spells to celebrate the Masitlatida and to sing the Necrocantus ... and all gods ... is given ...

The power of this curse emerges from the action of deposition that was performed during the cursing ritual. That power is brought to bear not just on the victims and their belongings, but also their social relations, as the curse forbids them from celebrating a local religious festival, thereby isolating them from their community.[30]

As outlined in Chapter 3, the manipulation and mutilation of the lead tablet was believed to contribute to the efficacy of a curse. On the supernatural level, this was believed to come from the physical actions of folding, rolling, piercing and so on, and they made use of the relationships created between the tablet and the victims by the writing of their names. Modern scholars might choose to deny the literal efficacy of such ritual actions – few would seriously argue that supernatural punishments were actually manifested on the victims named on the tablets – but nevertheless it is probable that these ritual actions *did* have some real effects. Manipulating and mutilating a lead tablet is a relatively demanding task, requiring an exertion of physical strength. Doing so could have resulted in a cathartic effect in the curser, perhaps producing feelings of released tension, regained control and justice served.[31] There is also the possibility, as argued by Kiernan, that curse tablets created psychosomatic symptoms in victims who knew, or merely suspected, that they had been cursed.[32] This has been observed by ethnographers in modern India and Africa,[33] and is arguably behind the illnesses reported by the Roman orator Libanius when someone placed a mutilated chameleon in his classroom.[34] Through this psychosomatic mechanism, spurred on by the fear and mistrust that can be created in networks of rumour and gossip, it is possible that victims of ancient curses actually did suffer physical symptoms because of the magical attacks perpetrated against them.

Knowledge is power

The knowledge of how to perform a cursing ritual is an aspect of the curser's power because it affected the way they perceived their ability to successfully achieve their aims. There is a spectrum of knowledge displayed on the curses from the western provinces, from non-literate scratchings to those produced in the Graeco-Egyptian tradition, full of magical words, drawings and long texts in multiple languages. In Chapter 3 we saw that curses at this end of the spectrum were likely to have been produced by freelance religious specialists with some level of training in those traditions, or, at the very least, access to written spell books or templates. Their claims to authority were based on access to this knowledge, especially the secret names given to the dizzying array of supernatural beings upon whom they could call, and the complex theologies into which they fit.[35] Knowledge of these systems did not spread widely, and so individuals writing their own tablets relied on whatever local traditions they were aware of, supplemented by their own creativity. Gordon has recently identified a six-stage scale of religious competence in the 'self-authored' curses from Italia, from the ability to write one or two names, to more accomplished texts making use of technical terminology and both religious and legal procedure.[36] With more knowledge, Gordon argues, cursers were increasingly able to make appeals to greater authorities, and make further justifications for what they were doing. Nevertheless, even those only able to write the names of their victim(s) were still demonstrating some awareness of the tradition of cursing, and by enacting the other stages of the ritual process were making claims about their connections to supernatural power.

At this point it is worth reemphasising the significance of the skill of literacy, something I explored briefly in Chapter 3. Although not strictly essential, as the pseudo-inscriptions from Bath attest, it is true that many cursers were literate to some degree, in Latin or, less commonly, Greek or Celtic, or perhaps knew someone who could be trusted to write on their behalf. The curse tablets show a great deal of variation in the literacy skill levels of the cursers, from rough, careless hands to confident, practised scripts (compare the two Bath curses in Figure 5.1).[37] Those tablets that display proficient hands were likely to have been written by someone with some level of education or training. This did not necessarily come from a formal educational setting, but could have been obtained working (or being forced to work) as a stonemason, metal worker or bookkeeper.[38] In any case, this training would have required an investment of time and money, and therefore carried with it a certain prestige. The ability to write gave a person an advantage over those who could not, and, in terms of the ability to write a curse tablet, opened the possibility of bringing supernatural power to bear on anyone around them.[39] I would argue that Servandus, the enslaved man who cursed the other enslaved people he lived with in Leicester, was doing just this (**SD 456**). His writing skills gave him the ability to perform the ritual of cursing, and therefore also gave him access to power unavailable to other, illiterate individuals.

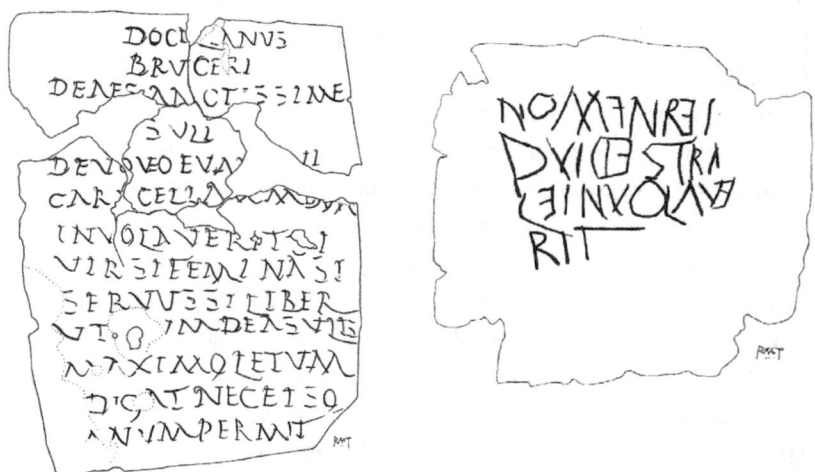

Figure 5.1 Two curses from Bath (not to scale). Images from Tomlin 1988, copyright Barry Cunliffe and Oxford University Committee for Archaeology.

Most of the curses from the Roman west were, unsurprisingly, written in Latin. However, around 100 tablets were written either wholly or partly in Greek, to which we can add another twenty or so that were either wholly or partly in Celtic. The linguistic elements of the curse tablets have been the subject of scholarly enquiry for over a century, and it is not my purpose to explore them here. However, there are interesting questions to be asked of the decision to write in either Greek or Celtic that do not have their answers in philology, but which do relate to the present discussions of agency and power.

The first, and perhaps most obvious reason why a person might have chosen to write their curse in Greek or Celtic is that it was their native language. Although we cannot know their exact numbers, it is safe to say that there were sizeable groups of people in Italia and the western provinces who either did not speak Latin, or for whom it was a second language.[40] In the case of Greek-speakers, many would have travelled west, whether voluntarily or not, from the regions where Greek was the dominant language. It is possible that the specialists who produced the Graeco-Egyptian style curses found in Rome, Carthage and Sousse had travelled from the east, but writing in Greek had other possible meanings in this tradition, which I will discuss below. 'Self-authored' Greek curses (i.e. those with none of the *voces magicae*, *charaktêres* or other features of Graeco-Egyptian cursing) are fewer in number and spread more thinly. Aside from four from Rome there are another seven Italian examples, all single finds from the mainland or Sicily.[41] Elsewhere there are three from Carthage and one each from Trier and Szombathely (Pannonia).[42] It is not inconceivable that the writers of these texts were Greek themselves, and so wrote their curse in the language they knew best. For Celtic speakers, we know that the Roman conquests of Northern Europe did not immediately wipe out the native languages of these regions. People continued to speak them into the imperial period, even if they were increasingly likely to be bilingual with Latin.

There may have been factors other than convenience at play in the choice to use a language other than Latin, especially in a context such as cursing, even for native speakers of the language. In the popular culture of the western Roman world, ideas about magical power were inextricably connected to the Greeks. Pliny the Elder's potted history of magic firmly situates the origins of such practices in the east: originally Persia, but quickly finding fertile ground in Greece.[43] In his speech of self-defence against a charge of magic, Apuleius points out what he calls a 'common error' of some people who think that the followers of various Greek philosophers were, in fact, practising magic.[44] This assumption seems to have been present even in the late republic, when Cicero could accuse Vatinius, and other Pythagoreans by association, of using Greek philosophical learning as a cover for dabbling in human sacrifice and necromancy.[45] Circe and Medea were well-known characters, and Roman writers often labelled other witches or their products as 'Thessalian'.[46] Considering these close connections between Greek culture and non-normative ritual practices, some cursers could have been inspired to use Greek because they associated that language with contacting the supernatural in these ways.[47] It is interesting that even on some curses where the main body of the text is in Latin, the *voces magicae* are written using the Greek alphabet. There are even a handful of tablets written in Latin but using the Greek alphabet (SD 436; **DT 231, 252**, 253, **267**, 269, **270, 304**). All but one of these is from Africa where, again, the influences from the Graeco-Egyptian traditions were felt most strongly. The single example from Uley, far away in Britannia, raises many difficult questions, but certainly suggests that such associations were not restricted to places where Greek speakers would be more common. It certainly seems that some people thought of Greek as a more powerful language, or one that was more appropriate for creating curses that were more comprehensible for the supernatural figures being invoked, even if that meant they were less understandable by humans.[48]

Around twenty cursers chose to communicate their curse to the gods using the Celtic language.[49] Two of these texts, the ones from Chamalières (SD 163) and Larzac (SD 158), are among the longest texts that survive in these languages and have therefore been significant pieces of evidence for linguists. For the purposes of this study, the linguistic details are not as important as the reasons why the cursers chose to write their curse in Celtic. At first thought, we might think that the choice to write in Celtic suggests the curser could not write Latin, but in fact the reverse is probably true. All the Celtic curses use the Latin alphabet – out of necessity, as there was no distinct Celtic writing system – and so the cursers must have had some familiarity with writing in Latin. Writing in Celtic must, therefore, have required a conscious rejection of the possibility of writing in Latin, even though they could have conceivably done so. Mullen has argued that these texts could be interpreted as individuals consciously marking out their own Celtic identity, especially as they were in communication with Celtic deities.[50] I would add to this argument the significant fact that, as far as can be determined, none of the Celtic curses appear to use translations of the stock formulas commonly found in their Latin counterparts.[51] By contrast, as Adams has pointed out, it is possible that Celtic words or phrases were used on these curses in the same way that 'Greek' *voces magicae* were used elsewhere: to add intentional obscurity to the text.[52]

The power of a curse emerged from the lived experience of practising the ritual. The active inscribing, manipulation, mutilation and deposition of the lead tablet all worked to create relationships, out of which was generated the power and agency that the curser could then claim to use in whatever way they intended. Individuals made the most effective curse they could, based on whatever knowledge was available to them in their own social contexts, and sought to increase their own agency, either to achieve aims that they were otherwise incapable of completing themselves, or to bolster efforts made through other channels.

Relationships

All recent theoretical work on agency has emphasized a crucial point: agency emerges from relationships, either between humans, or between humans and things.[53] In other words, agency is not an essential quality that a human or thing 'has', but is the result of the ways in which they interact with the world around them. As I have argued here and in Chapter 3, cursing rituals can be framed as ways for the cursers to produce particular kinds of agency by interacting with a variety of things: lead tablets, nails, graves, sacred springs and so on. However, it was not just relationships between humans and things that were created or transformed as part of cursing rituals, but also social relationships between humans, especially cursers and their victims. In this section, I will argue that engaging in cursing rituals gave cursers a way to negotiate their position within their community, as well as to take active steps to alter both their own social relations and those of their victims. When studying other contexts, social anthropologists have argued that sorcery practices are intimately connected to social relations, the structure of social orders and the processes by which these are all defined.[54] Others have argued that sorcery is fundamentally conservative, as it patrols the boundaries of what is acceptable and punishes those who transgress, such as thieves and adulterers.[55] Social anthropology and classical studies have differed on this point; in the study of the ancient world, magic is often seen as isolated from mainstream society, having little to do with normal social relations.[56] In this part of the chapter I will show that this view is incorrect, and that cursing did have an important role in influencing social relations.

The central social relationships involved in ancient cursing rituals are those between the cursers and their victims. The performance of a cursing ritual would have been an important moment in the ongoing development of these relationships, as one party was trying to influence the other in ways that could have serious ramifications in real life, as we have already seen. Where the cursers were able to identify their victims by name, it is reasonable to suggest that they knew them in some capacity. Following on from this, the act of cursing certain named victims is an attempt by the curser to define their social relationships with those around them by identifying people that they believed were opposed to them.

By pushing this interpretation further, we see that the grouping of several victims together on a single curse becomes an act of creating bounded social groups with a common cause. With this in mind, we can more satisfactorily explain the theft curses that give long lists of suspects, despite reporting the theft of relatively small, inexpensive objects such as cloaks or small quantities of cash (**SD 206, 303, 456**). As was discussed earlier, on these curses, the cursers are naming the people whom they already believed were their enemies or rivals. In this way, the ritual helped the cursers work out their place in their community, and to take active steps to change their relationships with those around them. Juridical curses did not mark out the main litigants as isolated opponents, but bound them together in groups with lawyers, wives and enslaved people, all named under titles such as *inimici* (**SD 468, 470, 473**). At Bad Kreuznach, where we seem to have evidence of multiple curses being placed as the trials progressed, and as certain individuals became more or less involved, we can interpret these successive curses as a process of drawing and redrawing the boundaries of this group identity. On circus curses, the cursers had ready-drawn lists of opponents that were already sorted into the colour-coded factions around which competitions were organized. Nevertheless, the cursers were still reaffirming the lines of faction rivalry by placing these curses, making it very clear to themselves who was on the 'right' side, and who was on the 'wrong'. From this perspective, the listing of names on curse tablets becomes an act of ordering. The cursers were taking a complex, difficult and perhaps even dangerous social situation and attempting to reorganize it in a way that both made sense to them and (potentially) helped resolve it. They may have already had loose versions of these lists in mind, but cursing allowed them to go further, literally solidifying the lines between two sides by carving their targets' names into sheets of metal, and then applying supernatural power to rework the situation into one where the boy gets the girl, where the right team wins a race, where the right side wins a trial, or where wrong-doers are punished for their crimes.

As this curser–victim relationship was the most important one for the cursing ritual, it was important to present it correctly. People who wrote erotic attraction spells were particularly interested in constructing relationships between themselves and their victims, for obvious reasons, and Winkler's analysis of ancient love magic is still a fundamental work on this point.[57] He interprets attraction spells as attempts by the curser to transfer their own feelings of intense desire onto their intended victim. In the text of many attraction spells, the effects that were intended to become manifest on the victim followed standard ancient descriptions of *eros* (fever, madness, burning, insomnia, loss of appetite and so on), which was considered a physical disease in antiquity.[58] Inducing such symptoms in the victim effectively reversed the situation that existed at the beginning of the ritual, putting the curser in the position of power over the victim, rather than the other way around. No longer suffering, the cursers on attraction spells are reimagined as calm and powerful manipulators of both their victims and the supernatural forces by whose involvement their curse did its work.

An example from Sousse illustrates not only the role-reversal that Winkler describes, but also another important aspect of the relationships affected by erotic curses (**DT 266**):

For you [the infernals] are supporting me so that Vettia, whom Optata bore, cannot sleep nor accept nourishment or food because of love for me ... I bind up the senses, wisdom and intellect and will of Vettia, whom Optata bore, so that she loves me, Felix whom Fructa bore, from this day, from this hour, so that she should forget her father and mother and all her friends and all men, but not love for me, Felix whom Fructa bore.

After some traditional symptoms of *eros*, the curse goes on to split Vettia from her family, friends and strangers in order to force her to Felix. If this curse had worked, it would have resulted in a radical rupturing of Vettia's social relationships, isolating her from the most important people in her life. Leaving aside Chapter 4's discussion of whether Vettia and the other women targeted by such curses were secluded virgins or sexually active women, the intention to end existing relationships and to create new ones is clear. The nuclear family, centred on the married couple and their children, was a fundamental building block of Roman society and a structure that, even allowing for substantial regional variation, nevertheless shaped the lives people across Italia and the western provinces in fundamental ways.[59] For women especially, the relationships they formed with their parents and husbands were essential for defining their social position, because, unlike men, their capacity for building individual public reputations was limited.[60] As a result, their position and reputation as daughters, wives and mothers were central to how they were perceived by others in their communities. While the man and woman did have some say over the person they married, it was still the case that the suitability of prospective spouses was a decision for members of the wider family, especially the older generation. Birth, wealth, social position and moral character were all weighed carefully, with the aim of creating a match that was beneficial for the social, economic and (in elite circles) political positions of both the original families and the new one that would be formed.[61] Attraction spells, especially these ones that mention the separation from parents and other family members, seek to subvert these courtship processes and intentions, erasing and redrawing the social relationships of everyone involved in a way that primarily benefitted the curser. Moreover, this would presumably be against the will of the woman and her family, making it an even more troubling break from their perspective.

Although the attraction spells are the most obvious manifestation of the redrawing of social relationships, other kinds of curses were aimed at achieving similar things. As shown earlier, the juridical and circus curses helped to solidify the lines already established by the case or race, with the different sides diametrically opposed. The cursers were opposed to the victims on the theft curses too, with the former suffering because of the misdeeds of the latter. This is a simplistic understanding of the relationships, however, and a closer analysis reveals more interesting facets. Competition, juridical and theft cursing rituals aimed to change the relative agency and power of victims and cursers, just as the attraction spells did. At the start of the ritual, cursers often envisioned themselves as the underdogs, or the innocent victims of wrongdoing, putting them in a position of powerlessness in relation to those who had done them wrong.[62] This is best summed up by two curses from Germania, found at Mainz (**SD 493**) and Groß-Gerau respectively (**SD 482**):

> Whoever has committed fraud regarding this money ... that (person) is the better (off) and we are the worse (off) ...

> Greatest of all gods, Atthis, lord, all of the twelve gods. I commend to the goddesses my unjust fate ...

The authors of other curses, relating to both theft and other motives, that ask the gods to avenge or pursue the victim, are in some sense admitting their own inability to do so without some outside help. This sense of powerlessness could have come from the real powerlessness of the likes of women, enslaved people, non-citizens, and even poor Romans, all of whom were at some disadvantage when it came to accessing official structures of power. In these situations, the cursers of the Roman curses were expressing their sense of distress, loss and powerlessness, perhaps in a similar way to the Sinhalese Buddhists who use cursing shrines in Sri Lanka.[63] The cursing rituals allowed the cursers to take these feelings and transform them into angry agency, with the input of power from supernatural beings or from the ritual itself. The Mainz curse mentioned above shows this (**SD 493**), as later in the text the victim is compelled by the pain of physical punishment to come to the temple and confess their crimes in public. Conducting the curse ritual has allowed the curser to move from a position of powerlessness to one of power over the victim.

In sum, curses gave the curser the potential ability to redraw their social connections to the people around them. By grouping together enemies, whether known or unknown, suspected or proven, they were ordering their social world into a shape that made sense to them, or that benefitted them in whatever aim they were pursuing. Attraction spells helped break existing ties and redraw their social landscape in ways that served them better. In many kinds of curse, the fundamental change in relationships was the reversal of power positions, as previously powerless cursers gained control over a situation and had the agency to direct things to their own advantage.

Identification

So far in this chapter has explored how relationships between people were presented, in terms of their social connections and relative ability to exercise power and agency. In this final section, I want to discuss the ways names and naming practices were used to present victims. By continuing to think about curse tablets from the perspective of power and relationships, we begin to appreciate the importance of naming for creating connections between individuals and their social contexts. Through conscious decisions to identify their victims in particular ways, cursers linked them to other people, including parents, spouses or enslavers. Naming was also an important strategy in the subversion of normal power structures that we have already seen in this chapter, as victims were rarely identified by markers of rank or privilege.

In the way they are treated, names could (and still can) stand for many different aspects of the person: body, mind, character, reputation and relationships. Of course, this is not a new revelation, nor something only revealed by curse tablets, as is readily attested by the massive body of scholarship on the social significance of names in ancient Mediterranean studies as well as other fields.[64] Personal names can present clues about any aspect of a person's identity, including gender, ethnicity, status, family and occupation. Names are central to the understanding of a person's place within their community, both for the individual themselves and the others around them. As with all other aspects of a person's identity, names are not static and unchanging, but flexible and fluid, changing over time and in different circumstances. The ways in which a person chooses to name themselves, and the ways in which people choose to name other people, can reveal or obscure, assert or deny particular identities. Individuals can go by different names at different times, depending on the circumstances: I can be 'Dr McKie' to my students, 'Stuart' to my wife and 'Dad' to my children. Some ways of naming a person are appropriate only at particular times, and accidentally using the wrong name or form of address can cause embarrassment or can be insulting or denigrating if done deliberately. At least one recent study has shown that forms of naming and address can reveal gender biases in particular communities, in this case the academic discipline of internal medicine, where women were consistently less likely to be addressed by their professional title than their male counterparts, thereby minimizing their expertise and contributing to the marginalization of female scholars.[65] Doing this deliberately is a kind of power, in that it attempts to limit the agency of women, making it harder for them to act in their social and professional contexts.

There was a clear concern for appropriate naming in the ancient world, something visible in several different places. Naming is a central narrative theme of Homer's *Odyssey*, with the name of Odysseus himself being obscured or revealed at key points in the poem's plot.[66] Austin has argued that there could be traces of 'name magic' here, in that those closest to the hero are unwilling to utter his name to protect it from malicious actions by his enemies.[67] Indeed, it is only after Odysseus reveals his true name to Polyphemus that the Cyclops is able to invoke his curse.[68] At least in Austin's view, this is an instance of the kinds of 'name taboo' that have been reported by anthropologists and ethnographers in various societies around the world, where names are often kept secret to protect the individual from disease or malign magic.[69] For a Roman example, we have the strange and contradictory stories about a secret name of the city, or perhaps its tutelary deity, which had to be preserved for the safety and security of Rome. In some versions, this name was revealed in 82 BC by a tribune of the plebs, Q. Valerius Soranus, who was duly executed for his transgression.[70] Whether these stories are true or not is somewhat beside the point: for our purposes it is enough that some Romans *believed* they were, and that knowledge of true or secret names could increase power over someone or something, even the city of Rome itself.

Naming on curse tablets can seem deceptively simple and has therefore been somewhat overlooked by most scholars. The direct targeting of names in curse formulas has been noted, as has the unusual use of maternal filiation in the Graeco-Egyptian tradition, but few scholars have thought about the social significance of the ways in which cursers named their victims.[71] In this section of the chapter, I aim to think more deeply about the importance of names on curse tablets, and especially they ways in which they link people into wider relationships.

As mentioned in the previous chapter, there were two methods by which victims could be identified on curse tablets: either by direct naming, or by using formulas such as 'whether man or woman'. Of the two, direct naming was the more common, as there were various means by which a person could learn who they needed to target: rival charioteers, rumoured thieves or known litigants. Directly naming the victims seems to have been considered more effective, as the treatment of names in some cursing formulas attests. Names directly stood for the victims themselves, who were not physically present when the ritual was enacted. The appearance of phrases such as 'kill these names' (**SD 469**) are clear demonstrations that the written words of the victims' names stood for their physical body, not just their person in some abstract sense. Naming their victims was so important to many cursers that they were the only thing they wrote on the tablet, making them the only part of the ritual that could be manipulated by nailing, folding or depositing, as well as the only permanent reminder that the curse had been placed. The direct and intimate connection between tablet and victim created by naming is well demonstrated by a curse from Bath (**SD 213**):

> I have given to the goddess Sulis the six silver coins which I have lost. It is for the goddess to exact (them) from the names written below: Senicianus and Saturninus and Anniola. The written page (has) been copied out. Anniola, Senicianus, Saturninus.

On this tablet, the victims' names are the targets of both the wrath of the goddess and the physical manipulation performed as part of the cursing ritual. First, Sulis was exhorted to extract the stolen coins 'from the names' (*a nominibus*) of three victims, which stand for the victims themselves. Then the names were inscribed on the tablet, in two different orders on the front and the back so that both instances of Anniola's name would be hit by the nail that was subsequently driven through the tablet (Figure 3.4). Elsewhere, I have argued that formulas such as this create permanent, enchained relationships between the victims, cursers and the gods, even when the victims' names were not actually known.[72] Even just some use of the word *nomen* seems to have been enough for the invoked beings to find the right victim, as in the curse from Bath that reads simply 'the name of the thief (*nomen furis*), whether slave or free, whether boy or girl' (**SD 307**). Here, and in these other examples, we see curse tablets conforming to ideas of 'name magic' like those found in the *Odyssey* and modern anthropological studies, in that the direct naming of victims allowed the curser to gain power over them and then influence them in whatever way they intended.

Most victims and cursers were identified by a single name. For many enslaved people and non-citizens, this was probably the only name they possessed and was therefore the only name by which they could be identified. Roman citizens had more complicated nomenclature, consisting of at least two, sometimes three or more elements for both men and women. However, the standard procedure for cursing Romans seems to have also been to use a single name. Out of 921 men named as cursers or victims on the curse tablets from the Roman west, only twenty-seven (3 per cent) were identified using their *tria nomina*, with a further 127 (13 per cent) given two names, leaving 767 with one name only.[73] For women, the data are similar: of the 257 women named as cursers and victims on the curse tablets, only forty-four (17 per cent) were given two or more names. A detailed onomastic study of all these names is beyond the scope of this book, but

Mullen has shown how the examination of the names on the Bath tablets can advance our understanding of things such as cultural change in the provinces.[74] My focus will remain on the social significance of the naming strategies used on curse tablets, in terms of the ways they construct relationships between victims, cursers and other members of the wider communities.

As just established, most victims were identified by single names, usually a *cognomen*.[75] This was the name by which most individuals would have been known to those around them and was therefore the most intimate name for each person.[76] The full Roman name would only have been used in the most formal settings, when it was important to convey something of the status and position of the person being named. This was important in other written texts, such as, for example, monumental stone inscriptions intended for public display.[77] Curse tablets were neither official documents nor were they publicly displayed, and so it would have made little sense to use full citizen names. Mullen has argued that at Bath and other sites in Britannia, Celtic *cognomina* were used alone because formal Roman names might have felt inappropriate in a conversation between Celts and their gods.[78] While there might be some merit in this argument for certain sites in the north-west, it cannot be true in places such as Mainz, where Celtic and Germanic *cognomina* were used in communication with the Phrygian goddess Mater Magna.

When further identification was included in curse tablets, the most common method was by reference to a parent. In 'self-authored' texts, this was usually the father, predominantly done in the standard Roman way, by either putting the father's name in the genitive or by using the word *filia* or *filius*. Patronymics were probably the only additional name by which Greek, Celtic and Germanic people would have been known, both before and after the Roman conquest, so it is not too surprising that they are found on curses from across the study area.[79] On those curses influenced by the Graeco-Egyptian traditions, individuals were more commonly identified by the mother, usually using a phrase like '*quem peperit Prima*' (whom Prima bore, **DT 247**). Various possible explanations for this practice have been suggested, from the greater accuracy afforded by matrilineal identification to influences from older Egyptian and West Asian traditions.[80] I follow Graf, Gager and Ogden in favouring the subversive, countercultural flavour that it afforded the curses.[81] In other words, identifying someone by naming their mother was contrary to normal social practice, and therefore subverted normal power structures, and such inversions may have been attractive to the freelance religious specialists who produced these texts, adding a level of mystique and exoticism to their products.

On curse tablets, women were occasionally identified as *uxor* (wife), usually when their husbands were also named, which gives the impression that they were only secondary victims, and that the husbands were the main targets (**SD 117, 214, 235, 299, 443, 473**). It also reinforces the presumption that women were dependent on their husbands for their social identity, effectively putting them in a subordinate social position and reducing their potential power, making them more vulnerable to the curse. Alongside spouses and children, other family relationships were sometimes mentioned.[82] As well as giving more detailed identification, adding these relationships situated the victim within webs of social relationships as members of wider family networks. This is an extension of the listing of victims discussed earlier in the chapter, in that, on one level, the cursers were assembling groups of connected enemies and treating them as a bounded entity. On another level, it spread the curse outwards onto parents, husbands, children and others, who might now all suffer for the wrongdoing of their relatives. This is certainly an important characteristic of sorcery in Sri Lanka, and has an effect on the form of magical attacks that have been performed there.[83] Several of the confession *stelae* from Roman Asia Minor also show that people could suffer from the wrong-doing of their relatives, and were anxious to appease the gods and free themselves from the illnesses or misfortunes that had been transferred onto them by association with the guilty party.[84] We might invoke the idea of 'name magic' again here; being named on a curse, even only tangentially as a relative of the main victim, was enough to drag a person into sharing some portion of their punishment.

After filiation, the only regularly occurring marker of identity present on curse tablets was the enslaved or freed status of an individual. In total, forty-four people are marked out as enslaved (using either *servus/a*, *ancilla* or *doulos*), and a further thirteen as freed (using either *libertus/a* or *apeleutheros*), almost always with their present or former enslaver also named.[85] Using these labels to identify victims has a similar effect to naming family connections, in that it places the victim within networks of other people, who may also be affected by the curse through association. Even more so than naming a woman as *uxor*, pointing out the enslaved condition of a victim reinforces their subordinate social and legal positions, emphasising their vulnerability to the power of the curse. Naming family connections and enslaved/freed status were often done together, as in the following examples from Bath (**SD 214**) and Cuma (**SD 62**):

> A petition. (I ask) you Victory (The Avenger?) ... Cunomolius (son) of Minicus, Minervina (his) wife, Cunitius (their) slave, Senovara (his) wife, Lavidendus

> (their) slave, Mattonius (their) slave, Catinius (son) of Exsactor ... Methianus ... I give ... enemy.
>
> (I give?) Marcus Heius Calidus, son of Marcus ... Blossia daughter of Gaius, Publius Heius Calidus son of Marcus; Chilo slave of Heius Marcus, Marcus Heius freedman of Marcus ... Gaius Blossius freedman of a woman, Bithus Atto slave of Heius Marcus, Blossia daughter of Lucius. I bind fast all these people to the infernal gods so that none of them has anyone ... is able to, and not ... anyone is able to do. I dedicate this(?) to the infernal gods so that they act accordingly.

On texts such as these we are seeing the Roman *familia* at its most extended, something that the curses are making good use of so they can drag in as many victims as possible.

Apart from connections to family members and enslavers, other markers of identification were rarely used, unlike on lapidary inscriptions where inclusion of an individual's ethnic origin, legal status or profession are much more common. Only four curse tablets from the entire study area state the ethnic or geographic origin of the victim. The first to consider is from fourth-century Trier (**dfx 4.1.3/16**):

> (I curse) Tiberius Claudius Trevirus, a German and the freedman of Claudius Similis. I ask you, lady Isis, thus you send him flowing, and whatever he has in goods, in sickness in the Megaron.

The victim is identified is very formally, using forms and containing information reminiscent of public inscriptions. His full *tria nomina* are given, along with his status as a freedman and the name of his former enslaver. He is identified as being a German, and that – combined with his freed status – makes it very likely that he originally came from beyond the frontiers. It is possible that Trevirus had prominently displayed his status and identity in some way, perhaps on a monumental inscription as was not untypical for wealthy freedmen – although none bearing his name have been found – and that the curser was using this to provide exceptionally accurate targeting information for their curse. In a Greek curse from the city of Rome, several wrestlers and athletes are given their cities of origin, such as 'Artemon, son of Nicolaus, the wrestler from Ephesus' and 'Agathandrus son of Aristarchus, the athlete from Kos' (**AE 2014, 213**). In a study of gladiatorial tombstones from Campania, Hope has suggested that matching fighters from different locations against each other might have added tension and drama to the event, so the geographic origins on this curse may have been a well-known part of the men's public persona.⁸⁶ The third of these curses, this time from Sisak in Pannonia, also gives geographic origin as part of more specific targeting information and alongside longer forms of the victims' names (**SD 529**): 'Gaius Domitius Secundus and Lucius Larcius and Secundus Valerius from Cibalae and Publius Citronius, Gaius Corellius from Narbo and Lucius Licinius Sura from Hispania and Lucilius Valens.' In this case, as with the other two, the purpose seems to be to provide further identification of the victims, so that the curse will be more likely to succeed. However, these geographical origins feel much more personal than in the previous two curses, rather than details that could be gleaned from publicly displayed texts. This perhaps suggests that the curser had a closer connection to the victims, although the nature of the tablet makes it hard to reconstruct the exact details. The men are described as enemies (*adversarii*), and the curse targets their speech, so a juridical motive is usually suggested. Marco Simón and de Llanza suggest that this curse may have been placed by one or more local people, engaged in some dispute with the Roman authorities, possibly identifying L. Licinius Sura with the man who was instrumental in Trajan's conquest of Dacia.⁸⁷ Finally, on the Celtic-language curse from Chamalières, also motivated by a trial, two of the victims are designated as *pelignon*, translated by both Lambert and Mees as 'stranger'.⁸⁸ What this means exactly is unclear, but the two men could have been from outside the Empire, or perhaps simply unfamiliar to the local community. In all four of these cases, the inclusion of the geographical origins of the victims is a conscious 'othering' of them, emphasizing their status as outsiders and newcomers to the local areas.

As well as ethnic origin, other common markers of identity in epigraphy were also only very infrequently used on curse tablets. Although soldiers are implicated on a few other curses, military rank as a marker of identity appears on just one tablet from Mainz (SD 495).⁸⁹ Apart from the enslaved and freed people, the only people identified by legal status, social rank, elected magistracies or other official positions are the procurator and legates of Hispania cursed in Ampurias, discussed in Chapter 4 and earlier in this chapter. On juridical curses, certain individuals are identified as advocates, judges or clerks because such information was relevant to the legal proceedings, and their positions made them obvious targets for the curse.⁹⁰ Two of the Bad Kreuznach curses (**SD 468, 473**) give the professions of some of their victims, either because it was a convenient way to identify them or because their jobs were related to the trial in some way. There are only nine other curses that mention a victim's profession, including a miller (**SD 5**), eight enslaved hairdressers (**SD 52**), doctors (DT 123,

Gager 79), a veterinarian (**SD 117**) and various staff on a farm in Pula (**SD 101 and 102**).[91]

Apart from these few exceptional cases, the hundreds of other victims were identified by only a single name. Without references to their ethnic affiliations, social rank, career successes or positions of privilege, the victims were envisioned as relatively equal. Regardless of their background, they were all uniformly vulnerable to the aggressive power of the curses and, if accused of wrongdoing, would all receive the same divine punishment regardless of social status, unlike in the human justice system of the time. Again, we can see a subversion of normal power structures here, as curses worked to flatten the hierarchies of Roman society, bringing everyone down to the same level. At the same time, curses envision a world where a person's agency is not limited by the power granted to others by their position in society. The only exceptions are the enslaved people, whose status would have afforded them no protection from the most severe punishments under the justice system. By using these markers of identity for their enslaved victims, especially where they also name their present or former enslavers, the cursers were picking up on and strengthening an identity of domination and control that had been forced onto them by others.

This section has made it clear that, far from being casual or incidental, naming held a great deal of significance for those who wrote curse tablets in the Roman west. As words that could stand for the whole person of their victim, names were essential for bringing them into the performance of the ritual, where they could be influenced in whichever way the curser envisioned. We can draw direct parallels between Roman curses and instances of 'name magic' in a variety of other cultural contexts. Because of their direct and intimate relationship with the individuals they stand for, names are considered as powerful tools in both malicious and beneficial ritual practices.

The social significance of people's names further enhances their importance in rituals such as cursing. Names stand for more than just the individual by themselves and can reveal a whole range of relationships and networks in which a person is embedded, as well as the ways in which they are presented to their communities. Names are essential for defining identity, especially when additional markers are added, for example *serva*, *liberta* or *uxor*. On the curse tablets, individuals were named simply and informally, with few additional details that would make them stand out. Where these were included, it was usually a connection to their household, either as a child, a spouse, or as a presently or formerly enslaved person. Public positions or careers are included much more rarely, and usually only when it is relevant to the motive of the curse.

This is the essential point: as displayed on curse tablets, markers of identification are only present insofar as they help the curser pursue their intentions.

Conclusions

This chapter began by pointing out that curse tablets all aimed at achieving a particular purpose. This observation might seem simple, even simplistic, but it is at the heart of the 'lived religion' approach to these objects. Performing a cursing ritual was an important moment in a curser's life, after which they expected the world around them to be altered in some way. For some this might have been a seemingly minor change, such as the return of some item of property or victory for a favoured chariot team. For others, much more may have been at stake: fortunes, security, even lives could depend on the outcomes of legal trials, personal disputes or courtships. Whatever their purpose, it seems likely that cursers came to cursing rituals because their ability to pursue their intentions through other means was hampered in some way. Cursing was a way to augment the deficient agency of individuals who were marginalized by the social and political structures of the Roman Empire, which were dominated by small, elite groups. Anyone outside those groups could be driven to cursing if they felt their ability to act was limited, but we might naturally think of women, non-citizens, and enslaved people as prime candidates. Unfortunately, the fact that most curse tablets were anonymous makes it difficult to make definitive statements about the kinds of people most likely to perform cursing rituals.

This chapter, and indeed this whole book, has also revealed the intensely social character of Roman cursing. As well as addressing whatever specific event provoked it, curse tablets were also fundamentally about defining a curser's place in their communities. Listing victims and grouping them together as 'enemies' was a process of drawing and redrawing social relationships, as was the abrupt, often violent desire to remove a woman from her family and join her to the man behind an attraction spell. The potential to reverse imbalanced power relationships, however they might be imagined by the cursers, was a central aspect of cursing rituals. Finally, the ways in which victims were named, and the parts of their identity that were suppressed or emphasized, defined these individuals, bringing into focus the parts of themselves that were most important to the success of the curse. Cursing was a lived, social experience, used by individuals as a tool to navigate complicated and shifting relationships with those around them.

6

Epilogue

Throughout this book, I have made the case for examining the lived experience of performing cursing rituals in the Roman west. Rather than charting the development of language across centuries, or asking big questions about the relationship between religion and magic, I have instead focused on the place of curses in the lives of the people who made them. On this scale, it has become absolutely clear that curse tablets were objects created by the experience of performing the ritual itself, steeped as it was in the physical, political, cultural and social contexts of the individual. Taking a 'lived religion' approach has in fact made it much easier to account for variation across time and space, as individuals creatively adapted and adopted the practice of cursing to suit their own needs in their own contexts.

At the most basic level, we must remain alive to the physical experience of the cursing ritual, in terms of the interaction between humans and the things involved. As a ritualized activity, curses emerged from mutual, relational interactions between bodies, a lead tablet, a stylus, sometimes a nail and the locations in which they came together: the water of a spring, the sand of an arena or the dirt of a grave. Curses were woven by the curser through a series of creative moments informed by the material experience of acting with and reacting to these things. Each ritual would have been a unique experience for the individual curser, and the final product of their actions would not necessarily have been exactly what was in their mind before starting. Knowledge of how, where and why to place a curse was unevenly spread around the regions and within communities: some cursers were able to consult religious specialists with training in elaborate Graeco-Egyptian traditions while others relied on the stories and wisdom of friends and family, or simply their own wits. Creative experimentation was a hallmark of ancient cursing rituals: every aspect of the process could be changed depending on a host of shifting factors.

If there is one unifying theme that cuts across all the curse tablets studied here, it is their aim. In one way or another, every curse intended to change the world in some observable, identifiable way. The first transformation was the turning of a blank sheet of metal into a potent curse, achieved by the performance of the ritual itself. Through the bringing together of the relevant objects, human bodies and supernatural forces, further transformations were affected by cursing, especially in the connections between people. Wrongdoers could be punished, races could be won, and lovers could be joined, but lurking beneath all of these was the intent to transform social relationships by breaking, forming or altering them. Many people used cursing rituals as a process for understanding their complex social world, navigating the factions and cliques that formed within towns, villages or even individual households. By drawing up lists of rivals or enemies, cursers were not just reflecting the world as it existed, but were redrawing and reorganizing it to create a picture that was more favourable for them. Social structures and hierarchies were inverted or levelled through the deliberate use of personal names or through the reversal of power relationships between those in superior and inferior positions. In this way, we can see that curses were not always about resolving short-term problems, but were an important moment in ongoing social relationships, closely connected to other forms of informal and sometimes malicious communication, such as rumour and gossip. Curses provided new opportunities for people to act in a world where power was uneven, and where individuals were not always free to successfully deploy their agency. Fundamentally, cursing was an attempt to gain control over a situation of crisis that the curser perceived themselves as otherwise powerless to resolve. It could work alongside other channels of action – lawcourts, courtship, rumour, gossip, direct confrontation – or could make up for them when they appeared to fail. In terms of agency, cursing speaks to an understanding of the world in which human activity is limitless in its ability to affect change. If a person knew how to do it, they could bring almost anything under their control, even the gods themselves. In a world where belief in the efficacy of magic was endemic, but also where positions of power were jealously guarded by a small group of elite men and women, it is easy to see why such rituals were considered potentially threatening.

So where do we go from here? This book has demonstrated the deeply social nature of ancient cursing rituals, comprehensively rejecting the image of curses being produced by lone practitioners, furtively scribbling down their intentions then sneaking into cemeteries under the cover of darkness. Instead, we see the reality of a process in which, from beginning to end, any number of people could have been involved, and about which a whole community could come learn through networks of gossip and rumour. The lived religion approach taken here has also challenged pan-Mediterranean narratives that makes cursing a constant presence in ancient societies. From the perspective of the individual, we no longer see overarching traditions of cursing that stretch across centuries, but instead short-lived flurries of activity clustered around moments of intense competition or crisis. Curses were emergency rituals that were only relevant to human lives in particular circumstances. As such, there is scope for further work in exploring the contexts in which curses flourished, however briefly. For reasons of space, I had to be selective in the geographical and chronological scope of this book, meaning that more than a thousand curses fall outside its boundaries. Nevertheless, the material from the Greek world, both before and during the Roman imperial period, can and should be analysed from these theoretical positions. Away from the field of curse tablet studies, the conclusions of this book have wider-reaching ramifications. As symmetrical archaeology and 'new materialism' continue to gain traction in our fields, the observations made here offer a convincing way to think about power in new ways. We cannot ignore the vast inequalities of the Roman world by putting everything and everyone on a totally flat ontological plain. Curse tablets reveal the lengths to which some people were willing to go, or were forced to go, to circumvent structures of power that limited their agency. Our models of ancient society must take these disparities into account, or they will not be fit for purpose.

From the conclusions drawn in this book, it has become clear how significant curse tablets were for ongoing relationships between the individual cursers and the world around them. Curses were available to people regardless of gender or status, and helped them navigate situations that seemed beyond their control. Cursing rituals had a fluid, shifting relationship with established religion and other power structures, and had enough scope for creativity to allow people to make the best possible curse to suit their needs. At times they drew on widely held notions of religious practice, divine power, human justice, crime and punishment and public identity, and at other times they directly reversed these concepts. Conclusions on this scale are important, but the individual lives of people should not be lost from view. Behind every curse is someone like the wife of Florus with whom we began: a woman trying to make sense of a desperate situation.

Appendix: Select Catalogue of Curses

The appendix contains most of the Greek and Latin curses discussed in the book. As it is the most up-to-date corpus, I have followed the order of SD where possible. Those not included in SD are listed by other major corpora in the following order: DT, SGD, Gager, NGCT, dfx, AE. The Leiden Epigraphic conventions have been followed and I have aimed to reproduce the layout of the original text wherever possible. English translations are my own unless indicated and all dates are AD. Because of the difficulties in providing translations, Celtic curses have not been included. For these, readers are directed to RIG 2.2.

Quotations from Tomlin (1988) reproduced with permission of Oxford University Committee for Archaeology and Roger Tomlin. Quotations from Gager (1992) reproduced with permission of Oxford Publishing Limited through PLSclear.

SD 1

Origin: Rome. Grave outside Porta Latina.
Date: First century.
Bibliography: DT 138; dfx 1.4.4/2; LCT 16.
Notes: rolled and tied with wire.

Danae ancilla no<v>icia
Capitonis hanc <h>ostiam
acceptam habeas
et consumas Danae
ne habe<a>s Eutychiam
Soterichi uxorem

Danae, new slave of Capito: may you receive this offering, and may you consume Danae. May you not have Eutychia, wife of Soterichos.

SD 3

Origin: Rome. Exact site unknown.
Date: First or second century.
Bibliography: DT 137; dfx 1.4.4/1; LCT 15.
Notes: written in ink on a lamp.

Helenus suom (=eius) nomen eimferis (=inferis)
mandat stipem strenam lumen
suom secum defert ne quis eum
solvat nisi nos qui fecimus

Helenus gives his name to the infernals. He brings with him a small offering, a new-year's gift, his lamp. May no-one release him except us, who have done this.

SD 5

Origin: Rome. A columbarium outside Porta San Sebastiano.
Date: Second to fourth century.
Bibliography: DT 140; dfx 1.4.4/4; LCT 18
Notes: Drawing of a standing daemon (Typhon-Seth?). Rolled.

		. . . ου	. . . .
		. . . μνε	filius . . . .
		arcum tenens.	qui . . . . . o ab hac ora ab hoc die ab hoc nocte
		φρι	t[. . . . .]mti c[. . . . .]ege
		αααααα	tere contere confr[in]ge e [t . . . t]rade
	stanz	εεεεεε	morti fili[u]m Aselles Praeseti[ci]um pristinarium 5
		ηηηηηηη	qui manet in regione nona ubi videtur arte sua
		ιιιιιι	facere et trade Plutoni praeposito mortuorum
. . . nos me		οοοοοοο	et si forte te contempserit patiatur febris
. . . iginio		ωωωωωωω	frigus tortionis palloris sudores obbripi-
. . . . . .	Typhon-Seth.	Ουσιρασι	lationis meridianas interdianas seru- 10
. . . ruep		Ουσιρινασιρι	tinas nocturnas ab hac ora ab hac die ab hac (nocte)
. . . nmae		Ουσιρινεμοφρι	e]t perturba eum ne repraeensionem abeat
. . . xerc e		Ευλαμον κατεχε	et si forte occansione invenerit praefocato eum
. . . nu . . .			Praestetium filium Asell[es in termas in] valneas in quocumque loco
. . . as			et pede frange Pr[aesetici]o Aselles et [si] forte te seducat per alique 15

Appendix: Select Catalogue of Curses

	Victor	Asella	Prae[se]	[? artificia] et rideat de te et exsultetur tibi
		mater	tici[us]	vince peroccide filium mares Praesete-
			pris[tina]	cium pristinarum filium [A]selles
	Protome.	Protome.	Protome. r[ius]	qui manet in regione [nona ed]e ede
				tacy tacy 20
...tene
...ne
...eieraes

...son of ... From this hour, from this day, from this night ... grind, crumble, break and ... hand over to death the son of Asella, Praeseticius the baker, who lives in Region Nine, where he is seen to practise his profession, and hand him over to Pluto, the chief of the dead and, if by chance he disregards you, he should suffer a fever, a cold, torture, paleness, weariness, shivering in the middle of the day, in the evening and at night, from this hour, from this day, from this night and confound him, so that he cannot recover and if by chance he should come upon an opportunity, you should strangle him, Praeseticius, son of Asella, in the warm baths, in the baths, in whatever place, and shatter the feet of Praeseticius son of Asella and, if by chance he leads you astray through some art and laughs at you and is boastful to you, subdue and kill the son of the sea, Praeseticius the baker, son of Asella, who is in Region Nine, now now, quickly quickly.
Victor, Asella mother. Praeseticius the baker.

SD 16

Origin: uncertain, but possibly a grave near Rome.
Date: Fourth or fifth century.
Bibliography: dfx 1.4.4/13; LCT 25.
Notes: Inscribed on the inside of a cinerary urn.

Deprecor vos sancti angeli
quomodo <ha>ec anima intus in-
[cl]usa tenetur et angust{i}atur
[et] non vede<t> [ne]que [l]umine ne[que] a[li]quem
[refri]gerium non <h>abet [sic a]nima
[mentes cor]pos Collecticii quem pepe[rit Agne[lla]
teneatur ard[eat]
de{s}tabes[cat] usque

[ad] infernum [se]mper
[du]ci[t]e Collecticum
quem peperet
Agnella

I pray to you, holy angels. Just as this soul is held inside, having been locked up, and is restrained and cannot see and has neither light nor any other consolation, so should the soul, mind and body of Collecticius, who Agnella bore, be held, burned, wasted away. Forever drag off Collecticius, who Agnella bore, all the way to the underworld.

SD 48

Origin: Rome. Grave, but otherwise unknown.
Date: First century.

Side A
Dite Pater Proserpina dia Canes Orcini Ustores inferi
Ossufragae Larvae Furiae Maniae Aves nocturnae
Aves Harpyiae Ortygiae Virga Ximaera Geryones
Siredonas Circe Gegantes Spinx vos precatur et
petit rogat vos numina deum inferum qui
suprascripti estis ea[m] Caeciliam Primam sive quo
alio nomine est uti eam Dite Pater deprimas
malisque doloribus eam adpetas aput te abducas
Proserpina Dia tu facias illam Caeciliam Primam
sive quo alio nomine est uti eam deprimas
adimas illae sanguinem de venis corpus calorem
animi illae Caeciliae Primae eripias canes Or[ci]ni
Orcini tricipites vos illius Caeciliae Primae exedit[is] iocinera
pulmones cor cum venis viscera membra medullas
eius diripiatis dilaceretis lumina eius C[a]e[c]iliae P[r]imae
a(d)ripiatis vosque Ustores inferi eius Caeciliae Primae
peruratis lumina stomachum cor eius pulmones
adipes cetera membra omnia illius Caeciliae Primae
peruratis <a>duratis vos neque vivere nec valere
possit eamque Caeciliam Primam ad vos
adducatis tradatis ea sua ossufragis inferis vos

illae Caeciliae Primae ossum frangant medullas
exedint iocinera pulmones dirimant vosque
Ossufragae inferae tradatis illam Caeciliam
Primam Aurorae Orchi sorori Aurora Orchi
soror tu illae Caeciliae Primae eripias somnum
soporem obicias illae amentiam dolores stupores
malam frontem [---] usque donec Caecilia Prima
pereat intereat extabescat deinde tu Aurora
Orcini soror tradas illam Caeciliam Primam
Larvabus et Furiabus inferis [---] illae Caeciliae
Primae obiciatis metum formidines dolores

Side B
Stupor et amentia omnisque d [---] faciant
ead[-]m[--]quae sibi [---]a[---] adipiscatur
turpidines p[---]ma[---]anantur eam
Caeciliam Primam [---]am[---]ea habeat semper
turpid(in)es uti illa Caecilia Prima ab inimicis suis
prematur opprima[tur] desuma[tu]r neque [--]adatur
aves nocturnae Aves Harpyiae vos illius Caeciliae
Primae exeditis co[r] ma[n]us intera[nea] omnia obiciatis
illae Caeciliae Primae omnibus [---]aia
aegraque consilia febres cotidianas tertianas
quartanas usque dum animam eius Caeciliae
Primae eripiatis [---]cae que[---]mas[---]s[-]ia Virga
deum inferum[---]ac[---]a tu
efficias illae Caeciliae Primae quem admodum
tu domas caedis uris [per]uris ad Inferos eos qui
ad superos omnia mala sc[el]eraque fecerunt
sic tu Caeciliam Primam [ill]am Virga uras peruras
caedas domes do[n]ec tamqu[a]m al oram egentes
omnibus fortunis mortua[m] ad t[e] abducas
Himaera [---] Caeciliam Primam morsu mordeas
uti sana numquam fiat adil[- ?]illam f[---]em
uti turgeas sic tamquam tym[p]anum doloribusque
malis intereat usque donec ea pereat uti abducas
numqua[m] ea[---] eam Caeciliam Primam
perura[s ---]em[---]prm

138   *Appendix: Select Catalogue of Curses*

mortua fiat [---]a Geryones Siredones Circe Solis filia
quemadmodum Minerva una tunica [---]e[---]abat eos
monstrinae Siredenae cantibus homines detinebant
Circe feralis medicamentis Ulixis socios [---]a[--]inem
[---]e[-]atis Caeciliam Primam isdem malis isdem
[-]oloris Caeciliam adiuvatis vitamque animam eius
[-]aARGAMA (?) eripiatis inferis tradatis
[---] Dite pater Properpina dia et Virga vos precatur is qui hoc
ma[n]datum dedit vestram [---]a [---]fano detes[---]m[---] eam
perficiatis perfectae pati[---]

Dis Pater, divine Proserpina, Hounds of Orcus, Infernal Corpse-burners, Bone-crushers, Ghosts, Furies, Spectres, Night Birds, Harpies, Ortygian birds, Scourge, Chimera, Geryon, Sirens, Circe, Giants, Sphinx: to you he prays and begs, he asks you, infernal powers who are written above, that Caecilia Prima, or if she has any other name, crush her, Dis Pater, and attack her with sad sorrows, drag her to you. Divine Proserpina, make sure to crush that Caecilia Prima, or if she has any other name, consume the blood from her veins, and snatch away her body and the fire of the soul of Caecilia Prima. You Hounds of Orcus, Three-Headed-Ones of Orcus, you should eat up the liver, lungs, heart and veins, intestines, limbs, marrow of that Caecilia Prima, tear out and rip to pieces the eyes of that Caecilia Prima, and snatch her up, you infernal Corpse-burners, that Caecilia Prima, burn up her eyes, stomach, heart, lungs, fatty tissue and all other limbs of that Caecilia Prima, you should burn up and scorch her, so that she can neither live nor be strong, and you should drag her, Caecilia Prima, to you and you should hand her over to the Infernal Bone-crushers, you should shatter the bones of that Caecilia Prima, you should eat up her marrow, you should pull apart her liver and lungs and you should hand her over to the Infernal Bone-crushers, that Caecilia Prima, and to Aurora, Sister of Orchus. You Aurora, Sister of Orchus, should snatch away sleep and slumber from that Caecilia Prima, you should expose her to madness, suffering, stupidity, mental disorder ... all the way, as long as Caecilia Prima should pass away, perish, melt away, then you Aurora, Sister of Orcus, should hand over that Caecilia Prima to the Ghosts and Infernal Furies ... expose that Caecilia Prima to dread, terror and suffering.

May they cause stupidity, madness and all (suffering?) ... for herself ... be overtaken, disgraces ... this Caecilia Prima ... she should be always held. Disgraces, so that that Caecilia Prima should be crushed, overthrown, consumed by her enemies, and not ... You, Night Birds and Harpies, should eat up that

Caecilia Prima and throw off the heart, hands and all innards of that Caecilia Prima ... and troubled thoughts, daily fevers, tertian fevers, quartain fevers, until you tear out the soul of this Caecilia Prima ... Scourge of the underworld gods ... may you prepare that Caecilia Prima, who you fully break, beat, burn, burn up in Hell, with all those who have committed wickedness and crimes against the gods, thus you, Scourge, should burn, burn up, beat and break that Caecilia Prima until you should lead her dead to you, just like those on a shore who have lost their fortunes. Chimera ... may you bite into Caecilia Prima with your teeth ... so that she will never be well again ... so that you swell up like a drum, and she should die from bad pain, until she dies so you can take her away. No more ... burn up this Caecilia Prima ... may she be dead ... Geryon, Sirens, Circe, daughter of the Sun, in the way that Minerva misled(?) them with a tunic ... the terrible Sirens detained men with songs, the deadly Circe transformed(?) the comrades of Ulysses with magic potions ... (you should inflict on?) Caecilia Prima the same evils, the same suffering, 'help' Caecilia, and you should tear out her life and soul ... you should hand her over to the infernals... Dis Pater, divine Proserpina and Scourge, the one who gave this command prays to you ... may you perform it perfectly ...

SD 52

Origin: Ostia, Italia. Grave.
Date: unknown.
Bibliography: dfx 1.4.3/1; LCT 13.
Notes: Five nail holes around the edges and one through the text.

Agathemeris Maniliae ser(va)
[Ac]hulea Fabiae ser(va) ornatrix
[C]aletuche Vergiliae ser(va) ornatrix
Hilara Liciniae [ser(va) or]natrix
Crheste Corn[eliae] ser(va) ornatrix
Hilara Seiae ser(va) ornatrix
Mosch<h>is ornatrix
Rufa Apeiliae ser(va) ornatrix
Chila ornatrix

Agathemeris, enslaved woman of Manilia, Achulea, enslaved hairdresser of Fabia, Caletyche, enslaved hairdresser of Vergilia, Hilara, enslaved hairdresser of Licinia, Chreste, enslaved hairdresser of Cornelia, Hilara, enslaved hairdresser of

Seia, Moschis, the hairdresser, Rufa, enslaved hairdresser of Apilia, Chila, the hairdresser.

SD 56

Origin: Minturno, Italia. Grave.
Date: first century.
Bibliography: DT 190; dfx 1.4.1/1; LCT 9.

Dii i<n>feri vobis com<m>e<n>do si quic<q>ua<m> sa<n>-
ctitat[i]s h<a>betes ac t<r>ad{r}o Tic<h>ene<m>
C<h>arisi<i> quodquid acat quod i<n>cida<n>t
omnia in adversa dii i<n>feri vobis
com<m>e<n>do il<l>ius mem<b>ra colore<m>
ficura<m> caput capilla umbra<m> cereb-
ru<m> fru<n>te<m> supe[rcil]ia os nasu<m>
me<n>tu<m> buc<c>as la[bra ve]rbu<m> v[ul?]tu<m>
col<l>u<m> iocur umeros cor fulmones
i<n>testinas ve<n>tre<m> bra<ch>ia dicit-
os manus u<m>b<i>licu<m> visica<m> femena
cenua crura talos planta<s>
ticidos (=digitos)
Dii i<n>feri si il<l>am vider[o] dabesce<n>te<m>
vobis sa<n>ctu<m> il<l>ud lib<e>ns ob an<n>u-
versariu<m> facere dibus par-
entibus il(l)ius[---]ta
peculiu<m> tabescat

Infernal gods, to you I commend, if you have any power, and I hand over Tyche of Charisius, (and) whatever she does, so that everything should attack against her. Infernal gods, to you I commend her limbs, colour, shape, head, hair, shadow, brain, forehead, eyebrows, mouth, nose, chin, cheeks, lips, words, face, neck, liver, shoulders, heart, lungs, intestines, belly, arms, fingers, hands, navel, bladder, thighs, knees, shins, ankles, soles, toes. Infernal gods, if I will see her waste away, I will gladly [offer] you that sacrifice every year to the *di parentes* (?) ... property should waste away.

SD 62

Origin: Cuma, Italia. Grave.
Date: First century.
Bibliography: DT 199; dfx 1.5.3/2; LCT 32.

M(arcum) Heium M(arci) f(ilium) Caled[um ...]
Blossiam G(ai) f(iliam) P(ubliam) Heium M(arci) f(ilium) Caled[um]
Chilonem Hei M(arci) s(ervum) M(arcum) Heium [M(arci?) l(ibertum?)---]
G(aium) Blossium ⊃ l(ibertum) Bithum Atton[em?]
[He]i M(arci) ser(vum) Blossiam L(uci) f(iliam)
[hos(?)] homines omnes infereis
[de]is deligo ita ut niq[uis]
[e]orum quemcumque [---]
[---]re possit ni[ve?---]
[---] quidq[uam agere?] p[ossit?] id ded[ico---? deis]
[infereis?] ut ea ita faci[ant]

(I give?) Marcus Heius Calidus, son of Marcus; ... Blossia, daughter of Gaius; Publius Heius Calidus, son of Marcus; Chilo, slave of Marcus Heius; Marcus Heius, freedman of Marcus; ... Gaius Blossius, freedman of a woman; Bithus Atto, slave of Heius Marcus; Blossia, daughter of Lucius. I bind fast all these people to the infernal gods so that none of them has anyone ... is able to, and not...anyone is able to do. I dedicate this(?) to the infernal gods so that they act accordingly.

SD 70

Origin: Calvi Risorta, Italia. Necropolis.
Date: First half of the first century.
Bibliography: DT 191; dfx 1.5.1/1; LCT 29.
Notes: Each line is written at 90 degrees to the previous.

Side A
Dite (=Dispater) inferi C(aium) Babu-
llium et foto<t>r<icem> eius
Tertia<m> Salvia<m>

Side B
Dite (=Dispater) [pr]om[i]s<s>um

Quartae Satiae
recipite inferis

Pluto and the underworld gods, (I hand over) Gaius Babullius and his fucker Tertia Salvia. Pluto, receive into the underworld the promise of Quarta Satia.

SD 72

Origin: Pompeii, Italia. Attached to the tomb of Publius Vesonius Phileros.
Date: Unknown.
Bibliography: dfx 1.5.4/3; LCT 209.
Notes: inscribed on a piece of slate.

hospes paullisper morare
si non est molestum et quid evites
cognosce amicum hunc quem
speraveram mi\<hi\> esse ab eo mihi accusato-
res subiecti et iudicia instaurata deis
gratias ago et meae innocentiae omni
molestia liberatus sum qui nostrum mentitur
eum nec di penates nec inferi recipient

Stranger, stay a short while if it is not too troublesome, and learn what to avoid. This man, who I hoped was a friend of mine, brought prosecutors to me and instigated legal proceedings. I am grateful to the gods and my innocence: I am free from all trouble. He who deceived us, may he not receive the Penates nor the underworld.

SD 101

Origin: Pula, Italia. Grave.
Date: Mid second century.
Bibliography: dfx 1.7.5/1; LCT 41.
Notes: folded.

Caecilius Honoratus
Mindius Donatus
Mindius Charmides
Mindius Zoticus

Mindius Hermes
Mindius Maleus
Mindus Narcissus
Mindius Eititeus
Marcius Soter
Decidius Hister
Decidia Certa
Minervius Epaphroditus
Lucifer disp(ensator)
Lucifer adiutor coloni
Vitalis disp(ensator)
Trophimus
Trophimus alius
Anconius qui vilicavit
Tertius
Amandus
Viator

Caecilius Honoratus, Mindius Donatus, Mindius Charmides, Mindius Zoticus, Mindius Hermes, Mindius Maleus, Mindius Narcissus, Mindus Eititeus, Marcius Soter, Decidius Hister, Decidia Certa, Minervius Epaphroditus. Lucifer the treasurer, Lucifer the helper of the farmer, Vitalis the treasurer, Trophimus, the other Trophimus, Anconius who worked as an overseer, Tertius, Amandus, Viator.

SD 102

Origin: Pula, Italia. Grave.
Date: Mid second century.
Bibliography: dfx 1.7.5/2; LCT 42.
Notes: folded.

[Mind]ius Narcissus
Mindius Maleus
Decidius Hister
Decidia Certa
Minervius Epaphroditus
Me[nande]r(?)
Lu[cifer d]ispensator

Lucifer alius
Amandus dispensator
Vitalis dispensator
Trophimus qui dispensavit
Anconius qui vilicavit
Viator colonus
[Sept]imius(?) Sabinianus
Flavius Hedistus
Annius Calvo
Annius Civilis

Mindius Narcissus, Mindius Maleus, Decidius Hister, Decidia Certa, Minervius Epaphroditus. Menander, Lucifer the treasurer, the other Lucifer, Amandus the treasurer, Vitalis the treasurer, Trophimus who managed the expenses, Anconius who worked as an overseer, Viator the farmer. Septimius Sabinianus, Flavius Hedistus, Annius Calvo, Annius Civilis.

SD 109

Origin: Marsala, Italia. Grave.
Date: Second or third century.
Bibliography: AE 1997, 737; NGCT 79 (trans); dfx 1.11.1/1.
Notes: The Latin is at 90 degrees to the Greek and might be unrelated.

Side A
Καταδέω Ζωπυρίωνα τᾶς Μυμβυρ παρὰ Φερσε-
φόναι καὶ Τιτάνεσσι καταχθονίοις καὶ παρὰ
π[ρ]ιχομένοισι νεκύοις *vacat* ἐς τοὺς ἀτελέστους καὶ παρ-
ὰ [-]αρίαις Δάματρος παρ' ἀπευχομέ[ν]α[ισ]ιν
καταδέω δέ νιν ἐμ βολίμωι α[ἴσθησιν ?]
αὐτοῦ καὶ ψυχὴν αὐτοῦ ὡς μὴ δύν[αται ---]ν
λαλία[ν] καταδέω δέ νιν ἐμ βολί[μ]ωι σ[ωφρο]-
[σ]ύν(αν) [α]ὐτὰν καὶ νοῦν καὶ ψυ[χήν]

Side B
[Καταδέω] δὲ ὅπως
[μὴ δύνανται] ἀντία
[λέγειν] μ⟨ή⟩τε πο[ιεῖν]
Iunius

Septumius
C Ac<i>nus
M An(n)ius
L Umbonius
M Nautius
M Rustius
L Nautius
Umbonia

I bind down Zopyrion son of Mumbur before Persephone and before the underground Titans and before the abominating (male) dead. <And I bind him down> also before the priestesses of Demeter and before (the) abominating (female dead). And I bind him down in lead, him and his mind and soul, so that he will be unable to speak in opposition. And I bind her down in lead . . . her and her mind and her soul.

I bind them down so that they will be unable to speak or act against (me)

Iunius, Septumius, Caius Acinius, Marcus Annius, Lucius Umbonius, Marcus Nautius, Marcus Rustius, Lucius Nautius, Umbona.

SD 117

Origin: Bologna, Italia. Exact context unknown.
Date: Fourth or fifth century.
Bibliography: dfx 1.1.2/1; Sánchez Natalias 2011 (trans); LCT 3.
Notes: Sánchez Natalías argues that this and the next tablet are part of the same curse. Between the *voces magicae* at the top is a drawing of a standing figure with crossed hands and six snakes coming from its head.

ΦωΡΒΗ	Ψιαο	τιωΡ
ΦωΡΒεΘ	Βραι	ΒαΡιω
ΦωΡΒεΝ	ω	ΒαθακαΡ
ΦωΡΒι		PHO
ΦωΡΒΙ	Por	ιαγαακ[---]
ΦωΡΡα	cel-	CHθ [-]o
	lus	
Porcellu	mo-	Porcel[lus]
	lomedicu	medicu[s--]

molomedicu interficite omn[e---]
corpus caput tente<s> oculus[---]
[mor(?)]t<u>os facite Porcellu<m> et [mau]-
rilla<m> u<xo>re<m> ipsius dite[---]
em corpus omnis menbra [---]
bisc[e]d[a] Porcelli qui iced[---]
[cada]t languat et ru[at---]

Porcello. Porcello the veterinarian. Porcello the physician. The veterinarian. Destroy his entire body, his head, teeth, eyes ... Let Porcello and his wife Maurilla be ... May all Porcello's body, limbs, entrails ... disintegrate, languish and collapse.

SD 117

Origin: Bologna, Italia. Exact context unknown.
Date Fourth or fifth century.
Bibliography: dfx 1.1.2/3 and 1.1.2/4; Sanchez Natalias 2011 (trans); LCT 5.
Notes: A drawing of a bound figure with crossed hands.

At 90 degrees to the rest of the text
[Po]rcellu[s et]
[m au]
rill[am]
ipsi us
molo medicus

On the arms of the bound figure
Porcellus
Porcellus

Below the figure
           mulo Porce[llus mu]-
            lo molomedico[---]
interficite eum occidite eni[ca]
te profucate Porcellu<m> et Mau
rilla<m> u<xo>re<m> ips[i]us anima cor-
nata epar isi[---]e mr
us

Another fragment

[------]
[---febres(?)] tercinias quartana[s-
pal(?)]oris frigora morb<os> em[---
--P]orcellus m<u>lomedicus [---
--a]rdor autus aton ad[---
---]aseimi amor[-]ab ace[---
---]gymni amorfus pant[---
---]meras ceoras macas[---
---]ctrias catapomas si[---
---]as enpractias leson[---
---]eisopeisos[-]t[---
---]e s[---]

Porcello the veterinarian and Maurilla his (wife). Porcello. Porcello. Veterinarian. Porcello the veterinarian. Destroy, crush, kill, strangle Porcello and his wife Maurilla. Their soul, heart, buttocks, liver . . .

. . . tertian, quartan (fevers?) . . . pallor, cold, disease . . . Porcello the veterinarian . . . fire . . .

SD 118

Origin: Bologna, Italia, exact context unknown.
Date: Fourth or fifth century.
Bibliography: dfx 1.1.2/2; Sanchez Natalias 2012b (trans); LCT 4.
Notes: folded. Between the *voces magicae* at the top is a drawing of a standing figure with crossed hands and six snakes coming from its head.

ΦωPBH	YIA	TIωP
ΦωPBEN	BIPA	BαPIω
ΦωPBEO	ω	BαθαcωP
ΦωPBI		KαNΦI
		PHO
ΦωPBω		OEBPNB
ΦωPBI		ιαYααkεPBε
	Fis	
ΦωPPω	tu<m>	LHO Fistu[m]

Fistu\<m\> sina	occi	sinator\<em\> d[-]
	dite	CAEQUEM[---
---t]ore\<m\> occi-	inic	TIU occi[dite]
[di]te eni-	ate	QUAN[---
[ca]te		

[occid]ite in\<i\>ca[te] Fi[stum]
Fistus diffloiscat (=diffluat) langu\<e\>at [m(?)]
ergat et disuluite omni[a]
menbra omnis (=omnia) viscida ipsius Fisti dis\<s\>olbite membra biscida la[ng]u\<e\>a[t]
runpite binas ipsiu[s]
runpite omnis (=omnia) menb[ra]
Fisti sinat[o]ris[---]

Crush, kill Fistus the senator. Crush, kill Fistus. Crush ... Fistus the senator ... Crush, kill Fistus the senator. May Fistus dilute, languish, sink and may all his limbs dissolve, all his entrails (?) of Fistus. Dissolve his limbs and entrails (?), may he languish. Burst his veins (?), break all his limbs. Fistus the senator ...

SD 119

Origin: unknown but possibly Campania, Italia. Possibly in water.
Date: First century.
Bibliography: dfx 1.5.6/1; LCT 35.
Notes: Pierced twice before folding. Both nails still in situ.

Column A.	*Column B.*
Philocomus	tabesca(n)t
Antioc\<h\>us	dom\<i\>nis non pla-
P\<h\>arnace\<s\>	cea(n)t
Sosus	eide\<m\> (=item) his quorum nom[ina] hic sunt
Erato	perea[nt] quo\<d\> e\<t\> pla-
Epidia	cean\<t\> peculio il\<l\>o-
	rum dicta facta
	ad inferos

May Philocomus, Antiochus, Pharnaces, Sosus, Erato (and) Epidia waste away: they have not pleased their master. These same (slaves), whose names are here, should pass away, and should be pleased with their property. Their words and deeds to the infernals.

SD 120

Origin: Mérida, Hispania. Exact context unknown.
Date: Unknown.
Bibliography: DT 122; dfx 2.3.1/1; Tomlin 2010: (trans); LCT 219.
Notes: Inscribed on a marble slab.

Dea Ataecina Turi-
brig(ensis) Proserpina
per tuam maiestatem
te rogo obsecro
uti vindices quot mihi
furti factum est quisquis
mihi im<m>udavit involavit
minusve fecit [e]a[s res] q(uae) i(nfra) s(criptae) s(unt)
tunicas VI [p]aenula
lintea II in[dus]ium I cuius no?]m[en?] ignaro
i[---]ius

Goddess Ataecina of Turibriga, Proserpina, I ask you by your majesty, I beg you to avenge the theft which has been done me, whoever has changed, stolen, diminished the things which are written below. Six tunics, two linen cloaks, a shift(?). Whose name, I do not know ...

SD 121

Origin: Alcácer do Sal, Hispania. Temple.
Date: Second half of the first century.
Bibliography: Tomlin 2010 (trans); dfx 2.3.2/1; LCT 220.

Domine Meagre
invicte tu qui Attidis
corpus accepisti accipias cor-

pus eius qui meas sarcinas
su{p}stulit qui me compilavit
de domo Hispani illius corpus
tibi et anima<m> do dono ut meas
res invenia<m> tunc tibi <h>osta<m>
quadrupede<m> do<mi>no Attis voveo
si eu<m> fure<m> invenero dom<i>ne
Attis te rogo per tu<u>m Nocturnum
ut me quam primu<m> compote<m> facias

Unconquered Lord Megarus, you who received the body of Attis, may you receive the body of him who robbed me from the house of that Spaniard. I give and donate his body and soul to you, that I may find my property. I then promise you a four-footed sacrifice, Lord Attis, if I find that thief. Lord Attis, I ask you through your Nocturnus, to make me master of it as soon as possible.

SD 132

Origin: Écija, Hispania. Grave.
Date: Second half of the first century.
Notes: Nailed after folding.

gregs an[t]oniani veneta et russea quadriga
lascivi veri quadriga lascivi vetii qua[d]riga
margaritei qua[d]riga margaritei quadriga gelotis quadriga urbici quadriga ila-
ri quadriga eleni quadriga basilisci
quadriga nomantini quadriga barba-
rionis qua<d>riga calidromi quadriga lupi agitatores piramus agi-
tator[e]s et quadrigas antoniani patricium martialem
successum atiarionem
vaicus narcisus at-
sertor
tota grex antoniani

The stable of Antonianus, the Blues and Reds, the Quadriga of Lascivus Verus, the Quadriga of Lascivus Vetius, the Quadriga of Margariteus, the Quadriga of Margariteus, the Quadriga of Gelus, the Quadriga of Urbicus, the Quadriga of Hilarus, the Quadriga of Helenus, the Quadriga of Basiliscus, the Quadriga of Nomantinus, the Quadriga of Barbario, the Quadriga of Callidromus, the Quadriga of Lupus, the charioteers, Piramus, the charioteers and Quadrigas of Antonianus, Patricus, Martialis, Successus, Atiario, Vaicus, Narcissus, Adsertor: the whole stable of Antonianus.

SD 134

Origin: Ampurias, Hispania. Grave.
Date: 75-85.
Bibliography: dfx 2.1.1/3; LCT 48.
Notes: Written left to right and bottom to top.

Side A
Consilium Fulvi
legati Olossi-
tani Campanus
Fidentinus Augus(ti)
[---]o[---]

Side B
Fulvus legatus Au-
gusti Rufus legatus
Augusti Maturus
proqurator Augusti
legati atvocati Ind[i]-
cetanorum

Council of the legate Fulvus, the Olossitani legates, Campanus Fidentinus, the imperial ...

Fulvus, Augustan legate, Rufus, Augustan legate, Maturus, Augustan procurator, legate, advocates for the Indicetani.

SD 135

Origin: Ampurias, Hispania. Grave.
Date: 75-85.
Bibliography: dfx 2.1.1/4; LCT 49.
Notes: Written left to right and bottom to top.

Side A
[Oloss]itani
Sempronius
Campanus Fi-
dentinus atve-
{ve}rsari<i>
mei inique
ne int[er]sint

Side B
[Ful]vus legatus
[Aug]usti Rufus lega-
[tus Aug]usti Matu-
[rus] procurator
[Aug]usti consilium
legati atvoca-
ti Indice-
tano-
{ti Indicetano}
-ru[m]

May my adversaries, the Olossitani, Sempronius Campanus Fidentinus, not oppose me unfairly.

Fulvus the Augustan legate, Rufus the Augustan legate, Maturus the Augustan procurator, council of the legate, advocates of the Indicetani.

SD 136

Origin: Ampurias, Hispania. Grave.
Date: 75-85.
Bibliography: Gager 52 (trans); dfx 2.1.1/2; LCT 47.
Notes: Written left to right and bottom to top.

Side A
Maturus proqura-
tor Augusti consi-
lium legati
legati Indiceta-
norum
{Indicetanoru[m]}

Side B
Olossita[ni]
Titus Aurelius
Fulvus lega-
tus Augusti
Rufus legatus Au-
gus[ti]

Maturus, Augustan Procurator; council of the legate, (that is) the legate for the Indicetani; (the advocate?) for the Indicetani.

The Olossitani; Titus Aurelius Fulvus, Augustan legate; Rufus, Augustan legate.

SD 140

Origin: Sagunt, Hispania. Exact context unknown.
Date: Late first century.
Bibliography: dfx 2.1.3/1; LCT 51.
Notes: shaped like a footprint (intentionally?) and wrapped around a coin of Vespasian.

Quintula cum Fortunali sit semel et numquam

Quintula should never again be with Fortunalis.

SD 142

Origin: Sagunt, Hispania. Exact context unknown.
Date: First or second century.
Bibliography: dfx 2.1.3/3; Tomlin 2010 (trans); LCT 216.

CR Felicio Aure[lian(?)]i
rogat et mandat pequnia\<m\> quae a
me accepit Heracla conservus meum
ut inst{t}etur \<h\>uius senus o[c]el\<l\>us et
[v]ires q\<u\>icumqui sunt ari demando pequniam \<h\>onori sacri-
cola\<e\>

Felicio (the slave?) of Aurelianus asks and entrusts the money which Heracla my fellow slave received from me, that his bosom be attacked, his eye and strength, whoever they are ... I entrust the money to the honour of the priest.

SD 157

Origin: Montfo, Gallia. Pit.
Date: First century.
Bibliography: dfx 4.4.1/1; LCT 226

Side A
quomodo hoc plumbu\<m\> non
paret decadet sic deca-
dat aetas membra vita
bos gran{o}um mer\<x\> eoru\<m\> qui
mihi dolum malu\<m\> fecerunt
idem Asuetemeos
Secundina que illum tulit
et Verres Tearus

Side B
et Amarantis et
hoc omnia vobis dii
interdico in omni-
bus sortebus tam celebrare
Masitlatida concinere necra-
cantum Col[--]scantum et
omnes deos [---]
ta datus[---]

Just as this lead disappears and falls, thus falls their youth, limbs, life, ox, grain and goods, those who did me wrong, namely Asuetemeos, Secundina who stole it, and Verres Tearus

and Amarantis and all that is yours, oh gods, I forbid (them) by all spells to celebrate the Masitlatida and to sing the Necrocantus ... and all gods ... is given ...

SD 160

Origin: Chagnon, Gallia. Grave.
Date: Second or third century.
Bibliography: DT 111-2; Gager 53 (trans); dfx 4.3.1/1-2; LCT 67-8.
Notes: two sheets originally attached as a diptych. Found with puppy skeleton.

Sheet 1
denuntio personis infra-
scribtis Lentino et Tasgillo
uti adsin<t> ad Plutonem
<et at Proserpinam hinc a[beant]>
quomodo hic catellus nemin[i]
nocuit sic imqueolosiccodma nec
illi hanc litem vincere possint
quomodi nec mater huius Catelli
defendere potuit sic nec advo-
cati eorum e[os d]efendere {non}
possint sic il[lo]s [in]imicos
atracatetracati gal-
lara precata egdarata
hehes celata mentis ablata
{et ad Proserpinam hinc abeant}

Sheet 2
aversos ab hac l[i]te esse <debent> quomodi hic catellus aversus
est nec surgere potest{i}
sic nec illi sic tra<n>specti sin[t]
quomodo ille
quomodi in hoc m[o]nimont<o> (=monumento) ani-

malia ommutuerun<t> nec surgere possun<t> nec illi mut[i]
Atracatertracati gallara
precata egdarata he-
hes celata mentis abla-
ta

I command that the persons written below, Lentinus and Tasgillus, be off from here to Pluto and Persephone. Just as this puppy harmed no one, so (may they harm no one) and may they not be able to win this lawsuit; just as the mother of this puppy could not defend it, so may their lawyers be unable to defend them, and so may those (legal) opponents ATRACATETRACATI GALLARA PRECATA EGDARATA HEHES CELATA MENTIS ABLATA

be turned back from this suit; just as this puppy is twisted away and is unable to rise, so neither may they; they are pierced through, just as this is; just as in this tomb, beings have been silenced and cannot rise up, may they not ... ATRACATERTRACATI GALLARA PRECATA EGDARATA HEHES CELATA MENTIS ABLATA

SD 173

Origin: Maar (Trier Nord), Gallia. Grave.
Date: Second century.
Bibliography: DT 103; dfx 4.1.2/1; LCT 57.
Notes: Inscribed on a cinerary urn, all except 'Aprilis Kaesio' written when the clay was wet.

a b c d e f g h i k l m n o p r r s t u x y z

		Artus fututor	Aprilis Kaesio
Art<e> ligo dercomogni <filium> fututor	Fututor		

Artus (is a) fucker ... I bid Artus the fucker, (son of?) Dercomognus.

SD 176

Origin: Trier, Gallia. Amphitheatre.
Date: Fourth or fifth century.
Bibliography: dfx 4.1.3/2.

quidquid adh[ibent P]-
aga[n]us et advo[ca]-
tus <h>a[b]es

Whoever Paganus and (his?) advocate summon, you have.

SD 183

Origin: Trier, Gallia. Amphitheatre.
Date: Fourth century.
Bibliography: dfx 4.1.3/9; LCT 222.

Side A
Yibalfoqorim
Charaktêres
Ydmxfus
Inabihtriaro vestro [rogo?]
[Di]anam et Martem
vinculares ut me vin-
dicetis de ququma (=cucuma?)
Eusebium in ungulas
obligetis et me
vindicetis

Side B
Depos<i>tum Eusebium

I ask Diana and Mars, the binders, that you may redeem me from the hothead. You should bind Eusebius in claws and liberate me.

Eusebius has been deposited.

SD 205

Origin: Lydney Park, Britannia. Temple of Nodens.
Date: Unknown.
Bibliography: DT 106; RIB 306; Gager 99; Adams 1998; dfx 3.15/1; LCT 289.

Devo
Nodenti Silvianus
anil<l>um perdedit
demediam partem
donavit Nodenti
inter <eos> quibus nomen
Seniciani no<n> <i>llis
petmittas sanita-
tem donec perfera<t>
usque templum [No]-
dentis

To the god Nodens: Silvanus has lost his ring and given half (its value) to Nodens. Among those who are called Senicianus do not allow health until he brings it to the temple of Nodens.

SD 206

Origin: Bath, Britannia. Sacred spring.
Date: Second or third century.
Bibliography: DT 104; RIB 154; Tab Sulis 4 (trans); dfx 3.2/1; LCT 242.
Notes: Letters within each word reversed. Curse and names in different hands.

qu[i] mihi vilbiam in[v]-
olavit sic liqu<esc?>at com[o]<do> aqua
[---] qui eam [invol]-
avit Velvinna Ex[s]-
upereus Verianus Se-
verinus A<u>gustalis Com-
itianus
Minianus Catus
Germanill[a] Iovina

May he who has stolen my brooch (or cutting tool?) from me become as liquid as water ... who has stolen it. Velvinna, Exsupereus, Verianus, Severinus, Augustalis, Comitianus, Minianus, Catus, Germanilla, Iovina.

SD 210

Origin: Bath, Britannia, sacred spring.
Date: Fourth century.
Bibliography: Tab Sulis 5 (trans); dfx 3.2/6; LCT 244.
Notes: Folded once. Possibly two different hands.

[D]ocimedis
[p]erdidi<t> mani-
cilia dua qui
illas involavi<t>
ut mentes sua<s>
perd[a<t>] et
oculos su[o]s
in fano ubi
destina<t>

Docimedis has lost two gloves. (He asks) that (the person) who has stolen them should lose his minds [sic] and his eyes in the temple where (she) appoints.

SD 213

Origin: Bath, Britannia. Sacred spring.
Date: Third century.
Bibliography: Tab Sulis 8 (trans); Gager 94; dfx 3.2/8; LCT 246.
Notes: Pierced through 'Anniola' on both sides.

Side A
[d]eae Suli donavi [arge]-
nteolos sex quos per[didi]
a nomin[i]bus infrascrip[tis]
deae exactura (=exactio) est
Senicianus et Saturninus {sed}
et Ann[i]ola carta picta persc[ritpa]

Side B
An<n>[i]ola
Senicianus
Saturninus

I have given to the goddess Sulis the six silver coins which I have lost. It is for the goddess to exact (them) from the names written below: Senicianus and Saturninus and Anniola. The written page (has) been copied out. Anniola, Senicianus, Saturninus

SD 214

Origin: Bath, Britannia. Sacred spring.
Date: Third century,
Bibliography: Tab Sulis 9 (trans); dfx 3.2/9; LCT 186.
Notes: Folded five times.

Side A
Pet<it>io
{rove} <rogo?> te
Victoria vind<ex>
{Cun} Manici
Cunomolius
Minervina ussor (=uxor)
Cunitius ser<v>us
Senovara ussor (=uxor)
Lavidendus ser<v>us
Mattonius ser<v>us
Catinius Exsactoris
fundo eo
Methianus
[---] dono

Side B
[---ini?]micus
tpiasu
gineninusu [-]
[-]igienunus

A petition. (I ask) you Victory the Avenger(?)...Cunomolius (son?) of Minicus, Minervina (his?) wife, Cunitius (their?) slave, Senovara (his?) wife, Lavidendus (their?) slave, Mattonius (their?) slave, Catinius (son?) of Exsactor...Methianus ...I give...

    enemy(?)

SD 215

Origin: Bath, Britannia. Sacred spring.
Date: Second century.
Bibliography: Tab Sulis 10 (trans); dfx 3.2/10; LCT 247.
Notes: Pierced after inscribing.

Side A
Docilianus
Bruceri
deae sanctissim<a>e
Suli
devoveo eum [q]ui
caracellam meam
involaverit si
vir si femina si
servus si liber
ut[i e]um dea Sulis
maximo letum
[a]digat nec ei so-
mnum permit-

Side B
tat nec natos nec
nascentes do-
[ne]c caracallam
meam ad tem-
plum sui numi-
nis per[t]ulerit

Docilianus (son) of Brucerus to the most holy goddess Sulis. I curse him who has stolen my hooded cloak, whether man or woman, whether slave or free, so that the goddess Sulis should inflict the greatest death upon him and not allow him sleep or children now and in the future, until he has brought my hooded cloak to the temple of her divinity.

SD 221

Origin: Bath, Britannia. Sacred spring.
Date: Third century.

Bibliography: Tab Sulis 16 (trans); dfx 3.2/15.
Notes: Pierced.

Side A
Nomen
furis qui
latera

Side B
rqvet
donat{u}-
ur

The name of the thief who ... is given.

SD 235

Origin: Bath, Britannia. Sacred spring.
Date: Second century.
Bibliography: Tab Sulis 30 (trans); dfx 3.2/22; LCT 188.
Notes: Circular plate with beaded rim. Folded twice.

Severianus fil(ius) Brigomall<a>e
Patarnianus filius
Matarnus ussor (=uxor)
Catonius Potentini
Marinianus Belcati
Lucillus Lucciani
Aeternus Ingenui
Bellaus Bellini

Severianus son of Brigomalla; Patarnianus (his?) son; Matarnus (and his?) wife; Catonius (son of) Potentinus; Marinianus (son of) Belcatus; Lucillus (son of) Luccianus; Aeternus (son of) Ingenuus; Bellaus (son of) Bellinus.

SD 236

Origin: Bath, Britannia. Sacred spring.
Date: Second or third century.
Bibliography: Tab Sulis 31 (trans); dfx 3.2/23; LCT 249.

Notes: Folded three times.

si cis (=quis) vome-
rem Civilis
involavit
ut an[imam] su{u}a<m> in tem-
plo deponat
[si? n]o[n] vom-
[erem-] ub
[---si se]rvus
si liber si li-
bertinus [--]
unan[--] o
finem faci
[a]m

If anyone has stolen Civilis' ploughshare, (I ask) that he lay down his life in the temple [?unless] ... the ploughshare, whether slave or free or freedman ... I make an end to ...

SD 246

Origin: Bath, Britannia. Sacred spring.
Date: Second or third century.
Bibliography: Tab Sulis 41 (trans); dfx 3.2/33; LCT 258.
Notes: Folded.

[------]
[---dir]ipuit ut [eo]rum pretium
[et e]xigas hoc per sanguinem et sa-
[nitatem sua]m et suorum nec ante illos pati[a]r-
[is bibere? nec m]anducare nec adsellare nec
[meiere? ---]ius hoc [a]b{i}so<l>verit

... has stolen, that ... the price [of them and] exact this through [his] blood and [health] and (those) of his family, and not allow them [to drink or] eat or defecate or [urinate] before he has ... released (?) this.

SD 247

Origin: Bath, Britannia. Sacred spring.
Date: Second or third century.
Bibliography: Tab Sulis 42 (trans); dfx 3.2/34; LCT 259.

[---]a[-]e[-]na[---]
[qui?---] fecit do[no?---]
[---i]n fano Su[lis?---]
[------]

... has done ... given ... in the temple of Sulis ...

SD 250

Origin: Bath, Britannia. Sacred spring.
Date: Second or third century.
Bibliography: Tab Sulis 45 (trans); dfx 3.2/37; LCT 261.
Notes: Folded once.

Side A
dea Suli [---]
[------]
[------]
[---]is qu[i---]

Side B
si servus si liber <si> quicumq[ue---]
erit non illi permittas nec
oculos nec sanitatem nisi caecitatem
orbitatemque quoad vixerit
nisi haec ad fanum [---pertulerit?]

To the goddess Sulis ... whether slave or free, <if> whoever he shall be, you are not to permit him eyes or health unless blindness and childlessness so long as he shall live, unless [he return?] these to the temple.

SD 259

Origin: Bath, Britannia. Sacred spring.
Date: Second or third century.

Bibliography: Tab Sulis 54 (trans); dfx 3.2/46; LCT 266.

Side A
B+

Side B
[------]
conq[u]aer[or] tibi Sulis Arminia
<ut> Verecundinum Ter[en]ti(?) c[ons]umas
qui argentiolos duos mihi[---]
[---]revavit no[n il]l[i p]er-
mittas nec sedere nec iacere [ne]c
[---] a[m]bulare n[ec]
somn[um nec] sanitatem [illu?]m
quantocius consumas et inter[u]m
det[-]aestact[---]nus
[---]mensi[-]ion[---]
[no]n perveniat

...I Arminia, complain to you, Sulis, [that] you consume Verecundinus (son of) Terentius, who has [stolen ...] two silver coins from me. You are not to permit [him] to sit or lie [or ... or] to walk [or] (to have) sleep [or] health, [since] you are to consume (him) as soon as possible; and again ... [not] to reach ...

SD 271

Origin: Bath, Britannia, sacred spring.
Date: Third century.
Bibliography: Tab Sulis 66 (trans); dfx 3.2/57; LCT 273.
Notes: Folded nine times.

Exsuperius
donat pannum ferri
qui illi innoc[entiam? ---]nfam
tusc[---] Su-
lis si vir [si femin]a s[i] ser<v>us
si liber ho[c]
ill[---]
et[---]er[---]

suas inv[o]la[veru]n[t] s[i] vir
si femina s[ati]sfecerit
sanguin[e] ill[o]rum hoc
devindices [si?] q[u]is aenum mihi involav[i]t

Exsuperius gives an iron pan(?). (The person) who ... innocence for him ... of (?) Sulis, whether man [or woman], whether slave or free ... this ... and ... have stolen his ..., whether man or woman, is to have given satisfaction with their blood. You are to reclaim(?) this [if] anyone has stolen the vessel from me.

SD 299

Origin: Bath, Britannia. Sacred spring.
Date: Third or fourth century.
Bibliography: Tab Sulis 94 (trans); dfx 3.2/73; LCT 274.

Uricalus Do[c]ilosa ux[or] sua
Docilis filius suus et Docilina
Decentinus frater suus Alogiosa
nomina{a} eorum qui iuraverunt
{qui iuraverunt} ad fontem deae Suli\<s\>
prid\<i\>e idus Apriles quicumque illic per-
iuraverit deae Suli facias illum
sanguine suo illud satisfacere

Uricalus, Docilosa his wife, Docilis his son and Docilina, Decentinus his brother, Alogiosa: the names of those who have sworn \<who have sworn\> at the spring of the goddess Sulis on the 12th of April. Whosoever has perjured himself there, you are to make him pay for it to the goddess Sulis in his own blood.

SD 302

Origin: Bath, Britannia. Sacred spring.
Date: Fourth century.
Bibliography: Tab Sulis 97 (trans); dfx 3.2/76; LCT 275.

Side A
90 degrees to rest of text: primurudeum

Basilia donat in templum Martis ani-
l<l>um argenteum si ser<v>us si liber
m<e>dius fuerit vel aliquid de hoc
noverit ut sanguine et liminibus et

Side B
omnibus membris configatur vel et-
iam intestinis excomesis <om>nibus habe<at>
is qui anilum involavit vel qui medius
fuerit.

Primurudeum. Basilia presents to the temple of Mars (her) silver ring. If slave or free man has been involved, or knows anything about it, he may be accursed in (his) blood and eyes and all his limbs, or even with all his intestines eaten away: he who has stolen the ring or was a witness is done for.

SD 303

Origin: Bath, Britannia. Sacred spring.
Date: Fourth century.
Bibliography: Tab Sulis 98 (trans); Gager 96; dfx 3.2/77; LCT 276.

Side A
seu gens seu C-
h<r>istianus quaecumque utrum vir
[u]trum mulier utrum puer utrum puella
utrum s[er]vus utrum liber mihi Annia[n]-
o ma{n}tutene de bursa mea s<e>x argente[o]s
furaverit tu d[o]mina dea ab ipso perexi[g]-
e[--- eo]s si mihi per [f]raudem aliquam inde p-
reg[u]stum(?) dederit nec sic ipsi dona sed ut sanguinem suum eputes qui mihi hoc inrogaverit

Side B
Postum[inu]s Pisso
Locinna [A]launa
Materna Gunsula
C[an]didina Eutic<h>ius

Peregrinus
Latinus
Senicianus
Avitianus
Victor
Sco[ti]us
Aessicunia
Paltucca
Calliopis
Celerianus

Whether pagan or Christian, whosoever, whether man or woman, whether boy or girl, whether slave or free, has stolen from me, Annianus (son of) Matutina (?), six silver coins from my purse, you, lady goddess, are to exact [them] from him. If through some deceit he has given me ... do not give thus to him, but reckon as(?) the blood of him who has invoked this upon me.

Postuminus, Pisso, Locinna, Alauna, Materna, Gunsula, Candidina, Euticius, Peregrinus, Latinus, Senicianus, Avitianus, Victor, Scotius, Aessicunia, Paltucca, Calliopis, Celerianus.

SD 304

Origin: Bath, Britannia. Sacred spring.
Date: Third or fourth century.
Bibliography: Tab Sulis 99 (trans); dfx 3.2/78; LCT 277.
Notes: Line 2 is written retrograde.

execro \<eum\> qui involaverit qui\<d\> Deomiorix de hos-
{i}pitio suo perdiderit quicumque \<e\>r[it?] deus illum
inveniat sanguine et
vitae suae illud redemat

I curse (him) who has stolen, who has robbed Deomiorix from his house. Whoever (stole his) property, the god is to find him. Let him buy it back with (his) blood and his own life.

SD 307

Origin, Bath, Britannia. Sacred spring.
Date: Third or fourth century.
Bibliography: Tab Sulis 102 (trans); dfx 3.2/81.
Notes: Three conjoining fragments. Folded.

numen (=nomen) fur-
ti si se[r]<v>us
si l[ibe]r
si puer si pue
lla [---]
[------]
[------]

The name of the thief, whether slave or free, whether boy or girl ...

SD 337

Origin: Caerleon, Britannia. Amphitheatre.
Date: First or second century.
Bibliography: Gager 100; dfx 3.6/1; LCT 283.
Notes: Ansate plaque, pierced.

Dom<i>na Ne-
mesis do ti-
bi palleum (=pallium)
et galliculas
qui <sus>tulit non
redimat ni<si>
v[i]ta sanguine{i} su[o]

Lady Nemesis, I give to you a cloak and pair of shoes. Let him who stole them not redeem (himself?) except with his life, his blood.

SD 339

Origin: London, Britannia. Found below Telegraph Street, Moorgate, in an uncertain context.
Date: Second half of the first century.

Bibliography: RIB 7; dfx 3.14/1; LCT 198.
Notes: Pierced seven times.

Tretia\<m\> Maria\<m\> defico (=defigo) et
illeus vita\<m\> et me\<n\>tem
et memoriam [e]t iocine-
ra pulmones interm{x}ix{i}-
ta fa\<c\>ta cogitata memor-
iam sci (=sic) no\<n\> possit{t} loqui
\<quae\> sicreta si\<n\>t neque sinit a-
mere possit neque [-]
[---]cl[a]udo

I curse Tretia Maria and her life and mind and memory and liver and lungs mixed up together, and her words, thoughts and memory; thus may she be unable to speak what things are concealed, nor be able to love, nor ... I shut.

SD 343

Origin: London, Britannia. Amphitheatre drain.
Date: Second or third century.
Bibliography: Tomlin and Hassall 2005 (trans); dfx 3.14/6; LCT 288.

[d]eae dea[na]e dono
capitularem et fas-
[c]iam minus parte
tertia si quis hoc feci[t]
[s]i p[u]er si [p]uella s[i]
[s]er[vus] s[i liber]
don[o eum] nec p[er]
me [vi]v[ere] possit

I give to the goddess Diana (my) headgear and band less one-third. If anyone has done this, whether boy or girl, whether slave or free, I give him, and through me let him be unable to live.

SD 345

Origin: Clothall, Britannia. Grave.
Date: Unknown.
Bibliography: RIB 221 (trans); dfx 3.9/1; LCT 195.
Notes: Pierced by five nails, four of which survive. Also holes for thin lead wire, some of which survives. Inscription written right to left and partly disguised by unusual letter forms.

vetus
quomodo sanies
signeficatur
Tacita deficta (=defixa)

Tacita, hereby accursed, is labelled old like putrid gore.

SD 350

Origin: Ratcliffe-on-Soar, Britannia. Found during field walking.
Date: Unknown.
Bibliography: Hassall and Tomlin 1993 (trans); Mullen 2013; dfx 3.19/3; LCT 294.
Notes: Written in mirror-image capitals.

nomine Camulorigi<s> et Titocun<a>e molam quam perdederunt
in fanum dei devovi cuicimque num[e]n (=nomen) involasit
mola<m> illam ut sa<n>guin suum mittat usque diem quo
moriatur q[ui]cumque invo[l]a[sit] <f>urta moriatur
et pavlatoriam quicumque [illam] involasit
et ipse {moriato} mo[ri]atur quicumqu<e> illam
involasit et vertogn de <h>ospito vel bissacio (=vissacio)
quicumque illam involasit a de{v}o moriotur (=moriatur)

In the name of Camulorix and Titocuna I have dedicated in the temple of the god the mule which they have lost. Whoever stole that mule, whatever his name, may he let his blood until the day he dies. Whoever stole the objects of the theft, may he die; and the feedbag, whoever stole it, may he die also. Whoever stole it and ... from the house or the saddle bags, whoever stole it, may he die by the god.

SD 352

Origin: Wanborough, Britannia. Exact context unknown.
Date: Second half of the second century.
Bibliography: Rea 1972 (trans); dfx 3.23/1; LCT 307.

[---]depre[co]r te peto [---] evene [---]
[---p]eto iudicio tuo qu[i de me p]eculans[---]
[---]tum ne {l}il<l>i permittas bibere n[ec]
[esse nec vigilare nec do]rmire nec ambulare neque ullam
[partem vivere sinas illiu]s gentisve unde ille nascit[ur]
[---]eita ulla nec alumen-
[tum] pr[e<a>]ve<h>emente<r> loquantur et r[-]
[---]ugabatur certum sciu[n]t
[---] si
[---] meuere[c]am[eue]
[---]m]eor

... I pray to you, I beg ... I beg to deliver to your judgement (the man who) stole from me, that you do not permit him to drink nor eat nor wake nor sleep nor walk and that you do not allow any part (of him) to live or of the family from which he springs ... nor nourishment ... they may speak very violently ... they know for certain ... if ...

SD 361

Origin: Uley, Britannia. Temple.
Date: Third or fourth century.
Bibliography: Hassall and Tomlin 1989: 329–31 (trans); Uley 43; dfx 3.22/16; LCT 300.
Notes: Folded.

Deo Mercurio
Docilinus quaenm
Varianus et Peregrina
et Sabinianus qu[i] peco-
ri meo dolum malum in-
tulerunt et in t[e]rra pro-
locuntur (=proloquuntur) rogo te ut eos

max[i]mo [le]to adigas nec
eis sanit[atem nec] som-
num perm[itt]as nisi
ad te quod m[ihi] admi-
ni[strav]erint
redem[e]rint

Docilinus to the god Mercury ... Varianus and Peregrina and Sabinianus who have brought evil harm on my farm animal and are pronouncing it in earth (?). I ask that you drive them to the greatest death, permit them neither health nor sleep unless they redeem from you what they have administered to me.

SD 441

Origin: Caistor St Edmund, Britannia. Found in the River Tas.
Date: Unknown.
Bibliography: Hassall and Tomlin 1982 (trans); dfx 3.7/1; LCT 284.
Notes: Rolled.

a Nase[---]
eve<h>it Vroc[---]
sius fascia<m> et armi[lla]-
s cap<it>olare spectr[um(?)]
cufia<m> duas ocrias x vas-
a stagnea si mascel si me-
mina (=femina) si puer si pu<e>lla duas
ocri<as> si vull<u>eris factae sang<uine>
suo ut <i>llu<m> requerat{at} Neptu<nu>s
e<t> amictus e<t> cufia <et> arm<i>lla[e---]
denarii xv cape<t>olare tunc sanguin<e>
fasciam tenet fur e
c<h>arta s(upra) s(cripta) ratio<n>e

Vroc ... sius carries off from Nase ... a wreath and bracelets, a cap, a mirror (?), a head-dress, a pair of leggings, ten pewter vessels, whether he be man or woman, boy or girl. If you want the pair of leggings, they shall become yours at the price of his blood, so that he, Neptune, shall seek him out, and a cloak and headdress and bracelets, fifteen denarii, a cap. Then the thief holds onto the wreath at the cost of his blood in accordance with the transaction on the above written sheet.

SD 443

Origin: Pagan's Hill, Britannia. Exact unknown, but near a temple.
Date: First half of the third century.
Bibliography: Hassall and Tomlin 1984 (trans); dfx 3.18/1; LCT 291.
Notes: Folded.

[Deo Mercu]ri[o?---]
[---]mitr[--]pio[---]
in (denari)is III milibus cuius [de]mediam
partem tibi <dono> ut ita illum [e]xigas a Vassicil-
lo [---]pecomini filio et uxore sua quoniam
[per]rtussum (=percussum) quod illi de hospitio m[eo---]
[pec]ulaverint nec illis [p]ermittas sanit[a]-
[tem] nec bibere nec ma[n]d[u]care nec dormi[re]
[nec nat]os sanos habe[a]nt ne{s}si hanc rem
[meam] ad fanum tuum [at]tulerint iteratis
[pre]c[i]bus te rogo ut [ab ip]sis nominibus
[inimicorum] meorum hoc [percu]ssum recipe-
[atur?] perven[ia]t

[To the god Mercury?] ... in three thousand denarii, of which (I give) you half portion on condition that you exact it from Vassicillus the son of [...]cominus and from his wife, since the coin which they have stolen from my house. You are not to permit them health nor to drink nor to eat nor to sleep [nor] to have healthy [children] unless they bring this [my] property to your temple. With repeated [prayers] I ask you that this [coin?] may come to be recovered [from the very] names of my [enemies].

SD 450

Origin: Broomhill, Britannia. Exact context unknown (metal detectorist find).
Date: Unknown.
Bibliography: Hassall and Tomlin 1994 (trans); dfx 3.5/1; LCT 282.

Notes: Written in mirror-image capitals.

Side A
s<i> se<r>vus si [l]ib[e]<r> [qu]-
i [f]uravit su[st]uli-
t [ne ei] dimitte
[male]fic<i>um d<u>m
tu vindi[c]a[s]

Side B
ante dies
nov[e]<m> si pa-
[g]a[n]us si
mil[e]s [qui]
su[s]tu<l>it

(whoever) has stolen (it), taken (it), whether slave or free, do not forgive him his evildoing until you punish him

within nine days, whether civilian or soldier, (whoever) has taken (it).

SD 451

Origin: Hamble Estuary, Britannia. Found by metal detectorist on foreshore.
Date: Second half of the fourth century.
Bibliography: Tomlin 1997 (trans); dfx 3.11/1; LCT 285.
Notes: Rolled.

domine Neptune
t<i>b<i> d<o>no <h>ominem qui
[so]l<i>dum involav[it] Mu-
coni et argenti[olo]s
sex ide<o> dono nomi<n>a
qui decepit si mascel si
femina si pu{u}er si pu{u}e-
lla ideo dono tibi Niske
et Neptuno vitam vali-
tudinem sangu<in>em eius
qui conscius fueris eius
deceptionis animus

qui hoc involavit et
qui conscius fuerit ut
eum decipias furem
qui hoc involavit sangu<in>em
ei{i}us consumas et d-
ecipias domin[e] Ne[p]-
tune

Lord Neptune, I give you the man who has stolen the solidus and six argentioli of Muconius. So I give the names who took them away, whether male or female, whether boy or girl. So I give you, Niskus, and to Neptune the life, health, blood of him who has been privy to that taking-away. The mind which stole this, and which has been privy to it, may you take it away. The thief who stole this, may you consume his blood and take it away, Lord Neptune.

SD 456

Origin: Leicester, Britannia. House, perhaps built into the wall of a bath-suite.
Date: Second or third century.
Bibliography: AE 2008: 792; Tomlin 2009 (trans).

d{a}eo Maglo <do> eu{u}m qui fr<a>udum
fecit de pa<e>d<ag>o<g>io <do> el{a}eum qui
furtum <fecit> de pa<e>da<g>o<g>ium {sa<g>um}
qui sa<g>um Servandi invola-
vit
S[il]vester Ri<g>omandus
S[e]nilis Venustinus
Vorvena
Calaminus
Felicianus
Ruf{a}edo
Vendicina
Ingenuinus
Iuventius
Alocus
Cennosus
Germanus
Senedo

Cunovendus
Regalis
Ni<g>ella
[[S[enic]ianus]]
do ant{a}e nonum diem
illum tollat
qui sa<g>um involavit
Servandi

I give to the god Maglus him who did wrong from the slave-quarters; I give him who (did) theft <the cloak> from the slave-quarters; who stole the cloak of Servandus. Silvester, Ri(g)omandus, Senilis, Venustinus, Vorvena, Calaminus, Felicianus, Rufedo, Vendicina, Iugenuinus, Iuventius, Alocus, Cennosus, Germanus, Senedo, Cunovendus, Regalis, Ni(g)ella, Senicianus (deleted). I give (that the god Maglus), before the ninth day, take away him who stole the cloak of Servandus.

SD 462

Origin: Krefeld-Gellep, Germania. Grave.
Date: Second half of the first century.
Bibliography: Blänsdorf 2014.
Notes: folded. First two lines are 90 degrees to rest of the text. Names written right to left.

como (=quomodo) hoc perversum scriptum est sic
illos dei spernent
Theudocsius
Lupicinus
Iustinianus
Leontius
Terentianus
Aelario
Hermoginis
Mastidius
conmo (=quomodo) <h>oc perversum
est sic no<n> pos[---]o
addi nilum (=nihilum)
cui possit

Just as this writing is perverse, so will the gods despise them: Theudocsius, Lupicinus, Iustinianus, Leontius, Terentianus, Aelario, Hermoginis, Mastidius. Just as this is perverse, so shall they not be able to(?) ... Nothing should be added to this.

SD 464

Origin: Cologne, Germania. Grave.
Date: Mid first century.
Bibliography: LCT 100.
Notes: Written retrograde.

Side A
Vaeraca sic res tua
perve<r>se agas quomodo hoc
perverse scriptu<m> est

Side B
Quidquid exop[ta]s nob[i]s
in caput tuum
eveniat

Vaeraca, thus it is with your case: you act perversely, even as this writing is perverse.

Whatsoever you wish for us shall come down on your head.

SD 467

Origin: Bad Kreuznach, Germania. Grave.
Date First or second century.
Bibliography: DT 95; dfx 2.1.4/2; LCT 73.
Notes: Folded.

Side A
Fructus Gra-
cilis et Aur<e>um
adi<u>torium
def[ero]

i[nfer]-
ris

Side B
sic non pos-
sit respo[nde]-
re qua<e>s[tionibus]

I bring Fructus Gracilis and Aureus the adiutorium to the infernals.

Thus may he not be able to respond to questioning.

SD 468

Origin: Bad Kreuznach, Germania. Grave.
Date: Second half of the first century.
Bibliography: DT 96; dfx 5.1.4/3; LCT 74.
Notes: Rolled.

Side A
inimicorum
nomina ad
[---]lum
inferos
[------]

Side B
inimicorum nomina
Optatus Silonis ad infe-
ros
Faustus Ornatus(?)
Terentius Attisso
Atticinus Ammonis
Latinus Valeri<i>
Adiutor Iuli<i>
Tertius Domiti<i>
Mansuetus Senodatium(?)
Montanus materiarius
Aninius Victor
Quartio Severi

Sinto Valentis
Lutumarus lanius
Similis Crescentis
Lucanus Silonis
Communis Mercatoris
Publius offector
Aemilius Silvanus

Right margin.
Cossus Matuini

The names of the enemies (are given) to ... the infernals.

The names of the enemies to the infernals: Optatus son of Silo, Faustus Ornatus, Terentius Attisso, Atticinus son of Ammo, Latinus son of Valerius, Adiutor son of Iulius, Tertius son of Domitius, Masuetus son of Senodatius, Montanus the timber merchant, Aninius Victor, Quartio son of Severus, Sinto son of Valens, Lutumarus the butcher, Similis son of Crescens, Lucanius son of Silo, Communis son of Mercator, Publius the dyer, Aemilius Silvanus, Cossus son of Matuinus.

SD 469

Origin: Bad Kreuznach, Germania. Grave.
Date: Second half of the first century.
Bibliography: DT 97; dfx 5.1.4/4; LCT 75.

Side A
data nomina
ad inferas larvas

Side B
dis manibus hos v(oveo?)
L(ucium) Celi(um) C(aium) Haeb[---]
et siquos alios hos[tes]
habeo
neca illa nom[ina]

These names have been given to the infernal evil spirits.

I vow these to the Manes: Lucius Celius, Gaius Haeb ... and if I have any other enemies. Kill these names.

SD 470

Origin: Bad Kreuznach, Germania. Grave.
Date: Second half of the first century.
Bibliography: DT 98; dfx 5.1.4/5; LCT 76.
Notes: Folded

Sinto Vale<n>tis sive alii inimici
Sinto Valentinus inim<i>cus sic com<o>di (=quomodo) plumbum
subsidet sic Sintonem et Martialem Sinto[nis]
et adiutorium Sintonis et quisquis contra
Rubrium fr[atre]m et me Quaritonem
si qui<s> contravenerit Sintonem et aduito-
rium eius Sintonis defero ad infero<s>
sic nusquam contra nos [inve]nisse(?) respon[sio]-
nis cum loquantur inimici sic [d]esumat
non parentem tanquam inferos

Sinto Valentis or any other enemies. Sinto Valentinus the enemy. Just as this lead will fall, so shall fall Sinto and Martialis of Sinto and the assistant of Sinto and whoever is against Rubrius my brother and me Quartio, if anyone will have opposed (us), I give Sinto and the assistant of Sinto to the infernals. Just as nowhere against us ... of an answer, when enemies speak. In the same way that he does not choose a parent, he does not choose the infernals.

SD 472

Origin: Bad Kreuznach, Germania. Grave.
Date: Second half of the first century.
Bibliography: DT 100; dfx 5.1.4/7; LCT 78.

Side A
Nomina
data [dela]-
ta le[gata]

ad inferos
u[t] illos per vim
[c]onrip[i]ant (= corripiant)

Side B
Silonia<m>
Surum Cae-
  nu<m>
Secundum
ille te
<s>ponsus pro-
cat il<l>um amo

The names have been given, delivered, entrusted to the infernals, so that they seize them by force.

Silonia, Surus, Caenus, Secundus. That which (or 'he who'?) has been vowed urges you. I love him.

SD 473

Origin: Bad Kreuznach, Germania. Grave.
Date: first half of the second century.
Bibliography: DT 101; dfx 5.1.4/8; LCT 79.
Notes: Folded.

inimici et inimici
Caranita[n]i Abilius Iu<v>enis
Sabinus ap<p>aritor Arria Dardisa Optatus
Silonis Privatu[s Se]veri Cossus Maesi
Marcus aerari[us] Atta Marci ux{s}or
Camula ux{s}o[r] Gamati Ambiti Val[erius]
Ciri Atticinus [Am]monis Terentius Atti-
so Iulia Attisonis Narcis<s>us Caliphon[t]is
Cali[pu]nti[s e]t Pudentis et Pude<n>s
[---]ssia[---]us Albus Vicinus
[---]nsi[---]

left margin
sic te morbo a<d>dicant dii m[anes]

right margin
[---]dii inferi[---]sunt

The enemies and enemies of Caranitanus: Abilius Iuvenis, Sabinus the clerk of the court, Arria Dardisa, Optatus son of Silo, Privatus son of Severus, Cossus son of Maesus, Marcus the coppersmith, Atta the wife of Marcus, Camula the wife of Gamatus Ambitus, Valerius son of Cirus, Atticinus son of Ammo, Terentius Attiso, Iulia (wife of) Attiso, Narcissus son of Caliphons, Calipuntis and Pudentus and Pudens ... Albus Vicinus ... thus should the eternal shades abandon you to sickness ... the infernal gods are ...

SD 477

Origin: Frankfurt, Germania. Grave.
Date: First half of the second century.
Bibliography: dfx 5.1.2/2; LCT 71.

Side A
[Do? i]nimicos Sexti ut
[s]ic non [p]ossint [con-
t]ra Sextum veni[re]
nec agero quicq[uam]
possint [u]t sic [sint?]
vani et muti q[uomo?]-
di et illi qui in
itoac

Side B
lotum loqui Va[le]-
ntinus et [Fron?]-
to et Ripanus et Le[---]
et Iuventin[us?]
et Luci[u]s et [---] Gar[---]
[F]rontonem [---]
[---]li adversari[---]
sint vani et m[uti]

[qu]omodi ista gar<r>u[la]
[avi]s [---]

(I give?) the enemies of Sextus, thus in this way they may not be able to go against Sextus nor do anything, thus in this way they should be useless and mute just as those, who in . . .

. . . to speak. Valentinus and Fronto and Ripanus and Le . . . and Iuventinus . . . and Lucius and . . . Fronto . . . the enemies . . . be useless and mute like this talkative bird(?)

SD 478

Origin: Frankfurt, Germania. Grave.
Date: Mid second century.
Bibliography: dfx 5.1.2/1; LCT 70.

Side A
rogo mane[s et(?) dii(?)]
inferni ut [Ma]-
rius Fronto [adv]-
ersariu[s] Sex[tii]
sit vanus neq-
ue loqui pos-
[s]it contra
[S]extum ut F[r]onto fiat
mutus q-
[um] (= cum) accesser[it]

Side B
Consular-
[e]m ut sit
mutus ne-
que poss[it]
loqui ne-
que qui[c]quam ag[e]-
re tanqu-
am nullo (=nullum)
ad inf[eros]
re[ligatum(?)]

I ask the spirits of the dead and the infernal gods that Marius Fronto, enemy of Sextus, be untrustworthy and not be able to speak against Sextus, thus Fronto is made mute when he will approach the consular legate, thus he is mute and not able to speak or to do anything, just as nothing has been bound to those below.

SD 479

Origin: Rottweil, Germania. Unknown context.
Date: Late first or second century.
Bibliography: dfx 5.1.7/1; LCT 230.
Notes: Written retrograde on ansate tablet. Some letters upside down. Pierced.

Side A
fib<u>lam Gnatae
qui involavit aut
qui melior est animi
conscios ut illum
aut illam aversum faci-
ant di<i> sicut hoc est

Side B
aversum et qui
res illaeus sus-
tulit

Whoever has stolen the brooch of Gnata, or whoever is an accomplice. As the gods make that (man?) or that (woman?) wrong like this (word) is

wrong, and whoever has stolen that thing.

SD 482

Origin: Groß-Gerau, Germania. House.
Date: Late first or second century.
Bibliography: AE 2004, 1006; LCT 228.
Notes: Folded. Found with an *as* of Vespasian.

Side A
deum max{s}ime Atthis Tyranne
totumque duodecatheum comme-

ndo deabus iniurium fas ut me vindic-
<e>tis a Priscil<l>a Caranti (filia) quae nubere er<r>a-
vit per matrem deum vestrae ut
[v]indicate sacra Pater[na]
P[ri]scil<l>[a]
pere[at]

Side B
per matrem deum intra dies C(?) cito
vindicate numen vestrum magnum
a Priscilla quae detegit sacra Pris-
cillam <n>usquam nullam numero nu[p]-
sit gentem tremente Priscilla
quam errante

Greatest of all gods, Lord Atthis, of all the twelve gods. I commend to the goddesses my unjust fate, that you may avenge me to Priscilla, daughter of Carantus, who married mistakenly. Through your great mother of the gods, avenge the secrets of Paternus (or the paternal secrets?). Priscilla should perish.

Through the mother of the gods, avenge your great divinity soon, within one hundred days, to Priscilla who betrays the sacred rituals. I consider Priscilla to be nothing and no-one. She married a scoundrel. Priscilla made such a mistake.

SD 483

Origin: Groß-Gerau, Germania, Unknown.
Date: First century.
Bibliography: AE 2007, 1049; LCT 229.
Notes: Rolled.

<h>umanum qui{s}
sustulit Verionis
palliolum sive res
illius qui illius minus
fecit ut illius mentes
memorias deiectas sive
mulierem sive eas cuius
Verionis res minus fecit

ut illius manus caput
pedes vermes cancer ver-
mitudo interet membr-
a medullas illius interet

The person who stole the cloak of Verio or his possessions, he who made his possessions smaller, thus his thoughts and memories have been destroyed, whether a woman or those who have reduced the property of Verio; worms, tumours and vermin will invade his hands, head and feet, they will invade his limbs and marrow.

SD 484

Origin: Mainz, Germania. Temple of Magna Mater.
Date: 65–130.
Bibliography: dfx 5.1.5/4; DTM 15; LCT 91.

Side A
pri

Side B
Five lines around edges.
Prima Aemilia Nar-
cissi agat quidquid co-
nabitur quidquid aget
omnia illi inver-
sum sit

Nine lines in centre
sic illa nuncquam
quicquam florescat

amentita surgat a-
mentita suas res agat
quidquid surget om-
nia interversum sur-
gat prima Narcissi
aga<t> como (=quomodo) haec carta
nuncquam florescent

May this befall Prima Aemilia, (the lover?) of Narcissus: whatever she will attempt, whatever she will do, let it all go wrong. Insanely she should rise, and insanely go about her business. Whatever shall rise, so shall all (her things?) rise wrongly. May this befall Prima, (the lover?) of Narcissus: just as this letter will never flourish, so shall she never flourish.

SD 486

Origin: Mainz, Germania. Temple of Mater Magna.
Date: 65–130.
Bibliography: DTM 5; LCT 85.
Notes: Rolled.

Side A
Bone sancte Atthis tyran-
ne adsi<s> advenias Libera-
li iratus per omnia te rogo
domine per tuum Castorem
Pollucem per cistas penetra-
les des ei malam mentem
malum exitum quandius
vita vixerit ut omni cor-
pore videat se emori praeter oculos

Side B
neque se possit redimere
nulla pe{r}cunia nullaque re
ne<que> abs te neque ab ullo deo
nisi ut exitum malum
hoc praesta rogo te per maiestatem tuam

Good holy Att(h)is, Lord, help (me), come to Liberalis in anger. I ask you by everything, Lord, by your Castor (and) Pollux, by the boxes of the sanctuary, give him a bad mind, a bad death, so long as he lives, so he may see himself dying all over his body, except the eyes and that he cannot redeem himself with money or anything else, neither from you nor from some other god, except with a bad death. Perform this, I ask you by your majesty.

SD 488

Origin: Mainz, Germania. Temple of Magna Mater.
Date: 65–130.
Bibliography: DTM 11; LCT 236.

Side A
mando et rogo
religione ut man-
data exagatis
Publium Cutium
et Piperionem et

Side B
Placida et Sacra
filia eius sic illorum
membra liquescan<t>
quatmodum hoc plum-
bum liquescet ut eo-
ru<m> exsitum sit

I hand over and ask with attention to ritual, that you require from Publius Cutius and Piperion the return of the goods entrusted to them. Also

Placida and Sacra her daughter: thus may their limbs melt away, as this lead will melt away, so that it is their death.

SD 490

Origin: Mainz, Germania. Temple of Mater Magna.
Date: 65–130.
Bibliography: DTM 4; LCT 87.
Notes: Possibly two different hands. Folded.

Side A
Tiberius Claudius Adiutor

in megaro eum rogo te Ma-
t[e]r Magna megaro tuo re-
cipias et Attis domine te
precor ut hu<n>c <h>ostiam accep-
tum <h>abiatis et quit aget aginat sal et aqua illi fiat ita tu
facias dom<i>na it quid cor eocnora (= iecinora)
c<a>edat

Side B
devotum defictum
illum menbra
medullas {aa}
nullum aliud sit
Attis Mater Magn[a]

Tiberius Claudius Adiutor: in his Megaron I ask you, Mater Magna that you may receive him into your Megaron. And Lord Attis, I beseech you, just as you (pl.) shall accept this offering, and what he does and undertakes, so shall it be as salt and water for him. So you should do, Lady, that which kills the heart (and) the liver.

Cursed and bound, those in limbs and marrow. Nothing else should be, Attis, Mater Magna.

SD 491

Origin: Mainz, Germania. Temple of Magna Mater.
Date: 65–130.
Bibliography: DTM 1; LCT 231.
Notes: Rolled. Each side written in a different hand.

Side A
Mater magna te rogo
p[e]r [t]ua sacra et numen tuum
Gemella fiblas meas quails
sustulit sic illam requis
adsecet ut nusquam sana si[t]
quomodo galli se secarunt

sic ea\<m?\> velis nec se secet sic uti
planctum ha[be]at quomodo
et sacrorum deposierunt
in sancto sic et tuam vitam
valetudinem Gemella
neque hosti\<i\>s neque auro neque argento redi-
mere possis a matre
deum nisi ut exitum
tuum populus spectet
Verecundam et Pater-
nam sic illam tibi com-
mendo Mater deum
magna rem illorum
in aecrumo deo vis qua-
le rogo co\<n\>summent[u]r
quomodo et res meas vire-
sque fraudarunt nec se
possint redimere
nec hosteis lanatis

Side B
nec plum{i}bis
nec auro nec ar-
gento redimere
a numine tuo
nisi ut illas vorent
canes
vermes adque
alia portenta
exitum quarum
populus spectet
tamquam quae {c} forro
[-] auderes comme[ndo]
duas
tamquaniuscauer{s}so
scriptas istas
ae riss[-]adricis[-]s[-]lon

a[-]illas si illas cistas
caecas aureas fecra
e[--] i [-]lo[--]as
ov[-]eis[-]mancas a

Mater Magna, I ask you, by your sanctuary and your divine power: Gemella, who has stolen my brooches, I ask you that she also cuts herself, so no part of her is healthy. Just as the galli have cut themselves ... so you should make her do. And may she not cut herself, so that she may lament. And just as they laid the holy objects in the temple, thus it should be with your life and your health, Gemella. Neither with sacrificial animals nor with gold nor with silver may you be able to redeem yourself from the Mother of the Gods unless the people watch your death. Verecunda and Paterna: thus I give that to you, great Mater Magna, their business ... as I ask that they are finished in the same way that they have cheated my fortune and my strength, and these should not be able to be redeemed with woollen offerings.

Neither through lead nor through gold nor through silver can they redeem themselves from your divine power, unless dogs, worms and other monsters devour them. May the people watch their death, just as ... two ... let justice turn back (?) ... these writings ... if those hidden golden boxes ...

SD 492

Origin: Mainz, Germania. Temple of Mater Magna.
Date: 65–130.
Bibliography: DTM 3; LCT 233.

Side A
rogo te domina Mater
Magna ut tu me vindices
de bonis Flori coniugis mei
qui me fraudavit Ulattius
Severus quemadmod[um]
hoc ego averse scribo sic illi

Side B
omnia quidquid agit quidquid
aginat omnia illi aversa fiant
ut sal et aqua illi eveniat

quidquid mi abstulit de bonis
Flori coniugis mei rogo te
domina Mater Magna ut tu
de eo me vindices

I ask you, Lady Mater Magna, that you avenge me in the matter of the fortune of my husband Florus. The one who has deceived me, Ulattius Severus: just as I write this wrongly, so shall

everything that he does, everything he undertakes, everything should go wrongly for him. Like salt and water shall it go for him. Everything he has taken away from me from the fortune of my husband Florus, I ask you Lady Mater Magna, that for this you avenge me.

SD 493

Origin: Mainz, Germania. Temple of Magna Mater.
Date: 65–130.
Bibliography: DTM 2; LCT 232.
Notes: Folded. Melted in a fire.

quisquis dolum malum adm[isit de] hac pecun[i]a [---]
ille melior et nos det[eri]ores sumus[---]
mater deum tu persequeris per terras per [maria per locos]
ar<i>dos et umidos per benedictum tuum et o[mnes--- qui de hac]
pecunia dolum malum adhibet ut tu perse[quaris illum--- quomodo]
galli se secant et praecidunt vir[i]lia sua sic il[le---] r s q
intercidat melore pec[tus ---] bisidis [ne]que se admisisse nec[---]
hostiis si[n]atis nequis t[---] neque sut[-]tis neque auro neque
argento neque ille solvi [re]fici redimi possit quomodo galli
bellonari magal[i] sibi sanguin[em] ferventem fundunt frigid[us]
ad terram venit sic et [---]cia copia cogitatum mentes [quem]-
admodum de eis gallo[r]u[m ma]glorum bellon[ariorum sanguinem/ritus?]
spectat qui de ea pecunia dolum malum [admisit sic illius]
exitum spectent et a[d qu]em modum sal in [aqua liques]-
cet sic et illi membra m[ed]ullae extabescant cr[a]s [veniat]
et dicat se admisisse nef[a]s d[e]mando tibi rel[igione]
ut me votis condamnes et ut laetus libens ea tibi referam
si de eo exitum malum feceris

Whoever has committed fraud regarding this money, ... that (person) is the better (off?) and we are the worse (off?) ... Mother of the gods, you will pursue (them?) across the lands, across [the seas], across the dry and wet places, through the one that you praise (= the dead Attis?) and [all] ... whoever has committed fraud regarding this money, you should pursue [them] ... [Just as] the galli cut themselves and chop off their genitals, so shall they ... cut their chest (?) ... and that he neither did anything wrong nor that he [... and you should not] allow, neither through sacrificial animals nor with ... nor with gold nor with silver, nor should that man be able to be saved or restored or redeemed. Just as the galli, the priests of Bellona and the magali shed hot blood (and) it comes to the earth cold, in this way also all the ... ability, thought, reason ... He/she will see the extent of the [powers] of the galli, the magali and the priests of Bellona ... [he/she who committed] the fraud of this money ... [so should] they watch his death. And just as salt [will become liquid] in (water), so shall his limbs and marrow waste away. Tomorrow [he should come], and say that he has committed the crime. I give to you the instruction in religious form, that you fulfil my vows and that I will happily and willingly reciprocate, when you have made over them a horrible death.

SD 494

Origin: Mainz, Germania. Temple of Magna Mater.
Date: 65–130.
Bibliography: DTM 6; LCT 234.

Quintum in hac tablua depon[o] aversum
se suisque rationibus vitaeque male consummantem ita uti galli bellonarive absciderunt concide-
runtne se sic illi abscissa sit fides fama faculit[a]s nec illi
in numero hominum sunt neque ille sit q[u]omodi et ille
mihi fraudem fecit sic illi sancta Mater Magn[a] et relegis[ti]
cuncta ita uti arbor siccabit se in sancto sic et illi siccet
fama fides fortuna faculitas tibi commendo Attihi d<o>mine
ut me vindices ab eo ut intra annum vertente[m ---] exitum
illius vilem malum

At 90 degrees to main text
ponit nom<en> huius mari-

tabus i si agatur ulla
res utilis sic ille nobis
utilis sit suo corpore
sacrari horr<e>bis

In this tablet I curse Quintus, who has turned away from himself and his life principles and has acted badly. Just as the galli or the priests of Bellona have cut themselves and lost their strength, so shall loyalty, reputation and ability be cut off, and just as they are not numbered among men, so should he not be. Just as he has betrayed me, so holy Mater Magna, take everything from him. Just as the tree in the temple will dry up, so shall his reputation, loyalty, his happiness, his ability dry up. To you I give the instruction, Lord Attis, that you free me from him, so that within the turn of a year ... his death, the low, evil.

He/she names the name of this man to the wives. If any useful thing is done, so he should be useful to us through his body. You should tremble at being cursed.

SD 498

Origin: Mainz, Germania. Temple of Mater Magna.
Date: 65–130.
Bibliography: DTM 12; LCT 237.
Notes: Rolled.

Side A
sic[--]s siccum quanmi
qu[omodo] di hoc liquescet
se [--- sic co]llum membra
me[du]lla peculium
d[e]l[i]ques[ca]nt

Side B
eoru<m> quamodum gallorum angat se [-]
s[ic i]lla aga<t> ut de se
[pr]obant(?) tu dom<i>na es fac ut X mensibus
exitum illorum
sit

Just as this is dry (?) ... just like this will melt away, thus may the neck, the limbs, the marrow, the property melt away from them. In the way that the galli torture themselves, so shall it go for her, just as she proves herself. You are the mistress: make her death come within ten months.

SD 520

Origin: Bregenz, Raetia. Grave.
Date: First century.
Bibliography: DT 93; dfx 7.1/1; LCT 103.

Side A
Domitius Niger et
Lollius et Iulius Severus
et Severus Nigri ser<v>us adve[rs]-
ar[ii] Bruttae et quisquis adversus eam loq<u>it omnes per[da]tis

Side B
[ro]g<o> vos omnes qui illi
malum [pa]ratis
dari [--]dm[-]o dari O[g]mio a[bs]u-
mi mort[e] [---]t [---]t
[--]nti et Nige[r]
[---]dim [--]o [---] Valerium
[---]a et Ni[g]er

Domitius Niger, Lollius, Iulius Severus and Severus, the slave of Niger, the opponents of Brutta and anyone else who speaks against her: you should destroy them all.

I ask that you should destroy all who inflict evil ... to be handed over in death to Ogmius ... and Niger ... Valerius ... and Niger.

SD 521

Origin: Bregenz, Raetia. Grave.
Date: First half of the second century.
Bibliography: dfx 7.1/2; LCT 104.
Notes: Written boustrophedon then folded.

Deo amc ea\<m\> re\<m\> impl-
e\<b\>id D(is)p\<at\>er ad era\<m\> Ogmius salute\<m\> cur (=cor) talus re[n\<es\>]
anum genita\<lia\> [l]c[---]m auri-
s cest{h}ula\<m\> utens(ilia)
dav \<it\>{i}spiridebus
ac ov\<o\>ediu\<nt\> {a}ei ne qui-
iat nubere ira de[i]

To the god ... Dis Pater will fulfil the matter to Aeracura(?). Ogmius will give (her) health, heart, ankles, kidneys, anus, genitals ... ears, little box(?) and other things to the spirits and they obey him, so she should not be able to marry, by the wrath of the god.

SD 522

Origin: Kempten, Raetia. House, perhaps under a threshold.
Date: Mid second century.
Bibliography: dfx 7.2/1; LCT 105.

Side A
Mutae tacitae ut mutus sit
Quartus agitatus erret ut mus
fugiens aut avis adversus basyliscum
ut e[i]us os mutu\<m\> sit mutae
mutae [d]irae sint mutae
tacitae sint mutae
[Qu]a[rt]us ut insaniat

Side B
ut Eriniis rutus sit et
Quartus Orco ut mutae
tacitae ut mut[ae s]int
ad portas aureas

Silent Mutes, thus Quartus should be mute, he should scurry around like a fleeing mouse or bird in the face of a basilisk, so should his mouth be mute, Mutes. May the Mutes be dreadful, may the Mutae be silent. May Quartus be driven mad, may Quartus be driven to the Furies and to Orcus. May the Mutae be silent, mute and silent at the golden gates.

SD 524

Origin: Peiting, Raetia, In the wall of a house.
Date: Second or third century.
Bibliography: dfx 7.4/1; LCT 106.
Notes: The text is partially inverted, partially retrograde and written from bottom to top.

Side A
Gemella supra mensuram naturae
domini tui Clementis iaces qu[are(?)] ut
te patitur sic tu patere [ver(?)]am eius [mensu(?)]-
ram patere audacter quod te iuve[t]

Side B
somnus te tuetur Gemella sub
iugum missa q<u>iesce [---] contineas te
non pe[cca]s ama Clementem
sicut ibi eum non videbis [sic ---]s qua
plumbum [---]a[---]

Gemella, you lie beyond the natural measure of your master Clemens, therefore as he suffers you, so you suffer his true measure, suffer desperately, since it helps you.

Sleep protects you, Gemella, keep quiet in your enslavement ... you should restrain yourself, do not err. Love Clemens, just as you will not see him there, thus ... with what, lead ...

SD 526

Origin: Mautern, Noricum. Cemetery, perhaps a shrine rather than a grave.
Date: Mid second century.
Bibliography: dfx 6.1/1; LCT 101.
Notes: Used as a seal for a small clay jar containing burnt material. The victim's name is written upside down.

Side A
Pluton sive{m} Iov-
em infernum dici opor{no}-
tet eracura Iuno
inferna acciet<e> ia<m> c<e>lerius
infra scribtum e<t> tradite {i}
manibus
Aurelium Sinnianum
C<a>eserianum

Side B
sic Silvia inversu<m> m-
aritu<m> c{e}ernis quom-
{m}odi nomen il<l>lius
scribtum est

Pluto, or if it is proper to say Jupiter of the Underworld, Aeracura, Juno of the Underworld, now quickly fetch the one named below and hand him over to the Manes. Aurelius Sinnanus Caesarianus.

Thus Silvia, you see your husband turned upside down, just as his name is written.

SD 527

Origin: Ptuj, Pannonia. Grave.
Date: Second half of the second century.
Bibliography: dfx 8.4/1; LCT 109.
Notes: Folded and pierced multiple times. Written boustrophedon and on the reverse the letters are sometimes reversed or written upside down.

Side A
Paulina aversa sit
a viris omnibus
et deficsa sit ne quid

Side B
possit mali facere
Firminam [cl]od[as] ab o-
mnibus humanis

Paulina should be turned away from all men and cursed, so that she cannot do any harm. You should close off Firmina from all men.

SD 529

Origin: Sisak, Pannonia. Found in the River Kupa.
Date: First half of the second century.
Bibliography: dfx 8.1/1; Barta 2017 (reading); LCT 107.
Notes: Folded both before and after writing.

Side A
advers{s}ar<i>o<s> nos{s}tro<s>
G(aius) Dometiu<s> Secundus
et Lucius Larcio
et Secun<d>o Valar<i>us
Ciba(lis) et P(ublius) Citronia
G(aius) Corelliu<s> Narbone
et L(ucius) Liccnius Sura <H>is{s}pan(ia)
et Luc{c}il{l}ius
Val{l}ente ne possi<nt>
contra s{s}e faceri
avertat illo<s> ame<n>te<s>
contra lucui (=loqui) ne am
li illorus muto o<s> fac(iat?)
G(aius) Dom<i>tius S{s}ecundo
et Lucius La<r>c<i>o L(ucius) Gida(lis) (=Cibalis)
M[u]ta Tagita[-]
[--] na illoru[m--]

Side B
Ma(n)data data s(upra)s(cripta)
Savo cura<m> aga<s>
deprema<s> adver<s>ar<i>o<s>
nos{s}tro<s> o<b>mut{u}<escant> ne
contra n[os] l[o]cuia(ntur)
{data deprementi}

(We curse?) our enemies: Gaius Domitius Secundus and Lucius Larcius and Secundus Valerius from Cibalae and Publius Citronius, Gaius Corellius from

Narbo and Lucius Licinius Sura from Hispania and Lucilius Valens. May they be unable to act against (us). May she send them away insane; may they not speak against (us) ... May she make their mouths mute. Gaius Domitius Secundus and Lucius Larcius from Cibalae. Muta Tacita ... their ...

The above-mentioned (names) are given and entrusted to Savus. Take care and force down our enemies, so that they become mute and do not speak against us. Given to the one who forces down.

SD 530

Origin: Petronell, Pannonia. Amphitheatre.
Date: Second half of the second century.
Bibliography: dfx 8.3/1; LCT 239.
Notes: Folded.

Sa<nc>te Dite pa-
ter et Vera-
cura et Cerber-
e auxilie q<u>i tenes
limina inverna sive
{sive} superna
ΔΜΟΗΡΜΗ [---] Σολουμ(?)νος σφραγες φορ(ε)
ται ν ρα το λ[εσθαι]
v[os] pre[co]r fa[ci]a[tis]
[Eudemum(?) --- a(?)]d r[egnum inf]-
ernum quam cel[e]ris<s>i[me]
infra dies nove<m> va-
sum reponat defigo Eudem[um]
nec[et]i[s] eum pes<s>imo leto ad inf[er]os
d[uca]tis eundem recol<l>igatis
m[anibu]s ministeria infernorum
d]eu[m quom]od<o> i[l]<l>e plu<m>bus po<n>dus h<a>bet sic et
[E]ud<e>mus h<a>beat v[o]s iratos inter la<r>vas
[---]ate ia<m> hostiat quam celeris<s>im<e>
m[---]

Holy Dis Pater and Veracura and Cerberus the helper, who hold the thresholds of the underworld and overworld DMOERME SOLOUMNOS SPHRAGES

PHORE TAI N RA TO LESTHAI. I beseech you; you should make Eudemus ... to the infernal kingdom as quickly as possible, in nine days he should put back the vessel. I curse Eudemus: you should kill him with the worst death, you should lead him to the infernals and bind him with the Manes, in service to the infernal gods. Just as this lead has weight, so should Eudemus have (the weight of?) your anger. Among the dead ... now he should make amends as soon as possible ...

SD 532

Origin: Budapest, Pannonia. Grave.
Date: Late second or early third century.
Bibliography: AE 2009, 1169; Lassanyi 2017 (trans).
Notes: Found with a bent stylus.

Iulia Nissa et Gaius Mutilius ne possit facere contra Oceanum contra Am(o)en<a>m ne possit Gaius contra Felic(i)o-
ne(m) facere Respect<ae> lingua ne possit adversus co<n>servos
facere Eunici Suri lingua ne possit adversus Oceanu<m>
loqui ne possit Gaius aut Iulia adversus Annia-
num facere et Decibali lingua et nomen ne possit adversus Oceanum facere <qu>o modo hoc ego aver-
so graphio scribo sic lingu<ae> illorum aversas ne pos<s>int
facere contra <h>os lena[-] ego supraposiui ne Gaius aut Iulia
Nissa et Eunicus Surus adversus Oceanum lin[gu]-
as obligatas ae[---]ne lingu<a> Asellionis ne [possit]
contra Am<o>ene<m> [---] facere[---]

Three lines inserted after lines 3, 4 and 5 respectively:
Ammionis(?) lingua ne possit adversus ne[---]us
Assellionis lingua et nomen ne possit a<d>versus Oc<e>anum facere
Anniani lingua ne possit [---]au[---]o

May Iulia Nissa and Gaius Mutilius be unable to do harm to Oceanus and Amoena. May Gaius be unable to do harm to Felicio. May Respecta's tongue be unable to do harm to her fellow slaves. May Eunicus Surus' tongue be unable to speak against Oceanus. May Gaius or Iulia be unable to do harm to Annianus and may Decibalus' tongue {and name} be unable to do harm to Oceanus. Just as I write this with a bent, twisted stylus, so too may their bent and twisted tongues be unable to do harm to these ... whom I mentioned above. May Gaius or Iulia

Nissa and Eunicus Surus be unable to ... their bound tongue against Oceanus ... may Asellio's tongue be unable to ... against Amoena.

May Ammio's tongue be unable to ... against. May Asellio's tongue {and name} be unable to do harm to Oceanus. May Annianus' tongue be unable ...

DT 161

Origin: Rome. A columbarium outside Porta San Sebastiano.
Date: 390–420.
Bibliography: Tremel 72.
Notes: Rolled. Drawings of Typhon-Seth, Osiris in sarcophagus, bound figures and heads on frames.

Column A
Εὐλάμων κατέχι Οὔσιρι
Οὔσιρι Ἅγι Οὔσιρι Μ[νε]
Φρι

Λό(γος)· ὑμῖς δέε Φ[υδρια δέε
Νυμφεε Ἀειδωναι ανεενκωρω·
εἶνα κατάσ
χητε [---]
[------]
[------]
[------]
[---] Εὐ
θύμιον ὃν καὶ Μάξιμον ὃν καὶ
Γίδαντα υἱὸν Πασχασίας καὶ
Εὐγένιον ὃν καὶ Κήρεον υἱὸν]
Βενερί[ας ἅμα]
καὶ Δομ[νῖνον]
ὃν καὶ Θώ[ρακα]
Εὐλάμων [κατέχι]
Οὔσιρι Οὔ[σιρι Ἀ]
γι Οὔσιρι [Μνε]
Φρι
τὸν υἱὸν
Φορτούνας·
ἀξιῶ ὑμᾶς
κατὰ τ[ῆς]

Column B
Λό(γος)· ὑμῖς δέε Φυδρια δέε
Νυμφεε Ἀ
ειδωναι ανεενκωρω· κατάσχητε
τούτους τοὺς ἵππους τοῦ
πρασείνου
Ἰούδηξ Εἰλειοδρόμος [---] απο [-]
Σῶλ Ἠπόνικος
Λαωμέδων Φοντᾶνον
Εὔπολον τοῦ πρασίνου
Ὀλυμπιονίκην Αὔρεον
[το]ῦ πρασείνου δεστρῖτοι
[Βαβυλ]όνιος Οὐράνιος
Πολ.[υϊδ]ής Σαγήταν
Κοπ[ίδων . . . .]κος
Ἀχ[ι]λλ[εὺς . . . .]σους
[------]
α [---]
αι [---]
[------]
καὶ ἀπόδους
τοὺς ἵππους
τοῦ πρασείνου
οὕσπερ γεγραμέ
νους ἐν τούτη τῆ
λεπίδει· ὅτι
ὁρκίζω σε κατὰ

Column C
[--] κ [---] δ [--] ασε [---]
[---] μάλ[ι]στα εἶνε [---]
[--- κατ]ὰ τοῦ [ὑ]πὸ τ[ὴν Ἀνάνκην
τοῦ κατέχον
τος]
κύκλα [---]
[---] βακαξιχ[υ]χ βαδε[τοφωθ
φθωσισιρω εἶνα κα
τάσ]χητε τούτους τοὺς [ἡνιόχους
τοῦ ---]
ἀπὸ τῆς σήμερον ἡ]μέρας καὶ
ὥρας [---]
βη[--- ἡ]νιόχου [---] υἱὸν
τ [---] τον
το [--- Ῥεστοῦτ]ον [τ]ὸν υἱὸν
Ῥεσ[το]ύτας καὶ [--- κ]
αταστρέψητε
αὐτοὺς καὶ [---] ἀπὸ τῆς σήμερον
[ἡμέρας καὶ ὥρας ἕως δ]
ωδεκάτης
[Λό(γος)· ὑμῖς δέε Φυδρια δέε
Νυμφε Ἀει]δω[ναι α]νεεν
κωρω [κατάσχητε Ἀρτέμιον ὃν
καὶ Ὀσπητον]
τὸν υἱ[ὸν Σαπήδ]α[ς] καὶ
Ἀσ[τέριον ὃ]ν

δυνάμε
ως ὑμῶν
εἴνα <κ>
ἀδυνάμους
ἀβοηθήτους
ποιήσητε
<[τ]ε> καὶ συνε
[δε]μένους
[οὕσ]περ καὶ
[παραδί]δω ὑμῖν
[ἐ]πὶ τὴν παρακαταχήκην καὶ
καταστρέψητε
[αὐτ]οὺς καὶ ποιήσητε αὐτοὺς
εἶνε λ [---] ορκουσηπα
[τ]ῶν ἵπον τοῦ πρασίνου· ὅτι
ὁρκίζο
[ὑμᾶς κ]ατὰ τοῦ ὑπὸ τὴν Ἀνάνκην
τοῦ κα
[τέχον]τος κύκλα
[καὶ Οιμη]νεβαινχυχ
[βα]χυχ βαχυχ
βαχαξιχυχ βαχα
ξιχυχ βαδετο
φθωσειρω
[κ]ατάσχητε τούτου[ς τ]ο[ὺ]ς
π[ρασίν]ου[ς
Εὐ]θύμιον ὃν καὶ Μάξιμον [ὃν]
καὶ Γίδαντα υἱὸν
[Π]ασχασίας ἅμα κ[αὶ Εὐ]γένιον
ὃν
[καὶ] Κήρε[ον υἱ]ὸν
[Βε]νερίας
[ἀπὸ τῆς σήμερον] ἡμέρας καὶ
ὥρας·
[ὅτι ὁρκίζο σε ἅγι]ε Εὐλάμων καὶ
ἅγιε
[---] η δρε ι να [---]
[---] υς [---]

τοῦ ὑπὸ τὴν Ἀναν
κην τοῦ κατέχοντος κύκλα Οὔσιρι
Μνε
[Μη]νεβαινχυχ
βαινχαδ[α]χχυχ
βαδετοφοθ
[φθ]ωσισιρω
εἴνα κατάσχ
ετε τούτους
[τοὺς ἵπ]πους
[------]
[------]
λ [---]
ἀπόδους εἶνε
συνεκλασμένο[υς]
ἐν τῷ εἰπικῶ·
ὅτι ὁρκίζο ὑμᾶς
ατὰ τῆς δυνάμεως
ὑμῶν εἴνα
[---] ωσιν
[------]
καὶ ε [---]
ηδω [---]
τε [---]
[------]

καὶ Σαπηδ[ῶσον] τὸν υἱὸν
[Εἰρήνης εἴνα] κα
τήσχητε [καὶ] συνδ[ήσ]ητε κ[αὶ
καταστ]ρέ
ψητε ἐ[ν] τῷ κίρκω τῆς [νέας] Βα
βυλονος· ὅ[τ]ι ὁρκίζο ὑμᾶς κατὰ
τοῦ ὑπὸ τὴν
Ἀνάνκην τοῦ κατέχοντος κύκλα
καὶ Οιμη
νεβαχυχ [β]αινχυχ [---]
χυχ [βαχα]χυχ βαδε[τοφωθ]
φθ[ω]
συσυρω [κα]τάσχητε [Ἀρτέμιον]
ὃν
καὶ Ὄσπητον τὸν υἱὸν Σαπήδας
μάλειστ[α] καὶ Ἀστέριον [ὃν καὶ
Σα]
πηδῶσ[ον] τὸν υἱὸν Εἰρήνης ἀπὸ
τ[ῆς]
σή[με]ρ[ον] Ἄρε[ως ἡμέρας]· ἤδη
ἤ
[δη ἤ]δη [τ]αχ[ὺ τα]χ[ύ]

(remaining lines are in a column between columns 1 and 2, at 90 degrees)
Εὐθύ
Μις
ὁ καὶ

Appendix: Select Catalogue of Curses 205

Μά
Ιμος
ὁ καὶ
Γίδας
[υ]ιὸς Πα
[σ]χασίας

EULAMON bind OUSIRI OUSIRI AGI OUSIRI MNE PHRI. The spell: (I invoke) you Phrygian goddess, Nymph goddess Aidonai living here so that you bind ... Euthemius, nicknamed Maximus Gidas, son of Paschasia, and Eugenius, nicknamed Cereus, son of Veneria, also Domninus, nicknamed Thorax (EULAMON bind OUSIRI OUSIRI AGI OUSIRI MNE PHRI) son of Fortuna. I urge you in your power, make them powerless, helpless and bind together those I deliver to you, and keep them in your power and cast them down and cause them to ... the horses of the Greens. Thus, I beseech you by the one who, under the power of Necessity, restrains the circles and OIMENEBAINCHUCH BACHUCH BACHUCH BACHAXICHUCH BACHAXICHUCH BADETOPHTHOSEIRO so that you bind these charioteers of the Greens, Euthymius, nicknamed Maximus Gidas, son of Paschasia, and also Eugenius, nicknamed Cereus, son of Veneria, from this day and hour. I beseech you holy Eulamon and you holy ...

The spell: (I invoke) you Phrygian goddess and Nymph goddess Adonai living here, that you bind these horses of the Greens: Iudex, Heliodromus ... Sol, Hipponicus, Laomedon, Fontanus, Eupolus of the Greens, Olympionica, Aureus of the Greens, Babylonius, Ouranius, Polyides, Sagitta, Cupid ... Achilles ... and footless, the horses of the Greens which are written on this metal tablet, So I beseech you by the one who, under the power of Necessity, restrains the circles OUSIRI MNE MENEBAINCHUCH BAINCHADACHCHUCH BADETOPHOTH PHTHOSISIRO so that you bind these horses ... are footless, collide in their team, so I beseech you in your power that you ...

... especially ... who, under the power of Necessity, restrains the circles ... BAKAZICHUCH BADEDOPHOTH PHTHOSISIIRO so that you bind the charioteers ... this day and hour ... charioteer ... son. ... Restutus, son of Restuta and ... throw them down and ... from this day and hour until the twelfth (race?). The spell: (I invoke) you Phrygian goddess and Nymph goddess Aidonai living here, that you bind Artemius, nicknamed Hospes, son of Sapeda, and Asterius, nicknamed Sapedosus, son of Irene, so that you bind and bind and destroy in the circus of (new) Babylon, So I beseech you by the one who, under the power of

Necessity, restrains the circles and OIMENEBACHUCH BAINCHUCH ... CHUCH BACHACHUCH BADETOPHOTH PHTHOSUSURO so that you bind Artemius, nicknamed Hospes, son of Sapeda, and especially Asterius, nicknamed Sapedosus, son of Irene, today on the day of Ares, now, now, now, quickly, quickly. Euthymius, nicknamed Maximus Gidas, son of Paschasia.

DT 198

Origin: Cuma, Italia. Grave.
Date Second or third century.
Bibliography: Jordan 2003 (trans).

Charaktêres
[Ορ--αια]οφιοφοριος [---]
ηθιτουτω [-] σουπεμονδεσ [---]
δαίμονες καὶ πνεύματα οἱ ἐν τῷ [τό]-
πῳ τούτῳ θηλυκῶν καὶ ἀρρενικ[ῶν]
ἐξορκίζω ὑμᾶς τὸ ἅγιον ὄνομ[α τοῦ]
Ερηκισιφθη αραραραχαραρα ηφθι[σικηρε]
Ιαω Ιαβεζεβυθ λανα ν βεσαφλαν [---]
[-]νκηιπαμμουροφαηντιναξο[---]
ὁ τῶν ὅλων βασιλεὺς ἐξεγέρθητι κ[αὶ]
ὁ τῶν φθιμένων βασιλεὺς ἐξαφέ[θητι]
μετὰ τῶν καταχθονίων θεῶν ταῦτα γὰρ
γείνεται διὰ Οὐαλερίαν Κοδράτιλλαν
ἣν ἔτεκεν Οὐαλερία Εὔνοια ἣν ἔσπειρε Οὐαλέριος Μυστικός Ὡς τὸ φῶς ἀγγέ-
λει θεοῖς τὰ κ[ατὰ] σκότος κατ' ἐπιταγὴν
[-]οτ[-]φερρο[---]ε υορσερχεμ[-]νε[--]
μελ[-]ει διάκοπτ[ε τὴ]ν στοργήν τὴν
φιλίαν δῆς αὐτὴν [εἰς Τάρ]ταρα τοῖς
δὲ ἐν φωτὶ δὸς α[ὐτὴν μ]εισεῖν (?) εἰς χό-
λον θεῶν εἰς φόβον εἰσ[ε]λθέτω
[ἡ Οὐαλερία Κοδράτιλλα ἣν ἔτεκ]εν
Β[αλερία Εὔνοια] ἣν ἔ[σ]πειρε Βαλέριος
Μυστικός μεισε[ίτω] αὐτήν λήθην
αὐτῆς λαβέτω Βετρούβιος
Φῆλιξ ὃν ἔτεκεν Βετρουβία Μαξιμιλ-

Appendix: Select Catalogue of Curses 207

[λα ὃ]ν ἔσπει[ρε Βετρού]βιος Εὐέλπιστος
[---]εχεαι Τυφῶν
μα[---]ον Βαρβαραουθ
αατα[-]αχων δότε {εἰς μ[εῖ-]
σος} Βετρουβίῳ Φήλικι ὃν ἔ[τεκ]ε Βετρουβία Μαξίμιλλα ὃν ἔσπειρε Β[ετ]ρού-
βιος Εὐέλπιστος εἰς μεῖσος ἐλθεῖν
καὶ λήθην λαβεῖν τῶν πόθων
Οὐαλερίας Κοδρ[α]τίλλης ἣν ἔσπειρε
Βα[λέριος Μυστ]ικ[ό]ς ἣν ἔτεκε Βαλερία
[Εὔνοια ---]το κατέχετε ὑμεῖς
[--- τα]ῖς λοιπαῖς τειμωρίαις
[---]ας ὅτι πρώτη ἠθέτησε
[Βετρούβιον Φ]ήλικα τὸν ἑαυτῆς ἄνδρα
[---] Ιακουβηειυντον[---]τα
[------]

OR...NAIAOPHIOPHORIOS...ÊTH TOUTÔ SOUPEMONDES...daemons and spirits in this place of (prematurely dead persons) female and male, I adjure you by the holy name of ERÊKISIPHTHÊ ARARARACHARARA ÊPHTHISIKÊRE IAÔ IABEXEBYTH LANA BESAPHLAN ... NKÊIPAMMOUROPHAÊNTINAXO ... King of the ... arouse yourself, and king of the dead ... with the underworld gods. For these things come about through Valeria Quadratilla, whom Valeria Eunoea bore, whom Valerius Mysticus begot. As the light announces to gods the things in darkness under orders of ... cut off the delight, the love (for her). Bind (?) her into Tartarus. And grant those in (the) light to (hate her?) Let Valeria Quadratilla, whom Valeria Eunoae bore, whom Valerius Mysticus begot, enter into hatred of gods, into fear. Let Vitruvius Felix, whom Vitruvia Maximilla bore, whom Vitruvius Eulpistus begot, hate her, come to have forgetfulness of her ... ECHEAI Typhon, MA ... ON BARBAEOUTH DATA ACHON, grant ... Vitruvius Felix, whom Vitruvia Maximilla bore, whom Vitruvius Euelpistus begot, to enter into hatred and to have forgetfulness of his desires for Valeria Quadratilla, whom Valerius Mysticus begot, whom Valeria Eunoea bore.... Control (her?) you ... with remaining (?) punishments ... because she first broke faith with Vitruvius Felix, her own husband...IAKOUBEEIUNTON...TA...

DT 222

Origin: Carthage, Africa. Grave (Bir ez Zitoun).
Date: Second or third century.
Bibliography: dfx 11.1.1/8; LCT 118.

Side A
Claudia Helenis
Clodia Successi
Clodia Steretia
Clodius Fortunatus
Clodius Romanus
Mu[rc]ius Crim[--]enius
Servilius Faustus
Valerius Extricatus
quomodi haec nomina a-
[d(?) inferos(?) dedi(?)]
[sic omnes(?)]
[adversu]s me ommute[scant]
[neque(?) lo[qui [possint(?) quomodo]

Side B
huic gallo lingua(m)
vivo extorsi et defi-
xi sic inimicorum
meorum linguas ad-
versus me ommutescant
sic qui [in(?)] me l[o]qui
osusve fuerit ad ni<hi>lo [-r]ediat res illius
[- ha]ec pr{a}ecatio ita
[---]erteta est ad [---]
[preco]r(?) vos muta [---]
[---] per ves[tr---]

90 degrees to rest of text
vec]turia<m> di<i> Manes ita uti
vost poniteque sic adversus

Claudia (of) Helena, Clodia (of) Successus, Clodia Steretia, Clodius Fortunatus, Clodius Romanus, Murcius Crim..enius, Servilius Faustus, Valerius Extricatus.

Just as I gave these names to the infernals, so shall all who oppose me become silent and not be able to speak. Just as I twisted out and bound the tongue from this live chicken, so shall the tongues of my enemies, having opposed me, become silent. Thus, anyone who dared to speak against me, their business shall go back to nothing ... this prayer thus ... is to ... I beseech you mute ... by your (?) ... victory, spirits of the departed, thus to use ... thus having opposed.

DT 230

Origin: Carthage, Africa. Grave (cemetery for Roman officials).
Date: Second or third century.
Bibliography: dfx 11.1.1/16; LCT 124.
Notes: Folded. Gaps left for names of curser and victim.

Side A
καταξιν [q]ui es <in> Aegupto magnus daemon
{et} aufer illae somnum usquedun veniat at me
et animo meo satisfaciat Τραβαξιαν omnipotens daemon adduc
    amante<m> aestuante<m> amoris et desideri<i> mei cau-
sa Νοχθιριφ qui <es> cogens daemon coge illa<m>
m[ec]un coitus   facere Βιβιριξι qui es
f[ort]issimus daemon urgue [c]oge illam venire ad me aman-
te<m> aestuante<m> amoris et desideri<i> mei
causa Ρικουριθ agilissime daemon in Aegupto {et} agita
   a suis parentibus a suo cubile et aerie quicumque caros habet et coge illa<m> me amare mihi conferre ad meu-
[m] desiderum

Side B
[------]
[---] vi cirie (=kyrie)
aut ab cr ---]t[---]
peper[--]it ap[---]rgiebs
de{o}um ep cam

90 degrees to rest of text
[------]
[------]
f[aci(?)]as

Kataxin, who is a great daemon in Egypt, take away sleep from her NN, all the while she should come to me NN and should satisfy my soul. Trabaxian, all powerful daemon, bring NN loving, burning with passion for the sake of my love and desire. Noxthirif, who is a summoning demon, summon her, NN, to me to have sex (with me) NN. Bibirixi, who is the strongest daemon, urge and summon her to come to me loving, burning with passion for the sake of my love and desire, NN. Rikourith, the most agile daemon in Egypt, drive NN from her parents, from her bed and and all whom she holds dear, and drive her, loving me, to me and to bring her together with me to my desire ... strength lord but to ... bore ... god ... you should make.

DT 231

Origin: Carthage, Africa. Grave (Bir ez Zitoun).
Date: Second or third century.
Bibliography: dfx 11.1.1/17; LCT 125.
Notes: folded. Latin text in Greek letters.

[---]περα[---]
[---κου]ωρουμ[-]
[--- κ]ουω ρορ[-]
[---]μαγνα ουτ
[---]διας[--]τ κουωμο-
[δο ---]ανουντιο ρεγις
[---]ι μορτους αβ ιλ-
[λα ---]ινητουρ ανιμα
[---]οκ λοκο σικ ετ
[---]τη δητινεατουρ
[ιν ομ]νε τεμπους ιν α-
[μωρ]ε ετ δεσιδερι[ο] Μαρ-
[τ]ιαλικι κουεμ πεπεριτ
Κορωναρια σερρουσεμ[--]λω
κνημεω τριπαρνωχι α-
[β]ρασαξ σχωομονοε ευ-
φνεφερησα μαλχαμα
ιαρεμμουθου χεννειθ
ατιουρο ουως περ ουωκ πρε-
[πο] σιτου σουπερ νεκεσσι-

[τατ]ης τερρε σικ ετ τε[-]
[---]δομινους αιη απερ
[--]ουτ ε[ξ] ακ διη οκ μομεντο
[---]ις[---]
[------]
[-]ατε ιλλ[α]ς ησου[---]
αμετ Μαρτιαλε ουτ ο<μ>-
μνι μουλιεβρι ωρας μ[ε] ιν
μεντε αβεατ ετ τωτα διε
[ιν α]νιμω αβεατ αμωρε με-
[ουμ ---] νιμ[---]
[---] τις μαγνα τυ[--]
[--- δομ]ινουμ ιαμ ιαμ[-]
[---]πεηια

... of whom ... great thus ... in what way ... I will declare the king's ... dead from her ... (her) soul is held back ... in this place, thus and ... of who is mother ... you, she should be held back for all time in love and desire for Martialis, who Coronaria bore. I beseech you through this charge over the necessities of the earth, thus and you ... lord ... thus, from this day, this moment ... she ... should love Martialis, so that at every hour she has me in her womanly mind and has my love in her soul all day ... you great ... lord, now, now ...

DT 234

Origin: Carthage, Africa. Grave (Bir ez Zitoun).
Date: Second or third century.
Bibliography: Tremel 53.

Ἐξορκίζω σε ὅστις ποτ' οὖν εἶ νεκυδαίμων ἄωρε κατὰ τ[--]
[---]καὶ τὰ [---] τα [ὀνό]ματα α[--] πων
βρουραβρουρα μαρμαρει μαρμαρει αμαρταμαρει απε-
ωρνομ φεκομφθω βαιεψων σαθσαθιεαω [---] ββαιφρι
ἵνα καταδήσῃς τοὺς ἵππους τοῦ οὐενέτου καὶ τοῦ συνζύγ[ου
αὐτοῦ πρασίνου ---] εους σοι [σεσημειωμ]ένα ἐν τοῖς θα[λ]α[σσίοις]
ὀστράκοις παρακατατέθηκα ἐν τούτω τῶ σκεύει Οὐιττᾶτον
Δηρεισῶρε Οὐικτῶρε Ἀρμένιον Νίμβον Τύριον Ἄμορε Πραικλ-
ᾶρον τὸν καὶ Τετραπλᾶ Οὐρεῖλε Παρᾶτον Οὐικτ[ῶρε
Ἰμβου]τρί[ουμ] Φονεῖκε Λικον καὶ τοῦ συνζύγου αὐτοῦ πρα-

σίνου Δάρειον Ἄγιλε Κουπείδινε Πουγιῶνε Πρ-
ετιῶσου Προυνικὸν Δαρδανον Εἴναχον Φλόριδον Πάρδον
Σερουᾶτον Φούλγιδον Οὐικτῶρε Προφικιον κατα-
{δησον αὐτοῖς δρόμον πόδας νείκην ὁρμὴν ψυχὴν ταχύτητα ἐκκόψον ἐκνεύρωσοω ἐξάρθρωσον αὐτοὺς ἵνα}
δησον αὐτοῖς τον δρόμον τὴν δύναμιν τὴν ψυχὴν τὴν ὁρμὴν τ-
ὴν ταχύτητα ἄφελε αὐτῶν τἠω νείκην ἐμπόδισον αὐτοῖς τοὺς πόδας ἔκκοψον ἐκνεύρωσον ἐξάρθρωσον αὐτοὺς ἵνα
μὴ δυνασθῶσιν τῇ αὔριον ἡμέρα ἐλθόντες ἐν
τῷ ἱπποδρόμω μήτε τρέχειν μέτε περιπατεῖν μέτε ν-
εικησαι μηδὲ ἐξελθεῖν τοὺς πυλῶνας τῶν ἱππαφ-
ίων μήτε προβαίνειν τὴν ἀρίαν μήτε τὸν σπάτιον μηδὲ
κυκλεῦσαι τοὺς καμπτῆρας ἀλλὰ πεσέτωσαν
σὺω τοῖς ἰδίοις ἡνιόχοις Διονυσίω τοῦ οὐενέτου καὶ Λα-
μυρῷ καὶ Ῥεστουτιάνω καὶ τοῦ συνζύγου αὐτοῦ
πρασίου Πρώτω καὶ Φηλεῖκε καὶ Ναρκισσω ἀνάγκα-
ν[---ἀρε[-]α[---]α[-]ν[---]κ
αμαει μεσαγρα μεσακτω ασβυρ ὀρεοβαβζαγρα μ-
ασκελλει φνουκενταβαωθ ασμφορνο
βεουουβεου [-] κατάδησον τοὺς ἵππους τοῦ οὐενέτου ὧν
τὰ ὀνόματά σοι σεσημειωμένα ἐν τού-
τω τῷ σκεύει ἐν ὀστράκοις θαλασσίοις παρακατατέθηκα Οὐιττᾶτον Δηρεισῶρε Οὐι-
κῶρε Ἀρμένιον Νίμβον Τύριον Ἄμορε Πραι-
κλᾶρον τὸν καὶ Τετραπλὰ Οὐιρεῖλε
Παρᾶτον Οἰκτῶρε Ἰμβουτρίουμ Φονεῖκε Λί-
κον καὶ τοῦ συνζύγου αὐτοῦ π-
ρασίνου Δάρειον Ἄγιλε Κουπείδινε
Πουγιῶνε Πρετιῶσον Προυνικὸν
Δάρδανον Εἴναχον Φλόριδον Πάρδον
Σερουᾶτον Φούλγιδον κατάδη-
σον αὐτοῖς δρόμον πόδας νείκην ὁρμὴν ψ-
υχὴν ταχύτητα ἔκκοψον ἐκ-
νεύρωσον ἐξάρθρωσον αὐτοὺς ἵνα μὴ
δυνασθῶσιν τῇ αὔριον ἡμέρα
ἐν τῷ ἱπποδρόμω μήτε τρέχειν μήτε περιπατεῖν μέτε νείκησαι
μηδὲ ἐξελθεῖν τοὺς πυλῶνας τῶν ἱππᾶ-

φιων μηδὲ κυκλεῦσαι το{υ}-
ὺς καμπτῆρας ἀλλὰ πεσέτωσαν
σὺν τοῖς ἰδίοις ἡνιόχοις
Διονυσίω τοῦ σὐενέτου καὶ Λα-
μυρῶ καὶ ῾Ρεστουτιάν-
ω καὶ τοῦ σονζύγου αὐτοῦ μρασί-
νου Πρώτω καὶ Φηλ-
εῖκε καὶ Ναρκίσσω κατάδησον α-
ὐτοῖς τὰς χεῖρας
ἄφελε αὐτῶν τὴν νείκηω
τὸν ἀπόβασιν κ-
αὶ τὴν ὁρασιν ἵνα μὴ δυνασθῶσιν Βλέπειν
τοὺς ἰδίους ἀντιπάλους
ἡνιοχοῦντες ἀ-
λλὰ μᾶλλον ἅρπασον αὐ-
τοὺς ἐκ τῶν ἰ-
δίων ἁρμάτων καὶ σ-
τρέψον ἐπὶ
τὴν γῆν ἵνα πεσέτωσ-
αν ἐμ παντὶ
τόπω τοῦ ἱππο-
δρόμου
συρόμενοι μά-
λιστα δ-
ὲ ἐν τοῖς καμπτ-
ῆρσι-
ν σὺν τοῖς ἰδί-
οις
ἵπποις ἤδη ἤδ-
η
ταχὺ ταχὺ
ταχέως

I beseech you, whoever you now are, spirit of an untimely dead man, down ... and ... the names ... BROURABROURA MARMAREI MARMAREI AMARTAMAREI APERORNOM PHEKOMPHTHO BAIEPSON SATHSATHIEAO ... BBAIPHRI in order that you bind the horses of the Blues and the ally of the Greens ... I have written to you on the wet (?) shards, these I have put down in this urn: Vittatus, Derisor, Victor, Armenios, Nimbus, Tyrios, Amor, Praeclarus, Tetrapla, Virilis Paratus, Victor, Imboutrious, Phoenix, Licus and these allied drivers of the Greens: Darius, Agilis, Cupido, Pugio, Pretiosus, Prounicus, Dardanus, Inachus, Floridus, Pardus, Servatus, Fulgidus, Victor, Prophicius {bind the race, the legs, the victory, the strength, the courage, the speed, break them, drive them mad, cut out their limbs from them} bind the race, the strength, the strength, the speed, take their victory, restrain their legs, break them, drive them mad, cut out their limbs from them, so that, on tomorrow's race day in the Circus, they cannot run, nor turn, nor win, and not even leave the starting boxes, nor go through the start, nor complete a lap(?) or turn around the post, but may they fall along with their drivers Dionysius of the Blues and Lamurus and Restitutianus and the allied drivers of the Greens, Protus and Felix and Narcissus. Necessity ... ARE[.]A[...]N[...]K AMAEI MESAGRA MESAKTO ASBYR OREOBABZAGRA MASKELLEI PHNOUKENTABAOTH SAMPHORNO BEOUOUBEOU Bind the horses of the Blues, whose names I have written to you on the wet (?) shards and have put in this urn, Vittatus, Derisor, Victor, Armenius, Nimbus, Tyrius, Amor, Praeclarus, Tetrapla, Virilis, Paratus, Victor, Imboutrious, Phoenix, Licus and the allied (horses) of the Greens: Darius, Agilis, Cupido, Pugio, Pretiosus, Prounicus, Dardanus, Inachus, Floridus, Pardus, Servatus, Fulgidus. Bind their race, feet, victory, strength, life, quickness, cut out their limbs, drive them mad, so that tomorrow in the circus they will neither run around (the turning point), nor win, nor even come out of the starting blocks, nor go around the turning point, but may they fall with their charioteers Dionysius of the Blues and Lamurus and Restutianus, and these allied charioteers of the Greens: Protus and Felix and Narcissus. Bind their hands, take away their victory, their success and their sight, so that they are not able to see their opponents when steering the car, but tear them from their cars and throw them to the ground, so that they fall and are dragged through the entire racetrack, but especially at the turning point, along with their horses. Now, now, quickly, quickly.

DT 247

Origin: Carthage, Africa. Amphitheatre.
Date: Second or third century.
Bibliography: Tremel 93; dfx 11.1.1/22; LCT 130.

Notes: Folded. Includes a drawing of a human-form demon with a snake's head, holding a staff or lance in the right hand and a lightning bolt (?) in the left.

[------]
[occi]-
dite
exter-
minate vulnerate Gallicu<m> quen
peperit Prima in ista <h>ora in am-
p<h>it<h>eatri corona et ar[-]a[--]a[---]
ludes orno [--] pe <h>oc ter[--]a[---]ias
gula[-]neiu   que p[---]ave
rite <h>oc tene il li manus obliga[---]
[---]obture   non liget ur[su] ursos
[---]   par ill[-]u[---]ra[-]orat
[---]   obliga illi pede[s] m[e]-
       m[br]a sensus me-
charaktêres   dulla
obliga Gallicu quen peperit Prima ut
neque ursu<m> neque tauru<m> singulis plagis oc-
cida[t n]eque binis plagis occid<a>t neque ternis
plagis oc[ci]dat tauru<m> ursu<m> per nomen
dei vivi omnipotentis ut perficeatis iam iam
cito cito allidat illu<m> ursus et vulneret illu<m>

... strike down, banish, wound Gallicus, who Prima bore, at this hour in the ring of the amphitheatre and ... games ... bind his hands ... may he not bind the bear, the bears ... bind his feet, limbs, senses, marrow. Bind Gallicus, who Prima bore, so that he cannot kill either the bear or the bull with a single blow, nor kill them with two blows, nor kill the bull or the bear with three blows. May you achieve this by the names of the living and almighty god now, now, quickly, quickly. May the bear crush him and wound him.

DT 250

Origin: Carthage, Africa. Amphitheatre.
Date: Fourth century.
Bibliography: Tremel 96; dfx 11.1.1/25; LCT 132.
Notes: Folded.

Side A

Βαχα[χυχ---] qui es Egipto magnu[s]
da<e>mon obliges perobliges Maurussum vena-
torem quem peperit Felicitas
Ιεχρι auferas somnum non dormiat
Maurussus quem peperit F[e]licitas
Παρπαξιν deus omnipotens adducas
ad domos infernas Maurussum quem
perperit Felicitas
Νοκτουκιτ qui possides tractus Ita-
li<a>e et Campani<a>e qui tractus es per
Ac<h>erus{h}ium lacum {perducas ad}
{domos Tartareas intra dies septe<m>}
perducas ad domos Tartareas Maurus-
sun quem peperit
Felicitas intra dies septe<m>
da<e>mon qui possides <H>ispani-
am et Africam qui solus per marem
tra<n>s{s}is pertrans{s}eas {h}animam et {i}spiri-
tum Maurussi quem peperit Felici-
tas pertranseas omnem remedium et
omnem filacterium et omnem tuta-
mentum et omnem oleum libutorium
et perducatis obl[i]getis pe[r]obligetis
[oblig(?)]etis apsumatis desumatis consu-
[m]at[i]s cor membra viscera interania
[M]auruss[i venatoris(?)] quem peperit
[Felicitas]

90 degrees to rest of text.
et te ad
[iu]ro quisquis inferne
[es] per h<a>ec sancta nomina Necessitatis

Side B
μασκελλει μασκελλω φνοθκεν [Σα]βαωθ ορεοβαρζαγ[ρα]
φηξικθων πυρκτων [---] φιτ [--]ι[-]τ[-]η[-]ω[-]ρ[--]
κερδερνσανδαλε κατανεικανδε[λε] depre<he>[ndatis]
[e]t facitatis pallidum m<a>extum tristem [---]

[---] mutum non se regentem Maurussum quem pe[pe]r[it] Felicitas
in omnem proelium in omni certamine evanescat ruat [---]tr[---]e
Maurussus quem peperit Felicitas desub amp<h>itiatri corona [---]
eatem au<gu>r<i>a{m}(?) patiatur Maurussus quem peperit Felici[t]as [vinc(?)]
    ere [non]
possit perversus sit perperversus sit Maurussus quem [p]e[pe]rit Fe[licitas---]
nec lac[ueos] possit super ursum mittere non alligare [ursum(?) possit]
[c]onliga[tum(?)] tenere omnino non possit manos illi et ro[bur(?)---]
[pe]des illi obligentur non possit currere lassetu[r---]e
[{h}a]nimam et {i}spiritum deponat in omnem pro<e>lium [in] omni[bus con]-
[g]ressionibus depannetur vapulet vulneretur [vincat(?)]ur [et(?) d(?)]e [ma]-
[n]us alienas inde [f]igatur tra<h>atur exiat Maurussu[s quem peperit]
F[elicit]as desub amp<h>itiatri corona facie<s> at terrae [iam iam(?)]
[ci]to cito depremite defigite perfigite consu[mite --- Mau]ru[s]-
[sum] quem peperit Felicitas ut(?) remis<s>e ferarum morsus [patiatur(?)]fe[--
    -]
[t]am tauros tam apros tam leones quae [---]l[--- Mau]-
[rus]sus quem peperit Felicitas occidere possit [nulla]m(?) [feram(?) ---]
[------]

BACHACHUCH ... who is a great daemon in Egypt, you should bind up, completely bind up Maurussus the beast hunter, who Felicitas bore. Iechri, you should take away sleep, Maurussus, who Felicitas bore, should not sleep. Parpaxin, omnipotent god, you should take Maurussus, who Felicitas bore, off to the infernal house. Noktoukit, who is master of the land of Italy and Campania, who is master of the Acherusian Lake, you should take Marussus who Felicitas bore off to the house of Tartarus within seven days. Daemon, who is master of Spain and Africa, who alone passes through the sea, pass through the soul and spirit of Maurussus, who Felicitas bore. Pass through every remedy and every amulet and every defence and every anointing of oil and you should carry off, bind up, completely bind up ... bind up, wear out, fight, devour the heart, limbs, organs and innards of Maurussus the beast hunter, who Felicitas bore, and I beseech you, whatever infernal you are, by these holy names of Necessity:

MASKELLEI MASKELLÔ PHNOYKEN SABAÔTH OREOBARZAGRA PHÊXIKTHÔN PYRKTÔN ... PHIT ... ITÊOR ... KERDERNSANDALE KATANEIKADELE You should seize and make him pale, sorrowful, dejected ... silent and unable to control himself, Maurussus who Felicitas bore. In every fight, in every struggle he should die, fall down ... Maurussus who Felicitas bore.

Beneath the ring of the amphitheatre ... Maurussus who Felicitas bore should be afflicted by the same prophecy. Maurussus who Felicitas bore should not be able to conquer, having been knocked down and destroyed, nor should he be able to throw nooses over the bear, nor should he be able to bind the bear, nor should he be able to bind together at all. His hands, strength and feet should be bound. He should not be able to run, he should be exhausted ... he should lay down his soul and spirit. In every fight, all contests he should be torn apart, flogged, wounded, beaten and bound and dragged away from the hands of others. Maurussus who Felicitas bore should go away, you will bring him to ground beneath the ring of the amphitheatre. Now, now, quickly, quickly weigh down, fix down, fix completely, devour ... Maurussus who Felicitas bore, so that, having been driven back, he may suffer the bites of wild beasts ... bulls, boars, lions, which ... Maurussus, who Felicitas bore, should not be able to kill any beasts ...

DT 251

Origin: Carthage, Africa. Amphitheatre.
Date: Second century.
Bibliography: Tremel 97; dfx 11.1.1/26; LCT 133.
Notes: Folded.

Column 1.
[Adiuro vos a]nim<a>e [---]n [-]asse <h>uius loci
[per] <ha>ec sancta nomina Psarchyrinχ oncrobrotescirvio arcadams
ter vo{o}s adiuro anim<a>e <h>uius loci
ere{re}cisipte araracarara
eptisicere [c]ycbacyc bacaci cyχ bacaχicyc obrimemao
saum
obriulem patatnaχ apoms
psesro iaω iossef iorbet
[i]opacerbet bolcoset date
interitu<m> <h>is venatoribus
Metret<a>e Syndicio Celsano
Atsurio Felici Cardario
Vincentio ne viribus suis placere possint
adi[u]ro vos per nomin[a]
[---] audita o[---]
[------]

Column 2.
[adiuro vos per <ha>ec no]mina neces-
[sitatis] temae [---]cerciel baciel
[---]aciχese amestubal
merteme perturacrini mascelli mascello fnycentabaot
zosagrac hunc epitto e-
reπton ypo ton lepta oreo-
peganyχ et per magnum C<h>aos vos adiuro
iabezepat erecisipte araracarara
eptisicere cog{g}ens enim vos et reges
d<a>emoniorum bacaχicyχdemenon
bacaχicyχ cogens enim vos et iu-
dices exsenγium animarum qui vos
in tachymorey vit<a>e iodicaverunt
criny arincbor cogens enim vos
et sangtus deus Mercurius in-
fe[rnu]s conge[ns] ipse se[-]s[---]
[------]

Column 3.
[---]ine fiat
descocemri obligate
<h>os venatores

I beseech you, spirits ... of this place, by these holy names PSARCHYRINCH ONCROBROTESCIRVIO ARCADAMS Three times I beseech you, spirits of this place ERECISIPTE ARARACARARA EPTISICERE CYCBACYC BACACI CYCH BACACHICYC OBRIMEMAO SAUM OBRIULEM PATANACH APOMS PSESRO IAÔ IOSSEF IORBET IOPACERBET BOLCOSET give death to these beast hunters: Metreta, Syndicius, Celsanus, Asturius, Felix, Cardarius, Vincentius, they should not be able to give pleasure with their strength. I beseech you by names... having been heard... I beseech you by these names of Necessity ... TEMAE ... CERCIEL BACIEL ... ACICHESE AMESTUBAL MERTEME PERTURACRINI MASCELLI MASCELLO FNYCENTABAOT ZOSAGRAC on this hidden thing under the urn OREOPEGANYCH and by great Chaos I beseech you IABEZAPAT ERECISIPTE ARARACARARA EPTISICERE for it compels you and the king of the daemons BACACHICHUCHDEMENON BACACHICHUCH for it compels you and the judges of the bloodless souls, who have judged you in ephemeral life ... It compels you and the holy infernal god Mercury. It compels you ... he should be made ... Kill these beast hunters.

DT 252

Origin: Carthage, Africa. Amphitheatre.
Date: Second century.
Bibliography: Tremel 98; dfx 11.1.1/27; LCT 134.
Notes: Folded. *Voces magicae* as edge text. Mix of Greek and Latin.

ερεκισιφθη αραρα[χ]αραρα εφθισικεκε
ευλαμω
ιωερβηθ ιωπακερβηθ ιωβ[ο]λθωσηθ βολκοδηφ
βασουμαπαντα θνυχθεθωνι ρινγχοσερσω
απομψπακερβωθ πακαρασαρα ρακουβα ααακαχοχ
ραβκαβ και συ θεοξηρ
ἄν[α]ξ κατάσχων τὸν καρπὸν
τῶν ἀποδομων καὶ τὸ ὁμοιων κατάσχες τοῦ Σαπαυτούλου ὃν ἔτεκεν Πονπονία δῆσον αὐτὸν καὶ ρε[---]ε
τὴν δύναμιν τὴν καρδίαν τὸ ἧπαρ τὸν νοῦν τὰς φρή-
νας ἐξορκίζω ὑμᾶς αλκ[-] αμηνηγεισειχεεε
βασίλ<ε>ιον ὑμῶν ἵνα βλεπ[-]{ε} ινπλικατε λακινια<μ>
Σαπαυτούλο ιν καβια κορονα αμπιθεατρι [---]

χυχβαχ	ευλαμω	ιωερβηθ	αω[--]ει[-]α[---]ρ
	υλαμωε	ιωπακερβηθ	πωκ[---]
βακαχυχ	λαμωευ	ιωβολχωσηθ	ιωκαδιανω
	αμωευλ	ιωαπο[---]	
βακαξιχυχ	μωευλα	ιωπακαρθαρ	
βαζαβαχυχ	ωευλαμ	ιωπασναξ	
μανεβαχυχ	αβεζεβεβιρω	ιωτοντρυ[--]σι	
βαδετοφωθ	ιω ιαω	αυβλυουλ	
βλιχχαιωχ	θευζυε	ευλαμω	
βρακ			

ισισισρω σισιφερμοχ χνοωρ αβρασαξ
σοροορμερ φεργαρβαρμαρ οφριουρινχ
ἐπικαλοῦμέ σε ὁ μέγας καὶ ἰσχυ[ρ]ὸς [καὶ δ]υ[να]-

τος κρατῶν καὶ δωμεύων καὶ κατόχων δεσμοῖς ἀλύτοις αἰωνίοις ἰσχυροῖς ἀδαμαντίνοις
καὶ πόσον ψυχὴν κράτησον καὶ κατασλ δ
κατάδησον ὑπόταξον προσκλίσον τὸν Σ[α]παυ[τού]λ[ον]
κατάδησον αὐτὸν σμαύρησον ιν πα [---]
ἵνα ἐξέλθε <ι>ς τόνδε τὸν τόπον μηδὲ τὴν πύλη[ν]
ἐξέλθε μέτε τὴν τυμηθη ἀπέλθ<ε>ιν{ι}
τὸν τόπον ἀλλὰ μίνη κατὰ<δησον> σοῖς δεσμοῖς
ἰσχυροῖς αἰωνίοιθ ἀδαμαντίνοις τὴν ψυ[χ]ὴν
τοῦ Σαπαυτούλου <ὃν> ἕνεκε {τὸν} Πονπωνία ε [--ο]υ-
ριανι πατιατουρ λακινια ιλλι ινπλικητουρ
οβλιγητουρ ουρσελλου<μ> νον ρεσπικια{ν}τ
{νον} λιγετ νημινεμ πουγνι ιλλι σολβαν-
τουρ νον σιτ ποτεστατις qua <νον> βουλνερητουρ
σανγουινητουρ Σαπαυτούλους κουρρερε νον
ποσσιτ οβλιγηντουρ ιλλι πεδες νερβια
ιλ<ι>α κοντρα γῆς κοντ<ρ>α [-] εντε σοῦ φακιτε
Σαπαυτούλου ομν [---] φαζελο[υ]νε συι
ιανουαριας ιν ομνι μομεντο ἤδ[η τα]χύ
ευλαμω
[ερεκισι]φθη αραραχ[αραρα ηφθισικερε]

EREKISIPHTHÊ ARARACHARARA EPHTHISIKEKE EULAMÔ IÔERBÊTH IÔPAKRBÊTH IÔBOLTHOSÊTH BOLKODÊPH BASOUMAPANTA THNUCHTHETHONI RINGCHOSERSÔ APOMPSIPAKERBÔTH PAKARASARA PAKOUBA AAAKACHOCH RABKAB (Gr.) and you god, who makes things dry, ruler, who holds back the fruit that has already grown, hold in the same way Sapautoulus who Pomponia bore, bind him, break his strength, his heart, his liver, his mind, his sense. I conjure you to the parapet by your divinity, that Sapautulos cannot see, (Lat.) entangle him in a cloth in the theatre, in the ring of the amphitheatre … (Gr.) I call on you, the great and strong and powerful ruler, who captivates and binds with unbreakable, eternal, strong and steely shackles. Put an end to his life, conquer, shake, bind, subdue, cast down Sapautoulos, tie him down, make him weak, so that … that he does not leave this place and does not go out of the gate, and does not want to leave this place, but he shall remain in his place through your strong, eternal, steely shackles. The soul of Sapautoulos, who Pomponia bore … (Lat.) He should suffer, he should be entangled by this cloth, he should be bound up. He should not see the bear, he should bind no-one, his fists should be destroyed, and there should be no force with which to wound, or to make blood flow. Sapautoulus should not be able to run, his feet, muscles and abdomen should be bound down in earth, bringing together of you and (?) Sapautoulus, make... January in every moment (Gr.) now, quickly EULAMÔ EREIKISPHÊTH ARARACH ARARA ÊPHTHISIKERE

DT 266

Origin: Sousse, Africa. Grave (nr. road from Kairouan).
Date: Second or third century.
Bibliography: dfx 11.2.1/4; LCT 144.
Notes: Folded.

[---o]pe commendo tibi quo[d]
[---]mella ut illiam inmittas dae-
[monibus?---]n aliquos infernales ut non per-
[mittatur?---] es me contemnere sed faciat
[quaecu]mque desidero Vettia quem peperit Optata vobis enim adiuvantibus
ut amoris mei causa non dormiat non ce-
bum non escam accipere possit
καρκε γενθιμοι μωκ θιεμδδ
ωκεεντι μοι θεψε
charaktêres obligo Vetti<a>e [quam]
peperit Optata sensum sap[i]entiam et [intel]-
lectum et voluntatem ut amet me Fe[licem]
quem peperit Fructa ex ha[c] die ex h[ac hora]
ut obliviscatur patris et matris et [omni]-
um suorum et amicorum omnium [et omnium]
virorum amoris mei {autem} <gratia> Fe[licis quem]
peperit Fructa Vettia que[m peperit Optata
solum me in mente habeat [--- insani-]
ens vigilans uratur frigat [---]
ardeat Vettia quam peper[it Optata ---]
[a]moris et desideri<i> m[ei causa---]
[------]

...I hand over to you who ... so that you send her to the daemons ... any infernals, so that she cannot be allowed ... to despise me, but should do whatever I desire. For you are supporting me so that Vettia, who Optata bore, cannot sleep nor accept nourishment or food because of love for me ... KARKE GENTHIMOI MÔK THIEMDD ÔKEENTI MOI THEPSIE I bind up the senses, wisdom and intellect and will of Vettia, who Optata bore, so that she loves me, Felix who Fructa bore, from this day, from this hour, so that she should forget her father and mother and all her friends and all men, but not love for me, Felix who Fructa bore. Vettia, who Optata bore, should have only me in her mind ... sleeping or waking, may she burn, may she roast ... may Vettia, who Optata bore glow ... with love and desire for me ...

DT 267

Origin: Sousse, Africa. Grave (nr. road from Kairouan).
Date: Second century.
Bibliography: dfx 11.2.1/5; LCT 145.
Notes: Folded.

[------]
[---]ηναρο[--]
[---]πζο[--]αχ[---]
[-]ε[---]ρωταρξο[---]
[κ]ειδεροσανδαλε
[ερ]εσχειγαλ
[δα]μναμενευς σεριροχε
[σε]μεσειλαμ σατραπερκμηφ
[-]εθμομαω μαρχαχον
χθαμαρζαξ ζαρακ[α]θαρα
θωβαρραβαυ θαρναχαχα
παραιθερε ακραμμαχαμαρει
λαμψουρη λαμψουχνι
σεσεργεοβαρφαραγγης
κωγιτε Βονωσα<μ> κουαμ
[π]επεριτ Παπτη αμαρε
[μ]η Οππιομ κουεμ πεπεριτ
Ουενερια αμωρε σακρω σινε
ιντερμισσιωνε [-] νον ποσσιτ

δορμειρε Βονωσα νεκουε ησσε
[---]Βονωσα νεκουε αλιουτ
[------]

90 degrees to rest of text
σεδ αβρομπατουρ ετ μη σωλυμ[---]
ο[υ]ιδερετ ομνιβους διηβους αδξ[---]
ουσκουε αδ διεμ μορτις σουε ι[---]

ÊNARO ...PZO .. AX ... E ...RÔTARXO ... KEIDEROSANDALE ERESCHEIGAL DAMNAMENEUS SERIROCHE SEMESEILAM SATRAPERKMÊPH ETHOMAÔ MARCHACHON CHTHAMARZAX ZARAKATHARA THÔBARRABAU THARNACHACHA PARAITHERE AKRAMMACHAMAREI LAMPSIOURÊ LAMPSIOUCHNI SESERGEOBARPHARAGGÊS compel Bonosa, who Papte bore, to love me, Oppius, who Veneria bore, with a holy, unbroken love. Bonosa should not be able to sleep nor eat ... Bonosa, and not others ... but should be broken up and only me ... should be seeing for all days ... until the day of her death ...

DT 270

Origin: Sousse, Africa. Grave (nr. road from Kairouan).
Date: Second century.
Bibliography: dfx 11.2.1/8; LCT 148.
Notes: Folded.

Αδ[ιουρ]ο επ [--] περ μαγνουμ δεουμ ετ
περ [αν]θέροτας [--] ετ περ εουμ κουι αβετ
αρχεπτορεμ σουπρα χαπουθ ετ περ σε-
πτεμ σθελλας ου{υ}θ εξ κουα ορα
οχ σομπ{π}οσουερο νον δορμιαθ Σεξ-
τίλλιος Διονισίε φιλιους ουραθουρ
φουρενς νον δορμιαθ νεκουε σεδεατ
νεκουε λοκουατουρ σεδ ιν μεντεμ αβ-
ιατ με Σέπθιμαμ Ἀμένε φιλια ουραθουρ φουρενς αμορε ετ δεσιδεριο
μεο ανιμα ετ χορ ουραθουρ Σεξτίλι Διονισίε φιλιους αμορε ετ δεσιδεριο μεο Σεπτίμες Ἀμένε φιλιε του αου-

τεμ Αβαρ Βαρβαριε Ελοεε Σαβαοθ
Παχνουφυ Πυθιπεμι φαχ Σεξτι-
λίουμ Διονισίε φιλιουμ νε σομνου-
μ χονθινγαθ σεθ αμορε ετ δεσιδεριο μεο ουραθουρ ουιιους σιπιριτους
ετ χορ χομβουρατουρ ομνια μεμ-
βρα θοθιους χορπορις Σεξτίλι Διονισίε φιλιους σι μινους δεσχενδο ιν α-
δυτους Ὀσυρις ετ δισσολουαμ θεν
θαπεεν ετ μιτταν ουθ α φουλ
α φλουμινε φερατουρ
εγω ενιμ σουμ μαγνους
δεχανους δει μαγνι δει
αχραμμαχαλαλα [-]ε

I beseech ... through the great god and through Anterotas ... and through him who has a hawk above his head and through the seven stars, so that Sextilius, son of Dionysia, from the hour I will set out here should not sleep, but should burn with insanity. He should not sleep nor sit nor speak, but should have me, Septima daughter of Amoena in mind. He should burn with insanity, love and desire for me, the spirit and heart of Sextilius, son of Dionysia should burn with love and desire for me, Septima daughter of Amoena. But you ABAR BARBARIE ELOE SABAOTH PACHNOUPHU PUTHIPEMI, make Sextilius, son of Dionysia, not touch sleep, but burn with love and desire for me, his spirit and heart should be burnt up, all the limbs and the whole body of Sextilius, son of Dionysia. If little, I descend into the Adyton of Osiris and will destroy the burial and send HIM, so that he is carried along the river. For I am the great chief of the god, great god AXRAMMAXALALA E.

DT 275

Origin: Sousse, Africa. in a libation tube for a grave (nr. road from Kairouan).
Date: Second century.
Bibliography: Tremel 25; dfx 11.2.1/12; LCT 152.
Notes: Rolled.

ΚΚΚΑΑΑΛΛΛ *charaktêres* ΘΦΙΟΠΑΙΑΙΑΟ
Privatianu<s> Supestianu<s> russei qui et Naucelliu<s> Salutare<s>
Superstite<s> russei servu<s> Reguli Eliu<s> Castore Repentinu<s>

226　　　　　*Appendix: Select Catalogue of Curses*

KKKAAAΛΛΛ *charaktēres* ΘΦΙΟΠΑΙΑΙΑΟ
Glaucu\<s> Argutu\<s> veneti Destroiugu\<s> Glauci cadant Lydu\<s>
Alumnu\<s> cada{n}t Italu\<s> Tyriu\<s> cadant Faru\<s> cada{n}t Croceu\<s> cada[n]t
Elegantu\<s> cada{n}t P{r}anc\<r>atiu\<s> Oclopecta Virbosu\<s> cadant
Adamatu\<s> cada{n}t Securu\<s> Mantineu\<s> Prevalente cadant
Paratu\<s> Vagarfita cadant Divite\<s> Gar\<r>ulu\<s> cadant Cesareu\<s>
Germanicu\<s> veneti cada{n}t Danuviu\<s> cada{n}t
KKKAAAΛΛΛ *charaktēres* ΘΦΙΟΠΑΙΑΙΑΟ
Latrone Vagulu\<s> cadant Agricola canda{n}t Cursore
Auricomu\<s> cadant Epafu\<s> cadant Hellenicu\<s> cadant
Ideu\<s> Centauru\<s> cadant Bracatu\<s> Virgineu\<s> cadant
Ganimede\<s> cada{n}t Multivolu\<s> cada{n}t E[o]lu\<s>
Oceanu\<s> Eminentu\<s> cada[nt V?]agu\<s> cada{n}t
Eucles cada{n}t Verbosu\<s> cadant
KKKAAAΛΛΛ *charaktēres* ΘΦΙΟΠΑΙΑΙΑΟ
Privatianu\<s> cadat vertat fragat male giret
KKKAAAΛΛΛ *charaktēres* ΘΦΙΟΠΑΙΑΙΑΟ
Naucelliu\<s> Supestianu\<s> russei cadat vert[at fran]gat
KKKAAAΛΛΛ *charaktēres* ΘΦΙΟΠΑΙΑΙΑΟ
Supestite\<s> russei servu\<s> Reguli cadat vertat fran[gat]
Salutare\<s> cadat vertat frangat
Eliu\<s> cadat vertat frangat vertat
Castore cadat vertat frangat vertat
Repentinu\<s> cadat vertat frangat
KKKAAAΛΛΛ *charaktēres* ΘΦΙΟΠΑΙΑΙΑΟ

Six lines wrap around edges, starting in top left.
Obligate et gravate equos veneti et russei ne currere possint nec frenis audire possint nec se mo\<v>ere possint
set cadant frangant dis[f]rangantur et agitantes veneti et russei vertant nec lora teneant nec agitare possint nec retinere equos possint nec ante se nec adversarios suos videat nec vincant vertant

Privatianus, Superstianus of the Reds and Naucellius, Salutaris, Superstes of the Reds, the slave of Regulus, Aelius, Castor, Repentinus. May Glaucus, Argutus of the Blues (and) Destroiugus of Glaucus fall; may Lydus fall, may Alumnus fall; may Italus (and) Tyrius fall; may Farus fall; may Croceus fall; may Elegantus fall;

may Pancratius, Hoplopecta (and) Verbosus fall; may Admatus fall; may Securus, Mantineus (and) Praevalens fall; may Paratus (and) Vagarfita fall; may Dives (and) Garrulus fall; may Caesareus fall; Germanicus of the Blues fall; may Danuvius fall; may Latro (and) Vagulus fall; may Agricola fall; may Cursor fall; may Auricomus fall; may Epafus fall; may Hellenicus fall; may Ideus (and) Centaurus fall; may Bracatus (and) Virgineus fall; may Ganimedes fall; may Multivolus fall; may Aeolus, Oceanus (and) Eminentus fall; may Vagus fall; may Eucles fall; may Verbosus fall. May Privatianus fall; may he be turned back, be broken, turn badly (around the turning post). May Naucellius Superstianus of the Reds fall, be turned back, be broken. May Superstites of the Reds, slave of Regulus, fall, be turned back, broken; may Salutaris fall, be turned back, be broken; may Aelius fall, be turned back, be broken, be turned back; may Castor fall, be turned back, be broken, be turned back; may Repentinus fall, be turned back, be broken.

Bind and weigh down the horses of the Blues and Reds, so that they can neither run nor obey the bridle nor move themselves, but may they fall and be broken and be broken apart, and may the charioteers of the Blues and Reds be turned back, and neither hold the reins nor be able to drive nor restrain the horses, nor see in front of themselves or their opponents, nor may they win but may they be turned back.

DT 300

Origin: Constantine, Africa. Grave.
Date: Third or fourth century.
Bibliography: dfx 11.3.1/1; LCT 183.
Notes: Drawings of daemons with large phalli and goat-like legs.

Side A
    [--]aviuli
    [--]tei gutur
        babo
        w
        o o os
[--]o
[--a?]tur
        desumatur
        ut facia<s> il<l>um sine

                    sensu sine memo-
                    ria sine <spi>ritu sine
            medul<l>a
    sit   vi mutuscus

Side B
[---]ento demando tibi ut ac<c>eptu<m h>abeas
[S]ilvanu<m> q(uem) p(eperit) Vulva facta et custodias
[---e]nto [de]-
mando ut fa-
cia<s> [il]lum mo-
rtu<um>
depona<s>
eum at
Tartara

... should be taken up, so that you make him without sense, without memory, without spirit, without marrow. May he be mute by force ...

... I hand over to you, so that you accept Silvanus, whom Vulva Facta bore, and you should defend ... I hand (him?) over, so that you kill him. You should lay him down in Tartarus.

DT 304

Origin: Sousse, Africa. Grave (Nr. road from Kairouan).
Date: First century.
Bibliography: dfx 11.2.1/33; LCT 172.

Fragment 1.	*Fragment 2.*
ενθω θ	σεριβ
ενηθι ιαω	ρα
βμομη β	ειφωχ
θ[--]θοπτεπιλ	οθμα
θιουθκι	ευο
ροσταφαμ	θ
θενθωεν	[------]
νεβενν	μαρσαμωθ
Ευλαμω θισ	[α]νοχ φρη

[-]Τοττινα<μ> με α[μαρε---]
ρ σινε μενδ[ακιο?---] ουτ
[αμε]τ με σολουμ[--- ουτ α]μετ με
[σολουμ] Τοττινα κου[αμ πεπεριτ---]
ιιαρυρεσ[-]
τσο

Fragment 4.
[------]
ουειδερετ σιμ[---]
[v]ον ποσ<σ>ιτ κουανδιε[---ομνιβους διηβ]-
ους ουιξηριτ [ουσκουε αδ διεμ μορτις σουε---]

ENTHÔ TH SERIB ENÊTHI IAÔ RA BMOMÊ B EIPHÔCH TH ...
THOPTEPIL OUMA THIOUTHKI EUO ROSTAPHAM TH THENTHÔEN
NEBENN MARSAMÔTH EULAMÔ THIS ANOCH PHRÊ (Compel?) Tottina
to love me ... without falsehood(?) ... so that she loves only me ... so that
Tottina, who ... bore loves only me ... was seeing ... cannot inasmuch as ...
should have lived all days, right up to the day of her death ...

SGD 139

Origin: Carthage, Africa. Fountain of 1000 amphorae.
Date: Second or third century.
Bibliography: *SEG* 9.838; Tremel 66.

[Αρθυ Λα]ιλαμ Σεμεσειλαμ αεηιουω βαχυχ βακαξιχυχ με-
νε βαιχυχ αβρασαξ βασζαβαχχχ
κύριοι θεοί κατάσχετα[ι π]οιήσαται ετε [---]ε
[------]
[------]
[---]καὶ οὐενέτου τὸ τοῦ Στραβωνιανοῦ Ἰάσων Ἕλλην
Φέροξ Γάνγης Ὁλόχρυσος σὺν τῷ ἰδ-
ίῳ Εὔανδερ σὺν τῷ ἰδίῳ Φ[οῖβ]ος σὺν τῷ ἰδίῳ Πατρί[κιος σὺν τῷ ἰδίῳ
[------]
τὴν σήμε]ρον ἡμέραν ἐν τ[ῷ] κίρκῳ μὴ ἰσχύειν μὴ τρέχειν μὴ πηδῆσαι μὴ πιάσαι μὴ
τὰς καμπτῆρας περι[κυ]κλεῦσα[ι μήτε] νεικῆ[σαι]
[------]

[---]απι [---] τ[--- τ]ὴν ἀρέαν τοῦ κίρκου
ποσάκις ἂν ἐξέλθωσιν
σὺν τοῖς ἰδίοις ἡνιόχοι[ς]
[------]
[---]δεσμο[---]εν
τῇ σήμηρον ἡμέρᾳ
καὶ ὑμᾶς ἐπικα[λοῦμαι---]
[------]
[---]αβρα-
σαξ βασζαβαχχ-
υχ κύριοι θεοί ποιήσατ[αί μ]οι τελεώ[σαται]
[------]
[---]ῥουσέ[ου?]
τὸ τοῦ Στραβω-
νιανοῦ σὺν τοῖς ἰδίοις ἡνι[όχοις ---]
[------]
[---]Ἕλλεν<α> Φέροκ[α? Ὁλόχ]ρυσ[ον -]
ναρον Π-
ατρίκιον Φοῖβον αμ[---]σι[---]σο
[------]
[------]
[---]ολας
πρ[---]πω[---]

ARTHU LAILAM SEMESEILAM AEÊIOUÔ BACHUCH BAKAXICHUCH MENE BAICHUCH ABRASAX BASZABACHCHCH mighty gods, bind, accomplish ... and from the Blues of Strabonianus: Jason, Hellen, Pherox, Ganges, Holochrysus with their (charioteer), Evander with their (charioteer), Phoebus with their (charioteer), Patricius with their (charioteer) ... today in the circus may they not be strong, may they not run, nor go through, nor press hard, nor turn around the turning point, nor win ... the circuit of the circus, they should go out with their charioteers often ... today and I call you ... ABRASAX BASZABACHCHUCH mighty gods, accomplish, complete ... from the Reds of Strabonianus with their charioteers ... Hellen, Pherox, Holochrysus ... Patricius, Phoebus ...

Gager 10 (trans)

Origin: Carthage, Africa. Grave (cemetery for Roman officials).
Date: Second or third century.
Bibliography: DT 242; Tremel 61.

Ἐξορκίζω σε ὅστ[ι]ς ποτ' εἶ νεκυδαίμ[ω]ν τὸν θεὸν τὸν κτίσαντα γῆν κ[α]ὶ
οὐρανὸν Ιωνα
ἐξορκίζω σε τὸν θεὸν τὸν ἔχοντα τὴν ἐξουσίαν τῶν χθονίων τόπων
Νειχαροπληξ ἐξορκίζω σε τὸν θε[ὸν ---] ο [--] ωαε [--] ο πνευμάτων α[---]β [ἐ]
ξορκί-
[ζω σε] τὸν θεὸν τῆς Ἀνάγκης τὸν μέγαν Αρουροβααρζαγραν ὀρκίζω σε τὸν
θεὸν τὸν πρωτόγονον τῆς Γῆς Εφονκεισαιβλαβλεισφθειβαλ ὀρκίζω σε τὸν θεὸν
τῶν
ἀνέμων καὶ πνευμάτων Λαιλαμ ὀρκίζω σε τὸν θεὸν τὸν ἐπὶ τῶν
τειμωριῶν παντὸς ἐνψύχ[ου ---] ραπωκμηφ ὀρκίζω σε τὸν θεὸν τὸν τῶν οὐρανίων στερεωμάτων δεσπότην Αχραμαχαμαρει ὀρκίζω σε τὸν θεὸν
τὸν χθόνιον τὸν δεσπόζοντα παντὸς ἐνψύχου Σαλβαλαχαωβρη ὀρκίζω σε τὸν
θεὸν τὸν νεκυαγωγὸν τὸν ἅγιον Ἑρμῆν, τὸν οὐράνιον Αων
κρειφτον ἐπίγειον ἀλέον [---] βνιν τὸν χ[θό]νιον Αρχφησον ὀρκίζω σε τὸν θεὸν τὸν ἐπὶ τῆς ψυχοδοσίας παντὸς ἀνθρώπου γεγεγεγεν κ<ε>ί-
μενον Ιαω ὀρκίζω σε τὸν θεὸν τὸν φωτίζοντα καὶ σκοτίζοντα τὸν κόσμον
Σεμεσειλαμ ὀρκίζω σε τὸν θεὸν τὸν πάσης μαγείας τὴν ἔωγ-
σιν ἀνθρωπίνην σειυπν [---] Σαβαωθ ὀρκίζω σε τὸν θεὸν τ[ὸν] τοῦ Σα[λο]-
μόνος Σουαρμιμωουθ ὀρκίζω σε τὸν θεὸν τὸν τοῦ δευτέρου στερεώ-
ματος ἐν ἑαυτῷ τὴν δύναμιν ἔχοντα Μαρμαραωθ ὀρκίζω σε τὸν θεὸν
τὸν τῆς παλινγενεσίας Θωβαρραβαυ ὀρκίζω σε τὸν θεὸν τὸν
τοὺς ληνοὺς ὅλους [-] α [---]ιευ ὀρ[κί]ζω σε τὸν θεὸν τὸν τῆς ἡμέρας ταύτης
ἦσσε
ὀρκίζω Αωαβαωθ ὀρκίζω σε τὸν θεὸν τὸν ἔχοντα τὴν
ἐξουσίαν τῆς ὥρας ταύτης ἦσσε ὀρκίζω Ἰσοῦ ὀρκίζω σε τὸν θεὸν τὸν τῶν
οὐρανίων στερεωμάτων δεσπόζοντα Ιαω ιβοηα ὀρκί-
ζω σε τὸν θεὸν τὸν οὐράνιον Ιθυαω ὀρκίζω σε τὸν θεὸν τὸν [τ]ὴν δι[ά]νοιαν
παντὶ ἀνθρώπω χαρισάμενον Νεγεμψενπυενιπη
ὀρκίζω σε τὸν θεὸν τὸν πλάσαντα πᾶν γένος ἀνθρώπ[ων] Χωοιχαρεαμων
ὀρκίζω σε τὸν θεὸν τὸν τὴν ὅρασιν παντὶ ἀνθρώπω χαρισάμενον Ηχεταρωψιευ ὀρκίζω σε τὸν θεὸν τὸν χαρισάμενον τοῖς ἀνθρώποις τὴν διὰ τῶν ἄρθρων κ<ε>ίνησιν Θεσθενοθριλ [-] Χε-
αυνξιν ὀρκίζω σε τὸν θεὸν τὸν πατροπάτορα Φνουφοβοην ὀρκίζω

σε τὸν θεὸν τὸν τὴν κοίμησίν σοι δεδωρημένον
καὶ ἀπολύσαντά σε ἀπὸ δ[εσμῶ]ν τοῦ βίου Νεθμομαω ὁρκίζω σε τὸν
θεὸν τὸν παντὸς μύθου κυριεύοντα Ναχαρ ὁρκί-
ζω σε τὸν θεὸν τὸν τοῦ ὕπνου δεσπόζοντα Σθομβλοην
ὁρκίζω σε τὸν θεὸν τὸν ἀέριον τὸν πελάγιον
τὸν ὑπόγειον τὸν οὐρ[ά]νιον τῶν πελάγων τὴν ἀρχὴν
συνβεβλημένον τὸν μονογενῆ τὸν ἐξ αὐ-
τοῦ ἀναφανέντα τὸν πυρὸς καὶ ὕδατος καὶ γῆς καὶ ἀέρος τὴν
ἐξουσίαν ἔχοντα Ωηιαωεεηαφετι προσ-
εξορκίζω σε κατὰ τὴν γῆν ὀνόματα Ἑκάτης τριμόρφου
μαστειγοφόρου δεδούλου λαμπαδούχου
χρυσοσανδαλιαιμοποτιχθονίαν τὴν ἱππειτρο
ακτι [--] φι ερεσχειγαλ νεβουτοσουαντ
εἴπω σοι καὶ τὸ ἀλιθινὸν ὄνομα ὃ τρέμει Τάρταρα
γῆ βυθὸς οὐρανὸς Φορβαβορφορβα-
βορφ ορορ βασυνετειρω μολτιηαιω φυλακή
ναπυφεραιω Ἀνάγκη μασκελλι
μασκελλω φνουκενταβαωθ ὀρεοβαρζαργρα
ησθανχουχηνχουχεωχ ἵνα
διακονήσῃς μοι ἐν τῷ κίρκῳ τῇ πρὸς ιζ' ἰδὼν
[ν]οεμβρίων καὶ καταδήσῃς
πᾶν μέλος πᾶν νεῦρον τοὺς ὤμους τοὺς καρποὺς
τοὺς ἀνκῶνας τῶν ἡνιόχων
τοῦ ῥουσσέου Ὀλύμπου καὶ Ὀλυμπιάνου καὶ
Σκοπτίου καὶ Ιουυένκου
βασάνισον αὐτῶν τὴν διανοίαν τὰς φρένας
τὴν αἴσθησιν ἵνα μὴ
νοῶσιν τι π[ο]ιῶσιν ἀπόκνισον αὐτῶν τὰ
ὄμματα ἵνα μὴ βλεπῶσιν
μήτε αὐτοὶ μήτε οἱ ἵπποι οὓς μέλλουσιν
ἐλαύνειν Αἴγυπτον
Καλλίδρομον καὶ εἴ τις σὺν αὐτοῖς ἄλλος
ζευχθήσεται Οὐαλε[ν]-
τεῖνον καὶ Λαμπαδ [---] νον καὶ Μαῦ-
ρον Λαμπαδίου
καὶ Χρύσασπιν Ἴουβαν καὶ Ἰνδόν
Παλμάτον καὶ
Σούπερβον καὶ [-] ηιον Βού-

βαλον Κην-
σοράπου Ἔρεινα καὶ εἴ τινα
ἄλλον ἵπ-
πον ἐξ αὐτῶν μέλλει ἐλαύ-
νε[ι]ν
καὶ εἴ τις ἄλλος ἵππος τού-
τοις μέλ-
λει συνζεύγνυσθαι
προ-
λαβέτωσαν ἐπὶ νεί-
κην μὴ ἔλθωσιν

I invoke you, whoever you are, spirit of one untimely dead, IÔNA, the god who established earth and heaven. I bind you by oath, NEICHAROPLÊX, the god who holds the power of the places down beneath. I bind you by oath ... the god ... of the spirits. I bind you by oath, great AROUROBAARZAGRAN, the god of Necessity. I bind you by oath, BLABLEISPHTHEIBAL, the firstborn god of earth on which you lie(?). I bind you, LAILAM, the god of winds and spirits. I bind you ... RAPÔKMÊPH (?) the god who presides over all penalties of every living creature. I bind you, lord ACHRAMACHAMAREI the god of the heavenly firmaments. I bind you, SALBALACHAÔBRÊ, the god of the underworld, who lords over every living creature. I bind you ARCHPHÊSON (?) of the underworld, the god who leads departed souls, holy Hermes, the heavenly AÔNKREIPH, the terrestrial ... I bind you by oath, IAÔ, the god appointed over the giving of soul to everyone, GEGEGEGEN. I bind you, SEMESEILAM, the god who illuminates and darkens the world. I bind you SABAÔTH, the god who [brought] knowledge of all the magical arts. I bind you SOUARMIMÔOUTH, the god of Solomon. I bond you MARMARAÔTH, the god of the second firmament who possesses power in himself. I bind you THÔBARRABAU, the god of rebirth. I bind you ... the god who ... the whole wine-troughs ... I bind you, AÔABAÔTH, the god of this day in which I bind you. I bind you ISOS (Jesus?), the god who has the power of this hour in which I bind you. I bind you, IAÔ IBOÊA, the god who lords it over the heavenly firmaments. I bind you, ITHUAÔ, the god of heaven. I bind you NEGEMPSENPUENIPÊ, the god who gives thinking to each person as a favour. I bind you, CHÔOICHAREAMÔN the god who fashioned every kind of human being. I bind you, ÊCHETARÔPSIEU, the god who granted vision to all men as a favour. I bind you, THESTHENOTHRIL CHEAUNIXIN, who granted as a favour to men movement by the joints of the body. I bind you,

PHNOUPHOBOÊN, the Father-of-father god. I bind you, NETHMOMAÔ, the god who has given you [the corpse] the gift of sleep and freed you from the chains of life. I bind you, NACHAR, the god who is the master of all tales. I bind you, STHOMBLOÊN, the god who is lord over slumber. I bind you, ÔÊ IAO EEÊAPH, the god of the air, the sea, the subterranean world, and the heavens, the god who has produced the beginning of the seas, the only begotten one who appeared out of himself, the one who holds the power of fire, of water, of the earth and of the air. I further bind you, AKTI...PHI ERESCHEICHAL NEBOUTOSOUANT, throughout the earth (by?) names of triple form Hekate, the tremor-bearing, scourge-bearing, torch-carrying, golden-slippered-blood-sucking-netherworldly and horse-riding one (?). I utter to you the true name that shakes Tartarus, earth, the deeps and heaven, PHORBABORPHORBABORPHOROR BA SUNETEIRÔ MOLTIÊAIÔ Protector NAPUPHERAIÔ Necessity MASKELLI MASKELLÔ PHNOUKENTABAÔTH OREOBARZARGRA ÊSTHANCHOUCHÊNCHOUCHEÔCH, in order that you serve me in the circus on the eighth of November and bind every limb, every sinew, the shoulders, the wrists, and the ankles of the charioteers of the Red Team: Olympus, Olympianus, Scorteus, and Iuvencus. Torture their thoughts, their minds, and their senses so that they do not know what they are doing. Pluck out their eyes so that they cannot see, neither they nor their horses which they are about to drive: the Egyptian steed Callidromus and any other horses teamed with them; Valentinus and Lampadius ... Maurus who belongs to Lampadius, Chrysaspis, Juba and Indus, Palmatus and Superbus ... Boubalus who belongs to Censorapus; and Ereina. If he should ride any other horse instead of them, or if some other horse is teamed with these, let them [not] outdistance [their foes] lest they ride to victory.

Gager 12 (trans)

Origin: Carthage, Africa. Grave (cemetery for Roman officials).
Date: Second or third century.
Bibliography: DT 241; CIL VIII 12511 (drawing); Tremel 60.
Notes: rolled. Charaktêres around all four edges.

Σεμεσιλαμ δαματαμενευς ληοννα
λλελαμ [-] λαικαμ ερμουβελη ιακουβιαι ωερβηθ
ιωπακερβηθ ηωμαλθαβηθ αλλασαν καταρα ἐξορκί-

ζω ὑμᾶς κατὰ τῶν μεγάλων ὀνομάτων ἵνα
καταδήσητε πᾶν μέλος καὶ πᾶν νεῦρον Βικτωρικοῦ
ὅ[ν] ἔτεκεν [γ]ῆ μήτηρ παντὸς ἐνψύχου τοῦ ἡνιόχου τοῦ
βενέτου καὶ τῶν ἵππων αὐτοῦ ὧν μέλλι ἐλαύνιν Σεκουνδινοῦ Ἰούβενιν καὶ Ἀτβοκᾶτον καὶ Βούβαλον καὶ Βικτωρικοῦ
Πομπηϊανοῦ καὶ Βαϊανοῦ καὶ Βίκτορος καὶ Ἐξιμίου κα-
ὶ τῶν Μεσσαλῶν Δομινάτορα καὶ ὅσοι ἐὰν συνζευχθῶσιν αὐτοῖς κατάδησον αὐτῶν τὰ σκέλη καὶ τὴν ὁπμὴν καὶ
τὸ πήδημα καὶ τὸν δρόμον ἀμαύρωσον αὐτῶν τὰ
ὄμματα ἵνα μὴ βλέπωσιν στρέβλωσον αὐτῶν
τὴν ψυχὴν καὶ τὴν καρδίαν ἵνα μὴ [π]νέωσιν ὡς οὗτ-
ος ὁ ἀλέκτωρ καταδέδεται τοῖς ποσὶ καὶ ταῖς χερσὶ{τ} καὶ τῇ
κεφαλῇ οὕτως καταδήσατ[ε] τὰ σκέλη καὶ τὰς χιρας καὶ τὴν
κεφαλὴν καὶ τὴν καρδίαν Βικτωρικοῦ τοῦ ἡνιόχου τοῦ βενέτου ἐν τῇ αὔριν ἡμέρα καὶ τοὺς ἵππους οὓς μέλλι ἐλαύνιν Σεκουνδινοῦ Ἰούβενιν καὶ Ἀτβοκᾶτον καὶ Βούβαλον καὶ Λαυριᾶτον καὶ Βικτωρικοῦ Πομπηϊανὸν καὶ
Βαϊανὸν καὶ Βίκτορα καὶ Ἐξιμίου[μ] καὶ τῶν Μεσσάλης
Δομινᾶτον καὶ ὅσοι ἐὰν αὐτοῖς συνζευχθῶσιν [ἔ]τι ἐ-
ξορκίζω ὑμᾶς κατὰ τοῦ ἐπάν[ω] τοῦ οὐρανοῦ θεοῦ
τοῦ καθημένου ἐπὶ τῶν Χερουβι ὁ διορίσας τὴν γῆν
καὶ χωρίσας τὴν θάλασσαν Ιαω αβριαω αρβαθιαω
σαβαω
αδωναϊ ἵνα καταδήσητε Βικτωρικ{τ}ὸν τὸν ἡνί-
οχον τοῦ βενέτου καὶ τοὺς ἵππους οὓς μέλλι ἐλαύνιν
Σεκουνδινοῦ Ἰούβενιν καὶ Ἀτουοκᾶτον καὶ Βικτωρικοῦ
Πομπηϊανὸν καὶ Βαϊανὸν καὶ Βίκτορα καὶ Ἐξιμίουμ
καὶ τῶν Μεσσάλης Δομ[ι]νᾶτον ἵνα ἐπὶ νείκην μ[ὴ]
ἔλ[θωσι]ν ἐν τῇ αὔριν ἡμέρα ἐν τῷ κίρκῳ ἤδη ἤδη
ταχὺ τα[χύ]

SEMESILAM DAMATAMENEUS IÊSNNALLELAM LAIKAM ERMOUBELÊ IAKOUB IA IÔERBÊTH IÔPAKERBÊTH EÔMALTHABÊTH ALLASAN. A curse. I invoke you by the great names so that you will bind every limb and every sinew of Victoricus – the charioteer of the Blue team, to whom Earth, mother of every living thing, gave birth – and of his horses which he is about to race; under Secundinus (are) Iuvenis and Advocatus and Bubalus; under Victoricus are Pompeianus and Baianus and Victor and Eximius and also Dominator who belongs to Messala; also (bind) any others who may be yoked with them. Bind their legs, their onrush, their bounding and their running; blind their eyes so they cannot see and twist their soul and heart so that they cannot breathe. Just as this rooster has been bound by its feet, hands, and head, so bind the legs and hands and head and heart of Victoricus the charioteer of the Blue team, for tomorrow; and also (bind) the horses which he is about to race; under Secundinus, Iuvenis and Advocatus and Bubalus and Lauriatus; under Victoricus, Pompeianus and Baianus and Victor and Eximius and Dominator who belongs to Messala and any others who are yoked with them. Also I invoke you by the god above the heaven, who is seated upon the Cherubim who divided the earth and separated the sea, IAÔ ABRIAÔ ARBATHIAÔ ADÔNAI SABAÔ, so that you may bind Victoricus the charioteer of the Blue team and the horses which he is about to race; under Secundinus, Iuvenus and Advocatus, and under Victoricus Pompeianus and Baianus and Victor and Eximius and Dominator who belongs to Messala; so that they may not reach victory tomorrow in the circus. Now, now, quickly, quickly.

Gager 36 (trans)

Origin: Sousse, Africa. Grave (nr. road from Kairouan).
Date: Third century.
Bibliography: DT 271.
Notes: Pierced then rolled. Text is a mix of Greek and Latin.

Horcizo se daemonion pneumn to enthade cimenon to onomati to agio Αωθ
Αβ[α]ωθ τὸν θεὸν τοῦ Αβρααν καὶ τὸν Ιαω τὸν τοῦ Ιακου Ιαω
Αωθ Αβαωθ θεὸν τοῦ Ισραμα ἄκουσον τοῦ ὀνόματος ἐντείμου
καὶ φ[οβ]εροῦ καὶ μεγάλου   καὶ ἄξον αὐτὸν πρὸς τὴν
cae apelthe pros ton Orbanon hon ethecn Urbana
Δομιτιανὴν ἣν ἔτεκεν Κ[αν]διδά ἐρῶντα μαινόμενον ἀγρυπνοῦντα ἐπὶ τῇ φιλίᾳ αὐτῆς καὶ ἐπιθυ[μ]ία καὶ δεόμενον αὐτῆς ἐπανελθεῖν
εἰς τὴν οἰκίαν αὐτοῦ σύμβιο[ν] γενέσθαι ὀρκίζω σε τὸν μέγαν θεὸν
τὸν αἰώνιον καὶ ἐπαιώνιο[ν] καὶ παντοκράτορα τὸν ὑπεράνω τῶν
ὑπεράνω θεῶν ὀρκίζω [σ]ε τὸν κτίσαντα τὸν οὐρανὸν καὶ τὴν θάλασσαν ὀρκίζω σε τὸν διαχωρίσαντα τοὺς εὐσεβεῖς ὀρκίζω σε
τὸν διαστήσαντα τήν ῥάβδον ἐν τῇ θαλάσσῃ ἀγαγεῖν καὶ ζεῦξαι
τὸν Οὐρβανόν ὃν ἔτεκεν Οὐρβανά πρὸς τὴν Δομιτιανάν ἣν ἔτεκεν
Κανδιδά ἐρῶντα βασανιζόμενον ἀγρυπνοῦντα ἐπὶ τῇ ἐπιθυμία αὐ-

τῆς καὶ ἔρωτι ἵν' αὐτὴν σύμβιον ἀπάγῃ εἰς τὴν οἰκίαν ἑαυτοῦ ὁρκίζω σε τὸν ποιήσαντα τὴν ἡμίονον μὴ τεκεῖν ὁρκίζω σε τὸν διορίσαν-
τα τὸ φ[ῶς] ἀπὸ τοῦ σκότους ὁρκίζω σε τὸν συντρείβοντα τὰς πέτρας
ὁρκί[ζω] σε τὸν ἀπορ<ρ>ήξαντα τὰ ὄρη ὁρκίζω σε τὸν συνστρέφοντα τὴν
γῆν ἐ[πὶ τ]ῶν θεμελίων αὐτῆς ὁρκίζω σε τὸ ἅγιον ὄνομα ὃ οὐ λέγεται ἐν
τῷ ισα [---] ω ὀνομάσω αὐτὸ καὶ οἱ δαίμονες ἐξεγερθῶσιν ἔκθαμβοι καὶ περί-
φοβοι [γ]ενόμενοι ἀγαγεῖν καὶ ζεῦξαι σύμβιον τὸν Οὐρβανόν ὃν ἔτεκεν
Οὐρβανά πρὸς τὴν Δομιτιανάν ἣν ἔτεκεν Κανδιδά ἐρῶντα καὶ δεόμενον αὐτῆς ἤδη ταχύ ὁρκίζω σε τὸν φωστῆρα καὶ ἄστρα ἐν οὐρανῷ ποιήσαντα διὰ φωνῆς προστάγματος ὥστε φαίνειν πᾶσιν ἀνθρώποις
ὁρκίζω σε τὸν συνσείσαντα πᾶσαν τὴν οἰκουμένην καὶ τὰ ὄρη
ἐκτραχηλίζοντα καὶ ἐκβρά[ζ]οντα τὸν ποιοῦντα ἔκτρομον τὴν [γ]ῆ-
ν ἅπας<αν καὶ> καινίζοντα πάντας τοὺς κατοικοῦντας ὁρκίζω σε τὸν ποιήσαντα σημεῖα ἐν οὐρανῷ κ[αὶ] ἐπὶ γῆς καὶ θαλάσσης ἀγαγεῖν καὶ ζεῦξαι
σύμβιον τὸν Οὐρβανόν ὃν ἔ[τ]εκεν Οὐρβανά πρὸς τὴν Δομιτιανήν ἣν
ἔτεκεν Κανδιδα ἐρῶντα αὐτῆς καὶ ἀγρυπνοῦντα ἐπὶ τῇ ἐπιθυμία αὐτῆς δεόμενον αὐτῆς καὶ ἐρωτῶντα αὐτὴν ἵνα ἐπανέλθῃ εἰς τὴν οἰκίαν
αὐτοῦ σύμβιο[ς] γενομένη ὁρκίζω σε τὸν θεὸν τὸν μέγαν τὸν αἰώνιον καὶ παντοκράτορα ὃν φοβεῖται ὄρη καὶ νάπαι καθ' ὅλην τὴν οἰκουμένην δί ὃν ὁ λείων ἀφείησιν τὸ ἅρπασμα καὶ τὰ ὄρη τρέμει
καὶ [ἡ γῆ] καὶ ἡ θάλασσα ἔκαστον ἰδάλλεται ὃν ἔχει φόβον τοῦ Κυρίου
α[ἰ]ω[νίου] ἀθανάτου παντεφόπτου μεισοπονήρου ἐπισταμένου τὰ
γ[ενόμ]ενα ἀγαθὰ καὶ κακὰ καὶ κατὰ θάλασσαν καὶ ποταμοὺς καὶ τὰ ὄρη
καὶ [τὴν] γῆ[ν] Αωθ Αβαωθ τὸν θεὸν τοῦ Αβρααν καὶ τὸν Ιαω τὸν τοῦ Ιακου
Ιαω Αωθ Αβαωθ, θεὸν τοῦ Ισραμα ἄξον ζεῦξον τὸν Οὐρβανόν ὃν
ἔτεκεν Οὐρβα<νά> πρὸς τὴν Δομιτιανάν ἣν ἔτεκεν Κανδιδά ἐρῶντα
μαι[ν]όμενον βασανιζόμενον ἐπὶ τῇ φιλία καί ἔρωτι καὶ ἐπιθυμία
τῆς Δομιτιανῆς ἣν ἔτεκεν Κανδιδά ζεῦξον αὐτοὺς γάμω καὶ
ἔρωτι συμβιοῦντας ὅλω τῷ τῆς ζωῆς αὐτῶν χρόνω ποίησον αὐτὸν ὡς δοῦλον αὐτῇ ἐρῶντα ὑποταχθῆναι μηδεμίαν ἄλλη[ν]
γυναῖκα μήτε παρθένον ἐπιθυμοῦντα μόνην δὲ τὴν Δομιτια[νάν]
ἣν ἔτεκεν Κανδιδά σύμβιον ἔχειν ὅλω τῷ τῆς ζωῆς αὐτῶ[ν χρόνω]
ἤδη ἤδη ταχὺ ταχύ

I invoke you, daimonion spirit who lies here, by the holy name AÔTH ABAÔTH, the god of Abraham and IAÔ the god of Jacob, IAÔ AÔTH ABAÔTH, god of Israma, hear the honoured, dreadful and great name, go away to Urbanus, to whom Urbana gave birth, and bring him to Domitiana, to whom Candida gave birth, (so that) loving, frantic and sleepless with love and desire for her, he may beg her to return to his house and become his wife. I invoke you, the great god, eternal and more than eternal, almighty and exalted above the exalted ones. I invoke you who created the heaven and the sea. I invoke you, who set aside the righteous. I invoke you, who divided the staff in the sea, to bring Urbanus, to whom Urbana gave birth, and unite him with Domitiana, to whom Candida gave birth, loving, tormented and sleepless with desire and love for her, so that he may take her into his house as his wife. I invoke you, who made the mule unable to bear offspring. I invoke you, who separated light from darkness. I invoke you, who crushes rocks. I invoke you, who breaks apart mountains. I invoke you, who hardened the earth on its foundations. I invoke you, by the holy name which is not spoken ... I will mention it by a word with the same numerical equivalent and the daimones will be awakened, startled, terrified, to bring Urbanus, to whom Urbana gave birth, and unite him with Domitiana, to whom Candida gave birth, loving and begging for her. Now! Quickly! I invoke you, who made the heavenly lights and stars by the command of your voice, so that they should shine on all men. I invoke you, who shook the entire world, who breaks the back of the mountains and casts them up out of the water, who causes the whole earth to tremble and then renews its inhabitants. I invoke you who made signs in the heaven, on earth and on sea, to bring Urbanus, to whom Urbana gave birth, and unite him as husband with Domitiana, to whom Candida gave birth, loving her, sleepless with desire for her, begging for her, and asking that she return to his house and become his wife. I invoke you, great, everlasting and almighty god, whom the heavens and the valleys fear throughout the whole earth, through whom the lion gives up its spoil and the mountains tremble with earth and sea, and (through whom) each becomes wise who possesses fear of the Lord who is eternal, immortal, vigilant, hater of evil, who knows all things that have happened, good and evil, in the sea and rivers, on earth and mountain, AÔTH ABAÔTH, the god of Abraham and IAÔ of Jacob, IAÔ AÔTH ABAÔTH god of Israma, bring Urbanus, to whom Urbana gave birth, and unite him with Domitiana, to whom Candida gave birth, loving, frantic, tormented with love, passion and desire for Domitiana, whom Candida bore; unite them in marriage and as spouses in love for all the time of their lives. Make him as her obedient slave, so that he will desire no other woman or maiden apart from Domitiana alone, to whom Candida gave birth, and will keep her as his spouse for all the time of their lives. Now, now, quickly, quickly.

Gager 78 (trans)

Origin: Rome. A grave near Via Latina.
Date: Fourth century.
Bibliography: NGCT 84.
Notes: Nail hole in the middle of the text. Folded.

Side A
Three lines of Charaktêres
Charaktêres Φανχοιβικυξ Πετριαδη
Κραταρναδ[η] κατάσχετε κύριοι
ἄνγελοι Κλ[ω]δίαν Βαλερίαν Σω-
φρόνην [καὶ] μὴ Πωλ[ειτορ]ίας τυ-
χ<ε>ῖν

Side B
Ἀρθυλαιλαμ Σεμεσιλαμ
Βαχυχ Βαχαξιχυχ Μενεβαιχυχ
Ἀβρασαξ κύριοι θεοί κατά-
σχετε τὴν [ἐργ]αστιλλαρί[αν] Κλω-
δίαν Βαλερίαν Σω[φρό]νην
καὶ μὴ ἀγέτω Πωλ[ιτορ]ίαν ἐ[ργ]ά-
στιλλ[ο]ν [καὶ] ἀψυχ[ία]ν [ἰδεῖν]

PHANOIBIKUX PETRIADÊ KRATARNADÊ, Lord Angels, restrain Clodia Valeria Sophrone and may she not succeed in buying Politoria.

ARTHULAILAM SEMISILAM BACHUCH BACHAXICHUCH MENEBAICHUCH ABRASAX, Lord Gods, restrain the matron of the workhouse, Clodia Valeria Sophrone and do not let her drag Poletoria (as a workhouse labourer), to suffer (?) the fate of lifelessness (there).

Gager 79 (trans)

Origin: Rome. A grave near the Porta Adreatina.
Date: c. 270–82.
Bibliography: SGD 129.

Column 1
κατάσχες Ἀρτεμίδω-
ρον τὸν ἰατρὸν τὸν
Ἀρτεμιδώρου υἱὸν τὸν

Column 2
τὰς Ῥωμαίων πύλασ-
ς ἀλλὰ κατάσχετε Ἀρτε-
μίδω[ρο]ν τὸν Ἀρτεμιδώ-

τῆς τρίτης χώρτης τῆς
εἰς τὰ πραιτώρια [-] ὑπηρετεῖ
ὁ Δημητρίου τοῦ ἀποθα-
νόντος ἀδελφός ὃς βού-
λεται νῦν ἐξελθεῖν ἰς
τὴν πατρίδα τὴν ἰδίαν
μὴ ἐάσητε οὖν αὐτόν
ἀλλὰ κ[α]τάσχετε τὴν Ὑ-
ταλικὴν γῆν ἐς ἀε[ὶ]
θεινώση[τ]ε [δὲ καὶ]

ρου υἱὸν τὸν ἰατρόν
Εὐλάμων
Λαιμειλα [-] σιων
Κρειοχερσοφριξ
Ομηλιεύς
Αξηιεύς
Αρηιεύς
καὶ Λάθε καὶ Θαμ[βος(?)]
κατάσχετε

Restrain Artemidorus the physician of the third Praetorian cohort. The brother of the deceased Demetrius, who has worked as his assistant, now wishes to depart to his own country. Do not permit him [to prevent the departure?], but restrain the land of Italy and strike the gates of Rome and also restrain Artemidorus the physician, the son of Artemidorus. EULAMÔN LAMEILA ... ÔN ... REIOCHERSOPHRIX OMÊLEIUS AXÊIEUS ARÊIEUS and LATHOS and THAMBOS, restrain.

Gager 93 (trans)

Origin: Centuripe, Italia. Grave.
Date: First or second century.
Bibliography: SGD 115.

Κυρεία ἐξάροις τὸν Ἐλε<ύ>θ[ε]-
ρον ἂν ἐ<κ>δεικήσσῃς με
ποῖσω ἀργύρε[ο]ν σπάδικα
ἂν ἐξάρῃς αὐτὸν ἐκ τό͂ ἀν-
θρωπείνου γένεος

Lady, destroy Eleutherus. If you vindicate me, I will make a silver palm, if you destroy him utterly from the human race.

dfx 4.1.3/16

Origin: Trier, Gallia. Context unknown.
Date: Fourth century.
Bibliography: LCT 64.

Tib(erium) Claudium Treverum natione
Germanum lib(ertum) Claudii Similis rogo
te dom<i>na Isis ut illum profluvio
mittas et quidquid in bonis
habet in morbum megarum

(I curse) Tiberius Claudius Trevirus, a German and the freedman of Claudius Similis. I ask you, lady Isis, so that you send him a flowing (of blood or diarrhoea?), and (may) whatever he has in health (fall) sick with a terrible disease.

dfx 11.2.1/36

Origin: Sousse, Africa. Grave.
Date: Third century.
Bibliography: LCT 175.
Notes: Rolled.

[------]
[obligo --- quam peperit ---]ns mentia[--- ut amet me]
[--- ex hac die ex] hac hora ex hoc m[omento ut obliviscatur]
[patris et matris et suorum omn]ium [et amicoru]m omnium et omnium vi[rorum ---]
[---]n[--- in]sanien[s --- ins]aniens vigilan[s --- ur]atur comburatur ardeat sp[iritus amore(?) et(?)]
[de]siderio meo obli[go] caelum terram aq[uas(?) ---] et {h}aera immobile<m> set dom[---]
amoris hui{i}us Veram adiuro te per mag[na(?) --- n]omina ei{i}us dei qui sub terra [sedet ---]
osorniophri oserchochlo erboonthi im[--]hr[---]mne(?) phiblo chnembo sar[basmisarab --- de]-
tinentem sempiternum amorem qui [---] ego Optatus commendo deo [--- Veram quam]
peperit Lucifera {et} nulli attendat nis[i] mihi soli neminem alium [in mente habeat nisi me]
Optatum quem peperit Ammia P[--]ia[--]a Saphonia consummatum consu[mmatum consummatum]
col<l>iga in sempiterno tempore

...I bind...who...bore...wisdom...so that she loves me...from this day, from this hour, from this moment, so that she forgets father and mother and all her relatives and friends and all other men...insane...insane...waking...she should burn, should burn up, her spirit should blaze with love and desire for me. I bind heaven, earth, water...and air...immovable, but...Vera of this love. I beseech you by great...names of that god, who abides below the earth OSORNIOPHRI OSERCHOCHLO ERBOONTHI...PHIBLO CHNEMBO SARBASMISARAB holding back eternal love which...I, Optatus, hand over to the god...Vera, who Lucifera bore. May she long for no-one else except me, may she have nobody else in mind except me, Optatus who Ammia bore...Saphonia. Having fulfilled, fulfilled, fulfilled. Bind (us?) together through all eternal time.

AE 2014, 213

Origin: Rome. Cremation burial near the catacombs of Santa Domitilla.
Date: Late first or second century.
Notes: Written retrograde. Pierced after folding, nail still in situ.

fragment 1.

Side A
[--- κ]ατορύσσω καὶ
δέδεκα καὶ καταδεσμεύω
εἰς ψυχρὸν τάφον εἰς πυρὰν και-
ομένην εἰς θάλασσαν βάλλω εἰς
ποταμόν εἰ[ς λο]υτρῶνα εἰς μέγαρο[ν]
Εὔφρονα Τρύφωνος Σιφύου υἱὸν Ἀλεξανδρέα καὶ Φίλιππον Ἐζανίτην
ἀθλητὴν καὶ Ἀπίωνα Ἀρίστωνος
Ἀλεξανδρέα ἐπικαλούμενον Πῶ[λο]ν
ἀθλη[τ]ήν [---]να[--]ω[---]

Side B
Ἀλεξανδρέα ἀθλητήν Ἀρτέμωνα
Νικολάου Ἐφέσιον παλαιστήν
Πρωτογένην Τρύφωνος Ἀλεξανδρέα
ἀθλητήν Τρύφωνα Λευκίου Ἀλεξανδρέα
ἀθλητή[ν] Ἀγά[θ]ανδρον Ἀριστάρχου
Κῷον ἀθλη[τήν] Μαρίωνα Διοδώρου

Τραλλιανόν Διονύσιον Σαρδιανόν
Μηνόφαντον Ἐφέσιον Λεύκιον Πινά-
ριον Ἡρακλείδου υἱὸν Ἀλεξανδρέα
[Ἀ]ντιπᾶν Τιμ[--- Ἀ]λεξανδρέα

fragment 2
[---] Ἀλε-
[ξανδρέα] ἀ[θλητήν ?] Ἄμμωναν
[---] Ἀλεξα[νδρέ]α παλαιστήν
[---]ην[---]νο[---]ν[-] Λεωνᾶν
[---]αλκαμ[---Ἀλεξ]α[νδ]ρέα παλαιστήν
[Ἀντίπα?]τρον παν[---]ε[---]ρας
[---] πόδας γ[ό]να[τα? ---]
[---]κρα [---]
[---]ι[---]
[------]
[------]
[------]
[------]

fragment 3
[---]μ[-]ι[---]
[--- λ?]οιποὺς τοὺς λ[---]
[---]μένους

...I bury and tie and bind down to a cold grave, to a burning pyre, to the sea, I throw into a river, into the baths, into a temple, Euphron, son of Tryphon, son of Siphyos the Alexandrian, and Philippus from Aizanoi the athlete, and Apion, son of Ariston the Alexandrian, called Polus the athlete...

...the athlete from Alexandria, Artemon, son of Nicolaus from Ephesus the wrestler, Protogenes, son of Tryphon, the Alexandrian athlete, Tryphon, son of Lucius the Alexandrian athlete, Agathandrus son of Aristarchus, the athlete from Kos, Marion, son of Diodorus from Tralles, Dionysius from Sardis, Menophantus from Ephesus, Lucius Pinarius, son of Heraclides the Alexandrian, Antipas son of... from Alexandria

...the Alexandrian athlete, Ammonas... the Alexandrian wrestler... Leonas son of... the Alexandrian wrestler... Antipatrosis... feet, knees...

...the rest...

Barta 2015 (trans)

Origin: Budapest, Pannonia. Grave.
Date: Second or third century.
Notes: Folded.

Ito (=Dis) Pater Hracura [Mer]-
quri{s} cu<l>leni ea nomin[a]
tib[i] dicto tradas dirov (=diris) ca-
nibus di manes tartaris
Marcum Marcia<m> C<h>ariton[em]
Secumdum quiquit (=quicum) qu[e]
a<d>versarius surgexe[rit]
cui tibi an<t>epistulam ad[fe]-
ret muta et tacita
cuomodo manes muti et ta-
citi sum s{e}ic cui tibi ant-
cpistulan atferent mu[ti]
et taciti cin<t> (=sint) adversa<rio>[s]
Bellici atcipiti (=accipite) Trice[rbe]-
ri et retenetc illu[---]
[--- i]os

Dis Pater, Aeracura, Mercury of Cyllene, I dictate the following names to you: hand them over to the dreadful dogs, (and) the infernal souls in Tartarus. Marcus, Marcia, Chariton, Secundus and whoever may act like an opponent, who will bring a counter-curse to you. Muta Tacita. Just as the infernal souls are mute and silent, so those who bring a counter-curse to you may be mute and silent. Three-headed Cerberus, catch the opponents of Bellicus and keep them . . .

Notes

1 Introduction

1. Categorization: Faraone 1991; Versnel 1991a; Gager 1992; Versnel 2010; linguistic analysis: Jeanneret 1918; Kropp 2008b; Urbanová 2018.
2. Gager 1992; Graf 1997b; Ogden 1999; Luck 2006.
3. Primiano 1995; 2012; McGuire 2008; Bowman and Valk 2012; Harvey 2013; Knibbe and Kupari 2020.
4. Primiano 1995: 46.
5. Bowman and Valk 2012: 5.
6. McGuire 2008: 12–13.
7. Knibbe and Kupari 2020: 167.
8. Albrecht et al. 2018; Rüpke 2018; Gasparini et al. 2020a.
9. Rüpke 2016: 44.
10. Gasparini et al. 2020b, 3.
11. Graham 2021: 40.
12. Bourdieu (1977); Giddens (1984). See Harris and Cipolla (2017: 38–50) for an overview of agency and structure as they apply to archaeology.
13. Dobres and Robb 2000b: 8.
14. Robb 2010: 494; Sørensen 2018: 96–7.
15. Gell (1998); Hodder (2012); Latour (2005).
16. Sax 2006: 478–9; J. Sørensen 2007: 287–8; Rüpke 2018: 7; Graham 2021: 147–9.
17. Graham 2021: 11–13. See Harris and Cipolla (2017: 129–51) and Harris (2020: 19–20) for summaries of 'new materialism'. For the application of what are presumably now 'old materialist' approaches to the study of ancient magic, see Wilburn (2012), Boschung and Bremmer (2015) and Parker and McKie (2018).
18. Graham 2021: 21, original emphasis.
19. Van Dyke 2015; Gardner 2017: 207–08; Harris and Cipolla 2017: 148.
20. Dowding 1996: 4–5; Crellin 2020: 124.
21. Harris and Cipolla 2017: 46.
22. Dowding 2017: 8–13.
23. Crellin 2020: 123.
24. Woolf 2020.
25. Gardner 2013: 10; 2017: 207–08.
26. Throughout this book I have preferred the term 'enslaved person' rather than 'slave', and 'enslaver' rather than 'master'. This is in line with scholarship on more recent systems of enslavement, especially in the Americas (Gabrielle Foreman et al, n.d.).

27 Malinowski 1922; Evans-Pritchard 1937; Douglas 1970b; 1973.
28 Kapferer 1997: 2.
29 Evans-Pritchard 1937: 426; Marwick 1965: 68–9; Feddema 1997: 213–15; Kapferer 1997: 39.
30 Evans-Pritchard 1937: 107; Scott 1990: 142–4; Eves 2000: 458–9; White 2000; Stewart and Strathern 2004; Ashforth 2005 67.
31 Douglas 1970: 118; Weiner 1991: 186; Kapferer 1997: 44–5.
32 Edmonds 2019: 53.
33 Gordon and Marco Simón 2010; Wilburn 2012; Piranomonte and Marco Simón 2012; Gordon, Marco Simón and Piranomonte 2020.
34 For a summary of the debate, see Cunningham 1999; Otto and Stausberg 2013.
35 Frazer 1922: 48–60.
36 In our discipline see, most recently, Otto 2013.
37 Versnel 1991b: 184–7; Sanzo 2020: 38.
38 Gordon 1999; Stratton 2007; Edmonds 2019.
39 Luck 2006: 4; Versnel 2012; Chadwick 2015: 37.
40 Bremmer 2015: 12; Sanzo 2020: 38.

2 Cursing and Religion in the Roman West

1 Jordan 1985: 151.
2 Jordan 2000: 6.
3 Tomlin 2014.
4 This is the case for many tablets recorded in Audollent's original collection, including most of those from the cemeteries at Carthage and Sousse.
5 Cunliffe and Davenport 1985: 43.
6 See Tomlin (1988: 84–8) for the palaeographic dating of the Bath curses.
7 SGD 1. 94–8. For other, very similar accounts of the spread of cursing around the ancient world, see Gager (1992: 25–30); Ogden (1999: 6–10); Kropp (2008b: 45–6); Sánchez Natalías (2012a); Urbanová (2018: 33–6, 401–12) and Sánchez Natalías (2019).
8 Gager 1992: 25–7; Nakamura 2004; Faraone, Garnand and López-Ruiz 2005.
9 The dating of the single Punic curse from Carthage, discussed by Faraone, Garnand, and López-Ruiz (2005: 165–70), is controversial, and suggestions range from as early as the seventh century BC to as late as the second century BC. It would be significant for the early history of cursing if it did indeed pre-date the earliest Greek examples, but the lack of secure, original archaeological context makes resolution of this question almost impossible.
10 Eidinow 2007a; 2007b.
11 Murano 2012; 2013; Massarelli 2014; 2019; McDonald 2015; Vitellozzi 2019.
12 Marco Simón 2019.
13 The Pompeiian curse is SD 71. The curses from republican Rome itself include the famous 'John Hopkins *defixiones*' (SD 10–14).
14 Bélanger Sarrazin et al. 2019. For the archaeological context, see De Winter (2018).
15 I borrow the term 'self-authored' from Gordon (2013: 256 n. 3).

16 The 'Sethian tablets' were published by Wünsch at the end of the nineteenth century and were included in Audollent's collection (Wünsch 1898; Audollent 1904 nos. 140-87). For the Anna Perenna texts, see Blänsdorf and Piranomonte (2012); Piranomonte (2012) and Blänsdorf (2015).
17 So says Blänsdorf (2012: 147), although Piranomonte (2015: 78) has disagreed.
18 Originally published by Wünsch (1910).
19 For the 'Epigraphic Habit', see MacMullen (1982); Meyer (1990) and Cherry (1995).
20 Deckers, Lewis and Thomas 2016: 427.
21 See Rüpke (2013); Hunt (2016); MacRae (2016); Flower (2017); Rüpke (2018); Gasparini et al. (2020) and Graham (2021) for important monographs and edited volumes from only the past few years.
22 To borrow McGuire's (2008: 4) description of 'lived religion' more broadly.
23 Goldberg 2009; Häussler 2012; Aldhouse-Green 2018.
24 The standard work on the imperial cult in the Roman West is still Fishwick (1987), but see also Woolf (1998: 216ff).
25 Rüpke 2018, 292-5.
26 2016: 63-9. See below and Chapter 3 for more discussion.
27 The literature is vast, but see Webster (1997); Woolf (2000); Webster (2001); Revell (2009); Goldberg (2009) and Mattingly (2011) for contributions specifically relevant to religion.
28 See Hingley (2005); Versluys (2014); Pitts and Versluys (2015) and Woolf (2017) for applications of 'globalization' theory to the Roman world.
29 For a particularly convincing exploration of religious resistance to Rome, see Webster (1997).
30 Rüpke 2018: 301, 321-6.
31 Rüpke 2018: 321-2.
32 See papers in Richardson and Santangelo (2011).
33 On female priests, see Allason-Jones (2011) and Hemelrijk (2015: 37-108).
34 Wendt 2016. Explored in more detail in Chapter 3.
35 Lucian, *Dial. Meret.* 4.
36 Cato, *Agr.* 5; Columella, *Rust.* 1.8.6.
37 Beard, North and Price 1998: 211-44; Ripat 2011.
38 Wendt 2016: 56-60.
39 On this see, especially, Stratton (2007: 71-106); Rives (2010); Spaeth (2014) and Paule (2017).
40 Frankfurter 2002: 161; Gordon 2019c: 1001-02.
41 Graham 2021: 21-8.

3 Rituals, Gestures and Movements

1 Although this has changed in the last decade or so, see Wilburn (2012); Blänsdorf (2015); Curbera (2015); McKie (2018) and Sánchez Natalías (2018).
2 On the materiality of (ancient) magical practices more broadly, see Wilburn (2012); Boschung and Bremmer (2015); Houlbrook and Armitage (2015) and Parker and McKie (2018).
3 Ingold 2000a.

4   See Harris and Cipolla (2017: 129–51) for a summary. Graham (2021) is the first to apply these ideas to Roman religion.
5   Bell 1992: 59.
6   Bell 1997: 165–70.
7   Barrett 1991; Barrowclough and Malone 2007; Graham 2021.
8   Graham 2021.
9   Graham 2021: 201.
10 Swenson 2015: 330.
11 Mitchell 2006: 393–4. This line of thinking has been extended recently, with the arrival of post-human theories in the study of the Roman world, see Iara (2020); Zapelloni Pavia (2020).
12 Mitchell (2006: 395) gives the example of Orange marches in Northern Ireland. This can be demonstrated in the ancient world too, with the example of the Sacra Via in Rome, which was given its name either because the most sacred shrines of Rome stood along it or because it was the route of many religious processions (Platner and Ashby 1929: 456–9).
13 This is certainly the case for the following: Barrett (1991); Briault (2007); Fontijn (2007); Morley (2007).
14 On the emotional dimension of curse tablets, see Salvo (2012; 2016).
15 Ov., *Fast.* 2.571–82; Apul. *Met.* 3.17 and 9.29.
16 *Ann.* 4.52, 12.65, 16.31. The Greek and Latin terms used by ancient authors for the various figures associated with cursing and other magical practices is wide and inconsistent. To avoid these problems, I have opted to borrow the term 'freelance religious expert/specialist' from Wendt (2016), which I think encompasses the range quite neatly.
17 See, for example, *PGM* IV. 296–466, V. 304–69.
18 I follow Gordon's (2013: 256) distinction here, which he is right to say has been undervalued in past scholarship.
19 See Chapter 4 for more detail.
20 Blänsdorf (2012: 147) and Piranomonte (2015: 78) have differed over whether there were specialists operating at the fountain of Anna Perenna, but, on balance, I have found Blänsdorf's arguments for self-authorship more compelling.
21 Dickie 2001; Frankfurter 2002; Rives 2010; Wendt 2016; Gordon 2019c.
22 Petron. *Sat* 131; Lucian, *Dial. Meret.* 4; Columella, *Rust.* 1.8.6.
23 Stratton 2007: 96–9; Blanco 2017.
24 Philostr. *VA*; Plin. *NH.* 30.1–20; Lucian, *Alex.*
25 Dickie 2001: 185–8; Wendt 2016: 46–60. Evidence for the existence of such figures at Rome stretches back into at least the middle republic, see Livy 25.1.6–8.
26 Gordon 2012: 39–42.
27 Dio Chrys. 32.9.6–10; Juv. 6.582–92; Tert. *Apol.* 23.
28 See Wendt (2016: 220–3) for further criticisms of the 'religious marketplace' model and the operation of freelance religious experts within it.
29 Africa: DT 299, **300**, SGD 149, 137; Italia: **SD 117-8, DT 198,** 123, Gager 118, NGCT 61; Gallia: **SD 160**, 166; Germania: dfx 5.1.5/1, Bélanger Sarrazin et al (2019); Hispania: SD 130; Danubian provinces: **SD 530**, SGD 82, 83.

30 Inscribed amulets are another matter. See Kotansky (1994); Tomlin (2011a) and Faraone (2018) for those with known provenances from the Roman west.
31 The phrase 'carta picta perscripta' (the written page has been copied out) on **SD 213** from Bath might suggest that the curse was copied onto lead by someone other than the curser, but it is far from certain.
32 There are practical reasons for this ordering too, as it would be impossible to write on a tablet after rolling or folding.
33 I have discussed this in relation to Bath and Mainz elsewhere: see McKie (2016: 18).
34 See Tomlin (1988: 82) for a detailed discussion.
35 Lee 2009.
36 Skaggs 2007; Skaggs et al. 2012.
37 Durali-Mueller et al. 2007.
38 Since at least Audollent (1904: xlix), but see, most recently, Lamont (2021).
39 Sánchez Natalías 2018: 11–13.
40 Cousins 2020: 139–40.
41 Papyrus curses: e.g. *Suppl. Mag.* 40, 43 and 45; for wax curses see Ov. *Am.* 3.7.27–30.
42 Muzzioli 1939: 46.
43 2018: 14. For more on the potential uses of lamps in Graeco-Roman magical practices, see Diosono (2020).
44 Williams (2012: 260–6) gives a full interpretation of the burial and the drama that unfolded between Phileros and Orfellius.
45 For further discussion of 'speaking' epitaphs, see Carroll (2007).
46 Sánchez Natalías 2016: 76.
47 See Tomlin (2010: 247–53) for the similarities between this text and the British theft curses.
48 Tomlin (1988: 80), citing **SD 259**, which reports the theft of two silver coins. The logical conclusion is that the tablet is unlikely to have cost more than the value of the thing being reported stolen, but that assumes the curser was thinking logically.
49 The role of rumour and gossip in ancient cursing is discussed in more detail in Chapter 4.
50 Woolf 2012: 198.
51 Plin. *N.H.* 28.10–11.
52 Beard 1991: 55–7. The issue of writing and power has been further explored by Moreland (2001; 2006).
53 Beard 1991: 41–3.
54 For examples, see MacMullen (1981: 31–4) and Beard (1991: 41–2).
55 Beard 1991: 46–7; Rüpke 2009: 36–8.
56 Examining the materiality of texts has been particularly fruitful: see Taylor (2011) and the articles in Piquette and Whitehouse 2013b.
57 Piquette and Whitehouse 2013a: 3.
58 Ingold 2000b: 401–04. I have discussed the ritual significance of writing elsewhere: see McKie (2016: 20–1).
59 An observation made through my own experimental work.
60 Although it is possible that some were written in ink: see Schwinden (2004: 15).
61 Tomlin 1988: 82.

62 Mees 2011: 87–8.
63 Bowman and Woolf 1994: 5–6.
64 Tomlin 1988: 247–52. The collection of tablets found at Le Mans appear to also be pseudo-inscriptions: see Chevet (2016: 21).
65 In some publications (see, for example, Hassall and Tomlin (1989: 330) and Tomlin (2002: 172)) Tomlin has suggested that these two may have been written by the same person. Although he has not issued a full, unambiguous retraction of this possibility, the comparison seems to have dropped out of his more recent discussions of these tablets (see, for example Tomlin (2010: 249–50, 268; 2011b: 152). No doubt the ambiguity will be resolved when the Uley tablets are published fully.
66 One line at the top of the second side of this tablet is in a different hand to the rest, but the sense is continuous.
67 Harris 1989: 272.
68 Responses to Harris began soon after publication, see particularly the contributions to Humphrey (1991). For the Vindolanda tablets, see Bowman and Thomas (1974; 2003) and Bowman, Thomas and Adams (1994). There are also the recently discovered writing tablets from London (Tomlin 2016).
69 A criticism developed by Bowman (1991: 123).
70 Moreland 2006: 141–2.
71 One good example is a gravestone (*AE* 1931: 112), which includes the line '*hic iacet corpus pueri nominandi* (here lies the body of the boy ... insert name).' The letter-cutter copied out the words verbatim, without realizing they were meant to insert a specific name (Carroll 2007: 47).
72 Piquette and Whitehouse 2013a: 6.
73 Tomlin 2002; Mullen 2013.
74 Sánchez Natalías 2020b.
75 On drawings, *charaktêres* and geometric patterns of words and letters on curse tablets, see Mastrocinque (2008); Dzwiza (2012); Nemeth (2013) and Sánchez Natalías (2020b).
76 The mistakes are not unexpected when people are writing in non-standard styles. From my own experimentation I noted how difficult this was to achieve, especially in cursive, which has far fewer symmetrical letter forms than upper case.
77 I have also discussed these actions elsewhere: see McKie (2016: 21).
78 McKie (2018).
79 See also the discussion by Corbeill (2004).
80 Kropp (2008: 85). The importance of naming will be discussed further in Chapter 5.
81 Dungworth 1998: 156.
82 *HN.* 28.10.
83 Pl., *Phdr.* 274-7; Arist., *Int.* 1.16a.
84 Ingold 2000b: 399–400.
85 Stoller 1989: 115–17.
86 Stoller 1989: 119.
87 Gell. *NA.* 10.4.4, discussed by Corbeill (2004: 15–20; 26). See also Kropp (2008: 210–14).
88 Particularly Kropp (2008; 2010), who has applied the 'speech-act' theories developed by Austin (1962) and Searle (1971).

89 Kropp 2010: 360–76.
90 Kropp 2008: 145–60.
91 Kropp 2010: 360.
92 Kropp 2008: 234–5. Power and cursing will be discussed further in Chapter 5.
93 Violating tombs and despoiling corpses were both illegal and could carry heavy penalties, including the death sentence (*Dig.* 47.12). However, it is not at all clear that depositing a lead tablet in a tomb would constitute a crime under these laws.
94 Sen. *Ep.* 41.1; Apul. *Met.* 6.3.
95 Macrob. *Sat.* 1.10.21.
96 Livy 5.21.16; Plin. *HN* 28.25; Plut. *Vit. Num.* 14.3–6; Suet. *Vit.* 2.5; Plut. *Quaest. Rom.* 14.
97 2004: 26–9. See also (Graham forthcoming).
98 See, among a huge bibliography, Cancik (1985–6); Elsner (2012); Jenkyns (2013) and Moser and Feldman (2014) specifically for their discussions of space and religion.
99 See Stambaugh (1978: 575–80) for discussion of access to Roman temples.
100 *PGM* IV 435 (at sunset), V 355–40 (while the moon is waning), VII 435–6 (late evening or the middle of the night).
101 Hunt 2016.
102 Graham 2021: forthcoming; Mylonopoulos 2008; Rieger 2020.
103 There are of course exceptions to these general trends, and lots of curses in a single location can skew the numbers significantly. To take two examples, all twenty-two Gallic amphitheatre curses come from late-antique Trier, and all but one of the Italian spring tablets are from the Fountain of Anna Perenna in Rome. To avoid confusing duplication, the Bath tablets are under 'spring', but not also 'temple'.
104 For example, *PGM* IV 296–466, 1390–1495, 2006–2125; V 304–69, VII 396–404, 451–8.
105 As argued by Edmonds (2014: 234).
106 Cousins (2020: 116–19). Sanchez Natalias (2019: 464) has made a similar observation, although with perhaps less nuance on the involvement of Romanization.
107 Bradley 1998; Fulford 2001; Merrifield 1987.
108 Cousins (2020: 64) has called it 'one of the most emphatically Roman spaces in the province'. See Revell (2009) and Goldberg (2009) for more discussion of the different cultural influences at the temple of Sulis Minerva.
109 Dungworth (1998: 155); Kerneis (2010); Kiernan (2004b: 131; 2004a: 108–10).
110 Kiernan 2004a. See McKie (2019) for further discussion on the comparison between curses and votives.
111 McKie 2018.
112 The work of the Hungarian healer discussed by Kis-Halas (2012) is a prime example. Thorough searches of the victim's home by the healer always turn up some piece of magical paraphernalia apparently placed there by an enemy or black magician.
113 *Lib.*, 1.245–50.
114 Eidinow 2017: 402–4.
115 *Ann.* 2.69.
116 *HN.* 28.4.19.

117 Gager 1992: 121. Cicero also tells an anecdote about C. Scribonius Curio, who blamed a sudden lapse of memory, which struck while speaking in court, on evil spells and curses (*Brutus* 217).
118 Ogden (1999: 51–2) calls this the 'magical arms race'. For amulets, see Gager (1992: 219–22); for protective gestures, see Eitrem (1953: 602) and Corbeill (2004: 32).
119 Veale 2017; Cousins 2020; Salvo 2020; Graham 2021, 173–200.
120 For a summary, see Marco Simón (2020).
121 For the relationships between curses and votive assemblages on these sites, see the following: Bath: Cunliffe 1988; Anna Perenna: Piranomonte 2012; Uley: Woodward and Leach 1993; Mainz: Witteyer 2013.
122 Recent scholarship on votive practice in the Roman world emphasizes the range of possible meanings behind such offerings: see especially the papers in Graham and Draycott (2017).
123 Alfayé and Sánchez Natalías 2020.
124 Wallace-Hadrill 2008.
125 Graham 2005.
126 Hope 2009: 98–101.
127 Graham 2005: 136–8.
128 Dolansky 2011: 133.
129 Delattre 1898: 221–39.
130 Ov. *Fast.* 2.565-6.
131 Plut. *Quaest. Rom.* 14; Cic. *De Leg.* 2.22, 48–57. For discussion of funeral cult, see King (2009; 2020: 128–47).
132 Gager 1992: 20; Edmonds 2019: 65; Ogden 1999: 17–18.
133 Hor. *Sat.* 1.8.23–50; Luc. *Phars* 6.562–9.
134 (King 2009, 109–12; 2020, 128–47).
135 Heintz 1998: 338.
136 Choppard and Hannezo 1893: 194–5.
137 Graham 2021: 199.
138 Sánchez Natalías 2020a.
139 Platner and Ashby 1929: 119.
140 Elkins 2014.
141 Egelhaaf-Gaiser 2007: 205–06.
142 Revell 2009: 124–5; Cousins 2020: 112–13.
143 Cunliffe 1969: 105; Cunliffe and Davenport 1985: 180.
144 Betts 2016.
145 Blänsdorf 2010: 143.
146 Gordon 2014: 777.
147 Patterson 2000: 88–92.
148 Amphitheatres: Caerleon, London, Carthage, Petronell, and Trier; Circuses: Carthage and Khoms.
149 Wiedemann 1992: 46–7.
150 Tert. *Apol.* 15.5; *Nat.* 1.10.47: see discussion by Coleman 1990: 67.
151 Cousins 2014: 57–8; 2020: 137–8.
152 Matter 1852: 28–9.

153 For the archaeological contexts, see Sousse: Cagnat 1903: 260; Carthage: Delattre 1888: 157, 1898: 218.
154 Luck 2000: 204.

4 Motives and Social Frameworks

1 Audollent 1904, xc; Faraone 1991; Versnel 1991a. Audollent's original categories were 'judicial and against enemies', 'against thieves, tricksters and slanderers', 'amatory' and 'against chariot racers and gladiators'.
2 This is certainly true after the categories were reworked by Faraone (1991): see Gager (1992); Ogden (1999); Eidinow (2007a) and Kropp (2008). Before then, Audollent's categories were used, but with less rigidity: see, for example, Preisendanz (1972), who divided curses into 'political', 'juridical', 'hate and love' and 'circus'.
3 Gager 1992; Eidinow 2007a.
4 Ogden 1999: 4.
5 Eidinow 2007a: 155.
6 Tomlin 1988: 80–1.
7 *Dig.* 47.17.
8 Woodward and Leach 1993: 314–15.
9 See especially Versnel (2010) for a forceful restatement of his case (where he also incorporates new curses found between 1991 and 2005) and Versnel (2012b).
10 Adapted from Versnel (1991a: 68).
11 Versnel (2010: 323, 331) and Versnel (1991b) *passim*. This distinction is questioned by some other scholars, including Ogden (1999: 38).
12 Something noted by Gordon (2013: 273–4).
13 Although it is worth noting that textiles were not cheap in the ancient world and could have been the most expensive thing a poor person owned. Diocletian's Edict on Maximum Prices values cloaks at between 2000 and 12000 *denarii*, a huge sum considering the same edict puts a farm labourer's wages at 25 *denarii* a day (for the edict, see Frank (1940: 310–421)). This could be a reason why thefts of clothing were so often reported on curses.
14 *Dig.* 47.2.9; see also Riggsby (2010: 187–90). Unless the thief came armed or at night, in which case the Twelve Tables state that it was legal to kill them (*Dig.* 9.2.4.1).
15 Versnel (2002: 49 n. 42) has expressed concern about the application of the term 'vengeance' to prayers for justice, on the basis that it does not always occur. Although this concern is valid when applied to some cases, I do not think it should prevent us from pointing it out on the many tablets where it does occur.
16 Although there has been some work on this, see Mattingly (2006: 315); Kerneis (2010) and Marco Simón (2020a: 133–4).
17 Watkin (2007: 2863) suggests that, as theft was considered the most heinous crime in medieval Welsh law, it could have been similar in the pre-Roman period. Pursuing this line of argument is difficult however, as there is no surviving evidence for law in Iron Age Britain, and there are serious questions over the applicability of medieval manuscripts to earlier periods.

18 *Dig.* 49.2.60, see also Rodger (1990: 158).
19 Bradley 1997: 206.
20 According to Ulpian (*Dig.* 1.18.13) it was the governor's responsibility to hunt and punish 'committers of sacrilege, bandits, kidnappers and thieves'.
21 Korporowicz 2012: 148.
22 Connolly 2010: 30–2, 138–9.
23 A possibility explored by Crouzet (2009).
24 *Dig.* 47.2.94. Legal scholars have argued that this may have been because many thieves did not have the assets to pay fines or compensation; see Buckland and Stein (1963: 583–4); Frier (1989: 165).
25 Harries 2007: 45.
26 Kiernan 2004b: 126.
27 Versnel 1999: 151–3; Chaniotis 2004: 13.
28 See especially the confession *stelae* from Asia Minor collected by Petzl (1994).
29 *Dig.* 47.34.
30 Gager 1992: 42; Gordon 2012: 56ff. All charioteers in the Roman Empire raced for one of the four coloured factions – Blue, Green, Red and White – the origins of which were obscure even to the Romans. For a detailed discussion of their history and organization, see Cameron (1976).
31 Gordon 2012: 57–9.
32 Cameron 1976: 6–10.
33 Humphrey 1986: 305, 320.
34 Gordon 2012: 57.
35 Cameron 1976: 45ff.
36 Plin, *Ep.* 9.6; Dio 47.2, 74.4; Juvenal 11.197-201; Suet. *Vit.* 14; Amm. Marc. 37.4.28–31.
37 Wann, Carlson and Schrader 1999: 280.
38 Wann and James 2019: 146–7.
39 Havard, Wann and Ryan 2013; Wann et al. 2001.
40 Wann et al. 1999.
41 Wann et al. 2011.
42 Cameron 1976: 77–8 with *Dig.* 48.19.28.3.
43 References to timings on competition curses: 'today': **SGD 139** (Carthage); 'tomorrow': Gager 11 (Sousse); DT 235-240, **Gager 12**, (Carthage), Gager 15 (Rome); '7th day before the Ides of November': **Gager 10** (Carthage); 'Mercury's Day': DT 253 (Carthage); 'Ares' Day': **DT 161** (Rome); 12th and 24th (day or race?): DT 160, **161**, 164, 167 (Rome).
44 Wann et al. 2011.
45 Over fifty were originally recovered from the *spoliarium* of the amphitheatre, but only these few could be opened and read. From Rome, there is a single curse against wrestlers and athletes (**AE 2014, 213**). On beast-hunts as entertainment in general, see Epplett (2014). For the amphitheatre at Carthage, see Rossiter 2016.
46 Dunbabin 1978.
47 Beschaouch 2006.

48 Dunbabin 1978: 79; Hoek and Herrmann 2013: 73.
49 See, for example, AE 1967, 549 and CIL VIII 369.
50 CIL VIII 10479, 51.
51 Rossiter 2016: 247–8.
52 Fagan 2011: 149–51, 219–21. The only one on record is the riot in Pompeii in AD 59, which had an underlying political cause alongside the events in the arena (Tac. *Ann.* 14.17).
53 Cicero (*Brut.* 217–18).
54 This strategy is also present on Classical Attic legal curses: see Eidinow (2007: 170ff).
55 Eidinow 2007: 186–9.
56 Marco Simón 2010: 405.
57 The last two of these identifications are uncertain but highly plausible. See Marco Simón (2010: 402–05) for a more detailed discussion.
58 Fulvus in AD 71 and again in 85, Rufus as suffect consul in AD 95.
59 Gager 1992: 142–3; Solin 1968: 26–8.
60 Marco Simón 2010: 408; Fabre, Mayer, and Rodà 1991: 162.
61 For detailed discussions of the judicial process in the capital, see Bablitz (2007) and Corbeill (2015). Considering that governors and legates would have had some experience of the system at Rome, provincial trials were naturally modelled on it.
62 Ov. *Am.* 3.7.27–30; Ap. *Met.* 3.17, 9.29.
63 Most notably Dickie (2000) but see also Spaeth (2014) and Stratton (2014).
64 Faraone (2001: 132; 2002: 402). Pachoumi (2013: 313) has already called this model into question.
65 Graf 1997b: 146. Edmonds (2014: 293) makes a similar argument against reading too much into the feelings displayed on these tablets.
66 Winkler 1990: 86ff.
67 Winkler 1990: 87–9.
68 Winkler 1990: 87.
69 Faraone 2001; 2002; Winkler 1990: 97.
70 Dickie 2000: 570–1; Pachoumi 2013: 307.
71 Williams 1999: 27, 48.
72 Ov. *Am.* 2.19.3–4; Mart. *Ep.* 3.33.
73 Ripat 2014: 342.
74 Treggiari 1991: 52–4.
75 There are a few homosexual curses from Egypt. Women seeking women: *SGD* 151, *PGM* XXXII; men seeking men: *PGM* XXXIIa, LVVI, *Suppl. Mag.* 54.
76 Ripat 2014.
77 That is not to say that there were no potentially magical means of attracting lovers in this region. See, for example, the Romano-British love charms on brooches (*RIB* 2421.1, 2421.50), finger-rings (*RIB* 2422.12; 2422.61) and gemstones (*RIB* 2423.4). My thanks to Adam Parker for alerting me to these objects.
78 Martial 1.90.6 and 7.30.3. In Pompeian graffiti it has a wide variety of uses, from aggressive threats, to banter between prostitutes and their clients, to male boasts: see *CIL* IV 4239, 2176 and 4029. For more on *fututor*, see Adams (1982: 118–22) and Williams (1999: 185–7).

79 On one occasion, Martial does call a woman a *fututor* (1.90), but in this case he is accusing her of fucking her female lover, so taking the penetrative role. In Martial, the feminine *fututrix* seems to only be used in conjunction with feminine nouns (*manus* 11.22 and *lingua* 11.61), rather than women, but it does appear on the curse from Calvi Risorta, mentioned above.
80 For different readings of the text, see Urbanová (2018: 269).
81 I am not convinced by the interpretation of Urbanová and Frydek (2016), who see this as a father cursing a daughter who has revealed the secrets of the family's household worship to her new husband.
82 Versnel 2010: 303–5.
83 This is particularly true of Versnel's work on the prayers for justice (1991a: 2010).
84 Gordon 2013: 267.
85 Sánchez Natalías 2012: 131; Urbanová 2018: 167.
86 A point made recently by both Otto (2013: 323) and Gordon (2015: 148–53).
87 Faraone 1991: 10–17.
88 Faraone 1991: 17–20.
89 He cites Brown (1970: 25), who had already pointed out the political role of chariot racing factions up to late antiquity. For this see, now, Gordon (2012).
90 Eidinow 2007.
91 Eidinow 2007: 227–35.
92 Thomas 1996: 35.
93 Eidinow 2007: 231.
94 Winkler 1990: 88–9.
95 Frankfurter 2014; Ripat 2014.
96 Eidinow 2007: 165–89.
97 Versnel 1999: 149; Eidinow 2007: 188.
98 See, in particular, Graf (1997a).
99 Gager 1992: 22–3; Gordon 2013: 70–1; Cousins 2014: 58. See Chapter 3, above, for catharsis in curse tablet rituals.
100 Plin. *HN.* 18.41.
101 Graf 1997a: 109–12.
102 Chaniotis 2004.
103 Potts 2017.
104 I am not the first to look to anthropological comparisons to illuminate the study of ancient magic: see, for example, Brown (1970); Versnel (1991b); Whitmore (2018); and Alvar Nuño (2019a).
105 Gager 1992: 3. This point was also noted by Bradley (1997: 219).
106 Malinowski 1922; Evans-Pritchard 1937; Douglas 1970b; 1973.
107 Kapferer 1997: 2012.
108 Kapferer 1997: 242, 249–53. The use of perishable objects in Sri Lankan cursing (and comparable rituals in many other societies across the world) should be a warning to Roman archaeologists and historians. As I have said before, there is no way of knowing how many people cursed their enemies by doing something other than inscribing a sheet of lead, and we can know little of further actions involving perishable items that accompanied cursing.
109 Kapferer 1997: 36. See also Feddema (1997: 213–15) who found similar motives for cursing in a different part of the island to Kapferer's study.

110 Brown 1970: 18.
111 Douglas 1970a: xxxiv. Evans-Prichard held these doubts about Azande magic, see (1937: 404, 424), as did Marwick about the Cewa (1965: 82).
112 As pointed out by (Brown 1970: 18).
113 Gossip and rumour, while closely connected, have slightly different meanings. Gossip tends to take place mutually within a group or network (Stewart and Strathern 2004: 38–9), whereas rumours tend to have a much wider circulation, spreading between and through many different social networks (Laurence 1994; Neubauer 1999). Nevertheless, these differences do not impact much on my argument here, so for simplicity's sake I will talk about them interchangeably.
114 For the basis of speech act theory, see Austin 1962; Searle 1971. A more recent treatment of speech act theory was written by Sbisa (2009).
115 Weiner 1991: 187–8.
116 Kapferer 1997: 44–5.
117 For Athens, see Hunter (1990); for Rome, see Laurence (1994) and Dufallo (2001). Alvar Nuño (2019a) has recently discussed the relationship between rumour, gossip and curses in the Roman world. From the literary sources, see Hor. *Epod.* 11.7 and Prop. 3.25.1 for two examples of the damage to reputation caused by being the target of gossip and mockery.
118 Hunter 1990: 301; Weiner 1991: 161–3.
119 Ripat 2014, 350–2.
120 The rumour mills of Rome seem to have been very well informed of the love lives of the political elite, as the biographies of Plutarch and Suetonius readily and frequently attest. Anthropologists have studied the interplay between romantic relationships and gossip; see, for example, Epstein 1969.
121 Winkler 1990: 97.
122 Frankfurter 2014: 323–5.
123 Alvar Nuño 2019a; 2020.
124 Weiner 1991: 187–8. This was briefly noted by Versnel (2002: 56), but as far as I am aware the significance of the point has not been fully realized by any scholar in the field.
125 Azande: Evans-Pritchard (1937: 424); Sri Lanka: Feddema (1997: 204) and Kapferer (1997: 46).
126 Feddema 1997: 204.
127 Feddema 1997: 212.
128 Feddema 1997: 212.
129 Gager 1992: 20; Ogden 1999: 17.
130 This is the case in modern Africa; see Stewart and Strathern (2004: 29–30). The large-scale trials or disputes at Ampurias and Bad Kreuznach certainly constitute such situations.
131 It is, for example, a central plank in Kiernan's argument for the psychosomatic effects of ancient cursing (2004b: 131), and also his argument for the votive nature of 'prayers for justice' (2004a: 108–10). I have discussed this point elsewhere; see McKie (2018: 119–20).
132 Versnel (2002: 70–1) points out that the priests themselves could be the origin point of gossip about cursing. They were also members of the community, and they may have known the details of individual petitions, about which they could easily drop hints to others.
133 Soweto: Ashforth (2005: 68); Sri Lanka: Kapferer (1997: 40).
134 Chaniotis 2004.

135 Versnel 1999: 149–53.
136 'Oratorical ineptitude' is one of the conventional *loci* of invective in ancient oratory; see Craig (2004: 190–1).
137 Estimations for circus capacities vary dramatically. Carthage is usually put at between 40,000–45,000 (Humphrey 1986: 303), with the Roman Circus Maximus varying between 150,000 and 485,000, although the lower range is more plausible (Humphrey 1986: 126). The circus as Sousse has never been excavated properly, but appears to be roughly the same size or slightly smaller than that at Carthage (Humphrey 1986: 319–20).
138 Gordon 2012: 47–8.
139 See the prosopography of charioteers collected by Horsmann (1998).
140 A similar formula is found on a tablet from Bolonia in Hispania (SD 128), which asks that Isis 'publicly take away the life' of the thief.
141 Gager 1992: 81; Kiernan 2004b: 126–7.
142 On listing in Graeco-Roman cursing, see Gordon (1999: 2021).
143 Kapferer 1997: 270–3.
144 Chaniotis 1995: 327–8.
145 Chaniotis 1995: 65.
146 Robinson 2007: 181.
147 This encompassed anyone not a senator, equestrian, decurion or military veteran. For more on the distinction between *honestiores* and *humiliores,* see Bauman (1996: 128ff).
148 Coleman 1990: 46–7.
149 Stewart and Strathern 2004: 23.
150 Ashforth 2005: 69–71.
151 Evans-Pritchard (1937: 426) reported many forms of protective magic among the Azande, and one of the most widespread rituals among Sinhalese Buddhists in Sri Lanka is aimed at breaking or countering malicious magical attacks (Kapferer 1997: 83–184).
152 Ashforth 2005: 12; Stewart and Strathern 2004: 64–6.
153 1999: 52.
154 2005: 71.
155 Cewa: Marwick (1965: 3); Sinhalese Buddhists: Kapferer (1997: 40).
156 This is certainly the case in some societies studied by modern anthropologists: see, for example, Heald's study of witchcraft and theft among the Gisu people of Uganda (1986: 67).
157 These formulas will be discussed further in Chapter 5.
158 Jordan 1985: 151.

5 Agency, Power and Relationships

1 Albrecht et al. 2018: 571–2; Rüpke 2018: 11–12.
2 See Harris and Cipolla (2017) for a summary of the debate. The recent back-and-forth in *Archaeological Dialogues* between Lindstrom (2015; 2017) Ribeiro (2016; 2019) and Sørensen (2016; 2018) gives a flavour of the rich but often convoluted state of the debate.
3 The foundational texts by these two are Bourdieu (1977) and Giddens (1984).

4 The scholarship that has followed, defining, debating and criticizing these theoretical models within the social sciences, is vast. However, it has been summarized and applied to archaeology by, among others, Dobres and Robb (2000); Dornan (2002); Gardner (2007); Robb (2010) and Barrett (2012).
5 Robb 2010: 494; Sørensen 2018: 96–7.
6 Graham 2021.
7 Rüpke 2018: 91.
8 As noted by other scholars on curse tablets. See, for example, Crouzet (2009: 32); Frankfurter (2014: 325) and Alvar Nuño (2017b: 315).
9 Faraone and Gordon 2019: 319, 325.
10 Gordon 1990: 224–31; Woolf 1998: 215ff; Rüpke 2018: 280–2.
11 Revell 2009: 152.
12 Some scholars have argued that the situation was relatively similar before the Roman conquest too, at least in some parts of northern Europe, with elites and priests such as the druids in control of whatever public religious system might have existed. See Creighton (2000: 161).
13 Fishwick 1987; Allason-Jones 2011; Hemelrijk 2015.
14 See, for example, Derks (1991; 1995).
15 Derks 1998: 231–2.
16 As discussed in Chapter 3, lead was a common and cheap material in the north-western provinces. At Bath the smallest amount of money reported stolen was two silver coins (**SD 259**), so it is possible that the whole ritual cost no more than this.
17 As discussed in Chapter 4. See also Kelly (1966: 43–68) and Garnsey (1970: 216–17).
18 Kapferer 1997: 225–6; Stewart and Strathern 2004: 12–13.
19 See Rothenhöfer (2016), who suggests that the tablet could be from Oescus, near modern Pleven in Bulgaria, where the *Legio V Macedonia* had its base. Rufus may have commanded this legion in the 70s or 80s AD. His career is listed on the arch of Trajan in Lepcis Magna, for which see *CIL* VIII 13, but the inscription does not specify which *Legio V* he commanded, meaning he could equally have been in Germania with the *Legio V Alaudae*.
20 Alvar Nuño 2017a; 2019a; 2019b.
21 Alvar Nuño 2019b: 407.
22 The Greek word is *ergastillarian* (ἐργαστιλλαρίαν), which Alvar Nuño (2019b: 411) suggests may be a new word formed by fusing the Latin *ergastulum* and the Greek *ergasterion* (ἐργαστήριον).
23 Identifying enslaved people on curse tablets is difficult, as they rarely named themselves as such. Some names, such as Servandus, might suggest enslaved status, and the fashion among Roman enslavers for giving Greek names to the people they enslaved might also help. Otherwise, we rely on contextual interpretation. See Alvar Nuño (2019b: 403–04).
24 Alvar Nuño 2019b: 203–05. See also Gordon (2019a: 175).
25 On the positions of slaves in Roman families see, among others, Saller (1987); Martin (2003) and Penner (2012).
26 Sánchez Natalías (2019a) has recently made a convincing argument that, at least in the Roman west, watery places were predominantly used as locations for deposition because of their sacred nature, rather than for persuasive analogy or sympathetic magic.

27 Other scholars have noted that this was also the case with votive rituals (Derks 1998; Osborne 2004).
28 King 2009: 2020.
29 For self-authored examples, see almost all the curses from Bad Kreuznach. For examples of professionally made tablets, the ones from Carthage that taper towards the end often include formulas 'giving' names to the dead spirits invoked.
30 The term *Masitlatida* is unattested elsewhere, but the conclusion that it is a festival of some kind makes the most sense considering the verb *celebrare*. For a more detailed discussion, see Marichal (1981).
31 See discussions in Chapter 3, and Salvo (2012: 255–61) and Cousins (2020: 137–8).
32 Kiernan 2004b. On the victim's experience of being cursed, see also Eidinow (2017).
33 See Kiernan 2004b.
34 Lib. 1.245–50. Discussed in more detail in Chapter 3.
35 Gordon 2012b: 151–3.
36 Gordon 2019b.
37 This is another place where curse tablets differ from lapidary inscriptions, which were created by professional stonemasons, and therefore do not tell us whether the dedicants themselves were literate.
38 Bowman and Woolf 1994: 5–6.
39 On the relationship between writing and power, see Moreland (2001; 2006).
40 On bi- and multilingualism in the Roman world see Adams (2003; 2007) and Mullen and James 2012). The outputs of the LatinNow project (https://latinnow.eu/) are adding greatly to this area of study.
41 Marsala and Messina on Sicily; Centuripe, Camarina, Reggio Calabria, Bordighera and Torano Castello on the mainland.
42 See Sánchez Natalías (2019b) for a more detailed mapping of Greek curses from the Roman west.
43 Pin. *NH*. 30.3–11.
44 Apul. *Apol*. 27.
45 *In Vat*. 14.
46 On Circe and Medea in Latin writers, see Luck (1999: 110–13); Stratton (2007: 87–90) and Rives (2010: 69). Lucan's Erichtho (*Pharsalia* 6. 413–830) is the most famous Thessalian witch from Latin literature.
47 On the varied history of Greek as a ritual language in pagan and Christian religions, see Blom (2012).
48 Faraone 2018: 8–11.
49 Sixteen of these are from Gallia and the rest are from Britannia: two from Bath, one from Uley and another from Dodford.
50 Mullen (2007a: 42) suggests that the cursers who wrote in Celtic at Bath were travellers from the continent who were demonstrating a specifically Gallic identity. Unfortunately, scholarly understandings of the distinctions between Insular and Continental Celtic languages are not refined enough for a firm conclusion.
51 For a discussion of the 'Celtic-ness' of these curses, and potential connections to later, medieval Celtic culture, see Mees (2009). It should be noted that this is a controversial work, particularly among Celticists: see the critical reviews by Reid (2012) and Raepsaet-Charlier (2014). More positive impressions are given by Melia (2011) and Wiley (2011).

52 Adams 2003: 194–9.
53 Gardner 2007: 1; Knapp 2010: 196; Robb 2010: 494–5; Harris and Cipolla 2017: 85; Sørensen 2018: 96–7; Graham 2021: 11–12.
54 Kapferer 1997: 237.
55 Marwick 1965: 221; Douglas 1973: 43.
56 Kropp (2008b: 236) put this most emphatically when she stated that cursing rituals had no social function in sustaining or creating communities.
57 Winkler 1990: 71–98. Aspects of his interpretations have not gone unchallenged: see, for example, Dickie (2000: 563–64); Pachoumi (2013: 301) and Edmonds (2019: 108).
58 Faraone 2001: 43–4.
59 Firmly demonstrated by Saller and Shaw (1984) and followed by most scholars since (e.g. Dixon 1992 and Rawson 2003), but see Martin (1996) for issues with their methodology. On families beyond Rome and Italy, see the papers in George (2005).
60 On Roman marriage and family life, see Treggiari (1991) and Dixon (1992). On curse tablets in Roman families, see the work already done by Frankfurter (2014) and Ripat (2014).
61 Treggiari 1991: 84–121.
62 Faraone (1991: 20) gives the classic 'underdog' reading of ancient curse tablets.
63 Kapferer 1997: 237–9. Salvo (2012) and Cousins (2020: 137–8) have both recently argued for similar interpretations of ancient prayers for justice.
64 Alongside invaluable catalogues of names, such as Kajanto (1965); Lőrincz and Mócsy (1994), Solin and Salomies (1994) and Delamarre (2007), my argument here also builds on work that explores the social significance of onomastics, such as, for example, Adams (1978), Dickey (2002) and Mullen (2007b).
65 Files et al. 2017. Anecdotal evidence suggests this is far more widespread and exists in other academic fields. After Dr Fern Riddell was called 'immodest' on Twitter for insisting that people use her professional title, female academics from a range of fields added titles to their handles, sharing their own stories of deliberate, denigrating misnaming under the hashtag #immodestwomen. See Riddell 2018 for a discussion of the event and a link to her original tweet.
66 Goldhill 1991: 24–36. My thanks to Kate Cook for pointing out this connection to me.
67 Austin 1972, although see Olson (1992) who argues that there is nothing magical in it, but instead that the caution comes from the anxiety over believing the lies of wandering strangers.
68 *Od.* 9.528–35.
69 Austin references Levi-Strauss' (1973: 278–9) work with indigenous groups in South America, to which I may add the article by Hand (1984) that lists a great number of beliefs and practices collected from Europeans and Americans of European descent.
70 Varro *apud.* Servius *Aen.* 1.277; Plin. *HN.* 3.65; Plut. *Quaest. Rom.* 61; Macrob. *Sat.* 3.9.2. See also discussion of this episode by, among others, Murphy (2004), Rüpke (2007: 132–4) and Cairns (2010).
71 The most recent in-depth study of names on Latin curses is Urbanová (2019), but this is concerned primarily with the syntax of names in curse formulas. See also Gordon (2021) on lists of names in Roman curses.
72 McKie 2019: 446–7.

73 Cursers are much more rarely named at all. Of the seventy named male cursers, only four give themselves two names, and none use the *tri nomina*.
74 Mullen 2007b.
75 There are only ten men named by *praenomen* alone.
76 Dickey 2002: 60.
77 Salomies 2001: 84.
78 Mullen 2007b: 47.
79 Mullen 2007b: 40; Meißner 2012: 181, 186.
80 See Curbera (1999: 196–200) for a summary of the debate.
81 Gager 1992: 14; Graf 1997b: 128; Ogden 1999: 61.
82 *Nepos* (grandson): SD 166; *frater/adelphos* (brother): **SD 299, 470, Gager 79**, DT 226; *adelphea* (sister): SGD 127; *noverca* (stepmother): SD 485. Mees (2009, 55ff) suggests that the Celtic word *dona* found on the Larzac tablet could be translated as foster-daughter, but this is not a conclusion shared by Lambert (see *RIG* 2.2 L-98).
83 Kapferer 1997: 45.
84 Chaniotis 2004: 12–13.
85 I have assumed here that the five separate curses (**DT 275**, 276, 277, 278, 282) that name 'Superstes, slave of Regulus' are referring to the same person. More enslaved people can be identified by the content or context of the curse (for example, the six victims who 'have not pleased their *dominus*' on **SD 119**), but I have not counted these here.
86 Hope 2000: 102.
87 Marco Simón and De Llanza (2008), although not universally accepted; see Kos (2018). For Sura's contribution to the Dacian Wars, see Cass. Dio 68.9.
88 *RIG* 2.2 L-100; Mees 2009: 10–28.
89 SD 436 (Uley) and **450** (Weeting-with-Broomhill) include the formula 'whether civilian or soldier' and SD 463 (Bodegraven) appears to target soldiers divided into *contubernia*. The word *milites* appears on SD 531 (Szombathely), but the rest of the text is too fragmentary for a full interpretation.
90 See Chapter 4 for examples.
91 I have not included charioteers and other performers here because the very nature of the competition curses on which they were targeted required their identification as such.

Bibliography

Adams, J. N. (1978), 'Conventions of Naming in Cicero', *CQ*, 28: 145–66.
Adams, J. N. (1982), *The Latin Sexual Vocabulary*. London: Duckworth.
Adams, J. N. (1998), 'Two Notes on RIB', *ZPE* 123: 235–6.
Adams, J. N. (2003), *Bilingualism and the Latin Language*. Cambridge: Cambridge University Press.
Adams, J. N. (2007), *The Regional Diversification of Latin, 200 BC–AD 600*. Cambridge: Cambridge University Press.
Albrecht, J., C. Degelman, V. Gasparini, R. Gordon, M. Patzelt, G. Petridou, R. Raja, A.-K. Reiger, J. Rüpke, B. Sippel, E. Rubens Uriciuoli, L. Weiss (2018), 'Religion in the Making: The Lived Ancient Religion Approach', *Religion*, 48: 568–93.
Aldhouse-Green, M. J. (2018), *Sacred Britannia: The Gods and Rituals of Roman Britain*. London: Thames and Hudson.
Alfayé, S., and C. Sánchez Natalías (2020), 'Magic in Roman Funerary Spaces', in R. Gordon, F. Marco Simón and M. Piranomonte (eds), *Choosing Magic: Contexts, Objects, Meanings: The Archaeology of Instrumental Religion in the Latin West*, 41–54. Rome: De Luca Editori d'Arte.
Allason-Jones, L. (2011), 'Priests and Priestesses in Roman Britain', in F. Santangelo and J. H. Richardson (eds), *Priest and State in the Roman World*, 429–43. Stuttgart: Steiner.
Alvar Nuño, A. (2017a) *Cadenas Invisibles: Los Usos de La Magia Entre Los Escalvos En El Imperio Romano*. Besançon: Presses universitaires de Franche-Comté.
Alvar Nuño, A. (2017b), 'Morality, Emotions and Reason: New Perspectives on the Study of Roman Magic', *Archiv Für Religionsgeschichte*, 18: 307–25.
Alvar Nuño, A. (2019a), 'Suppressing Leaks: Magical Solutions to Gossip and Accusation in the Roman World', *Magic, Ritual, and Witchcraft* 14 (2): 189–210.
Alvar Nuño, A. (2019b), 'The Use of Curse Tablets among Slaves in Rome and Its Western Provinces', *Religion in the Roman Empire* 5 (3): 398–416.
Alvar Nuño, A. (2020), 'Ritual Power, Routine and Attributed Responsibility: Magic in Roman Households, Workshops and Farmsteads', in R. Gordon, F. Marco Simón and M. Piranomonte (eds), *Choosing Magic: Contexts, Objects, Meanings: The Archaeology of Instrumental Religion in the Latin West*, 77–91. Rome: De Luca Editori d'Arte.
Ashforth, A. (2005), *Witchcraft, Violence and Democracy in South Africa*, Chicago: University of Chicago Press.
Audollent, A. (1904), *Defixionum Tabellae Quotquot Innotuerunt: Tam in Graecis Orientis Quam in Totius Occidentis Partibus Praeter Atticas in Corpore Inscriptionum Atticarum Editas*, Paris: Fontemoing.
Audollent, A. (1908), 'Rapport sur des "Tabellae Defixionum" récemment découvertes a Sousse (Tunisie)', *BCTH* 3: 4–6.
Audollent, A. (1910), 'Bandeau de plomb avec inscription trouvé a Haidra (Tunisie)', in Chatelain, E. (ed.), *Mélanges offerts à m. Émile Chatelain*, 545–56. Paris: Librairie Ancienne Honoré Champion.

Austin, J. (1962), *How to Do Things with Words: The William James Lectures Delivered at Harvard University in 1955*. Oxford: Oxford University Press.

Austin, N. (1972), 'Name Magic in the "Odyssey"', *California Studies in Classical Antiquity*, 5: 1–19.

Bablitz, L. (2007), *Actors and Audience in the Roman Courtroom*. London and New York: Routledge.

Barrett, J. (1991), 'Towards an Archaeology of Ritual', in P. Garwood, D. Jennings, R. Skeates and J. Toms, *Sacred and Profane: Proceedings of a Conference on Archaeology, Ritual and Religion. Oxford 1989*, 1–9. Oxford: Oxford University Committee for Archaeology.

Barrett, J. (2012), 'Agency: A Revisionist Account', in I. Hodder (ed.), *Archaeological Theory Today*, 2nd edn, 146–66. Cambridge: Polity.

Barrowclough, D. and C. Malone eds, (2007), *Cult in Context: Reconsidering Ritual in Archaeology*. Oxford: Oxbow.

Barta, A. (2015), 'Ito Pater, Eracura and the Messenger: A Preliminary Report on a New Curse Tablet from Aquincum', *ACD* 51: 101–33.

Barta, A. (2017), 'The Siscia Curse Tablet from a Linguistic Point of View: A New Autopsy', *GLB* 22: 23–41.

Bauman, R. (1996), *Crime and Punishment in Ancient Rome*. London and New York: Routledge.

Beard, M. (1991), 'Writing and Religion: Ancient Literacy and the Function of the Written Word in Roman Religion', in J. Humphrey (ed.), *Literacy in the Roman World. JRA Supplementary Series* 3, 35–58. Ann Arbor: Journal of Roman Archaeology.

Beard, M., J. North and S. Price. (1998), *Religions of Rome*. Cambridge: Cambridge University Press.

Bélanger Sarrazin, R., A. Delattre, D. Demaiffe, N. De Winter, A. Martin, G. Raepsaet and M. T. Raepsaet-Charlier (2019), 'Une Tablette de Défixion Récemment Découverte à Tongres', *Latomus* 78: 471–81.

Bell, C. (1992), *Ritual Theory, Ritual Practice*. Oxford: Oxford University Press.

Bell, C. (1997), *Ritual: Perspectives and Dimensions*. Oxford: Oxford University Press.

Beschaouch, A. (2006), 'Que Savons-Nous Des Sodalités Africo-Romaines?', *CRAI*, 150 (2): 1401–17.

Betts, E. (2016), 'Places of Transition and Deposition: Phenomenon of Water in the Sacred Landscape of Iron Age Central Adriatic Italy', *ARP* 14: 63–83.

Betz, H. D. (1992), *The Greek Magical Papyri in Translation Including the Demotic Spells*, 2nd edn. Chicago: Chicago University Press.

Blanco, M. (2017), 'Women and the Transmission of Magical Knowledge in the Graeco-Roman World: Rediscovering Ancient Witches', in E. Suarez, M. Blanco, E. Chronopoulou and I. Canzobre (eds), *Magike Techne: Formacion y Consideracion Social Del Mago En El Mundo Antiguo*, 95–110. Madrid: Dykinson.

Blänsdorf, J. (2012a), *Die Defixionum Tabellae des Mainzer Isis- und Mater Magna-Heiligtums: Defixionum Tabellae Mogontiacenses (DTM)*, Mainz: Generaldirektion Kulturelles Erbe.

Blänsdorf, J. (2012b), 'The Social Background of the Defixion Texts of Mater Magna at Mainz and Anna Perenna at Rome', in M. Piranomonte and F. Marco Simón (eds), *Contesti Magici = Contextos Mágicos: Atti Del Convegno Internazionale, Roma, Palazzo Massimo, 4–6 novembre 2009*, 147–60. Rome: De Luca Editori D'Arte.

Blänsdorf, J. (2014), 'Das Verfluchungstäfelchen Aus Gelduba (Gellep Bei Krefeld) Grab 5486', *ZPE* 192: 181–6.

Blänsdorf, J. (2015), 'The Curse Inscriptions and the Materia Magica of the Anna-Perenna-Nymphaeum at Rome', in D. Boschung and J. Bremmer (eds), *The Materiality of Magic*, 293–308. Paderborn: Wilhelm Fink.

Blänsdorf, J. and M. Piranomonte (2012), 'Sale IX.49. La Fontana di Anna Perenna', in R. Friggeri, M. G. Granino Cecere and G. L. Gregori (eds), *Terme Di Diocleziano: La Collezione Epigrafica*, 617–39. Milan: Electa.

Blom, A. (2012), 'Linguae Sacrae in Ancient and Medieval Sources', in A. Mullen and P. James (eds), *Multilingualism in the Graeco-Roman Worlds*, 124–40. Cambridge: Cambridge University Press.

Boschung, D. and J. Bremmer eds, (2015), *The Materiality of Magic*. Paderborn: Wilhelm Fink.

Bourdieu, P. (1977), *An Outline of a Theory of Practice*. Cambridge: Cambridge University Press.

Bowman, A. (1991), 'Literacy in the Roman Empire: Mass and Mode', in J. Humphrey (ed.), *Literacy in the Roman World: JRA Supplementary Series 3*, 119–31. Ann Arbor: Journal of Roman Archaeology.

Bowman, A., and J. D. Thomas (1974), *The Vindolanda Writing Tablets. Northern History Booklet*. Newcastle upon Tyne: Graham.

Bowman, A., and J. D. Thomas (2003), *The Vindolanda Writing-Tablets (Tabulae Vindolandenses). Vol. 3. Tabulae Vindolandenses*. London: British Museum.

Bowman, A., J. D. Thomas and J. N. Adams (1994), *The Vindolanda Writing-Tablets (Tabulae Vindolandenses II)*. London: British Museum.

Bowman, A., and G. Woolf (1994), 'Literacy and Power in the Ancient World', in A. Bowman and G. Woolf (eds), *Literacy and Power in the Ancient World*, 1–16. Cambridge: Cambridge University Press.

Bowman, M., and Ü Valk eds, (2012), *Vernacular Religion in Everyday Life: Expressions of Belief*. Sheffield: Equinox.

Bradley, K. (1997), 'Law, Magic, and Culture in the "Apologia" of Apuleius', *Phoenix* 51 (2): 203–23.

Bremmer, J. (2015), 'Preface: The Materiality of Magic', in D. Boschung and J. Bremmer (eds), *The Materiality of Magic*, 7–19. Paderborn: Wilhelm Fink.

Briault, C. (2007), 'The Ultimate Redundancy Package: Routine, Structure and the Archaeology of Ritual Transmission', in D. Barrowclough and C. Malone (eds), *Cult in Context: Reconsidering Ritual in Archaeology*, 293–6. Oxford: Oxbow.

Brown, P. (1970), 'Sorcery, Demons, and the Rise of Christianity from Late Antiquity to the Middle Ages', in M. Douglas (ed.), *Witchcraft: Confessions and Accusations*, 17–46. London: Routledge.

Buckland, W. W., and P. Stein (1963), *A Text-Book of Roman Law from Augustus to Justinian*, 3rd edn. Cambridge: Cambridge University Press.

Cagnat, R. (1903), 'Les Tablettes magiques d'Hadrumete', *JS* 256–64.

Cairns, F. (2010), 'Roma and Her Tutelary Deity: Names and Ancient Evidence', in C. S. Kraus, J. Marincola and C. Pelling (eds), *Ancient Historiography and Its Contexts: Studies in Honour of A. J. Woodman*, 245–66. Oxford: Oxford University Press.

Cameron, A. (1976), *Circus Factions: Blues and Greens at Rome and Byzantium*. Oxford: Oxford University Press.

Carroll, M. (2007), '"*Vox Tua Nempe Mea Est*": Dialogues with the Dead in Roman Funerary Commemoration', *ARP* 11: 37–76.

Chadwick, A. (2015), 'Doorways, Ditches and Dead Dogs: Excavating and Recording Material Manifestations of Practical Magic amongst Later Prehistoric and Romano-British

Communities', in C. Houlbrook and N. Armitage, *The Materiality of Magic: An Artefactual Investigation into Ritual Practices and Popular Beliefs*, 37–64. Oxford: Oxbow.

Chaniotis, A. (1995), 'Illness and Cures in the Greek Propiatory Inscriptions and Dedications of Lydia and Phrygia', in P. van der Eijk, P. Horstmanshoff and P. Schrijvers (eds), *Ancient Medicine in Its Socio-Cultural Context*, 323–44. Amsterdam: Rodopi.

Chaniotis, A. (2004), 'Under the Watchful Eyes of the Gods: Divine Justice in Hellenistic and Roman Asia Minor', in S. Colvin (ed.), *The Graeco-Roman East: Politics, Culture, Society*, 1–43, Yale Classical Studies. Cambridge: Cambridge University Press.

Cherry, D. (1995), 'Re-Figuring the Roman Epigraphic Habit', *AHB* 9: 143–56.

Chevet, P. (2016), 'Le Sanctuaire Antique Du Site Des Jacobins Au Mans', *Archéopages* 43: 18–23.

Choppard, L., and G. Hannezo. (1893), 'Nouvelles Découvertes Dans La Nécropole Romaine d'Hadrumète', *BCTH*, 193–202.

Coleman, K. M. (1990), 'Fatal Charades: Roman Executions Staged as Mythological Enactments'. *JRS* 80: 44–73.

Connolly, S. (2010), *Lives Behind the Laws: The World of the Codex Hermogenianus*. Bloomington: Indiana University Press.

Corbeill, A. (2004), *Nature Embodied: Gesture in Ancient Rome*. Princeton: Princeton University Press.

Corbeill, A. (2015), '"A Shouting and Bustling on All Sides" (Hor. Sat. 1.9.77–8): Everyday Justice in the Streets of Republican Rome', in I. Ostenberg and J. Bjørnebye (eds), *The Moving City: Processions, Passages and Promenades in Ancient Rome*, 89–98. London: Bloomsbury.

Cousins, E. (2014), 'Votive Objects and Ritual Practice and the King's Spring at Bath', in H. Platts, John Pearce, C. Barron, J. Lundock and J. Yoo (eds), *TRAC 2013: Proceedings of the Twenty-Third Annual Theoretical Roman Archaeology Conference, London 2013*, 52–64. Oxford: Oxbow.

Cousins, E. (2020), *The Sanctuary at Bath in the Roman Empire*. Cambridge: Cambridge University Press.

Craig, C. P. (2004), 'Audience Expectations, Invective, and Proof'. In J. G. F. Powell and J. Paterson (eds), *Cicero the Advocate*, 187–213. Oxford: Oxford University Press.

Creighton, J. (2000), *Coins and Power in Late Iron Age Britain*. Cambridge: Cambridge University Press.

Crellin, R. J. (2020), 'Posthumanist Power', in R. J. Crellin, C. N. Cipolla, L. M. Montgomery, O. J. T. Harris and S. V. Moore (eds), *Archaeological Theory in Dialogue: Situating Relationality, Ontology, Posthumanism, and Indigenous Paradigms*, 115–30. London: Routledge.

Crouzet, Y. (2009), 'Les Tablettes de Bath et Uley: Un Placebo Juridique', *REL* 87: 25–33.

Cunliffe, B., and P. Davenport (1985), *The Temple of Sulis Minerva at Bath: Volume 1 The Site*. Oxford: Oxford University Committee for Archaeology.

Cunningham, G. (1999), *Religion and Magic: Approaches and Theories*. Edinburgh: Edinburgh University Press.

Curbera, J. (1999), 'Maternal lineage in Greek magical texts', in D. R. Jordan, H. Montgomery and E. Thomassen (eds), *The World of Ancient Magic: Papers from the First International Samson Eitrem Seminar at the Norwegian Institute at Athens*, 195–204. Bergen: The Norwegian Institute at Athens.

Curbera, J. (2015), 'From the Magician's Workshop: Notes on the Materiality of Greek Curse Tablets', in D. Boschung and J. Bremmer (eds), *The Materiality of Magic*, 97–122. Paderborn: Wilhelm Fink.

Daniel R. W., and F. Maltomini eds, (1990–2), *Supplementum Magicum*, 2 vols. Opladen: Westdeutscher Verlag.

De Winter, N. (2018), 'De Opgraving Aan Het Regulierenplein te Tongeren', *Signa* 7: 73–6.

Deckers, P., M. Lewis and S. Thomas. (2016), 'Between Two Places: Archaeology and Metal-Detecting in Europe', *Open Archaeology* 2 (1). https://doi.org/10.1515/opar-2016-0031.

Delamarre, X. (2007), *Nomina Celtica Antiqua Selecta Inscriptionum (Noms de Personnes Celtiques Dans l'epigraphie Classique)*. Paris: Editions Errance.

Delattre, A.-L. (1888), 'Fouilles d'un cimetiere romain a Carthage en 1888', *RA* 12: 151–74.

Derks, T. (1991), 'The Perception of the Roman Pantheon by a Native Elite: The Example of Votive Inscriptions from Lower Germany', in N. Roymans and F. Theuws (eds), *Images of the Past: Studies on Ancient Societies in Northwestern Europe*, 235–65. Amsterdam: Instituut voor Pre- en Protohistorische Archeologie.

Derks, T. (1995), 'The Ritual of the Vow in Gallo-Roman Religion', in J. Metzler, M. Millett, N. Roymans and J. Slofstra (eds), *Integration in the Early Roman West*, 111–27. Luxembourg: Musée National d'Histoire et d'Art.

Derks, T. (1998), *Gods, Temples and Ritual Practices: The Transformation of Religious Ideals and Values in Roman Gaul*. Amsterdam: Amsterdam University Press.

Dickey, E. (2002), *Latin Forms of Address: From Plautus to Apuleius*. Oxford: Oxford University Press.

Dickie, M. (2000), 'Who Practiced Love-Magic in Classical Antiquity and the Late-Roman World?', *CQ* 50: 563–83.

Dickie, M. (2001), *Magic and Magicians in the Greco-Roman World*. London and New York: Routledge.

Diosono, F. (2020), 'Lamps as Ritual and "magical" Objects in Archaeological Contexts', in A. Mastrocinque, J. E. Sanzo and M. Scapini (eds), *Ancient Magic: Then and Now*, 139–57. Stuttgart: Franz Steiner Verlag.

Dixon, S. (1992), *The Roman Family*. Baltimore: Johns Hopkins University Press.

Dobres, M.-A., and J. Robb eds, (2000a), *Agency in Archaeology*. London and New York: Routledge.

Dobres, M.-A., and J. Robb (2000b), 'Agency in Archaeology: Paradigm or Platitude?', in M. A. Dobres and J. Robb (eds), *Agency in Archaeology*, 3–18. London and New York: Routledge.

Dornan, J. L. (2002), 'Agency and Archaeology: Past, Present, and Future Directions', *Journal of Archaeological Method and Theory* 9: 303–29.

Douglas, M. (1970a), 'Introduction: 30 Years After Witchcraft, Oracles and Magic', in M. Douglas (ed.), *Witchcraft: Confessions and Accusations*, xiii–xxxviii. London: Tavistock.

Douglas, M. ed., (1970b), *Witchcraft: Confessions and Accusations*. London: Tavistock.

Douglas, M. (1973), *Natural Symbols: Explorations in Cosmology*, 2nd edn, London: Barrie and Jenkins.

Dowding, K. (1996), *Power*. Minneapolis: University of Minnesota Press.

Dowding, K. (2017), *Power, Luck and Freedom: Collected Essays*. Manchester: Manchester University Press.

Dufallo, B. (2001), 'Appius' Indignation: Gossip, Tradition, and Performance in Republican Rome', *TAPhA* 131: 119–42.

Dunbabin, K. M. D. (1978), *The Mosaics of Roman North Africa: Studies in Iconography and Patronage*, Oxford Monographs on Classical Archaeology. Oxford: Clarendon Press.

Durali-Mueller, S., G. P. Brey, D. Wigg-Wolf and Y. Lahaye (2007), 'Roman Lead Mining in Germany: Its Origin and Development through Time Deduced from Lead Isotope Provenance Studies', *Journal of Archaeological Science* 34 (10): 1555–67.

Dzwiza, K. (2012), 'The Catalogue and Statistical Analysis of the Charaktêres Project: A First Introduction', in M. Piranomonte and F. Marco Simón (eds), *Contesti Magici = Contextos Mágicos: Atti Del Convegno Internazionale, Roma, Palazzo Massimo, 4–6 novembre 2009*, 307–8. Rome: De Luca Editori D'Arte.

Edmonds, R. (2014), 'Bewitched, Bothered and Bewildered: Erotic Magic in the Graeco-Roman World', in T. Hubbard (ed.), *Companion to Greek and Roman Sexualities*, 286–300. Oxford: Blackwell.

Edmonds, R. (2019), *Drawing Down the Moon, Magic in the Ancient Greco-Roman World*. Princeton: Princeton University Press.

Eidinow, E. (2007a), *Oracles, Curses and Risk Among the Ancient Greeks*. Oxford: Oxford University Press.

Eidinow, E. (2007b), 'Why the Athenians Began to Curse', in R. Osborne (ed.), *Debating the Athenian Cultural Revolution: Art, Literature, Philosophy, and Politics 430–380 BC*, 44–71. Cambridge: Cambridge University Press.

Eidinow, E. (2017), 'Ancient Greco-Roman Magic and the Agency of Victimhood', *Numen* 64 (4): 394–417.

Epplett, C. (2014), 'Roman Beast Hunts', in P. Christesen and D. Kyle (eds), *A Companion to Sport and Spectacle in Greek and Roman Antiquity*, 574–90. Chichester: Wiley Blackwell.

Epstein, A. L. (1969), 'Gossip, Norms and Social Network', in J. C. Mitchell (ed.), *Social Networks in Urban Situations: Analyses of Personal Relationships in Central African Towns*, 117–27. Manchester: Manchester University Press.

Evans-Pritchard, E. E. (1937), *Witchcraft, Oracles and Magic among the Azande*. Oxford: Clarendon Press.

Eves, R. (2000), 'Sorcery's the Curse: Modernity, Envy and the Flow of Sociality in a Melanesian Society', *The Journal of the Royal Anthropological Institute* 6 (3): 453–68.

Fabre, G., M. Mayer and I. Rodà (1991), *Inscriptions Romaines de Catalogne*, Paris: Gerone.

Fagan, G. (2011), *The Lure of the Arena: Social Psychology and the Crowd at Roman Games*, Cambridge: Cambridge University Press.

Faraone, C. A. (1991), 'The Agonistic Context of Early Greek Binding Spells', in C. A. Faraone and D. Obbink (eds), *Magika Hiera: Ancient Greek Magic and Religion*, 3–32, Oxford: Oxford University Press.

Faraone, C. A. (2001), *Ancient Greek Love Magic*. Cambridge, MA, and London: Harvard University Press.

Faraone, C. A. (2002), 'Agents and Victims: Constructions of Gender and Desire in Ancient Greek Love Magic', in N. Nussbaum and J. Sihvola (eds), *The Sleep of Reason: Erotic Experience and Sexual Ethics in Ancient Greece and Rome*, 400–26. Chicago and London: University of Chicago Press.

Faraone, C. A. (2018), *The Transformation of Greek Amulets in Roman Imperial Times*. Philadelphia: University of Pennsylvania Press.

Faraone, C. A., B. Garnand and C. López-Ruiz (2005), 'Micah's Mother (Judg. 17:1–4) and a Curse from Carthage (KAI 89): Canaanite Precedents for Greek and Latin Curses Against Thieves?', *JNES* 64: 161–86.

Faraone, C. A., and R. Gordon (2019), 'Curses in Context 1: Curse Tablets in Italy and the Western Roman Empire: Development, Aims, Strategies and Competence', *Religion in the Roman Empire* 5 (3): 319–34.

Feddema, J. P. (1997), 'The Cursing Practice in Sri Lanka as a Religious Channel for Keeping Physical Violence in Control: The Case of Seenigama', *Journal of Asian and African Studies* 32: 202–22.

Files, J. A., A. P. Mayer, M. G. Ko, P. Friedrich, M. Jenkins, M. J. Bryan, S. Vegunta, C. M. Wittich, M. A. Lyle, R. Melikian, T. Duston, Y.-H. H. Chang and S. N. Haynes (2017), 'Speaker Introductions at Internal Medicine Grand Rounds: Forms of Address Reveal Gender Bias', *Journal of Women's Health* 26 (5): 413–19.

Fishwick, D. (1987), *The Imperial Cult in the Latin West: Studies in the Ruler Cult of the Western Provinces of the Roman Empire*. Leiden: Brill.

Flower, H. (2017), *The Dancing Lares and the Serpent in the Garden: Religion at the Roman Street Corner*. Princeton: Princeton University Press.

Fontijn, D. (2007), 'The Significance of "Invisible" Places', *World Archaeology* 39 (1): 70–83.

Frank, T. (1940), *An Economic Survey of Ancient Rome: Volume V, Rome and Italy of the Empire*. Baltimore: John Hopkins Press.

Frankfurter, D. (2002), 'Dynamics of Ritual Expertise in Antiquity and Beyond: Towards a New Taxonomy of Magicians', in P. Mirecki and M. Meyer (eds), *Magic and Ritual in the Ancient World*, 159–78. Leiden: Brill.

Frankfurter, D. (2014), 'The Social Context of Women's Erotic Magic in Antiquity', in K. B. Stratton and D. Kalleres (eds), *Daughters of Hecate: Women and Magic in the Ancient World*, 319–33. Oxford: Oxford University Press.

Frazer, J. (1922), *The Golden Bough: A Study in Magic and Religion. Abridged*. London: MacMillan.

Frier, B. W. (1989), *A Casebook on the Roman Law of Delict*. Atlanta: Scholars Press.

Gabrielle Foreman, P. et al (n.d.), 'Writing about Slavery/Teaching about Slavery: This Might Help', Available Online: https://docs.google.com/document/d/1A4TEdDgYslX-hlKezLodMIM71My3KTN0zxRv0IQTOQs/mobilebasic (Accessed 13 May 2021).

Gager, J. (1992), *Curse Tablets and Binding Spells from the Ancient World*. Oxford: Oxford University Press.

Gardner, A. (2007), 'Introduction: Social Agency, Power and Being Human', in A. Gardner (ed.), *Agency Uncovered: Archaeological Perspectives on Social Agency, Power and Being Human*, 1–15. Walnut Creek, CA: Left Coast Press.

Gardner, A. (2013), 'Thinking about Roman Imperialism: Postcolonialism, Globalisation and Beyond?', *Britannia*: 44: 1–25.

Gardner, A. (2017), 'On Theory Building in Roman Archaeology: The Potential for New Approaches to Materiality and Practice', in A. Van Oyen and M. Pitts (eds), *Materialising Roman Histories*, 203–9. Oxford: Oxbow.

Garnsey, P. (1970), *Social Status and Legal Privilege in the Roman Empire*. Oxford: Clarendon Press.

Gasparini, V., M. Patzelt, R. Raja, A.-K. Rieger, J. Rüpke and E. Urciuoli eds, (2020a), *Lived Religion in the Ancient Mediterranean World: Approaching Religious Transformations from Archaeology, History and Classics*. Berlin: De Gruyter.

Gasparini, V., M. Patzelt, R. Raja, A.-K. Rieger, J. Rüpke and E. Urciuoli (2020b), 'Pursuing Lived Ancient Religion', in V. Gasparini, M. Patzelt, R. Raja, A.-K. Rieger, J. Rüpke and E. Urciuoli (eds), *Lived Religion in the Ancient Mediterranean World: Approaching Religious Transformations from Archaeology, History and Classics*, 1–8. Berlin: De Gruyter.

Gell, A. (1998), *Art and Agency: An Anthropological Theory*. Oxford: Oxford University Press.

George, M. ed., (2005), *The Roman Family in the Empire: Rome, Italy, and Beyond*. Oxford: Oxford University Press.

Giddens, A. (1984), *The Constitution of Society: Outline of the Theory of Structuration*. Cambridge: Polity.

Goldberg, D. M. (2009), 'The Dichotomy in Romano-Celtic Syncretism: Some Preliminary Thoughts on Vernacular Religion', in M. Dreissen, S. Heeren, J. Hendriks, F. Kemmers and R. Visser (eds), *TRAC 2008: Proceedings of the 18th Annual Theoretical Roman Archaeology Conference*, 187–202. Oxford: Oxbow.

Goldhill, S. (1991), *The Poet's Voice: Essays on Poetics and Greek Literature*. Cambridge: Cambridge University Press.

Gordon, R. (1990), 'The Veil of Power: Emperors, Sacrificers and Benefactors', in M. Beard and J. North (eds), *Pagan Priests: Religion and Power in the Ancient World*, 199–231. London: Duckworth.

Gordon, R. (1999a), 'Imagining Greek and Roman Magic', in V. Flint, R. Gordon, G. Luck and D. Ogden (eds), *Witchcraft and Magic in Europe: Ancient Greece and Rome*, 161–275. London: Athalone Press.

Gordon, R. (1999b), '"What's in a List?" Listing in Greco-Roman Malign Magical Texts', in D. Jordan, H. Montgomery and E. Thomassen (eds), *The World of Ancient Magic: Papers from The First International Samson Eitrem Seminar at the Norwegian Institute at Athens*, 239–77. Athens: Norwegian Institute at Athens.

Gordon, R. (2012a), 'Fixing the Race: Managing Risks in the North African Circus', in M. Piranomonte and F. Marco Simón (eds), *Contesti Magici = Contextos Mágicos: Atti Del Convegno Internazionale, Roma, Palazzo Massimo, 4–6 novembre 2009*, 35–62. Rome: De Luca Editori D'Arte.

Gordon, R. (2012b), 'Memory and Authority in the Magical Papyri', in B. Dignas and R. R. R. Smith (eds), *Historical and Religious Memory in the Ancient World*, 145–80. Oxford: Oxford University Press.

Gordon, R. (2013), 'Gods, Guilt and Suffering: Psychological Aspects of Cursing in the North-Western Provinces of the Roman Empire', *ACD* 49: 255–81.

Gordon, R. (2015), 'Showing the Gods the Way: Curse-Tablets as Deictic Persuasion', *Religion in the Roman Empire* 1: 148–80.

Gordon, R. (2019a) 'A Babel of Voices: Styling Malign Magic in the Roman World', *Magic, Ritual, and Witchcraft* 14 (2): 155–88.

Gordon, R. (2019b), 'Do the "Vernacular" Curse-Tablets from Italy Represent a Specific Knowledge-Practice?', *Religion in the Roman Empire* 5: 417–39.

Gordon, R. (2019c), 'Subordinated Religious Specialism and Individuation in the Graeco-Roman World', in M. Fuchs, A. Linkenbach, M. Mulsow, B.-C. Otto, R. Parson and J. Rüpke (eds), *Religious Individualisation: Historical Dimensions and Comparative Perspectives*, 905–1009. Berlin: De Gruyter.

Gordon, R. (2021), 'The Performativity of Lists in Vernacular Curse-Practice under the Roman Empire', in R. Lämmie, C. Scheidegger Lämmie and K. Wesselmann (eds), *Lists and Catalogues in Ancient Literature and Beyond: Towards a Poetics of Enumeration*, 107–45. Berlin: De Gruyter.

Gordon, R. and F. Marco Simón eds, (2010), *Magical Practice in the Latin West: Papers from the International Conference Held at the University of Zaragoza, 30 Sept.–1 Oct. 2005*. Leiden: Brill.

Gordon, R., F. Marco Simón and M. Piranomonte eds, (2020), *Choosing Magic: Contexts, Objects, Meanings: The Archaeology of Instrumental Religion in the Latin West*. Rome: De Luca Editori d'Arte.

Graf, F. (1997a), 'How to Cope with a Difficult Life: A View of Ancient Magic', in P. Schäfer and H. G. Kippenberg (eds), *Envisioning Magic: A Princeton Seminar and Symposium*, 93–114. Leiden: Brill.

Graf, F. (1997b), *Magic in the Ancient World*. Cambridge, MA, and London: Harvard University Press.

Graham, E.-J. (2021), *Reassembling Religion in Roman Italy*. London and New York: Routledge.

Graham, E.-J. (forthcoming), 'Mobility, Kinaesthesia, Imagined Movement and the Making of Place in the Sanctuaries of Ancient Italy', in E. Angliker and M. Fowler (eds), *Archaeology of Ritual in the Ancient Mediterranean: Recent Finds and Interpretative Approaches*, 1–26. Liege: Kernos Supplements.

Hand, W. (1984), 'Onomastic Magic in the Health, Sickness and Death of Man', *Names* 32 (1): 1–13.

Harries, J. (2007), *Law and Crime in the Roman World. Key Themes in Ancient History*. Cambridge: Cambridge University Press.

Harris, O. J. T. (2020), 'What Do We Mean by Relational Anyway?', in R. J. Crellin, C. N. Cipolla, L. M. Montgomery, O. J. T. Harris and S. V. Moore (eds), *Archaeological Theory in Dialogue: Situating Relationality, Ontology, Posthumanism, and Indigenous Paradigms*, 15–33. London: Routledge.

Harris, O. J. T., and C. N. Cipolla (2017), *Archaeological Theory in the New Millennium: Introducing Current Perspectives*. London: Routledge.

Harris, W. (1989), *Ancient Literacy*, Cambridge, MA: Harvard University Press.

Harvey, G. (2013), *Food, Sex and Strangers: Understanding Religion as Everyday Life*. Durham: Acumen Publishing.

Hassall, M. W. C, and R. S. O. Tomlin (1982), 'Inscriptions', *Britannia* 13: 396–422.

Hassall, M. W. C, and R. S. O. Tomlin (1984), 'Inscriptions', *Britannia* 14: 333–56.

Hassall, M. W. C, and R. S. O. Tomlin (1986), 'Inscriptions', *Britannia* 17: 428–54.

Hassall, M. W. C, and R. S. O. Tomlin (1989), 'Inscriptions', *Britannia* 20: 325–45.

Hassall, M. W. C, and R. S. O. Tomlin (1992), 'Inscriptions', *Britannia* 23: 309–23.

Hassall, M. W. C, and R. S. O. Tomlin (1993), 'Inscriptions', *Britannia* 24: 310–22.

Hassall, M. W. C, and R. S. O. Tomlin (1994), 'Inscriptions', *Britannia* 25: 293–314.

Häussler, R. (2012), 'Interpretatio Indigena: Re-Inventing Local Cults in a Global World', *MediterrAnt* 15: 143–74.

Havard, C. T., D. L. Wann and T. D. Ryan (2013), 'Investigating the Impact of Conference Realignment on Rivalry in Intercollegiate Athletics', *Sport Marketing Quarterly* 22 (4): 224–34.

Heald, S. (1986), 'Witches and Thieves: Deviant Motivations in Gisu Society', *Man* 21: 65–78.

Hemelrijk, E. A. (2015), *Hidden Lives, Public Personae: Women and Civic Life in the Roman West*. Oxford: Oxford University Press.

Hingley, R. (2005), *Globalizing Roman Culture: Unity, Diversity and Empire*. London: Routledge.

Hodder, I. (2012), *Entangled: An Archaeology of Relationships Between Humans and Things*. Oxford: Wiley-Blackwell.

Hoek, A. van den, and J. Herrmann (2013), 'Thecla the Beast Fighter: A Female Emblem of Deliverance in Early Christian Popular Art', in A. van den Hoek and J. Herrmann (eds), *Pottery, Pavements and Paradise: Iconographic and Textual Studies on Late Antiquity*, 65–106. Leiden: Brill.

Hope, V. M. (2000), 'Fighting for Identity: The Funerary Commemoration of Italian Gladiators', *BICS* Supplement 73: 93–113.

Horsmann, G. (1998), *Die Wagenlenker Der Römischen Kaiserzeit: Untersuchungen Zu Ihrer Sozialen Stellung*. Stuttgart: Franz Steiner Verlag.

Houlbrook, C. and N. Armitage eds, (2015), *The Materiality of Magic: An Artefactual Investigation into Ritual Practices and Popular Beliefs*. Oxford: Oxbow.

Humphrey, J. (1986), *Roman Circuses: Arenas for Chariot Racing*. London: Batsford.

Humphrey, J. edn (1991), *Literacy in the Roman World. JRA Supplementary Series 3*. Ann Arbor, MI: Journal of Roman Archaeology.

Hunt, A. (2016), *Reviving Roman Religion: Sacred Trees in the Roman World*. Cambridge: Cambridge University Press.

Hunter, V. (1990), 'Gossip and the Politics of Reputation in Classical Athens', *Phoenix* 44: 299–325.

Iara, K. (2020), 'The Materiality of Divine Agency in Imperial Rome', in I. Selsvold and L. Webb (eds), *Beyond the Romans: Posthuman Perspectives in Roman Archaeology*, 55–66. Oxford: Oxbow.

Ingold, T. (2000a), 'Making Culture and Weaving the World', in P. Graves-Brown (ed), *Matter, Materiality and Modern Culture*, 50–71. New York: Routledge.

Ingold, T. (2000b), *The Perception of the Environment: Essays on Livelihood, Dwelling and Skill*. London and New York: Routledge.

Jeanneret, M. (1918), *La langue des tablettes d'exécration latines*. Paris: Neuchâtel.

Jordan, D. (1985), 'A Survey of Greek Defixiones Not Included in the Special Corpora', *GRBS* 26: 151–97.

Jordan, D. (2000), 'New Greek Curse Tablets (1985–2000)', *GRBS* 41: 5–46.

Jordan, D. (2003), 'Remedium Amoris. A curse from Cumae', *Mnemosyne* 56 (6): 666–79.

Kajanto, I. (1965), *The Latin Cognomina*. Helsinki: Helsingfors.

Kapferer, B. (1997), *The Feast of the Sorcerer: Practices of Consciousness and Power*, Chicago: University of Chicago Press.

Kapferer, B. (2012), *Legends of People, Myths of State: Violence, Intolerance and Political Culture in Sri Lanka and Australia*. New York and Oxford: Berghahn Books.

Kelly, J. (1966), *Roman Litigation*. Oxford: Oxford University Press.

Kerneis, S. (2010), 'La Question Enchantée Les Jugements Des Dieux Dans l'île de Bretagne (II e– IV e Siècle)', *RD* 88 (4): 483–98.

Kiernan, P. (2004a), 'Britische Fluchtafeln Und "Gebete Um Gerechtigkeit" Als Öffentliche Magie Und Votivritual', in K. Brodersen and A. Kropp (eds), *Fluchtafeln: Neue Funde Und Neue Deutungen Zum Antiken Schadenzauber*, 99–114. Frankfurt: Antike Verlag.

Kiernan, P. (2004b), 'Did Curse Tablets Work?', in B. Croxford, H. Eckardt, J. Meade and J. Weekes (eds), *TRAC 2003: Proceedings of the 13th Annual Theoretical Roman Archaeology Conference*, 123–34. Oxford: Oxbow.

King, C. W. (2009), 'The Roman Manes: The Dead as Gods', in M. Pu (ed.), *Rethinking Ghosts in World Religions*, 95–114. Leiden: Brill.

King, C. W. (2020), *The Ancient Roman Afterlife: Di Manes, Belief and the Cult of the Dead*. Austin: University of Texas Press.

Knapp, A. (2010), 'Beyond Agency: Identity and Individuals in Archaeology', in S. Steadman and J. Ross (eds), *Agency and Identity in the Ancient Near East: New Paths Forward*, 193–200. London: Equinox.

Knibbe, K., and H. Kupari (2020), 'Theorizing Lived Religion: Introduction', *Journal of Contemporary Religion*, 35 (2): 157–76.

Korporowicz, Ł. J. (2012), 'Roman Law in Roman Britain: An Introductory Survey', *Journal of Legal History* 33 (2): 133–50.

Kos, M. Š. (2018), 'Who Was L. Licinius Aura, Hispanus, on a Curse Tablet from Siscia?', *AFAM* 8: 828–38.

Kotansky, R. D. (1994), *Greek Magical Amulets: The Inscribed Gold, Silver, Copper, and Bronze Lamellae*. Opladen: Westdeutscher Verlag.

Kropp, A. (2008a), *Defixiones: Ein Aktuelles Corpus Lateinischer Fluchtafeln: Dfx*. Speyer: Kartoffeldruck-Verlag Kai Brodersen.

Kropp, A. (2008b), *Magische Sprachverwendung in Vulgärlateinischen Fluchtafeln (Defixiones)*, Tübingen: G. Narr.

Lambert, P.-Y. (2002), *Recueil des inscriptions gauloises (R.I.G). 2.2. Textes Gallo-latins sur instrumentum*. Paris: Éditions du CNRS.

Lamont, J. (2021), 'Cold and Worthless: The Role of Lead in Curse Tablets', *TAPA* 151 (1): 35–68.

Lassanyi, G. (2017), *On Secret Paths: Dark Spells in Aquincum*. Budapest: BHM Aquincum Museum.

Latour, B. (2005), *Reassembling the Social: An Introduction to Actor Network Theory*. Oxford: Oxford University Press.

Laurence, R. (1994), 'Rumour and Communication in Roman Politics', *G&R* 41: 62–74.

Lee, R. (2009), *The Production, Use and Disposal of Romano-British Pewter Tableware*, BAR British Series 478. Oxford: Archaeopress.

Lévi-Strauss, C. (1973), *Tristes Tropiques*, trans. J. Weightman and D. Weightman. New York: Penguin.

Lindstrom, T. C. (2015), 'Agency "in Itself": A Discussion of Inanimate, Animal and Human Agency', *Archaeological Dialogues* 22: 207–38.

Lindstrom, T. C. (2017), 'Agency: A Response to Sørensen and Ribeiro', *Archaeological Dialogues* 24: 109–16.

Lőrincz, B., and A. Mócsy (1994), *Onomasticon provinciarum Europae latinarum*. Budapest: Archaeolingua Alapítvány.

Luck, G. (1999), 'Witches and Sorcerers in Classical Literature', in V. Flint, R. Gordon, G. Luck and D. Ogden (eds), *Witchcraft and Magic in Europe: Ancient Greece and Rome*, 91–158. London: Athalone Press.

Luck, G. (2000), *Ancient Pathways and Hidden Pursuits: Religion, Morals and Magic in the Ancient World*. Ann Arbor: University of Michigan Press.

Luck, G. (2006), *Arcana Mundi: Magic and the Occult in the Greek and Roman Worlds*. Baltimore: John Hopkins University Press.

MacMullen, R. (1981), *Paganism in the Roman Empire*. New Haven and London: Yale University Press.

MacMullen, R. (1982), 'The Epigraphic Habit in the Roman Empire', *AJPh* 103 (3): 233–46.

MacRae, D. (2016), *Legibile Religion: Books, Gods, and Rituals in Roman Culture*, Cambridge, MA: Harvard University Press.

Malinowski, B. (1922), *Argonauts of the Western Pacific: An Account of Native Enterprise and Adventure in the Archipelagos of Melanesian New Guinea*. London: Routledge.

Marco Simón, F. (2010), 'Execrating the Roman Power: Three Defixiones from Emporiae (Ampurias)', in R. Gordon and F. Marco Simón (eds), *Magical Practice in the Latin West: Papers from the International Conference Held at the University of Zaragoza, 30 Sept.–1 Oct. 2005*, 399–423. Leiden: Brill.

Marco Simón, F. (2019), 'Early Hispanic Curse Tablets: Greek, Latin – and Iberian?', *Religion in the Roman Empire* 5 (3): 376–97.

Marco Simón, F. (2020a), 'Domino Neptuno Corulo Pare(n)Tur: Magic and Law in the Romano-Celtic World', in A. Mastrocinque, Joseph E. Sanzo and M. Scapini (eds). *Ancient Magic: Then and Now*, 123–37. Stuttgart: Franz Steiner Verlag.

Marco Simón, F. (2020b), 'Magical Practice in Sanctuary Contexts', in R. Gordon, F. Marco Simón and M. Piranomonte (eds), *Choosing Magic: Contexts, Objects, Meanings: The Archaeology of Instrumental Religion in the Latin West*, 25–40. Rome: De Luca Editori d'Arte.

Marco Simón, F., and I. R. De Llanza (2008), 'A Latin Defixio (Sisak, Croatia) to the River God Savus Mentioning L. Licinius Sura, Hispanus', *Vjesnik Arheoloskog Muzeja u Zagrebu* 41: 167–98.

Marichal, R. (1981), 'Une Tablette d'exécration de l'oppidum de Montfo (Hérault)', *CRAI* 125: 41–51.

Martin, D. (1996), 'The Construction of the Ancient Family: Methodological Considerations', *JRS* 86: 40–60.

Martin, D. (2003), 'Slave Families and Slaves in Families', in D. L. Balch and C. Osiek (eds), *Early Christian Families in Context: An Interdisciplinary Dialogue*, 207–30. Grand Rapids, MI, and Cambridge: Willian B. Eerdmans.

Marwick, M. (1965), *Sorcery in Its Social Setting: A Study of the Northern Rhodesian Ceŵa*. Manchester: Manchester University Press.

Massarelli, R. (2014), *I Testi Etruschi Su Piombo. Biblioteca Di Studi Etruschi, 53*, Rome: Fabrizio Serra editore.

Massarelli, R. (2019), 'The Etruscan Defixiones: From Contexts to Texts', *Religion in the Roman Empire* 5 (3): 363–75.

Mastrocinque, A. (2008), 'Les Formations Géométriques de Mots Dams La Magie Ancienne', *Kernos* 21: 97–108.

Mattingly, D. (2006), *An Imperial Possession: Britain in the Roman Empire 54 BC–AD 409*, London: Penguin.

Mattingly, D. (2011), *Imperialism, Power and Identity Experiencing the Roman Empire*. Princeton: Princeton University Press.

McDonald, K. (2015), *Oscan in Southern Italy and Sicily: Evaluating Language Contact in a Fragmentary Corpus*, Cambridge Classical Studies. Cambridge University Press.

McGuire, M. (2008), *Lived Religion: Faith and Practice in Everyday Life*. Oxford: Oxford University Press.

McKie, S. (2016), 'Distraught, Drained, Devoured, or Damned? The Importance of Individual Creativity in Roman Cursing', in M. Mandich, T. Derrick, S. Gonzalez Sanchez, G. Savani and E. Zampieri (eds), *TRAC 2015: Proceedings of the 25th Annual Theoretical Roman Archaeology Conference 2015*, 15–27. Oxford: Oxbow.

McKie, S. (2018), 'The Legs, Hands, Head and Arms Race: The Human Body as a Magical Weapon in the Roman World', in A. Parker and S. McKie (eds), *Material Approaches to Roman Magic: Occult Objects and Supernatural Substances*, 115–26. Oxford: Oxbow.

McKie, S. (2019), 'Enchained Relationships and Fragmented Victims: Curse Tablets and Votive Rituals in the Roman North-West', *Religion in the Roman Empire* 5: 440–55.

Mees, B. (2009), *Celtic Curses*. Woodbridge: Boydell Press.

Mees, B. (2011), 'Words from the Well at Gallo-Roman Châteaubleau', *Zeitschrift Für Celtische Philologie* 58: 87–108.

Meißner, T. (2012), 'Celtic and Germanic Names and Naming Traditions', in T. Meißner (ed.), *Personal Names in the Western Roman World: Proceedings of a Workshop Convened by Torsten Meißner, José Luís García Ramón and Paolo Poccetti, Held at Pembroke College, Cambridge, 16–18 September 2011*, 179–98. Berlin: Curach Bhan.

Melia, D. F. (2011), 'Review of "Celtic Curses" by Bernard Mees, Woodbridge, Suffolk: Boydell 2009', *Folklore* 122 (1): 113–14.

Meyer, E. A. (1990), 'Explaining the Epigraphic Habit in the Roman Empire: The Evidence of Epitaphs', *JRS* 80: 74–96.

Mitchell, J. (2006), 'Performance', in C. Tilley, W. Keane, S. Küchler, M. Rowlands and P. Spyer (eds), *Handbook of Material Culture*, 384–401. London: SAGE Publications.

Moreland, J. (2001), *Archaeology and Text*. London: Duckworth.

Moreland, J. (2006), 'Archaeology and Texts: Subservience or Enlightenment?', *Annual Review of Anthropology* 35: 135–51.

Morley, I. (2007), 'Time, Cycles and Ritual Behaviour', in D. Barrowclough and C. Malone (eds), *Cult in Context: Reconsidering Ritual in Archaeology*, 205–09. Oxford: Oxbow.

Mullen, A. (2007a), 'Evidence for Written Celtic from Roman Britain: A Linguistic Analysis of Tabellae Sulis 14 and 18', *Studia Celtica* 41: 31–45.

Mullen, A. (2007b), 'Linguistic Evidence for "Romanization": Continuity and Change in Romano-British Onomastics: A Study of the Epigraphic Record with Particular Reference to Bath', *Britannia* 38: 35–61.

Mullen, A. (2013), 'New Thoughts on British Latin: A Curse Tablet from Ratcliffe-on-Soar', *ZPE* 187: 266–72.

Mullen, A., and P. James eds, (2012), *Multilingualism in the Graeco-Roman Worlds*. Cambridge: Cambridge University Press.

Murano, F. (2012), 'The Oscan Cursing Tablets: Binding Formulae, Cursing Typologies and Thematic Classification'. *AJPh* 133 (4): 629–55.

Murano, F. (2013), *Le Tabellae Defixionum Osche*, Rome: Fabrizio Serra.

Murphy, T. (2004), 'Privileged Knowledge: Valerius Soranus and the Secret Name of Rome', in A. Barchiesi, J. Rüpke and S. Stephens (eds), *Rituals in Ink: A Conference on Religion and Literary Production in Ancient Rome*, 127–37. Stuttgart: Franz Steiner Verlag.

Muzzioli, G. (1939), 'Urna Inscritta Del Museo Del Terme (Con 2 Tav.)', *SMSR* 15: 42–50.

Nakamura, C. (2004), 'Dedicating Magic: Neo-Assyrian Apotropaic Figurines and the Protection of Assur', *World Archaeology* 36: 11–25.

Nemeth, G. (2013), 'Audollent's Demons', *Eirene* 49: 123–34.

Neubauer, H.-J. (1999), *The Rumour: A Cultural History*, London: Free Association Books.

Ogden, D. (1999), 'Binding Spells: Curse Tablets and Voodoo Dolls in the Greek and Roman Worlds', in V. Flint, R. Gordon, G. Luck and D. Ogden (eds), *Witchcraft and Magic in Europe: Ancient Greece and Rome*, 3–90. London: Athlone Press.

Olson, S. D. (1992), '"Name-Magic" and the Threat of Lying Strangers in Homer's Odyssey', *ICS* 17 (1): 1–7.

Osborne, R. (2004), 'Hoards, Votives, Offerings: The Archaeology of the Dedicated Object', *World Archaeology* 36: 1–10.

Otto, B.-C. (2013), 'Towards Historicizing "Magic" in Antiquity', *Numen* 60: 308–47.

Otto, B.-C., and M. Stausberg (2013), *Defining Magic: A Reader*, London and New York: Routledge.

Pachoumi, E. (2013), 'The Erotic and Separation Spells of the Magical Papyri and Defixiones', *GRBS* 53: 294–325.

Parker, A., and S. McKie eds, (2018), *Material Approaches to Roman Magic: Occult Objects and Supernatural Substances*. Oxford: Oxbow.

Paule, M. T. (2017), *Canidia: Rome's First Witch*. London and New York: Bloomsbury.

Penner, L. (2012), 'Gender, Household Structure and Slavery: Re-Interpreting the Aristocratic Columbaria of Early Imperial Rome', in R. Laurence and A. Strömberg (eds), *Families in the Greco-Roman World*, 143–59. London: Continuum.

Petzl, G. (1994), *Die Beichtinschriften Westkleinasiens*. Bonn: R. Habelt.

Piquette, K., and R. Whitehouse (2013a), 'Introduction: Developing an Approach to Writing as Material Practice', in K. Piquette and R. Whitehouse (eds), *Writing as Material Practice: Substance, Surface and Medium*, 1–14. London: Ubiquity Press.

Piquette K. and R. Whitehouse eds, (2013b), *Writing as Material Practice: Substance, Surface and Medium*. London: Ubiquity Press.

Piranomonte, M. (2012) 'Anna Perenna: Un Contesto Magico Straordinario', in M. Piranomonte and F. Marco Simón (eds), *Contesti Magici = Contextos Mágicos: Atti Del Convegno Internazionale, Roma, Palazzo Massimo, 4–6 novembre 2009*, 161–74. Rome: De Luca Editori d'Arte.

Piranomonte, M. (2015), 'The Discovery of the Fountain of Anna Perenna and Its Influence on the Study of Ancient Magic', in G. Bąkowska-Czerner, A. Roccati and A. Świerzowska (eds), *The Wisdom of Thoth: Magical Texts in Ancient Mediterranean Civilizations*, 71–85. Oxford: Archaeopress.

Piranomonte, M. and F. Marco Simón eds, (2012) *Contesti Magici = Contextos Mágicos*. Rome: De Luca Editori d'Arte.

Pitts, M. and M. J. Versluys eds, (2015), *Globalization and the Roman World: World History, Connectivity and Material Culture*. Cambridge: Cambridge University Press.

Platner, S., and T. Ashby (1929), *A Topographical Dictionary of Ancient Rome*. Oxford: Oxford University Press.

Potts, J. (2017), 'Corpora in Connection: Anatomical Votives and the Confession Stelai of Lydia and Phrygia', in J. Draycott and E.-J. Graham (eds), *Bodies of Evidence: Ancient Anatomical Votives Past, Present and Future*, 20–44. London: Routledge.

Preisendanz, K. (1972), 'Fluchtafel (Defixion)', in *Reallexikon Für Antike Und Christentum*, 8: 1–29. Stuttgart: A. Hiersemann.

Primiano, L. N. (1995) 'Vernacular Religion and the Search for Method in Religious Folklife', *Western Folklore* 54: 37–56.

Primiano, L. N. (2012), 'Manifestations of the Religious Vernacular: Ambiguity, Power and Creativity', in M. Bowman and Ü Valk (eds), *Vernacular Religion in Everyday Life: Expressions of Belief*, 382–94. Sheffield: Equinox.

Raepsaet-Charlier, M. T. (2014), 'Bernard Mees, Celtic Curses. Woodbridge, The Boydell Press, 2009 [Review]', *AC* 83: 364–65.

Rawson, B. (2003), '"The Roman Family" in Recent Research: State of the Question', *Biblical Interpretation* 11 (2): 119–38.

Rea, J. (1972) 'A Lead Tablet from Wanborough, Wilts', *Britannia* 3: 363–367.

Reid, J. K. (2012), 'Celtic Curses. By Bernard Mees. Woodbridge, UK: The Boydell Press, 2009. Pp. Viii + 229; 12 Illustrations. $105', *Journal of English and Germanic Philology* 111 (2): 224–26.

Revell, L. (2009), *Roman Imperialism and Local Identities*. Cambridge: Cambridge University Press.

Ribeiro, A. (2016), 'Against Object Agency. A Counterreaction to Sørensen's "Hammers and Nails"', *Archaeological Dialogues* 23: 29–35.

Riberio, A. (2019), 'Against Object Agency 2. Continuing the Discussion with Sørensen', *Archaeological Dialogues* 26: 39–44.

Richardson, J. H., and F. Santangelo eds, (2011), *Priests and State in the Roman World*, Stuttgart: Steiner.

Riddell, F. (2018), 'We need #ImmodestWomen when so many men are unable to accept female expertise', *New Statesman*, 16 June. Available online: https://www.newstatesman.com/politics/feminism/2018/06/we-need-immodestwomen-when-so-many-men-are-unable-accept-female-expertise (accessed 10 September 2021).

Riggsby, A. M. (2010), *Roman Law and the Legal World of the Romans*. Cambridge: Cambridge University Press.

Ripat, P. (2011), 'Expelling Misconceptions: Astrologers at Rome', *CPh* 106: 115–54.

Ripat, P. (2014), 'Cheating Women: Curse Tablets and Roman Wives', in K. B. Stratton and D. Kalleres (eds), *Daughters of Hecate: Women and Magic in the Ancient World*, 340–55. Oxford: Oxford University Press.

Rives, J. (2010), 'Magus and Its Cognates in Classical Latin', in R. Gordon and F. Marco Simón (eds), *Magical Practice in the Latin West: Papers from the International Conference Held at the University of Zaragoza, 30 Sept.-1 Oct. 2005*, 53–77. Leiden: Brill.

Robb, J. (2010), 'Beyond Agency', *World Archaeology* 42 (4): 493–520.

Robinson, O. F. (2007), *Penal Practice and Penal Policy in Ancient Rome*. London: Routledge.

Rodger, A. (1990), 'The Jurisdiction of Local Magistrates: Chapter 84 of the Lex Irnitana', *ZPE* 84: 147–61.

Rossiter, J. (2016), 'In ampitζatru Carthaginis: The Carthage amphitheatre and its uses', *JRA* 29: 239–58.

Rothenhöfer, P. (2016), 'Römische Offiziere Auf Einer Tabella Defixionum: Ein Außergewöhnliches Dokument Magischen Schadenzaubers Gegen Einen Legionskommandeur Und Weitere Mitglieder Des Offizierkorps', *Epigraphica* 78: 235–51.

Rüpke, J. (2007), *The Religion of the Romans*. Cambridge: Polity.

Rüpke, J. (2009), 'Dedications Accompanied by Inscriptions in the Roman Empire: Functions, Intentions, Modes of Communication', in J. P. Bodel and M. Kajava (eds), *Religious Dedications in the Greco-Roman World: Distribution, Typology, Use: Institutum Romanum Finlandiae, American Academy in Rome, 19–20 Aprile, 2006*, 31–41. Rome: Institutum Romanum Finladiae.

Rüpke, J. edn (2013), *The Individual in the Religions of the Ancient Mediterranean*. Oxford: Oxford University Press.

Rüpke, J. (2016), *On Roman Religion: Lived Religion and the Individual in Ancient Rome*. Ithaca: Cornell University Press.

Rüpke, J. (2018), *Pantheon: A New History of Roman Religion*. Princeton: Princeton University Press.

Saller, R. P. (1987), 'Slavery and the Roman Family', *Slavery and Abolition* 8 (1): 65–87.
Saller, R. P., and B. D. Shaw (1984), 'Tombstones and Roman Family Relations in the Principate: Civilians, Soldiers and Slaves', *JRS* 74: 124–56.
Salomies, O. (2001), 'Names and Identities: Onomastics and Prosopography', in J. P. Bodel (ed.), *Epigraphic Evidence: Ancient History from Inscriptions*, 73–94. London: Routledge.
Salvo, I. (2012), 'Sweet Revenge: Emotional Factors in the "Prayers for Justice"', in A. Chaniotis (ed.), *Unveiling Emotions: Sources and Methods for the Study of Emotions in the Greek World*, 236–66. Stuttgart: Franz Steiner Verlag.
Salvo, I. (2016), 'Emotions, Persuasion and Gender in Greek Erotic Curses', in E. Sanders and M. Johncock (eds), *Emotion and Persuasion in Classical Antiquity*, 264–79. Stuttgart: Franz Steiner Verlag.
Salvo, I. (2020), 'Experiencing Curses: Neurobehavioral Traits of Ritual and Spatiality in the Roman Empire', in V. Gasparini, M. Patzelt, R. Raja, A.-K. Rieger, J. Rüpke and E. Urciuoli (ed.) *Lived Religion in the Ancient Mediterranean World*, 157–80. Berlin: De Gruyter.
Sánchez Natalías, C. (2011), 'The Bologna *Defixio(nes)* Revisited', *ZPE* 179: 201–17.
Sánchez Natalías, C. (2012a), 'A Cartography of Defixiones in the Western Roman Empire', in M. Piranomonte and F. Marco Simón (eds), *Contesti Magici = Contextos Mágicos: Atti Del Convegno Internazionale, Roma, Palazzo Massimo, 4-6 novembre 2009*, 123–34. Rome: De Luca Editori D'Arte.
Sánchez Natalías, C. (2012b), '*Fistus difloiscat languat* . . . Re-reading of Defixio Bologna', *ZPE* 181: 140–48.
Sánchez Natalías, C. (2016), 'Epigrafía Pública y Defixiones: Paradigmas (y Paradojas) Del Occidente Latino', *ACD* 52: 69–77.
Sánchez Natalías, C. (2018), 'The Medium Matters: Materiality and Metaphor in Some Latin Curse Tablets', in A. Parker and S. McKie (eds), *Material Approaches to Roman Magic: Occult Objects and Supernatural Substances*, 9–17. Oxford: Oxbow.
Sánchez Natalías, C. (2019a), 'Aquatic Spaces as Contexts for Depositing Defixiones in the Roman West', *Religion in the Roman Empire* 5: 456–67.
Sánchez Natalías, C. (2019b), 'Mapping Katadesmoi in the Western Roman Empire', in C. Noreña and N. Papazarkadas (eds), *From Document to History: Epigraphic Insights into the Graeco-Roman World*, 151–64. Leiden: Brill.
Sánchez Natalías, C. (2020a), 'Other Public Spaces as Magical Contexts', in R. Gordon, F. Marco Simón and M. Piranomonte (eds), *Choosing Magic: Contexts, Objects, Meanings: The Archaeology of Instrumental Religion in the Latin West*, 69–76. Rome: De Luca Editori d'Arte.
Sánchez Natalías, C. (2020b), 'Paragraphics and Iconography', in R. Gordon, F. Marco Simón and M. Piranomonte (eds), *Choosing Magic: Contexts, Objects, Meanings: The Archaeology of Instrumental Religion in the Latin West*, 103–24. Rome: De Luca Editori d'Arte.
Sánchez Natalías, C. (forthcoming), *Sylloge of Defixiones from the Roman West*. Oxford: Archaeopress.
Sanzo, J. E. (2020), 'Deconstructing the Deconstructionists: A Response to Recent Criticisms of the Rubric "Ancient Magic"', in A. Mastrocinque, J. E. Sanzo and M. Scapini (eds) *Ancient Magic: Then and Now*, 25–46. Stuttgart: Franz Steiner Verlag.
Sax, W. S. (2006), 'Agency', in J. Kreinath, J. Snock and M. Stausberg (eds), *Theorising Rituals*, 473–81. Leiden: Brill.

Sbisa, M. (2009), 'Speech Act Theory', in J. Verschueren and J.-O. Östman (eds), *Key Notions for Pragmatics*, 229–44. Amsterdam: John Benjamins.

Schwinden, L. (2004), 'Blei Mit Tintenschrift', in M. Reuter and M. Scholz (eds) *Geritzt Und Entziffert: Schriftzeugnisse Der Römischen Informationsgesellschaft*. Stuttgart: Theiss.

Scott, J. C. (1990), *Domination and the Arts of Resistance: Hidden Transcripts*, New Haven, CT, and London: Yale University Press.

Searle, J. (1971), *Sprechakte: Ein Sprachphilosophischer Essay*. Frankfurt: Suhrkamp.

Skaggs, S. (2007), 'Lead Isotope Analysis of Roman Carthage Curse Tablets', in M. D. Glascock, R. J. Speakman and R. S. Popelka-Filcoff (eds), *Archaeological Chemistry: Analytical Techniques and Archaeological Interpretation*, 311–35. Washington, DC: American Chemical Society.

Skaggs, S., N. Norman, E. Garrison, D. Coleman and S. Bouhlel (2012), 'Local Mining or Lead Importation in the Roman Province of Africa Proconsularis? Lead Isotope Analysis of Curse Tablets from Roman Carthage, Tunisia', *Journal of Archaeological Science* 29 (4): 970–83.

Solin, H. (1968), *Eine Neue Fluchtafel Aus Ostia*. Helsinki: Societas Scientiarum Fennica.

Solin, H. and O. Salomies (1994), *Repertorium Nominum Gentilium et Cognominum Latinorum*. Hildesheim: Olms-Weidmann.

Sørensen, J. (2007), 'Acts That Work: A Cognitive Approach to Ritual Agency', *Method & Theory in the Study of Religion* 19: 281–300.

Sørensen, T. F. (2016), 'Hammers and Nails. A Response to Lindstrøm and to Olsen and Witmore', *Archaeological Dialogues* 23: 115–27.

Sørensen, T. F. (2018), 'Agency (Again): A Response to Lindstrøm and Ribeiro', *Archaeological Dialogues* 25: 95–101.

Spaeth, B. (2014), 'From Goddess to Hag: The Greek and the Roman Witch in Classical Literature', in K. B. Stratton and D. Kalleres (eds), *Daughters of Hecate: Women and Magic in the Ancient World*, 41–70. Oxford: Oxford University Press.

Stambaugh, J. (1978), 'The Functions of Roman Temples', *ANRW* 16.1: 554–609.

Stewart, P. J., and A. J. Strathern (2004), *Witchcraft, Sorcery, Rumors, and Gossip*. Cambridge: Cambridge University Press.

Stratton, K. B. (2007), *Naming the Witch: Magic, Ideology, and Stereotype in the Ancient World*. New York: Columbia University Press.

Stratton, K. B. (2014), 'Magic, Abjection and Gender in Roman Literature', in by K. B. Stratton and D. Kalleres (eds), *Daughters of Hecate: Women and Magic in the Ancient World*, 152–82. Oxford: Oxford University Press.

Swenson, E. (2015), 'The Archaeology of Ritual', *Annual Review of Anthropology* 44: 329–45.

Taylor, J. (2011), 'Tablets as Artefacts, Scribes as Artisans', in K. Radner and E. Robson (eds), *The Oxford Handbook of Cuneiform Culture*, 5–31. Oxford: Oxford University Press.

Thomas, J. (1996), *Time, Culture and Identity: An Interpretative Archaeology*. London and New York: Routledge.

Tomlin, R. S. O. (1988), 'The Curse Tablets', in B. Cunliffe (ed.), *The Temple of Sulis Minerva and Bath: Volume 2 The Finds from the Sacred Spring*, 59–278. Oxford: Oxford University Committee for Archaeology.

Tomlin, R. S. O. (1993), 'The Inscribed Lead Tablets: An Interim Report', in A. Woodward and P. Leach (eds), *The Uley Shrines: Excavations of a Ritual Complex on West Hill, Uley, Gloucestershire 1977–9*, 113–30. London: English Heritage and British Museum Press.

Tomlin, R. S. O, (1997), 'Inscriptions', *Britannia* 28: 455–474.
Tomlin, R. S. O. (2002), 'Writing to the Gods in Britain', in A. Cooley (ed.), *Becoming Roman, Writing Latin? Literacy and Epigraphy in the Roman West*, 165–79. Portsmouth, RI: Journal of Roman Archaeology.
Tomlin, R. S. O. (2008), 'Inscriptions', *Britannia* 39: 369–90.
Tomlin, R. S. O. (2009), 'Inscriptions', *Britannia* 40: 313–64.
Tomlin, R. S. O. (2010), 'Cursing a Thief in Iberia and Britain', in R. Gordon and F. Marco Simón (eds), *Magical Practice in the Latin West: Papers from the International Conference Held at the University of Zaragoza, 30 Sept.–1 Oct. 2005*, 245–73. Leiden: Brill.
Tomlin, R. S. O. (2011a), 'Protective Spells in Roman Britain', in M. Corbier and J.-P. Guilhembet (eds), *L'Ecriture Dans La Maison Romaine*, 137–44. Paris: de Boccard.
Tomlin, R. S. O. (2011b), 'Writing and Communication', in L. Allason-Jones (ed.), *Artefacts in Roman Britain: Their Purpose and Use*, 133–52. Cambridge: Cambridge University Press.
Tomlin, R. S. O. (2014), '"Drive Away the Cloud of Plague": A Greek Amulet from Roman London', in R. Collins and F. McIntosh (eds), *Life in the Limes: Studies of the People and Objects of the Roman Frontiers*, 197–205. Oxford: Oxbow.
Tomlin, R. S. O. (2016), *Roman London's First Voices: Writing Tablets from the Bloomberg Excavations, 2010–14*, London: MOLA.
Tomlin, R. S. O., and M. W. C. Hassall (2005), 'Inscriptions', *Britannia* 26: 473–97.
Treggiari, S. (1991), *Roman Marriage: Iusti Coniuges from the Time of Cicero to the Time of Ulpian*. Oxford: Clarendon Press.
Tremel, J. (2004), *Magica Agonistica: Fluchtafeln im antiken Sport*. Hildesheim: Weidmann.
Turner, E. (1963), 'A Curse Tablet from Nottinghamshire', *JRS* 53: 122–4.
Urbanová, D. (2018), *Latin Curse Tablets of the Roman Empire*. Innsbruck: Innsbrucker Beitrage zur Kulturwissenschaft.
Urbanová, D. (2019), 'Between Syntax and Magic: Some Peculiarities of Nominal Syntax in Latin Curse Tablets', in L. van Gils, C. Kroon and R. Risselada (eds), *Lemmata Linguistica Latina: Volume 2 Clause and Discourse*, 155–73. Berlin: De Gruyter.
Urbanová, D. and M. Frydek. (2016), 'Priscilla Caranti – Einige Bemerkungen Zum Möglichen Entstehungsszenario Des Fluchtäfelchens Aus Gross-Gerau', in A. Szabo (ed.), *From Polites to Magos. Studia György Németh Sexagenario Dedicata (Hungarian Polis Studies Nr. 22)*, 343–50. Budapest: University of Debrecen.
Van Dyke, R. (2015), 'Materiality in Practice: An Introduction', in R. Van Dyke (ed.), *Practicing Materiality*, 3–32. Tucson: University of Arizona Press.
Veale, S. (2017), 'Defixiones and the Temple Locus: The Power of Place in the Curse Tablets at Mainz', *Magic, Ritual, and Witchcraft* 12: 279–313.
Versluys, M. J. (2014), 'Understanding Objects in Motion: An Archaeological Dialogue on Romanization', *Archaeological Dialogues* 21 (1): 1–20.
Versnel, H. S. (1991a), 'Beyond Cursing: The Appeal to Justice in Judicial Prayers', in C. A. Faraone and D. Obbink (eds), *Magika Hiera: Ancient Greek Magic and Religion*, 60–106. Oxford: Oxford University Press.
Versnel, H. S. (1991b), 'Some Reflections on the Relationship Magic-Religion', *Numen* 38: 117–97.
Versnel, H. S. (1999), 'Κολασαι Τους Ημας Τοιουτους Ηδεως Βλεποντες "Punish Those Who Rejoice in Our Misery": On Curse Texts and Schadenfreude', in D. Jordan, H. Montgomery and

E. Thomassen (eds), *The World of Ancient Magic: Papers from The First International Samson Eitrem Seminar at the Norwegian Institute at Athens*, 125–62. Athens: Norwegian Institute at Athens.

Versnel, H. S. (2002), 'Writing Mortals and Reading Gods: Appeal to the Gods as a Dual Strategy in Social Control', in D. Cohen (ed.), *Demokratie, Recht Und Soziale Kontrolle Im Klassischen Athen*, 37–76. Munich: Oldenburg.

Versnel, H. S. (2010), 'Prayers for Justice, East and West', in R. Gordon and F. Marco Simón (eds), *Magical Practice in the Latin West: Papers from the International Conference Held at the University of Zaragoza, 30 Sept.–1 Oct. 2005*, 275–354. Leiden: Brill.

Versnel, H. S. (2012a), 'Magic', in S. Hornblower, A. Spawforth and E. Eidinow (eds), *Oxford Classical Dictionary*, 4th edn, 884–5. Oxford: Oxford University Press.

Versnel, H. S. (2012b), 'Response to a Critique', in M. Piranomonte and F. Marco Simón (eds), *Contesti Magici = Contextos Mágicos: Atti Del Convegno Internazionale, Roma, Palazzo Massimo, 4–6 novembre 2009*, 33–45. Rome: De Luca Editori D'Arte.

Vitellozzi, P. (2019), 'Curses and Binding Rituals in Italy: Greek Tradition and Autochtonous Contexts', *Religion in the Roman Empire* 5 (3): 335–62.

Wann, D. L., J. D. Carlson and M. P. Schrader (1999), 'The Impact of Team Identification on the Hostile and Instrumental Verbal Aggression of Sport Spectators', *Journal of Social Behavior and Personality* 14 (2): 279–86.

Wann, D. L., F. G. Grieve, R. K. Zapalac, J. R. Lanter, J. A. Partridge, S. E. Short, P. M. Parker and M. Short (2011), 'What Would You Do for a Championship: Willingness to Consider Acts of Desperation among Major League Baseball Fans', in B. Geranto (ed.), *Sport Psychology*, 161–73. New York: Nova.

Wann, D. L., J. L. Hunter, J. A. Ryan and L. A. Wright (2001), 'The Relationship between Team Identification and Willingness of Sport Fans to Consider Illegally Assisting Their Team', *Social Behavior and Personality: An International Journal* 29 (6): 531–36.

Wann, D. L., and J. James (2019), *Sports Fans: The Psychology and Social Impact of Fandom*. London and New York: Routledge.

Wann, D. L., R. R. Peterson, C. Cothran and M. Dykes (1999), 'Sport Fan Aggression and Anonymity: The Importance of Team Identification', *Social Behavior and Personality: An International Journal* 27 (6): 597–602.

Watkin, T. G. (2007), 'Ceremonies, Survivals and Syncretism: Ritual Searches in Roman Law and the Native Law of Wales', in F. D'Ippolito (ed.), *Filia: Scritti per Gennaro Franciosi*, 2851–64. Naples: Satura Editrice.

Webster, J. (1997), 'Necessary Comparisons: A Post-Colonial Approach to Religious Syncretism in the Roman Provinces', *World Archaeology* 28 (3): 324–38.

Webster, J. (2001), 'Creolizing the Roman Provinces', *AJA* 105 (2): 209–25.

Weiner, A. (1991), 'From Words to Objects to Magic: "Hard Words" and the Boundaries of Social Interaction', in F. R. Myers and D. L. Brenneis (eds), *Dangerous Words: Language and Politics in the Pacific*, 161–91. Prospect Heights: Waveland Press.

Wendt, H. (2016), *At the Temple Gates: The Religion of Freelance Experts in the Roman Empire*. Oxford: Oxford University Press.

White, L. (2000), *Speaking with Vampires: Rumor and History in Colonial Africa*. Berkeley and Los Angeles: University of California Press.

Whitmore, A. (2018), 'Phallic Magic: A Cross Cultural Approach to Roman Phallic Small Finds', in A. Parker and S. McKie (eds), *Material Approaches to Roman Magic: Occult Objects and Supernatural Substances*, 17–32. Oxford: Oxbow.

Wilburn, A. (2012), *Materia Magica: The Archaeology of Magic in Roman Egypt*. Ann Arbor: The University of Michigan Press.

Wiley, D. M. (2011), 'Celtic Curses by Bernard Mees', *Speculum* 86 (2): 529–30.

Williams, C. (1999), *Roman Homosexuality: Ideologies of Masculinity in Classical Antiquity*. Oxford: Oxford University Press.

Williams, C. (2012), *Reading Roman Friendship*. Cambridge: Cambridge University Press.

Winkler, J. (1990), *The Constraints of Desire*. New York and London: Routledge.

Woodward, A., and P. Leach (1993), *The Uley Shrines: Excavations of a Ritual Complex on West Hill, Uley, Gloucestershire 1977–9*. London: English Heritage in association with British Museum Press.

Woolf, G. (1998), *Becoming Roman: The Origins of Provincial Civilisation in Gaul*. Cambridge: Cambridge University Press.

Woolf, G. (2000), 'The Religious History of the Northwest Provinces', *JRA* 13: 615–30.

Woolf, G. (2012), 'Reading and Religion in Rome', in J. Rüpke (ed.), *Reflections on Religious Individuality: Greco-Roman and Judaeo-Christian Texts and Practices*, 193–208. Berlin: De Gruyter.

Woolf, G. (2017), 'Roman Things and Roman People: A Cultural Ecology of the Roman World', in A. Van Oyen and M. Pitts (eds), *Materialising Roman Histories*, 211–16. Oxford: Oxbow.

Woolf, G. (2020), 'The Rulers Ruled', in K. Berthelot (ed.), *Reconsidering Roman Power: Roman, Greek, Jewish and Christian Perceptions and Reactions*. Rome: École française de Rome. Available online: https://books.openedition.org/efr/4773 (accessed 27 April 2021).

Wünsch, R. (1898), *Sethianische Verfluchungstafeln Aus Rom*. Leipzig: Teubner.

Wünsch, R. (1910), 'Die Laminae Litteratae Des Trierer Amphitheaters', *BJ* 119: 1–12.

Zapelloni Pavia, A. (2020), 'Decentralising Human Agency: A Study of the Ritual Function of the Votive Figurines from Grotta Bella, Umbria', in I. Selsvold and L. Webb (eds), *Beyond the Romans: Posthuman Perspectives in Roman Archaeology*, 41–54. Oxford: Oxbow.

Index

Africa (modern) 25, 43, 93, 98, 99, 102, 112
agency 4–7, 10, 20, 24–5, 58, 105–7, 109, 110, 116, 120–1, 128, 129, 131–2
  see also power
amphitheatre 17, 49, 54, 58, 69–71
Ampurias 14, 16, 57, 73–4, 82, 91, 107–8, 127
amulets 13, 19, 21, 27, 50, 90, 98–9
Anna Perenna 17, 47, 51
anthropology 7, 10, 50, 88–90, 92–3, 98, 102, 117, 122–3
Athens/Attica 13, 86, 90
attraction spells 11, 75–8, 81, 91, 99, 111, 118–20, 129
Audollent, A. 10, 60, 62, 83–4, 101

Bad Kreuznach 14, 16, 31, 56–7, 71–3, 80–2, 86, 91, 99, 117–18, 127
Bath 9, 14, 16–18, 56, 88, 124
  curses from 31, 38, 40–1, 62, 66, 90–1, 113, 123, 125–6
  experience at 13, 32, 35–6, 45, 48–9, 55, 93, 107
  specialists at 29, 33
beast hunters 28, 69–71, 85, 99
binding 40–2, 44, 48, 61–2, 63, 85
Bologna 14, 108

Carthage 9, 14, 18, 67–71
  curses from 16, 31, 42, 69
  deposition at 52–4, 57
  specialists at 21, 27–8, 33, 39
catharsis 42, 56, 72, 87, 112
Celtic (language/texts) 9, 18, 35, 37, 113, 127
Celtic (people/names) 114–16, 124
cemeteries 45, 47–9, 71, 97, 110–1, 131
  curses from 40, 42, 72–4, 80, 95
  deposition in 52–7, 93
Chagnon 14, 42, 72
charaktêres 16, 17, 27–9, 39, 75, 81, 114
charioteers 42, 67–71, 94–5, 122

Cicero 52, 87, 115
circuses 27–8, 67–71, 85–6, 94–5, 118, 119
  deposition in 48–9, 54–6
Clothall 14, 39, 42
communication 44–5, 51–6, 107, 110, 116, 124, 131
competition curses 39, 42, 67–71, 85–6, 94–5, 99, 100, 101–2, 118, 120, 132

daemons 75, 99, 109–10
dead (the) 32, 41, 44, 52–4, 56, 94, 104, 110–11
deposition 30, 31, 46–57, 62–3, 71–2, 73–4, 81, 93, 107, 109–12
displaying curses 32–3, 49–50, 93, 124
Douglas, M. 7, 88
drawings on curses 27, 39, 61, 113

Eidinow, E. 61, 85–6
emotion 25, 33, 42, 44, 56, 64, 77–8, 86
enslaved people 6, 68, 80–1, 95, 106–7, 113, 120, 123
  as cursers 64, 100, 108–9
  as victims 66, 72, 79, 108–9, 125, 127–8
enslavers 108, 121, 125–6
Eros 75, 77, 118–19
Evans-Pritchard, E. E. 7, 88–9

factions 28, 67–70, 82, 86, 118
family 52, 66, 71–2, 76, 99, 119, 125–6
Faraone, C. 60, 62, 75, 77, 83–4, 85–6, 106
folding 30, 40–3, 112, 123
Frankfurt 14, 42, 94
freelance religious experts/specialists 20–1, 26–8, 33, 37, 39, 71, 75–7, 108, 110–11

Gordon, R. 28, 67–8, 83, 86, 95, 106, 113
gossip 7, 10, 43, 48, 90–3, 98–9, 108–9, 131
  see also rumour

Graeco-Egyptian traditions 16, 21, 26–8, 39, 48, 75, 110, 112–13, 115, 124
graves, *see* cemeteries
Greek language 13, 18, 37, 113–15
Greek Magical Papyri (*PGM*) 26–8, 31, 41, 47, 75
Groß-Gerau 14, 63–4, 81, 120

juridical curses 42, 71–5, 85–6, 91–2, 94, 99–100, 101–2, 117–18, 119–20, 127
justice 64–7, 87, 93–4, 97, 128

knowledge, religious 6, 20–2, 27, 29, 58, 74, 113–16

language 18, 43, 63, 113–16
   see also Celtic; Greek; Latin
Latin 16, 18, 31, 44, 114, 116
law 64–7, 96
lawyers 71–2, 74, 94, 117
lead, lead alloy 5, 12–13, 24, 30–2, 33, 35, 41–2, 53–4, 55, 111–12
Leicester 15, 64, 100, 113
Libanius 50, 87, 112
listing 67, 72, 96, 99–100, 117–18, 125–6, 129, 131
literacy 18, 29, 37, 44, 113–16
London 15, 54, 92

Maar 15, 32, 80
magic 20–1, 37–8, 43, 60, 75, 98, 115
   anthropology of 7, 50, 97
   definition and debate 8–9, 63, 86–8
   see also freelance religions experts; Graeco-Egyptian traditions; Greek Magical Papyri
magistrates 64–5, 67, 73–4, 107–8, 127
Magna Mater/Mater Magna 1, 81, 110, 124
Mainz 1, 9, 15, 16, 18, 45, 51, 55
   curses from 1, 31, 36–8, 95–6, 98–9, 111, 120, 127
   specialists at 29, 33
Malinowski, B. 7, 88
Mars 18, 54, 66
materiality 23–4, 26, 30–4
Mautern 15, 40, 79
Mercury 56, 94, 110, 110
Minturno 15, 53, 96
Montfo 15, 31, 111–12

name magic 122–3, 125, 128
names 36, 124–32, 134
   listing/grouping of 72, 99–100, 117–18
   targeted by curse 32, 40–1, 44
new materialism 5–6, 23–4, 132

Ovid 26, 32, 52, 75, 78

Petronell 15, 31, 54, 64
pewter 31–2, 35
piercing 41–3, 111–12
Pliny the Elder 31–2, 34, 41, 43, 50, 87, 115
Pompeii 15, 16, 32–3
Porta San Sebastiano 17, 27, 57
power 4–6, 105–6, 131
   and relationships 104–5, 118, 120, 125
   of ritual action 24–5, 30, 43
   sources of 109–16
   structures of 106–9, 125, 128
prayer 34, 43–5, 53
prayers for justice 46, 61, 62–7, 81, 94
priests/priestesses 1, 5, 19, 34, 106–7
psychosomatic symptoms 50, 112
punishment 33, 44, 63–7, 81, 87, 93–4, 96–7, 102, 110, 120, 128

Ratcliffe-on-Soar 15, 29, 37
relationships 2, 7, 33, 57, 60, 73, 75–82, 85, 90, 99, 116–20, 131–2
   and agency 5, 105, 116
   and power 6, 106, 121, 129
   targeted by curse 96, 125
religion 18–20, 24, 34, 130
   and magic 8–9, 88
   as lived experience 3–4, 5, 25, 45, 74, 85, 104
reputation 86, 90–1, 94–7, 102, 106, 119
risk 67–9, 85–6, 95
Rolling 30, 40–2, 53–4, 112
Rome 9, 15–18, 19, 57, 67–8, 69, 75, 82, 90, 122
   curses from 32; 78–9, 108, 126
   specialists at 21, 27–8, 33, 36 114
   see also Anna Perenna; Porta San Sebastiano
rumour 2, 7, 43, 50, 79–80, 90–3, 98–100, 108–9
   see also gossip

sacrifice 5–6, 20, 24, 42, 53, 55, 98–9
secrecy 46, 57, 90, 92–3, 102
separation spells 75, 78–81, 91
sorcery 7–8, 89, 92, 97, 102, 117, 125
Sousse 9, 15, 16, 53, 57, 67–9, 75, 82
    curses from 76, 118–19
    specialists at 21, 27–8, 33, 39, 114
space 4, 25, 45–6, 54–6
Sri Lanka 89–90, 92–3, 97, 99, 102, 120, 125
Sulis Minerva 45, 109–10, 123

temples 34–5, 44–5, 102, 109–10
    authorities at 20, 29–30, 87, 106–7
    curses from 1–2, 33, 66, 93–6, 98–9, 120
    deposition in 46–7, 49–50, 51–2, 54–5
theft curses 16, 25, 33, 56, 60–1, 62–7, 82, 87–8, 90–1, 93–4, 96–7, 99–102, 108, 110, 117, 119–20, 123
transformation 10, 24–6, 30, 44–5, 54, 116–17, 120, 131
Trier 15, 17, 18
    curses from 54, 80, 115, 126
    specialists at 27–8

Uley 9, 15, 16–17, 29, 35, 43, 61, 63, 82, 88, 107
    curses from 37, 42, 93–4, 115
    deposition at 51–2, 56–7

venatores, see beast hunters
Versnel, H. 8, 60–1, 63, 65, 67, 81, 94
Victoria/Victory 19, 66, 125
voces magicae 16, 17, 27–9, 39, 75, 108, 110–11, 115–16
votives 18, 21, 33, 49–53, 55, 58, 107, 110

Winkler, J. 77, 86, 91, 118–19
witches/witchcraft 21, 27, 48, 53, 75, 93, 115
    anthropology of 7, 89, 98–9
women 26, 82, 86, 123
    as cursers 1, 76, 78–80
    as victims 76–9, 118–19, 125
    disadvantaged 6, 64, 106–7, 120–2, 129
writing 5, 29–40, 44, 58, 111–16, 122–3

www.ingramcontent.com/pod-product-compliance
Lightning Source LLC
Chambersburg PA
CBHW052215300426
44115CB00011B/1693